INHABITED VOICES

MYTH AND HISTORY IN THE POETRY OF GEOFFREY HILL, SEAMUS HEANEY AND GEORGE MACKAY BROWN

DAVID ANNWN

iii

First published in 1984
by Bran's Head Books Limited
45, Milk Street, Frome, Somerset

© *David Annwn 1984*

ISBN 0 905220 46 3

Printed at the
Hunting Raven Press
45 Milk Street, Frome,
Somerset

75 · $\frac{1}{3}$ʋʋ

CONTENTS

INTRODUCTION

> The facts of our history — what Edwin Muir called the
> Story — are there to read and study: the neolithic folk,
> Picts, Norsemen, Scots, the slow struggle of the people
> towards independence and prosperity. But it often seems
> that history is only the forging, out of terrible fires, of a
> mask. The mask is undeniably there; it is impressive and
> reassuring, it flatters us to wear it.
>
> Underneath, the true face dreams on, and the Fable is
> repeated over and over again.
>
> (George Mackay Brown)

> Myths were things of utility to Tudor and Stuart politicians.
>
> (Geoffrey Hill)

> In many ways the fury of Irish republicanism is associated
> with a religion like this, with a female goddess who has
> appeared in various guises. She appears as Mother Ireland...
> I think the republican ethos is a feminine religion in a way.
>
> (Seamus Heaney)

Seamus Heaney, Geoffrey Hill and George Mackay Brown possess a keen awareness of myth and mythological patterns. Moreover, as these three quotations imply in their different ways, the relation between history and myth is continually scrutinised and restated in their work. But what does one mean by myth — especially the kind of myth that the three poets write about? One might examine it as a social force or ethos such as Fascism or the idolatry surrounding pop or film stars. Alternatively, one might explore how certain myths originated in naturalistic metaphor (the thunderbolts of Zeus) or exemplary tales. There are the mythic qualities embodied by psychological archetypes and, on a different level, myths seen as functions of linguistic values. This study touches upon certain of these areas at times, but I start my definition of myth with those categories of stories which somehow or other involve supernatural elements. One must allow each writer considered here an acute literary intelligence, but one could fall into the habit of misconstruing the writer's intentions by tracing every scallop-shell back to Aphrodite or every oak tree to Zeus. Whether or not my critical viewpoint has been influenced by Intentionalist theory, I have tried to sense each writer's drift whilst remaining aware of a large field of conscious and unconscious echoes in his work. Perhaps fortunately, none of the three would disclaim his use of ancient and modern myth. Nor would he claim to have erected a 'watertight' mythopoesis totally unreliant on previous patterns.

History, too, demands some kind of definition at this stage. How does each poet view the usual accepted span of selective and linear history from the Paleolithic to the Atomic Age and beyond? Does the poet conceive any historical scheme governing time and events such as the cyclical, recurrent or karmic models? Secondly, my use of the word 'history' involves the artist's re-telling of that reality, whether by epistle, hymn, rendition of a fragment or a ballad. Thirdly, and perhaps less importantly for this work, I have had to take into account the artist's personal (imagined or actual) history which is, of course, related to the other questions. Heaney is at pains to point out that life and work must be 'intertwined, a continuum', and includes sections of poetry which seem to be largely biographical in his work. Mackay Brown, on the other hand, writes: 'In the whole fabric of what I've written there are only one or two unimportant shreds of myself.' One suspects that Hill would encourage such a line of inquiry even less. I do not feel that my definitions of the poets' or my own sense of history and histories should be too staunch or detailed at this point. It is in considering the local details of the poetry that I seek to delineate some of the poets' historical concerns. For to attempt to do otherwise might prove to be an act of abstraction — an imposing of an unwieldy schema on the work or the supposed extraction of an 'ideological blueprint'.

II

It will be useful here to provide a brief introduction to the genre in which each of the poets works. Hill was at Keble College, Oxford, in 1953 and was keenly aware of 'The Movement' poets and, if one might read between the lines of his essay on Silkin, saw a need to react against them. Be that as it may, a clinical voice very like the distanced and clinical voices of Auden and Spender is there in his work. His verse participates in a scholastic scrupulosity, searching and dismissing various layers of rhetoric. His persona looks upon tombs, 'composed forms' and his dubiety itself is studied, fair-minded but at times over-fastidious. The gods are ciphers, codes, structures of thought and language: they are most dangerous when taken at face value, and must be continually questioned, tested, modified or 'defused'. Like allegorical figures in a Baroque painting, they stand between Mannerism and Neo-Classicism, between the aesthete and the philosopher, inviting critical and spiritual appraisal. In reaction, the naturalist is thrown back into a flurry of human primitivism:

> Until I could cry 'Death! Death!' as though
> To exacerbate that suave power;
>
> ("Three Baroque Meditations")

But this provides no escape and the poet's 'vixen' tongue is soon 'cleansed". The gods are one of the ways in which man has composed his existence, exteriorised psychic tensions and manipulated others. The reader watches as Hill stages each drama, each exercise in argument, rhythm and tone. They are beset with paradoxes, ornate cul-de-sacs of thought,

because the narrator's logic and the 'Knack of tongues' are unanswerable.
Man is tempted into inversion, the life of self denial and martyrdom,
but an insistence on the descent into darkness and death is itself a self-
deceiving elevation of the ego: 'Darkness/above all things/the Sun/
makes/rise'. These gods are drawn from the mock-heroic statuary of
Swift and Pope; they have been de-mythologised yet can still be used
for moralising or satire. As lopped sculptures, gargoyles or dead forms
'living' in the air, they become dumb observers of the brutality perpet-
uated in their names. They are the 'sometimes-abandoned' formulae
which men accept to the extent to which it proves expedient:

> The bells
> In hallowed Europe spilt
> To the gods of coin and salt
> The sea creaked with worked vessels.
>
> ("Of Commerce and Society")

The dead 'maintain their ground' in Hill's work, but they can be lifted
away and abused. Hill's observer is not like Hamlet, the parabalist of
Heaney's work, but simply that — an observer, disembodied and recording the trials of Lazarus, 'mystified, common man of death'. Hill's
handling of myth is fluid, begetting monstrous and blazing legendary
forms acting out a series of dramas. The effect gained is a little like
watching a Symbolist miracle-play whilst listening to a peculiarly
Empsonian commentary. Wainwright says that Henri Focillon provides
another analogy:

> Romanesque art had perceived [all created things] only
> through a mesh of ornament and in a monstrous disguise.
> It had combined man with beast and beast with chimera...
> The very profusion and variety of these incessantly meta-
> morphosed beings betray the impatience of their struggle
> to break out from the labyrinth of abstract style and to
> achieve life...

Wainwright calls to mind the master mason of *Mercian Hymns* and then
comments,

> The 'spectacles' may be frozen and sometimes unbear-
> ably bright, but they are not ordered or illuminated by
> a clear humanist vision, by reason, or by consoling
> Christianity. But their world is endlessly fecund, a blind
> animalised thriving of copulation upon an earth of sickly
> richness imaged in such poems from *King Log* as "Annun-
> ciations" ('the loathly neckings') and "The Imaginative
> Life".

The ambiguities, 'double-takes' and after-images in Hill's work are
legion and at times they seem to backfire and prove a little preposterous.
This is especially conspicuous because Hill, in his essays, advocates and
exhibits a keen linguistic intelligence — his infatuation with Coleridge's
'moral copula' might well be extended to a more 'moral' use of verb and

adjective in his own work. To pretend that "September Song" is a more adequate address to tragedy and atrocity than an over-stated cry of suffering is, I think, merely a play on words. However, where Hill's poetry does contrast its verbal and Imagist pyrotechnics with unadorned human utterance as in "Funeral Music" and *Mercian Hymns* a rare power is achieved. Hill can strike up a blaze of splendid images when he juxtaposes historical and mythological conventions. The blood sacrifice to the impassive gods remains a central motif in his work.

George Mackay Brown studied G.M.Hopkins' work for an MA at Newbattle Abbey when Edwin Muir was the warden there. He emerged into the anthologies at the time of MacDiarmid's second 'Scottish Renaissance'. While he clearly admires the work of Sidney Goodsir Smith and fellow Orcadian Robert Rendall, his verse has a bleak and simple power of its own. He found himself at once drawn to and aesthetically distanced from Orcadian life. It comes as no surprise that he cites Borges and Mann as two writers who have influenced his work. Muir expressed a certain reservation about Brown's more 'cold and abstract and theoretical style', where he felt 'the theme has not entered your imagination'. This seems to be a misunderstanding of Brown's basic stance, which is sometimes nearer to the cold strength of "Under Ben Bulben" than to the playful domestic voice of "Scarecrow in the Schoolmaster's Oats" or "A Child's Calendar". At one extreme there is in Brown's work a view of life as an illusion or a series of masks. He provides us with a referential 'grid' for his sense of myth in *Magnus*. The sacrificial act is the pivot, the 'Axle-Tree' of his writing, for Christ, Magnus and John Barleycorn symbolize a fact which is at the centre of Nature. Folk motifs are elevated to the stature of the numinous; the poor family of Everyman appears in Brown's mythological structure alongside Christ, Mary and Magnus. Art itself holds an order analogous to that of religion:

> Rood
> The lesser mysteries rooted also
>   in that first garden
> apple fraught, with pure rinsings.
>   ("The Lesser Mysteries of Art")

There are distinct echoes of Muir's world of pre-Christian innocence here, where the whole superstructure of dogma falls in a child's laughter. Recurrences, patterns, threads in the whole 'weave of time' are continually utilised. There is also a mystical thread of imagery and rhythm, starting with the villagers' incantations and repetitious ballads, and ending with a dense verse reminiscent of Gnostic texts:

> 'I am the Bringer of Dew,'
> 'I am the Dove'
> 'I am the Swarm of Bees.'
> 'I am the Grain of Dust from the Floor
>   of Heaven....'
>   ("The Golden Door")

Hill has given voice to similar lines involving a gently-modulating awe:

> You are the castaway of drowned remorse,
> you are the world's atonement on the hill.
> This is your body twisted by our skill
> into a patience proper for redress.

("Lachrimae Verae")

One must, however, state the limitation of this apparent similarity — Hill is engaged here with a contemplative mysticism of particular times and places, especially 15th and 16th century Europe, whereas Brown's imagery is absorbed into a sense of timelessness. Brown's later verse in *Winterfold* gains a strength of understatement varied with occasional bluntness recalling Eliot and Pound: 'She was a very luxurious lady/She rotted my leg'; 'With a golden key I opened a door/On a bowl of dead rose leaves'. ("Seven Translations of a Lost Poem") Like Heaney, he is a poet of a particular locality; whether this is the geographical Orkney or an Orkney of the mind is up to the reader to decide. (One suspects the two are inextricably interwoven for Brown.) In his stories and poems the fishermen and crofters occupy the foreground much as Heaney's peat-digger and ploughman dominate certain poems in his work. *Fishermen with Ploughs* remains an example of how Brown can weave a whole mesh of symbols and myths into a cyclical time-scheme governing the life of these people.

The 1960s and 1970s have seen an unprecedented convergence of technological advancement, religious furore and ecological concern. I believe that this change in lifestyle is embodied in a substantial way in Seamus Heaney's work. Edna Longley has characterised the chief concern of this age as 'a search for new gods'. Nerthus, the goddess of the boglands, is not simply an 'emblem befitting adversity' for Heaney. His sensibility has searched for expression outside a simple acceptance of Catholic ritual or a celebration of the weird and awful aspects of ecclesiastical sculpture, and has come to confront one of the primeval Mothers — the goddess of the boglands. Heaney draws our attention to the dead disposed in ditches and marshes and the doctrines which led them on. He sees Hill's 'ancient troughs of blood' and acknowledges that 'no bloodless myth will hold'. He wishes at one point 'to consecrate' the 'cauldron bog', to resurrect the corpses of the labourers and to purge the collective guilt that their memory and the present horror of Ireland inspire.

Heaney, an admirer of the English alliterative tradition, of Anglo-Saxon verse and Spenser, found himself ranked in the early 60s with a number of Irish contemporaries who shared Kinsella, Clarke, but especially Patrick Kavanagh as immediate influences. He also shared their troubled homeland — it was enough to give his verse an air of imminent crisis. Because of this, and perhaps because of the Irish literary tradition in general, Heaney is not enraged by the 'tongue's atrocity' or 'Pentecost's ashen feast'. In "Midnight" the narrator yearns for a more 'atrocious tongue' which will provide outlet for those life-styles and instincts which seem to be on the verge of extinction and which will articulate the fury of his 'backward look'. It is this onomatopoeic tongue — that of Joyce and Merriman, that of Kavanagh in "The Great Hunger" and that which lies 'vestigial, forgotten like the coccyx' or a Brigid's Cross yellowing in some outhouse — which Heaney uses. His poems continually draw our attention to the fact that this voice is often local, linked to the particular curve of a river or sound of a breeze. It is a language closely related to the Gaelic of the great houses and their secret culture that Corkery illuminates in *The Hidden Ireland*. This is not to say that Heaney does not, like Hill, condemn certain modes of speech. If Hill mistrusts the poetaster, the aesthete who savours each 'specimen-jar, fed with delicate spawn' and who sits at the banquet of the Word, Heaney mistrusts the rhetoric of, among others, the journalist:

> Who proved on their pulses 'escalate',
> 'Backlash' and 'crack down', 'the provisional wing,'
> 'Polarization' and 'long-standing hate.'
>
> ("Whatever You Say Say Nothing")

If Hill mistrusts the (supposed) Patron considering his lilies and the artist's nightly vixen-skill, Heaney condemns that rhetoric which offers itself as the voice of sanity and those who suck the fake taste, 'the stony flavours:/Of those sanctioned, old, elaborate retorts'. Brown too rails against the intrusion of the media which means that the islanders find themselves repeating 'some discussion they have heard on TV the night before. Number, statistics, graph are everything.'

Hill, one feels, suspects the rhetoric of the ancient world as much as that of the new.

The gods and spirits of Heaney's work are those of the soil and the inland lakes and rivers. They feed on their dark inheritance — the stratified dead, the mingling speech patterns and cultural detritus. However, because of the sense of wide-ranging historical schism and mythological quest in Heaney's work I have devoted a chapter to an introduction to his poetry.

What differences and affinities both hold these poets' work in creative tension with each other and help to illuminate that which makes them exciting and important writers? At first there does not seem to be a great deal of similarity in mythological interest: Cernunnos flexing in the arms of the king-gardener, Nerthus rising out of the Irish peat and the gentle, repetitious prayers of Eynhallow monks to their Lady of the Sea are culled from completely distinct traditions. However, all three poets share a common interest in the Catholic and Protestant faiths and in the Pagan 'survivals' which can be glimpsed within these traditions. Heaney in a poem like "The Other Side" shows himself as fascinated by the different dogmas as Brown is when he contrasts the beliefs and life-style surrounding kirk and chapel. The festivals of the Christian year are attended by violence which has become almost a ritual in "Funeral

Music": 'With an equable contempt for this World/'In honorem Trinitatis.' Crash...' The hopes and strictures of the Church of England have become part of the living mind of the generations in *Mercian Hymns* and they are in attendance at the tomb: '(Et exspecto resurrectionem mo mortuorem'/dust in the eyes, on clawing wings, and lips)' (XXIV). Brown and Heaney too record the 'holy wars', the conflict between the individual will and doctrine and the penalty of disobedience:

> Among tilted bottles, fists, faces
> — A cold drunken wheel —
> James saw the hangman put his red shirt on Wilma.
> ("Witch")

Such a poem brings to mind the interest in the feminine part of human nature, the women of the Irish and Orcadian communities and the confrontation of male and female power which we find in Brown's and Heaney's poetry. Women determine a man's life in Brown's work. They are mother, lover, midwife, and dresser of the corpse. They spur men on to jealousy and war, wait at the seashore for the boats that do not return and keen like gulls at a funeral. The figures of Valkyries, Muses, the Christian saints and the fertility goddesses merge and alternate in the stories of Orcadian life. Heaney too possesses the Celtic sympathy with womankind. The strange girl running with the cows, the young mother mourning her illegitimate child's drowning and the bride who lets the groom sleep on her knee on the ride to the airport are all part of the female compassion, strength and sexuality which somehow bind myth, history and life together. Heaney perceives a sexual drama in the clearing of a ditch or the planting of a stake into the bog. The whole bogland becomes a 'wet centre' like the wells and other passages to secret forms of life and to the darkest mysteries of existence. The pump, water-bringer for a community in "Rite of Spring", becomes an oral and vaginal opening, stirring and gushing to the climax: 'Her entrance was wet, and she came'. Sexuality for Heaney reaches down into the minutiae and microscopic levels of life and into the non-human world. To the croft-women in Brown's "The Statue in the Hills" Mary is: 'Our Lady of Dark Ploughs/Our Lady of Furled Boats.' Her power and the aura of women generally spreads out into nature, but sexuality, though necessary for the harvest, is not as all-pervasive for Brown. Magnus realises his power whilst celibate and there is a beauty of a transcendent quality which surrounds the virginal brother and sister who die untouched by the finger of carnality. This tendency to appreciate the asexual aspects of spirituality also pervades Brown's views of the monks. Apart from a few glimpses of the 'ghost-bride' in *Mercian Hymns*, Hill seems to distance his dramas of sexual tension from nature as a whole. "The Turtle Dove" and "The Troublesome Reign" find two nameless lovers moving in a social world of gesture and reciprocal remorse. Venus is re-born as a shark in "Metamorphoses" but she does not gain any of the fleshliness or desire that Heaney would have given such an image. The central divine presence is male in Hill's work — Offa, Sebastian Arruruz, The Stone Man, a rakish Christ, the Humanist, or Ovid carefully weighing up the options in a new Third Reich.

History as a power struggle, as invasion, conquest, settlement and re-settlement concerns all three writers. They examine the position of the craftsman and of the common man of labour and death within the context of societies torn and disrupted by violence. For Heaney there are the memories of the Elizabethan colonists of Lee and Blackwater, the Viking prows and warring tribes of early Ulster. Brown is concerned with the settlement of Orkney by a ravaged people, the battle between pirate and kingsman, Bonny Prince Charlie and the Redcoats and the attempts by farmers to avoid conscription. Hill studies the dead forms of Towton, the furious zeal of Plantagenets and Calvinists to assert their faiths by the sword, and depicts the England of Offa trembling under the certitude of a sadistic tyrant. The farmers and master-masons have to continue. Bards must sing out their verses from battle-swept decks and the poet in his cell must try to compose a stance before his torturers. Hill and Heaney are, it seems, more concerned with the last war and subsequent violence. The hunting boys in "Dawn Shoot" move in a world where there are still grim echoes of hoarse sentries and parachutists. The boy in Hymn XXVII listens shivering to the 'battle anthems' on the radio in the camoflaged nissen hut and imagines his own fantastic engagements. Interestingly enough though, Brown writes a whole section about Bonhoeffer in *Magnus* and Hill has dedicated a poem to the same martyr. They share an interest in self-sacrifice, even though their poetic worlds and views are very different. Ironically, in spite of Brown's real beliefs and Hill's sardonic distance from anything he writes, their mystical songs do at times share common themes.

History has its 'still-points'; its recurrences. Sustaining myths of a more passive kind are recorded by the three writers. Heaney's vision of a teeming and fearful natural world haunted by sounds and hidden presences is not so different from the more orderly but thriving circles of life in Brown's islands. Both Irishmen and Orcadian share an interest in the ballad and the fiddler's tune, though Brown has allowed his form to be influenced by these. Hill's is the more enclosed and private landscape — his art does indeed seem to be more sculptural. The music to his words is at times a 'florid, grim' one or a stately series of tear-inspiring pavanes. His humour is as subtle as Heaney's and as cutting as Brown's, but lacks the lighter inflections of the other twos' wit; it is a dark and mordant humour amused by its attempts to escape its self-defeating formulations.

In this book I have enlarged upon the various themes outlined here. There are strange overlappings which relate Brown's, Hill's and Heaney's work at unexpected moments. At other times their views and voices throw each other's work into stark relief. Whatever similarities I have drawn attention to, I acknowledge the strengths of their distinct and powerful apprehensions of myth and history. A consideration of their masteries of language and of their skills and a comparison of their visions confirm their individual importance. They also reveal the relevance of their personal and poetic myths in the Britain, Orkney and Ireland of today.

Lastly, in addition to the question 'Why choose to bring these poets together?' one might ask 'Why not other poets who are just as engaged in mythic patterns today? Why not David Jones, John Heath-Stubbs, C.H.Sisson, Ted Hughes?' My answer must be that I discounted other possible poets either because there seemed to be too little common ground between them and the three I have covered, or because, as in the case of David Jones, the volume of their work demands a book to itself, or simply because, in some cases, I did not find that their dealing with myth and history combined with their sense of form in any unified way: it is vital that a writer's presentation of his mythos is attended by poetic excellence — it is this criterion as much as sound reasoning, historical insight and vivid re-telling which makes the work of Hill, Heaney and Brown continually relevant to the world around them. I have accordingly taken into account the search for new forms, the successful folding of traditional themes into modern verse and their startling power to communicate. The subject matter of this study shows how seriously each of the three has conceived of his role in this context. The search for and through 'new gods' has long been considered a crucial one.

INFLUENCES

Patterns are difficult to unravel; in talking of influences we have not only to consider the wide-ranging impact of certain famous writers, but also the surfacing of various types of cultural and symbolic language in the work of the three poets. George Mackay Brown, using the most ancient of oral and literary conventions, concentrates both on tribal narrative:

> Their axes kept them that year from the dragon.
> Logs throttled a mountain torrent.
> A goatherd gaped on lumbering tons.
> *(Building the Ship)*

and saga forms, and he is interested in how these conventions have been used in modern verse. He draws upon the chivalric world, its particular brand of Christian thought and Troubadour tradition:

> And Armod the Iceland poet,
> "I am curious about their verse.
> The formal plots,
> Rose and marble and nightingale.
> This is not the poetry we know."

Yet there is a mystical strand in his writing which seems to have more in common with Traherne than the *Roman de la Rose*. He comments on the folk-tale, ballad and seasonal rituals of the peasants from the viewpoints of medieval officials. There is the great gulf between customs and beliefs stretching back to prehistory and the rational, often exploitative impulse of centralised power. Brown also has recourse to the Late Romantics' use of folk motif and legend, especially to Yeats. The vitality of Gerard Manley Hopkins' religious vision also makes itself felt in his work. No doubt Muir's vision of country life has affected him, but Brown's use of Catholic litany and motif is much closer to the tenets of doctrine than is Muir's.

Seamus Heaney, in style, is immediately recognisable as modernist. The comparison with D.H.Lawrence and Ted Hughes and their modes of capturing the animal and plant world has to be taken into account. But Heaney is aware of the great fathoms of pre-literate time, the rites of the Neolithic people and the Celts, their stone circles and monuments. To put the pagan world of Northern Europe into perspective, he also quotes its recorders: Greek, Latin and English, who speculated and peered into the recesses of the 'barbarian' consciousness. He delves into the origins of Anglo-Saxon verse and Viking remains in Dublin and considers their importance for a modern world. He adopts the figure of the wan-

1

dering teacher, parabalist, 'smeller of rot' and urchin of the wild. Like
an Old Testament hermit he uses a narrator wandering out of the fast-
nesses of nature to tell of 'centres' and the lies of civilisation. He explores the Shakespearian and Elizabethan uses of myth and the ways in
which they conflict with the Irish spirit of Aisling. The extensive sub-
stratum of early Irish literature, life and custom lie beneath his work:
the nature-spirits, goddesses, giants, bogeys of the peasants. He draws
connections between the Iron-age 'bog-burials' of Ireland and Denmark.
There is a druidic voice to his work, possibly that of the filid, and he
draws a contrast between earth-worshipping peoples and the sky-worshipping invaders. He is familiar with the writers of the Celtic Twilight,
but identifies more with the disavowal of the sentimental Irish peasant
and heroic myth by Clarke, Kavanagh and others. Joyce's 'seismic
sense' of language is also felt in his work. In reading 'Of red slobland
around the bones' in "The Digging Skeleton" one remembers Bloom's
'gland' of kidney laid in the frying pan. Heaney, in his dealing with the
disgusting, rejected, obscene aspects of life, defines another kinship
with Joyce, Beckett and the French 'realists', with Rabelais and possibly J.C.Powys. Psychoanalysis and modern science acknowledging in-
visible patterns of forces comprising the Material Universe have influenced his style and subject matter. These patterns have progressively
tested scientists' intelligence. Since Pound's understanding of man as
'a patterned integrity, a knot through which pass the swift strands of
simultaneous ecological cycles, recycling transformations of solar
energy,' we have gained subtler, finer pictures of what happens when
atoms, quark and charm group. The thronging, whining, unseen world
of Heaney's poems is a more delicate and microscopic view of Nature,
than the model of the Vortex.

The worship of reason and the Rise of the Enlightenment bred their
own ironies, but the ironies of unthinking belief had already existed for
centuries for those who could see them. Geoffrey Hill does not aspire
to capture vanished patterns or use a poem as a spell against machinery;
the brutalities of ancient ideologies and their rhetoric is too much on
his mind. He cannot weigh 'the beauty and the atrocity', for, on one
hand the exact qualities are irrecoverable, and on the other, the Word is
treacherous, an unfaithful tool. Perhaps more than either of the preced-
ing poets Hill dwells upon the successive meanings which congregate
around images. The whole repertoire of symbols from those of the early
mystics to those of the Post-Symbolists are at his disposal. The voice of
the Renaissance humanist and the victim of Nazi oppression sound side
by side in his work. Each poetic setting reveals a new set of ironies, a
new cluster and commerce of symbols and concepts modifying each
other. Within the cells of thought contained in sequences like "Funeral
Music" and "Lachrimae", there is a great variety of metaphysical speculation; yet the limitations and irony of the arguments are often laid
bare through historical hindsight. The language is often hermetic and

dense, wound inside itself, to a certain extent reminiscent of the prose of Mill and Newman. The elegance itself becomes ostensibly self-regarding, recalling the closed symbolic language of French poets in the 1890's. There is a great interest in religious forms: the sermon, the hymn, the confessio and the conflicting thought of Gnosticism, Neo-Platonism and heresy. Yet beneath all the Baroque prose and Augustan musing there are the layers of ancient shadow, perhaps all the more menacing and jarring for this contrast:

> By blood we live, the hot, the cold,
> To ravage and redeem the world:
> There is no bloodless myth will hold.
>
> (*Genesis*)

Hill, more than Brown or Heaney, has profited from a reading of Medieval and Renaissance mystics: da Todi, Rolle, San Juan de la Cruz and Robert Southwell. Heaney and Brown have dealt with martyrs, but Hill has no intention to 'make germinate' the studied actions of the saints. Brown reports the efficacy of Magnus's death and Heaney wishes to 'consecrate the cauldron bog', but Hill suspects all such formulation. The word is no cure: 'The Word has been abroad, is back, with a tanned look.' It subsists upon the mire of the dead and is at its very worst when used as a remedy or fillip to purge mental demons. Hill and Brown share an interest in the density of art, usefully symbolised by the Masque, where all gesture is stylised in a medium not dissimilar to heraldry. Both artists are able to elevate images to the level of the numinous in a stark and abstract way. Images of religious devotion are always offset by other ideas in Hill's work. The religious faculty is not seen as an embracing of a unified cosmos but as a cultural and often exploitative force generated by society. Hill invests these oppositions and schisms in his work with a rare power and fastidious craftsmanship. When T.S.Eliot wrote in "Tradition and the Individual Talent" that

> . . .the historical sense compels a man to write not
> merely with his own generation in his bones, but
> with a feeling that the whole of the literature of
> Europe from Homer and within it the whole of the
> literature of his own country has a simultaneous
> existence and composes a simultaneous order.

it was to have a tremendous impact upon modern writing as a whole. The contemporaneity of history, that which he called 'the mind of Europe' and 'the present moment of the past' brought the whole of Western civilisation and thought to bear on a writer's work. The pitch and attention of the writings of Heaney, Brown and Hill have been developed and exercised in relation to, and sometimes in reaction to, these perspectives. Eliot's sense of the necessity of 'humility of the man before Tradition, and of the poets' conscious mind before his limited technical problems' is fully acknowledged in Hill's dealing with history, and Hill consistently writes with a mind aware of Eliot's viewpoint and

3

an ear attuned to the music and cadences of the older poet's verse. The concept of the 'auditory imagination' has been described and used extensively by Heaney. But it is above all in the area of history, and in the role of the poet-as-historian, that Eliot has wielded the largest influence on these writers. The pressures of the past become a present tension in their work. The myths of the ancient Orcadians and Vikings are living issues, and the spirit of Offa endures:

> . . .from the middle of the eighth century
> until the middle of the twentieth (and
> possibly beyond

In "Deus est Amor" Pound wrote: 'The essence of religion is the present tense'. It is a sentence which could have appeared in any of Eliot's essays. What then are those broad and distinctive notions of myth and history possessed by Pound and Yeats which define them as important influences on the poets under consideration? In the case of Yeats, the impact of his thought runs largely counter to the Eliotic stance. Eliot found Yeats' poetry too otherworldly, and we know that Yeats found Eliot's earlier work limited to this world: the squalor of suburbia and London. Yeats' scheme of history is not the continuous present; on both a literary and an actual level history was to Yeats as it is to Brown, a series of recurrences. Pound on the other hand agreed with Eliot — there was 'a permanent basis for humanity', and this became a premise for the *Cantos*. Yet Pound's individual mythological and historical emphases differ from Eliot's, especially in regard to the vital issues of Paganism and sexuality. Another broad difference between Yeats and Pound on one side and Eliot on the other is the idea of poetry as magic. Pound laboured to locate the effective formulae: magical, poetical and economic, which would overcome the schisms of his time, much as Heaney and Brown seek to establish the assuaging ceremony of words, the poem as a spell to offset decay. Yeats saw his poetry as a kind of magic, rather than vice versa.

There are other links between Yeats and Pound and the younger poets which make necessary a discussion of their influence. Pound's views of sub-atomic life and the 'vortex', his use of irreducible linguistic formulae and ideas on the relation between the environment and speech are of importance to Heaney. The alchemical process embodied in *The Cantos* and his 'humanised gods' and holy centres are useful to bear in mind when considering Brown. Pound's 'collage' method and poetic juxtapositions can be informitavely compared to Hill's form in *Mercian Hymns*. In Yeats' case, we find that his interest in an art and a mythology 'rooted in the earth', in fairy and folk tale, psychic phenomena and the rhythms of life in the Irish countryside prove to be vital influences to all three poets. Here, I have touched only on a few basic emphases in Pound's and Yeats' work which make them important above and beyond the obvious and wide-ranging influence of Eliot.

4

Ezra Pound

In dealing with Pound's utilisation of mythological figures and motifs one is faced with an enormous body of work: the Greek writers spanning eight centuries, the Latin writers, Medieval and Renaissance Classicists, Dante and the Troubadour poets, Confucius, Mencius, and English Romantics, especially Browning and Keats. His knowledge of European cults – the mystery religions, Albigensians and fertility beliefs – was extensive. I am here indebted to Dekker's *Sailing After Knowedge*, and Boris de Rachewitz's fine essay, "Pagan and Magical Elements in Ezra Pound's Work", which not only order the material coherently and inclusively, but provide valid and careful approaches to a daunting subject.

Dekker initially discusses the sculptural imagination that Pound favours, and this leads him to examine Pound's use of sexual principles. Into the pre-Christian world of "Canto VIII" is introduced the Male force (the sculptor, the ploughman), working on a Female power (Tellus, the mountain). Heaney comes closest to this image, for he uses the idea of the ploughman and the Female soil, the phallic coulter cleaving the furrow. But Brown too writes of the Ploughman's societies and the mysteries which surround the Male cult. Both poets have emblems of the primeval duality of sexual power:

> He is the Winter Tree dragged by a peasant. . .
> He is the hollow in the rock.

Here in "Creator" the Spirit of Christ both transcends and yet adopts male and female characteristics: the yoni and lingam of the Hindus. Heaney's narrator in "Kinship" finds a reminder of origins in a turf-spade:

> the shaft wettish
> as I sank it upright.

Dekker comments on Pound's 'poetry of first principles', where the act of transformation is as vital a part of the poet's craft as the sculptor's. This is of special relevance to the poets under consideration. Entities blur and merge, a carter into a Celtic god, a hidden boy to an oracle, a turnip to a slashed head, so much that in Heaney's work metaphor is a primary structural device. In "Bone Dreams" we're never sure who breathes through the words: goddess and navigators and human narrator are twined together. A parallel, but not identical, process can be seen in Brown's work. We never decide whether the paupers in the barn are the Holy Family or whether the village women are actually ancient repositories of power. There is a gap between life and vision in Brown, and this gulf is spanned only by the miracle, or at a lesser level, by art, the folding process. There is no such doubt in transformation in either Heaney's or Pound's work. Gods do float in the azure air and pagan experience is still accessible in the bog. Hill too uses metamorphoses: statements and thoughts that merge and separate again, luminous moments where gods appear:

> In a brief cavort he was

5

> Cernunnos, the branched god, lightly concussed.
> (*Hymn XV*)

Indeed, in *Mercian Hymns*, Hill uses a technique in the transformation of character that is reminiscent of Pound's collage method. Instead of, for example in "Canto III", the scene of 'The panisks, little rural Pans from Cicero's *De Natura Deorum*, the dryas, oak-spirits passim from Greek heritage, the maelids from Ibycus, the gods upon the clouds from Poliziano;' in "Hymn I" we have holly groves from druidic tree-lore, the M5 from Britain in the 60's, the 'desirable new estates' from post-war Britain and 'martyrologist: the friend of Charlemagne' from Medieval histories. Indeed, in "Hymn II", the writing almost becomes cubistic or at least reminiscent of an abstract design from the 1910's.

Dekker goes on to discuss fertility ritual, especially the blood ceremony in the early *Cantos*. The blood-rite of Odysseus in Hades, which Pound uses as a metaphor for translation, also belongs to fertility ritual, especially as it celebrates the story of Adonis. The ceremony of fertility underlies the whole structure of *The Cantos*. In "Canto XXXIX", Odysseus, like the vegetable god, must descend after knowledge that is the 'shade of a shade'. Another fine example is "Canto XLVII", where 'the female does manifest and experience the divine through the sexual act:'

> The light has entered the cave
>
> Io! Io! —
> . . .By prong have I entered these hills:
> That the grass grow from my body.

Heaney's "Bog Poems" are infused with this consciousness. We find both the recognition of the blood-letting in ritual and the sexual association in these poems:

> Who will say 'corpse'
> to his livid cast?
> Who will say 'body'
> to his opaque repose?
> (*The Graubelle Man*)
> . . .I will stand a long time.
> Bridegroom to the goddess,
>
> She tightened her torc on him
> And opened her fen. . .
> (*The Tollund Man*)

Of course, Heaney does not quote a specific ritual because the actual words and actions of the Irish and Danish Iron-age are not available. He does, however, cite Diodorus Siculus and Tacitus: their comments on the land and people. Often, in dealing with Greek myth, Pound found himself using fables which were, in themselves, (im)moral: that is, they 'deal memorably with archetypal situations which give rise to moral problems'. It is in response to such problems that Heaney becomes the weigher of 'beauty and atrocity':

> (I). . .who would connive

in civilised outrage
yet understand the exact
and tribal, intimate revenge.
(*Punishment*)

Hill too is aware of the sexual and sacrificial aspects of myth. From a definition of the bloodless and ineffective myths in "Genesis", he goes on to examine the role of martyr, in poems of increasing concentration, until we reach "Lachrimae", themselves poems of metamorphoses and of comparison between erotic and metaphysical love. In "The Trouble-some Reign", a sexual obsession seems to be at the very core of the Universe:

She was his, then;
Her limbs grasped him, satisfied, while
his brain
Judged every move and cry from its
separate dark.

But though Hill's verse is involved at times in moral quandaries concerning the Christian message in particular, we can never be sure about the direction of the thought. In some ways one feels Pound's and Heaney's intentions are simple in relation to Hill's goals. After all, in "Canto LXXXII" we find Whitman singing through Pound and the longed-for mate becomes an Earth Bride. Whitman sings through Heaney no less; the linguistic quests of both Irishman and American modern are far from simple, but they are not as concerned with the stance of self-doubt as Hill is. Pound trusts the visionary revelation of Homer's words in a way that, one suspects, Hill would disdain.

George Mackay Brown has a vision of sacrifice at the heart of his work, whether it be revealed in the spirit of John Barleycorn, Saint Magnus, or Christ. The moral dilemma, though present, is ultimately waived, for as the hart forgives the hunter so Christ and Magnus forgive their persecutors and the Harvest prevails. The sexual act, though it is admitted into the circles of Brown's poems, does not become the central symbol. The "House of Love" is only the fifth door in "The Seven Houses"; each house is of equal worth. In Magnus's case chastity was given the principal importance because of his particular mission. To Brown the 'mixing of the hair' is an aid to man's life, but the lover is only one woman on a journey from mother to mourner. It is true that his poetry recalls Heaney's when it continually seeks to reconcile male and female, sea and earth, but one feels that Brown conceives of the 'elemental darknesses' as sexless. To Heaney and Pound the dark is 'ruminant', fecund; the light of day and sun male and potent.

In "Psychology and the Troubadours", Pound wrote his own definition of myth:

I believe in a sort of permanent basis for humanity, that is to say, I believe that Greek myth arose when someone having passed through a delightful psychic experience tried to communicate it to others and found it necessary to screen himself from persecution. Speaking aesthetically, the myths are explications of mood, you may stop there or you may probe deeper. Certain it is that these myths are only intelligible in a vivid and glittering sense to those people to whom they occur. I know, I mean one man who understands the Laurel and another who has, I should say met Artemis.

There is nothing new in this formulation — men have been posing this kind of framework for myth since the 1820's, and Blake may have understood it before that. Hill, in his "Mystical Songs" probing the essence of Christ's teaching, Heaney's narrator seeing Nerthus in a bog-oak, and Brown's Magnus transported by religious delight, savouring the textures and metaphors of the Mass, are influenced by this evaluation of myth. When a woman sees Mary in a sea-hollowed rock, or Hill draws Venus in the guise of a shark, we realise how far-reaching the experience is.

Once realised, however, as we have already discussed, the myth transmogrifies. Indeed, Dekker correctly identifies metamorphosis as an integral part of Pound's conception of myth, and also of Pound's conception of his own poetry. The era provided stimuli — Jung was undermining the picture of the single, stable ego, and scientists were developing a picture of molecular structure where man was simply part of that great sub-atomic field: the Universe (or as Brown infers in *Magnus*, man, bread, sun and earth, are fundamentally one.)

Dekker finds two kinds of metamorphosis in Pound's plan. Firstly, the way in which folk-patterns remain while generations wax and wane, change being a constant of the Universe. Heaney has noted similar patterns:

> He talked about persistence,
> A congruence of lives. . .

These lines from "Belderg" show how the Irishman is both committed to finding and comparing the patterns. He traces language back to a 'ban-hus' and delves amongst skulls till he finds the Vikings, part of his own heritage. He mourns the passing of certain patterns in "Ancestral Photograph"; in certain poems, particularly "Bone Dreams" and "Kinship", the shapes of older existences govern the work. There is no need for examples of how the pattern of communities and their life-styles is a structural feature of Brown's work, for it is so patently the warp and weft of his accomplishment. One has only to look at any of his poems to see the results of this: the heraldic images, repetitive phrases, and the insistence on the recurrance of human types under the mask. One cannot actually prove Pound's influence, only point out its possibility, or likelihood. For one thing, Brown's patterns are too localised within the setting of Orkney and Shetland to permit overmuch speculation about external influences.

Mercian Hymns is Hill's only work where patterns of generation influence both form and content. It could be that Hill seeks to ridicule this idea of surviving patterns by some of the odd transferences of time and place in this work:

> Troll-wives, groaners in sweetness, tooth-bewitchers.

> *(Hymn XXVI)*

This humourous linking of a Saxon charm against tooth-ache with modern confectionary, and especially a domestic lifestyle which cultivates kitsch furniture and unhealthy eating habits, is such an example. But other examples might reveal that Hill is in deadly earnest, and that thought patterns recur: Offa could be a modern statesman. Pound was relying on a 'permanent basis in humanity' rather like Jung's Collective Unconscious. Heaney's narrator seeks to lead a Belfast funeral rite into a Neolithic burial chamber; there are echoes there which might reawaken a national conscience. Brown states and re-states the patterns of John Barleycorn seeking to realign man's sympathies from an obsession with material gains back to the elements. They both share an idea of that 'permanent basis'. But Hill finds no hope in this. The self-delusions and savagery surviving in men's minds make such patterns merely neutral structures in time. Hill places his emphasis on the patternless anonymities of death — there illusions and traces of culture are shorn away. Even the poet's efforts to be 'unfashionable' are finally doomed, since 'clear vision' and poetic integrity are illusions in themselves:

> A blinded god believes
> That he is not blind.

> ("Doctor Faustus")

The terror of the Faust legends is not only that God is a tyrant who denies man the heights of his aspirations but that Faust, the artist and articifer, in claiming vision is a potential tyrant too.

Secondly, Pound used the kind of metamorphoses that Ovid used as an organising feature of *The Metamorphoses*. That is, the supernatural changing of people into animals, plants etc. Dekker relates this to Pound's reliance on the natural image and writes:

> . . .this approach to reality instructs us that, though the
> roots of things are in heaven, we worship best by under-
> standing their particular manifestations on earth. . .from
> 'this' point of view, the pagan gods are always, whether by
> patronage or metamorphosis, more concretely involved
> with this world than is the Christian god or a Neo-Platonic
> one.

This protean quality is an interesting dividing line between different writers. David Jones, who manages, not to have one foot in the pagan world and one in the Christian but rather to bring them together in one person and one timeless moment (the Mass), holds both options in his work. He has the shape-shifting goddess — Virgin on one hand and the structural motif of the order of the signs on the other, and he binds them well together, mainly through the medium of human perception.

9

Brown cannot do both of these. He can, as a Catholic, rely on the successive signs: the Hoy statue of Mary, the worshipped stone, the pagan bonfires, the Ploughman's societies, all born out of a common reverence for nature. Additionally, he can dwell upon the Biblical metaphor of men as vessels and God as the potter, but this remains a self-consciously literary artifice — merely an instructive image. However, he cannot show men fluidly changing shape. Even the Siberian shaman, though partaking of Nature's voices, remains human. Christ alone transcends human agency and may, by recourse to his sacrificial example, possess power. The Protean change remains pagan:

> a jobber amongst shadows.
> Old work-whore, slave-
> blood,

> . . .a straggle of fodder
> stiffened on snow
> comes first-footing

> the back doors of the little
> barons. . .
>
> *(Servant Boy)*

Heaney handles Viking relics and a narrator's changing form with a sureness which is born of, at once, a keen eye for mental impression and chemical constituents, and a sense of the magic and phenomena of Nature. If one likes, he is using the sciences of perception in their most contemporary aspects, but also affirming Mystery, the central pagan presence. The Christian God is mystery too, but the Bible provides a generally lucid blueprint, even if only by metaphor, whereas Heaney's immediate statement is one of wonder:

> A stagger in air
> as if a language failed
>
> *(The Backward Look)*
> Was it wind off the dumps
> or something in heat

> dogging us. . .
> the possessed air. . .
>
> *(Summer Home)*

It is as if the wild found another tongue as eloquent as its spoilt and awed witch's bastard: '. . .the isle is full of noises, sounds and sweet airs, that give delight and hurt not'.

Hill gives magic and dogma equal status:

> And now the sea-scoured temptress, having failed
> To scoop out of horizons what birds herald:
> Tufts of fresh soil: shakes off an entire sea,
> Though not as the dove, harried. Rather, she,

> A shark. . .
>
> *(Metamorphoses)*

She remains a story, like Christ; an archetype; perhaps an experiment, but one read in a book, not part of an actual nature though the formation is a little crude. Perhaps it might be said that Heaney starts from the mystery of nature and uses the movements, forms, noises that he intuits there to breathe life through the old figures, while Hill seems to start with the article, the convention, the written myth, and gradually work outward to expose the ironies of human thought which they reveal. His Ovid of *The Amores* is found in the Third Reich, celebrating the 'love-choir'. No chance for metaphysical change here; any reference to this man as the recorder of miracles brings us back to his grip on his real position:

> Things happen
> Too near the ancient troughs of blood.
> *(Ovid in the Third Reich)*

His 'fiction' is seen as a distraction, an illusion 'difficult' to sustain in such a state.

Dekker writes of metamorphosis being 'a revelation of the godhead but . . . . . . not something that exists apart from the natural world' in Pound's work.

> It is rather a more dramatic sign of the divinity which is
> imminent in the objects around him, whether they be
> works of art or of Nature. . .We perceive that there is a
> permanent body of wisdom which survives in myth, in
> ritual, and in the craftsman's lore; and this wisdom survives
> to a large extent because it can assume new forms accord-
> ing to the demands of a new time and locality. But what-
> ever form it takes, it embodies something of the growing
> world.

I would only add that this growing world is presented to us in a kind of 'timeless present'. The reader is involved with what Dekker calls 'a constancy of vision'. To Heaney, the bog victims provide useful symbols of timelessness, against which he can pose his own life in Part II of *North*. Brown, because of his obsession with the Mass and the repetitive lives of men, shows history turning a cartwheel in *Fishermen with Ploughs*. Hill discerns that thought defeats itself, progress is an illusion as potent as the very way in which we narrate history and the dead are an inescapable presence. Offa vanishes at the end of the *Hymns*, but he has only existed in one man's brain, where swords co-exist with maroon GTs. He starts with the statement 'No manner of address will do". In "Funeral Music" the brutal facts of life are unanswerable. Poetry is merely part of that reality and, in itself, answers nothing, and is itself unanswerable. There is one constant:

> . . .the dead maintain their ground –
> That there's no getting round.
> *(The Distant Fury of Battle)*

Yet this fact is far from being simply terrifying, as is pointed out in that same poem.

It is often said that Pound found his practical philosophy in the Far East and his 'spiritual philosophy' in the Near East and the Mediterranean. As to the first, save for a few mentions of Hindu salesmen and Oriental symbols in Brown, there is surprisingly little consideration of Far Eastern thought in these three poets. Especially surprising, since Yeats followed at least two gurus, and because of the influence of Snyder, Watts and others on Californian life at a time when Heaney was there. Hill seems to give little attention to the fact that his religious formulations and ideas of self-defeating thought were long ago dealt with by the Buddha.

The 'spiritual' side of Pound's formula was a compound of Neo-Platonism, Pythagoreanism and Gnosticism. The influence of G.R.S. Mead, with his fascination for Apollonius of Tyana (hero of *Rock-Drill*), John Heyden ("Canto LXXXVII"), and the Rosicrucian Erigena, are also felt in his work. Neither can we forget that Pound spent a good deal of time reconciling the pagan and courtly views of Eros, just as Brown has written of the spectacular meeting of Earl Rognvald with Lady Ermengarde of Narbonne. Not only do two totally different ideas of beauty enter the mind of the Earl — the Northerners' and the Southerners' — but also sacred and profane love mingle:

> They trembled as their lips
> Welded holy and carnal love in one flame.
> *(Port of Venus)*

and:

> What can I give
> For the cup and kisses brought to my mouth?
> Nothing.
> This red hand, a death-dealer.
> *(Twelfth Century Norse Lyrics)*

But one must remember that this overlapping is perhaps only coincidental. Pound taught Troubadour poetry whilst in London and had long been an expert on the Provencal lyric before he started the *Cantos.* One suspects that Brown reached Narbonne in his imagination, not by way of Ventadorn, but by the *Orkneyinga Saga.* He may never have read the Troubadours in their own tongue.

There is also Pound's use of much-repeated keywords such as: ὕδωρ (water), χϑονός (earth) and different languages, primarily for music and the special tonalities of natural sensibility, but also to stress that certain formulations (mythological or otherwise) are irreducible, unique and antique (and must be treated as such). Of course, Heaney and Hill use a Latin quotation here and there, and a poetic quotation from Spenser or Shakespeare, but the nearest to this irreducible antique flavour is Heaney's use of place-names. Brown does not report trows in native Gaelic, and Hill does not make Offa speak Anglo-Saxon. For Pound this would have been a loss of mythical dimensions. For when Pound wrote

12

in 1912 of 'our kinship to the vital universe, to the tree and living rock', he knew that through the medium of language Nature had created, by its sounds and colours, man's sense of myth. Brown describes the process in "The Seven Poets", but he never really lets it come fully into play in his own work (save in his use of place and croft names).

There is little to suggest that Pound's use of Egyptian hieroglyphics and Sumerian and Chinese pictograms, has affected the work of any of the three writers. Yet, as Pound remembers various painters such as Botticelli and Giotto, or sculptors like Duccio and Gaudier Breszchka, to give his vision visual and tactile dimension, so Heaney recalls Breughel and Goya; Brown paints verbal pictures which resemble Medieval paintings and heraldries; Hill talks of the 'ornate heartlessness of much mid-fifteenth century architecture' and equates it to the 'florid grim music' of "Funeral Music". They may not have the ideogram, but Heaney uses his 'parables', Brown his ballads, allegories and charms, and Hill his dense hymn and pavan forms.

Rachewitz points out Pound's interest in the alchemists' hermetic key to palingenesis. In an early poem, "De Aegypto", Pound 'pretends' mystical experience, and this:

> assumes full depth of meaning in the late Canto XC, where
> Isis, the lunar goddess of ancient Egypt, is placed in asso-
> ciation with Kwannon, the compassionate bisexual
> Bodhisattva:
>> Isis Kuanon
>> from the cusp of the moon.

Mystical experience is linked very closely to Alchemy in Pound's writing. He is 'constantly at work breaking down outworn symbols into their original components, restoring some of their earlier power', and intentionally follows the process described by Zosimus, Olympiodorus and other Greek alchemists, in which the descent into the underworld can only be accomplished in one's own body, which represents the earth. By purging the body one may find the philsophers' stone. This process is probably behind the patterns of transmutation and resurrection, as well as the gradually-refining crystal motif we find in the *Cantos*, and gradually acquires symbolic significance. As Rachewitz says

> Pound progressively refines his materials as if by calcin-
> ation in hermetic fire until the time we reach the Pisan
> Cantos, the work itself has become as crystal:
>> Serenely in the crystal jet
>> as the bright ball that the fountain tosses. . .
>>> as diamond clearness
>>>> *(Canto LXXIV)*

The inner nature of this process is also important when we consider how Pound hypostatises certain psychic forces within himself into a private pantheon, and also how he humanises his gods

Brown has also humanised his gods. Christ becomes Everyman in his

13

poetry, and the Holy Family, and family. He also betrays an interest in alchemy; the successive trains of changing images: coats, circles, stones, doors, masks, the constant injunctions of unity, especially wine-brewing, all prove to be metaphors for this process. In *Magnus*, the coat of life suddenly appears, flawless and pure, before his death. The gold of butter and grain, the red of wine, represent the pattern of suffering, death and resurrection in Nature — they parallel Pound's crystal ball. Heaney too, in "Churning Day", enumerates the tools and containers making the transformation of milk possible. As in the work of Jung, the labour here has a psychic as well as physical effect:

> our brains turned crystals full of clean deal churns

Such rhetoric of purification would seem empty for Hill. Even martyrs suffer from a subtle form of egotism in "Lachrimae".

Rachewitz links this alchemy motif in Pound's work to his infusion of gods with human attributes. Hence his preference for Ovid over Apuleius. The reason is made clear in "The Spirit of Romance", when, referring to Ovid's *Metamorphoses*, he concludes: 'the marvellous thing is made plausible, the gods are humanised, their annals are written as if copied down from parish registers'. We remember Heaney's carter-god in "Kinship", and Brown's constant references to the Holy Family being lowly poor folk. These truly are names out of parish registers. But for Hill the gods are deceptive systems, blind because they are unable to halt their manipulation of the mankind that made them. They are used by church and state to control their subjects and as such they can never be human. In "Picture of a Nativity", men are 'slack serpents' and beasts to the Christ-child. He is victim to the abstract purity which men have attributed to him. The gods are expedient, and require blood. True piety and unselfishness are contradictions in themselves.

Rachewitz also shows how Pound overlaps mythological motifs such as the Mithraic sunboats with historical events such as the destruction of the main Albigensian sites — Chaise Dieu, Mont Segur and Excideuil. He illustrates how Pound uses symbols from different mythological frameworks to throw light on each other. For example:

> In the Pisan Cantos, the sun rising out of darkness is
> identified with the creative Word, the Paraclete and
> Logos, a vision reinforced by the Chinese pictograph
> K'ou depicting a mouth which Pound interprets as:
> > mouth is the sun that is god's mouth
> > (*Canto LXXVII*)

This is later thematically rhymed with a reference to Wondjina, an Australian deity.

In Hill's "Of Commerce and Society", the Heads of State at Verseilles in 1919 become the Apostles at the Last Supper. Shelley and the whole Classical world seem dead or lost amidst 'frothed shallows'. Auschwitz looms. Thus Hill mixes dates and mythological motifs, but in a way that has more in common with the Augustan poets' Classical metaphors for contemporary man and events than with Pound's. For his conventions are assembled, not to reinforce a sense of mythic actuality, but to modify and add new perspectives to the way in which we view events in time. It is such a mode of writing that Hughes refers to in the words:

> Imagine hearing somewhere in the poem being recited
> the phrase 'crucifixion of Hitler'. The word 'Hitler' is as
> much a hieroglyph as the word 'crucifixion'. Individually
> the two words bear the consciousness of much of our
> civilisation. . .and in conjunction. . .they challenge our
> static ideas of good and evil.

Heaney uses such names and events with a purpose closer to Pound's:

> Balor will die
>
> and Byrthnoth and Sitting Bull
>
> Hercules lifts his arms
>
> (*Hercules and Antaeus*)

Here we have an Anglo-Saxon hero, an Indian medicine-man and an Irish giant set side by side to emphasise the death of those cultures which have stayed at an early stage of growth. Of course, belief and recorded time converge in Brown's work with his use of 17th century records in *A Spell for Green Corn*, and in the reported events surrounding the life of Magnus. The myths of Barleycorn and the goddess in his work are ever present in the peasants' life-styles; as such they enhance a feeling of a timeless continuum.

The Cantos are crowded with references to cosmic centres, the fertility cults of Adonis, Tammuz, the chthonic trinity of Eleusis and various agrarian as well as sexual rites. Though largely pre-Christian in origin, it is interesting to see how Pound relates them to a Christian setting. He, it seems, approves of Church ritual insofar as it retains traces of the older pagan meaning. 'The Church in sanity', he writes in a letter of June 18th, 1954, 'RETAINED symbols, look at Easter show in Siena Cathedral (Egypt etc.) Ceres, Bacchus and damn the blood washings. . .' He talks of the pagan origin of the symbolic ritual of the 'Mass and its artifacts, mitre and crozier etc.'

To examine the Triple-Goddess in Pound's work and that of Heaney and Brown would require a chapter in itself. Pound seems to dip rather liberally into the assortment of Goddesses from Greece and Asia Minor, whereas Heaney limits himself to Celtic and Nordic goddesses, and Brown to the nameless and un-named predecessors of Mary. Heaney, Brown and Pound also share the reverence for 'centres'. When Kenner writes: 'For the net is drawn tight, each sacred place remembers others', we recall Heaney's flax-dam and flax-poisoned waters in "Summer 1969". True, his centres are wilder and more organic than Pound's; the older poet chose cities and great works of art as vortices of power. Brown too chooses shrines and churches, especially on islands, as 'centres'. As for the survival of gods and pagan ritual in new guises ('For the gods persist – Christ is Tammuz again. . .'), Brown, like David Jones, would place emphasis on the progress of belief, up to and including the Marian religion. In *Magnus* Brown shows the shortcomings of the Neolithic and Aztec religions. Heaney, however, looks back to the ceremonies and mysteries of Celtic lore without which contemporary religion seems shallow. The haunters of Gallarus seem ecstatic and fulfilled characters in comparison to the women in "Poor Women in a City Church". The Mysteries of the Greek religions had a similar attraction for Pound. Hill alone mistrusts the gods, no matter from which direction and how far back they come. Their survival merely prolongs man's manipulation through emblems and symbols.

W.B.Yeats

Both Yeats and Pound were interested in mythological symbol and both knew of Plotinus's system of vortices, cones and crescents. However, entering Yeats' sphere of mythological interest is a daunting prospect. He belonged both to the Theosophists and the Hermetic Students of the Golden Dawn, and was deeply involved in Irish mysticism and folklore. The Dublin Hermetic Society, of which he was a founder-member, wanted to restore 'unity of being'. The Neo-Platonic strain in his work is obvious: the Hermetic Society dealt with a hidden philosophy of which all known religions were but manifestations. This doctrine had supposedly been shielded through the ages by the Gnostics, Hermetic and Rosicrucian orders, and also by individuals like Paracelsus, Bruno, Vaughan and Boehme. On a more materialistic plane, as Ellman writes, Yeats thought that communism, socialism, fascism and democracy were myths, for only myths could 'rouse great masses to action'. Not that this was the language of degradation, for Yeats was determined to pit a myth of his own against these other myths. This was to be 'The Castle of Heroes' – a new cult through which 'truths of the spirit' might be disseminated to the materialistic nation. The 'Heroes' would 'unite the radical truths of Christianity to those of a more ancient world.' The Hermetic Students had a great interest in pre-Christian Ireland, read John Rhys on Celtic heathendom, and worked out parallels between the Irish gods and Graeco-Roman ones. Seeking to avoid the 'myth' of fascism, Yeats was nearing an aristocratic fascism, backed by the rabble-rousing 'blueshirts'. He was even to write songs (which had to be censored) for this Irish equivalent of Nazi youth. Add to these elements Yeats' interest in ghosts, fairies and dreams, the Pre-Raphaelite 'Twilight' and Irish heroic legend, and one begins to sense the range of his ideas. In his notebooks from 1896–98 he listed his poetic subjects in a geometrical diagram as follows:

> a. classical divinities
> b. Celtic divinities, heroes
> c. forms of evocation and magical rites

d. character and personality traits

e. philosophic formulae

f. elements, colours

g. symbolism of Tarot cards

These subjects were set in the centre of a Cabalistic rose.

Perhaps the best approach is that taken by Austin Clarke in his *The Celtic Twilight and the Nineties*, in which he traces Yeats' and other Irish writers' apprehensions of fairies and spirits to that of Tennyson, who, Clarke says, 'was the first to write of them imaginatively'. He quotes Tennyson's lines about the fairy-circle from *The Idylls of the King*, and compares it with Yeats' "The Hosting of the Sidhe". Yeats had written several poems on Indian subjects, such as the small dramatic scene "Anashuya", and "The Indian to his Love", and Clarke draws our attention here to the influence of Sir Edwin Arnold's "The Light of Asia". This leads Clarke to stress the influence of the Romantic tradition upon Yeats' writing, especially that of Rossetti, Morris and Shelley. "The Wanderings of Oisin" is a good example of how a strictly Irish legend can be given the trappings of English Romanticism, through the medium of a young Irish poet's brain. There are, however, other important features of Yeats' life which demand consideration here. J.B. Yeats lost his faith in Christianity and as a result elevated poetry to the heights of religion, independent both of faith and scepticism. This could have allied poetry with non-Christian beliefs in his son's mind, in relegating them both to the status of coveted and secret knowledge. In 1888 Yeats made a collection of fairy-stories in which he asserts that the Irish peasantry, because of their distance from the centres of the Industrial Revolution, had preserved a 'rapport with the spiritual world and its fairy denizens which had elsewhere disappeared'. This underlines the constant need that Yeats felt to embed his mythology in Irish soil. At one point he said to T.Sturge Moore, 'all my art theories depend on just this rooting of mythology in the earth.' It is an idea both Heaney and Brown have profited from. However stylised or imaginatively-distanced their myths become at times, they are nearly always recognisable as Irish or Orcadian myths. The towns are Rackwick and Dublin, not Athens, and the goddesses are Bog-queens and Ladies of the Hoy shore-line, not Artemis or Demeter — at least not in their present forms.

Again, as in the case of Pound, we must take into account the international movements of Symbolism and Imagism which hardened and defined many personal mythic motifs in the minds of artists. Yeats wrote:

...for the elemental beings go
About my table to and fro
In flood and fire and clay and wind
They huddle from man's pondering mind;
Yet he who treads in austere ways
May surely meet their ancient gaze.
Man ever journeys on with them

> After the red rose-embroidered hem.
> Ah, faeries, dancing under the moon,
> A Druid land, a Druid tune!
>> (*To Ireland in the Coming Times*)

The poem shows an earnest desire to link those experiments of seances and psychic speculation with the Irish faery tales. Kathleen Raine says:

> Yeats had perceived that the phenomena of the seance
> are similar to the visions 'seen' by country people: the
> 'otherworld' of faery is the same as the 'otherworld' of
> the dead.

Brown never tries to make a link between the two psychic mysteries of this world and Orcadian trows. It is true that trows carry a real fiddler into the mound, but Brown never asks himself 'Do I believe in trows as I do in dreams?' Nor does he ask, 'Do I believe in trows as I do the Holy Mass?' Heaney, however, does link these layers of belief. His mermaid is, at least on one level, as real as the drowned bastard of "Limbo". The feminine Irish spirit of the wild is as real as the young girl who runs naked, 'astray among the cattle'. Mental illness, dreams, strange over-lappings of human and animal life as in "Bye-child", are manifestations in today's world of what we choose to call myth, the supernatural or the world of the spirits.

In 1896 Yeats prophesied that 'another Leda would open her knees to the swan and begin a new age. The bird's rape of the human, the coupling of god and woman, the moment one. . .epoch ended and another began. . .' We see here, not only Yeats' conscious attempt to unify the traditions he was drawing from, but also his attempt to link his myth or frame of reference to the world of time. For Yeats believed in spiritual revelation but, as Raine writes, 'a revelation accessible to all times because reality is omnipresent; the Christian appeal to history was no part of his system'. Leda was as alive in 1896 as Queen Victoria or Madame Blavatsky.

Stylistically, Yeats spent years considering how a cultivation of the Heroic Age could shape a distinctly Anglo-Irish style. When Lady Gregory's two books, *Cuchulian of Muirthemne* and *Gods and Fighting Men,* were published, he acclaimed them as an artistic breakthrough. Not only did they reveal ancient Ireland as preserved in the imaginative life of the people, but they communicated the legends in a fresh, vital way. We must never make the mistake of confining Yeats' mythology to the Heroic legends. His professed belief in spirits and fairies was never removed from his conviction that the Irish peasant was receptive to the supernatural:

> And he saw young men and young girls
> Who danced on a level place,
> And Bridget his bride among them,
> With a sad and gay face.
>> (*The Host of the Air*)

18

Indeed, his interest in the people and the spirit world generally outpaced his use of Heroic legend as the Celtic Twilight artists knew it. By the time of "A Coat" he is persuaded to walk naked and leave his coat of embroideries 'out of old mythologies' behind. However this abandonment is exercised only to take up a new kind of myth in poems like "The Phases of the Moon", "The Double Vision of Michael Robartes", "The Second Coming" or "Blood and the Moon". It is in these poems that a language dealing with ritual, cosmic forces, and incantations of ancient formulae, is refined. For instance, in Robartes' third speech in "The Phases of the Moon", we find:

> Twenty-and-eight the phases of the moon.
> The full and the moon's dark and all the crescents
> Twenty-and-eight, and yet but six and twenty
> The cradles that a man must needs be rocked in:
> Fot there's no human life at the full of the dark. . .

It is this mixture of folk-knowledge, esoteric doctrine and general philosophy which infuses the mature Yeats' work. This, and the gentle, discursive voice of the narrator, is perhaps his largest contribution to Brown's work:

> Who stood between the cold Plough and the embers
> In the door of death, knew that this masquerade
> Was a pure seeking past a swarm of symbols,
> The millwheel, sun and scythe, and ox and harrow. . .
> (*The Masque of Bread*)

Mysticism and folklore shine from these lines. Yeats' love of colour and number are also found in Brown's work:

> I made seven circles, my love
> For your good breaking.
> I make the grey circle of bread
> And the circle of ale
> And I drive the butter round in a golden ring. . .
> (*Country Girl*)

They also share in common poems called "When You are Old", choosing, in their different ways, to translate Ronsard's "Sonnet to Helen". Alan Bold calls Brown's attempt 'a Yeatsian pastiche', but, though Brown is clearly influenced by Yeats here, he has made the poem his own.

Yeats never completely escapes the high Celtic tradition. Clarke sees a significance in the fact that the last two legendary poems, written in 1939 a few weeks before Yeats' death, were "Cuchulain Comforted" and "The Black Tower". Even where the poem is not engaged with a mythological scenario, the flux of images often produces pagan motifs; for example, the centre and the beast ("The Second Coming"), a winged horse ("Easter 1916") and the labyrinthine repetition in "The Tower". This is not the place to examine the rich texture of the mythical and legendary motifs in Yeats' poems, but it is relevant to mention the

gold mosaic, holy fire, perne and gyre, the mackerel-crowded seas and
golden bough of "Sailing to Byzantium". This allegorical bric-a-brac,
drawn from the dazzling interiors of the Romantic and Pre-Raphaelite
poets' palaces, could symbolise all manner of artistic or mental artifices
and splendour. It immediately anticipates Brown:

> . . .I entered the golden door
> (There my throne stood, withering)
> I passed through rooms
> of flowers, flagons, chessboards
> And a room with a fountain.

> . .'I am the Grain of Dust from the Floor of Heaven'
> 'I am the Emerald.'
> 'I am the Temple Lamp. . .'
> (*The Golden Door*)

In a letter to O'Leary, Yeats wrote:

> If I had not made magic my constant study, I could
> not have written a single word of my Blake book, nor
> would *The Countess Kathleen* have ever come to exist.
> The mystical life is the centre of all that I do and all that
> I think and all that I write.

Kathleen Raine concluded: 'For Yeats, magic was not so much a kind of
poetry, as poetry a kind of magic, and the object of both alike was the
evocation of knowledge from beyond normal consciousness.' This viewpoint is an extreme one, but there is a basis for it. Pound himself once
wrote to John Quinn about Yeats:

> I think the term 'fantastic' in my cable was the just
> one. . .I notice with Yeats he will be quite sensible till
> some question of ghosts or occultism comes up, then
> he is subject to a curious excitement, twists everything
> to his theory, usual quality of mind goes.

But Pound did desire his poetry to have an element of magic about
it. Kenner writes of how Pound believed that whatever entered the
'mind's ecology' made a difference and that to offer men's minds a reading of historical patterns might consolidate or might alter those patterns.
Heaney too desires to alter the structures of mens' thoughts, but much
as he writes of men taking power from Nature into Art, and much as
Brown talks of the Word as a 'spell for green corn', one wonders if any
of these poets takes poetry as a kind of magic in the way Yeats did. I
shall talk later in detail of Heaney's conscious and unconscious use of
the shaman figure, the filid or wild hermit of the woods. He traces the
Latin word 'dives', for poet, to a sense of divining, chanelling a cosmic
force: . . .The pluck came sharp as a sting.

> . . .broadcasting
> Through a green aerial its secret stations.
> (*The Diviner*)

Is the poet by implication another organic 'aerial' of cells and nerve-endings for a force moving through him?

Ernest Fenellosa's notebooks concluded that language springs from creative metaphors in which man and nature come into a close bonding; these are intertwined with mythologies and primitive poetries. Therefore 'all words act, enact, verbwise, the propositions; they are chanellers of force'. Language partakes of and imitates nature since, as Kenner writes 'metaphor is the revealer of nature. . .the known interprets the obscure, the Universe is alive with myth.'

One feels these are fundamental ideas in Heaney's way of looking at reality. But due to many pressures we have long separated the magician and poet, at least in this country. The stance 'poet-as-shaman' has become a cheap pose, ridiculed by those who find Ginsberg or Snyder chanting mantras laughable. We have no qualms about tracing Yeats to a seance or revealing his Theosophical interests, but to talk of Heaney's cry:

> I could risk blasphemy,
> Consecrate the cauldron bog
> Our holy ground. . .
>
> *(The Tollund Man)*

as a statement of fluctuating belief would not be considered valid by most contemporary critics. The lines are merely a technique of narrative spoken by a fictive voice. The fact that this verse constitues a temptation and that its potential nature is real 'blasphemy' might afford us food for thought, especially as Heaney has spoken, if briefly, about his Catholicism. I do not think Hill, Brown or Heaney consider themselves to be involved in the black or white arts, merely that there are areas of religious confrontation within their work.

Ireland is the 'Holy Land' to Yeats too, but ironically so. He was born into an Ireland of religious division and was ever-conscious of the lore and beliefs which, by their age, dwarfed Christianity. He saw the religion of the peasant as being a kind of amalgam of old pagan and doctrinaire Christian belief. To Crazy Jane, 'All things remain in God' and the women of his poetry generally judge events by the rule of passion, which is the dance itself and which is timeless. Christian Love therefore is bound to be considered narrow and exclusive:

> Why should I seek for love or study it?
> It is of God and passes human wit.
> I study hatred with great diligence,
> For that's a passion in my own control,
> A sort of besom that can clear the soul
> Of everything that is not mind or sense.
>
> *(Ribh Considers Christian Love Insufficient)*

It is this sense in Yeats of deeper passions, older beliefs and spiritual forces, which are unsatisfied in Christianity which informs much of his verse (though he, like Pound, sees survivals of the pagan in Christian ritual). This is a basic premise in Heaney's work too, whereas Brown would disagree. To the Catholic artist the Christian story is the fulfilment of the collective strivings of Creation. Thus Jones finds Christ placing himself in the order of signs. Brown finds images of Christ's life everywhere. Christ has, by His Life, Death and Resurrection, folded the whole breadth and length of humanity's history in a moment: the Mass. Yeats' Magi are unsatisfied by 'Calvary's turbulence' and turn again to 'the uncontrollable mystery on the bestial floor.' (The bestiality of the miracle and its uncontrollable nature, if one likes it's 'blindness', remind one of Hill's reservations.) Oisin ending his wanderings returns to a natural world and a Christianised Ireland. He finds people bowed down with a consciousness of sin and guilt and he falls weakened and exhausted in the world of St.Patrick. An apocalyptic element is also linked with the insufficiency of the Christian vision in Yeats' work as it is in Heaney's. At the end of *Fishermen with Ploughs*, however, we still find Teresa hugging her rosary-beads and seeing Mary 'move' in the stone.

As 'the centre cannot hold' in "The Second Coming", so we find a 'rough beast' slouching towards Bethlehem and birth. We have already mentioned Heaney's and Pound's interest in centres: Yeats found them in fairy-rings, Byzantiums of the mind and in psychic rings connected to the pernes and gyres. Emerson writes, 'The poet is the sayer, the namer, and represents beauty. He is sovereign, and stands at the centre'. Both he and Yeats saw poets as possessed of a demon, though they both may have meant totally different things. As it is, like Blake they had both read the Neo-Platonists down the ages, Plotinus, Swedenborg and Boehme. When Heaney writes:

> Any point in that wood
> Was a centre. . .

and,

> You had to come back
> To learn how to lose yourself,
> To be a pilot and stray — witch,
> Hansel and Gretel in one.

in "The Plantation", one can almost hear the echoes of Emerson's essay "Circles", or Yeats' idea that, according to Olney,

> The circle is thus the figure that encompasses both God
> and man, both the 'transpersonal' unconscious and the
> private unconscious and that, in itself, connects, as all
> varieties of occult would agree, the above with the below.

Yet one can take the likenesses too far. Yeats wrote that in the line of thought running through Pythagoras and Plato 'we encounter an ultimate reality that is formalistic and that displays a series of perfect formal correspondences. . .' Brown, with his exact circles drawing sea and land together might agree with this, but Heaney would find its neatness and concision deceptive. There is nothing neat or concise in the worlds of Whitman or Jung, and Heaney cares too much about the erratic qualities of certain patterns of thought and emotion to sacrifice them to this shapeliness.

Yeats' 'centres' were anyway regarded as under threat. The war, the stirrings of urban democracy, communism and fascism, added to this sense of coming crisis. But in Yeats' terms this was a limited vision. His views of relativism, the principles of Yin and Yang, flux and re-flux and movement in the gyres, made him think of the necessity for the recognition of a more ancient and impassive notion. In "Lapis Lazuli" the ageless Chinese sages play on in spite of the tragic scene below' 'Their ancient, glittering eyes, are gay.' A crisis may arrive and return but it is only to be expected; peace too will come again. These sages could be the Taoist immortals, devotees of Chinese Buddhism or Madame Blavatsky's psychic contacts in Tibet, but their wisdom is stressed. Cromwell in "The Curse of Cromwell", remembers another knowledge that proves:

> . . .that things both can and cannot be;
> That the swordsman and the ladies can still
> [keep company. . .

The old order's seasonal and hierarchic reassertion is a major theme in Yeats' verse just as the figure of the Laird recurs through Brown's work.

However, even in Cromwell's soliloquy there is a suggestion that Yeats' mythos is changing. Finally, only the horses and dogs understand his talk. D.M.Hoare comments on the retreat from actuality, especially in the direction of dream and fantasy in Yeats' early work and how this again changed. She traces the change in the Cuchulain theme from a tale straight out of Curtin's *Myth and Folklore of Ireland*, through the 'heart-mysteries' of *At the Hawk's Well* (1917), to its status as an emblem imbued with the writer's own ideas. In the "Death of Cuchulain" (1939), there is a grim and tragic irony as the masterful heroic image is reduced to a mound of refuse, old iron, old bone, old rags. 'All that great past is a trouble of fools.' Perhaps this is why two subsequent generations of Irish writers have dwelt upon the stubborn and bloody realities of Irish history and culture, instead of placing such a great emphasis on heroic legend. Perhaps, in time, Heaney will do the same with the Bog victims and Brown to Magnus or Rognvald. It remains to be seen. Hill's characters are, in many cases, already exhausted emblems used to imply the specious nature of other conventions or ideas.

Tuohy writes, 'Irish legend' only appears interesting now 'when coloured by Yeats' own beliefs and his own personal relationships. Cuchulain takes his place in a cycle of plays as the poet's Anti-Self: by that time, not only the Celtic gods and heroes, but friends like John O'Leary were all a part of Yeats' personal mythology.' The recurrence of the voyage, the perilous tower, the warrior's choice or the old hard philosophising about life in Yeats' poems reveals that he was concerned to 'place' his work in the tradition of legendary conventions. They are the most ancient of patternings passed down from the stories of oral poets and singers and help give Yeats' work the feel of a timeless past in which supernatural events mingled with the heroism of mortals. Brown more than the other poets seems to have utilised these conventions too. Yeats, at least originally, looked to *The Tain* and Brown to the *Orkney-inga Saga*; it is feasible that the link stops here. But motifs such as the rose, doves, dancers, stone-circles, and the Holy City, recur in their work. The Empedoclean-Heraclitean gyres and cycles and cones go on reversing into one another in Yeats' work; we remember Brown's quern-stones turning under the Pentland Firth and the women weaving 'the warp and weft of time'. Eliade recalls the link between 'feminine inititiations, spinning and sexuality':

> It is the Moon that spins the Time, she who 'weaves'
> the lives of humanity: the goddesses of fate are spinners.

This 'one weave of time' as Brown calls it in *Winterfold*, together with the series of masks all men wear and the identification of sea with land, produce a unity of vision which is analogous to the unity which the machinery of Yeats' *A Vision* promulgates.

There is also the strong attraction of Indian mysticism: the dual influence of the Swami Shri Purohit and Mohini Chatterji is felt in Yeats' writing. Pound studied Confucius, Mencius and the Classical Chinese school. T.S.Eliot finished *The Waste Land* with sentences from *The Upanishads*. There seems surprisingly little trace of such philosophy in the work of the contemporary poets. Brown shows the occasional group of Chinese men drinking tea and a wily Hindu merchant in his short stories, but the vast wealth of Chinese and Indian learning lies very well hidden in their poetry — if it lies there at all.

Both Yeats and Pound were men obsessed with stone, the uncut and the sculpted. In this perhaps they have participated in and passed on a symbol of resistance and of the essence of all things:

> In a house of withered webbed stone
> The harp is hidden. . .

> . . .Fold hands.
> Bid the stone enter. . .
> > *(Seven translations of A Lost Poem)*
> . . .dressed some stones with his own mark.
> Which he tells of with almost fear;

> And of strange affiliation
> To what was touched and handled there,
> > *(Cairn-Maker)*
> Arnor has sailed to the quarries in Eday
> With chisel. . .
> That stone is red as fire, roses, blood. . .
> > *(Viking Testament)*
> Grass resurrects to mask, to strangle,
> Words glossed on stone, lopped stone-angel;
> > *(The Distant Fury of Battle)*

24

Gaudier-Breszchka, so Pound thought, could see the form in stone before he touched it. Heaney, for one, would agree with this. As the sea
and wind 'peel acres', so the artist sculpts his mark in "Synge on Aran".
The memory of the first artists at Carnac and Stonehenge, and in
Brown's case, Maes Howe, stir in these lines. Hill sees the rune in stone
as potentially brutal, for it outlasts man like the principles which move
him to action:

> ghosting upon stone
> Creatures of such rampant state, various
> Ceremony of possession.

But, with Heaney and Pound, the lapidary associations and identifications between the land and the Word are basic. The land shapes
language and moulds mythological metaphor. Both speech and the soil
contain strata, and when Graves, in the second volume of *The Greek
Myths* traces the origins of the names of gods, he is examining geographical data too. Albright ends his book, *The Myth against Myth*:

> Yeats resigned himself, not to God, but to a world
> without artifice, the wild thickness of things:
>> Not such as are in Newton's metaphor
>> But actual shells of Rosse's level shore.
> But of course the shells mean more because they are
> contractions of metaphors than they would have meant
> if they had been simple deposits of calcium carbonate. . .

Thoughts and ideas overlap throughout an artist's life. It is feasible that
Yeats at last came to a vision of the sufficiency of the 'land as an image'
which Pound and Heaney could never doubt.

The senses of these five poets differ quite radically, in discerning the
direction and quality of their visions. Heaney 'digs' for his landscape
and his narrator is a 'skull-handler', a delver. The 'unknown' is his goal,
whether it be supernatural, psychological or social — this is the Dark,
which surrounds the farms, villages and the minds of his countrymen.
Brown talks of the flames and darknesses of elemental matter, but his
vision of God is of light, with all the trappings of candles, flowers and
doves. Pound too asserts the potency of light and its configurations.
Light must enter the cave or the womb, and candles must float out
into the bay, before the mystical experience arrives. For Brown and
Pound, there must be a flash of light at the heart of the winter darknesses to produce the summer yield. The damp and dark earth is the
preservative and medicinal essence in Heaney's work: the sky-worshippers brought greed and dissolution. There is the splendour of light and
reverence for darkness found in Yeats: he shows a readiness to com-
mune with the spirits of the dead and consider the unseen sprites of
air. His cities of the imagination are as resplendent as Pound's walls of
stars in *The Pisan Cantos*, but his darknesses are as wet and mysterious
as those found in Heaney's poems.

There are a few strands left untied. Hill's use of the second person singular sounds remarkably like Pound's early work at times. Yeats' interest in the Tarot may have directed Brown to drawing such scenes as those found in "The Masque of Princes" or "White Emperor". Pound's use of fragments and paraphrases of documents may well have influenced Hill's hymn-form and "Lachrimae", or Brown's runes and official records. All five interleave historical details and statements in their poetry. The art of translation is especially considered in Pound's, Brown's, and Heaney's poems.

All five poets are aware of the concepts of reincarnation, cyclical time, and the continuous present. Whether the younger poets are aware of Plotinus', Pythagoras' and Vico's ideas of time is difficult to assess. Brown has written a book of verse which in its very span describes a cycle of time. Hill overlaps and compares different moments in time in *Mercian Hymns*, but he acknowledges that history evades the writer's grip. Yeats draws from fields of literature and experience in examining chronological perspectives, sometimes in contrast to his own ideas, but he does not exhibit the same utilisation of historical form, metre and language as Pound, though he uses the ballad, heroic legend and elegy forms, at times quoting from the work of previous masters.

Finally, both Yeats and Pound viewed modern history with something approaching despair. Hill too, while thought, power and expression remain loaded with darker threats, sees no way out. "Lachrimae" and "Mystical Songs" remain as brilliant exercises within certain forms. No desire to break out of those forms is shown, and even when he tries, as in "Funeral Music", it proves a hopeless effort. Brown's mistrust of machines almost echoes R.S.Thomas's strict condemnation at times, though on the whole his vision is lighter. Somehow, he seems to find faith easier to hold, and even if, as at the end of *Fishermen with Ploughs*, his people must enter a dark age again, hope is not exhausted. Heaney too deals with the new beginnings, even if the violence of his imagery is, at times, stark and uncompromising. There is at least a 'meagre' heat at the end of "Exposure" and a little destiny to hug. These are the poets' various conclusions, governed, to some extent, of course, by their different backgrounds and experience.

Myth and history are bound together in the minds of these men; often, the form and content of their work is a statement of this. As I said at the beginning, patterns are difficult to unravel, and I have not been exhaustive in this study of influence. I hope that the channels of commitment described here lead easily on to the more thorough considerations of the following chapters.

Beneath the weight of irony found in Hill's early poetry there is a steady and keen sense of schism. The world of cold, hard, often brutal facts is decisively separated from the perceived and imagined worlds where thoughts and words shield their creators:

> Words glossed on stone, lopped stone-angel;
> But the dead maintain their ground —
> That there's no getting round —
> *(The Distant Fury of Battle)*

Hill is aware that the human discipline of history is a very inexact and misleading practice. It deceptively elevates certain events in drawing them from the whole mass of past life. Poetry, also, shares this power of distortion as it attempts to 'resurrect' dead voices, and inasmuch as it attempts to vocalise feeling or thought at all. Thus, Hill's use of certain artistic conventions, whether sculptural, literary or rhetorical, is imbued with a consciousness of their tendency to delude.

The past has 'passed down' certain events and conventions. The events are lost — like a person's childhood, irrecoverable. They can be aesthetically reproduced but such attempts are external to, and a reinterpretation of, the original conventions. On the other hand, laws, architecture, artifacts, forms of government and, more important in Hill's work, forms of thought, sometimes remain. These are mere fragments isolated from the texture of ordinary life, but they do provide starting-points or clues. Hill peruses and centres his art on such fragments. Admittedly, the conventions are as composed and artificial as Hill's own medium. For example, a record of a king's exploits is a work of selection and refining too, arranged to present a limited, often largely false view of his reign. But Hill is alert to such difficulties and his verse embodies an intelligence checking and rechecking its own rhetoric, often deprecatingly. A recognition of this gap between convention and fact, role and man or supposedly 'meaningful' existence and life's confusing ambiguities, is a first step in approaching Hill's often cryptic work.

Heaney, in his essay "Now and in England", writes of the 'stiff and corbelled rhetoric' of Hill's earlier work, lacking the vigour of 'common speech' to 'squeeze out' of its words. Perhaps Hughes, in talking of the phrase 'the crucifixion of Hitler' in his essay "Myth and Education", is closer to the point:

> The word 'Hitler' is as much of a hieroglyph as the word
> 'crucifixion'. . .And in those who possess both stories, the
> collision of those two words, in that phrase cannot fail to

detonate a psychic depth-charge.

Hill takes this approach to its extreme, and at that pole, if handled subtly and aptly, his finished product does not demand the verve and colour of vernacular. Out of the shadings lying beneath, and energy running through, the words, are created mazes of thought, various channels for meditation. Often, the maze is not open-ended, and turns back on itself. His more obvious placing of Plato and the Third Reich together to cause an ideological friction is by no means his most polished method. We can see the same 'machinery' at work beneath a poem like "The Bidden Guest". Both Heaney and Brown have written of worshippers, surrounded by candles, praying in church, but never has the depth of their rhetoric so exhibited itself. There is the conventional sigh of reverent fervour from the hymnals: 'O quiet dead!', the Blakean parable:

But one man lay beneath his vine
And, waking, found that it was dead.
And so my heart has ceased to breathe
(Though there God's worm blunted its head. . .)

and a retreat from God and pursuit heavily reminiscent of "The Hound of Heaven":

. . .But now I hear
Like shifted blows at my numb back,
A grinding heel; a scraped chair.

Yet, it is part of Hill's accomplishment that he never lets mere echoes or juxtaposed rhetoric compose his entire approach. Just as much as the verbal hieroglyphs strike resonances from each other, there is an underlying mystery to his work, a language as cryptic as the secret correspondences of the Symbolist poets. Trying to extricate views of God from one of Hill's poems is like trying to isolate God and death in a poem by Rilke or Wallace Stevens. Intention is consciously both underlined and obscured by Hill's language and images and there is an essentially private quality about certain of the correspondences. These poems cannot be explained away — the very intractability of their form states this. However, one can go some way towards exploring the particular atmospheres which pervade the early work by a description of the 'props' with which Hill builds his poetic worlds.

Because of the tension between the environment and what men have made of it, life, in Hill's work, can become a series of artifacts. One remembers Brown's seven houses, series of doors or successive coats. In Hill's verse the days of the week become seven pits, a man becomes characterised by his own martyrdom or a jumble of titles, devotions or songs. The death of a linear notion of history lends to a stylisation of environment, where life becomes a moral drama viewed with the continuous qualifications of a narrator. Life is a plain on which all men are visible in their chosen postures. Men are vulnerable, victims of law, expectations, a predatory nature and their own egotistical designs and limited visions. Stone looms, outlasting all but the 'out-numbering' dead. Often statues are seen as immovable, obsolete but enduring the 'weatherings' of fashion and the storms of human suffering. Air and water hem man in and confound him with their beauty and violence. But the delineation of these elements is subtler than this. If stone, the essence of matter, 'Pitched to extremities, in the rock's vein. . .' (*Metamorphoses*), shows both the extremity of nature and human creation, then water reveals the possibility of real inspiration and imagination without reference to the flesh. However, none can totally desert their humanity, their animal nature, and attain an art unflawed by self-interest:

> Water
> Silences all who would interfere;
> Retains, still, what it might give. . .
> (*The White Ship*)

The sea, like art, the great leveller, has 'drowned' many — promised, refused and given great wealth. It offers the artist an opportunity to create a 'new world', but far too many men having failed turn back to the older beliefs and doctrines with their fixity and often unbearable 'truths'. Moby Dick, Melville's great white 'myth', is hunted across the oceans by an Ahab who has allied himself with Satan. But, as numerous commentators have decided, the 'myth' is unrealised. It remains too amorphous. The whale is an immense symbol for God or the devil or selflessness,

> And I renounced, on the fourth day,
> This fierce and unregenerate clay,
> Building as a huge myth for man
> The watery leviathan. . .
> (*Genesis*)

The creature is too 'watery', and the albatross (also named for its whiteness — the colour of eternity) 'goes wild and lost, Upon a pointless ocean tossed'. Thus the crossbow kills the 'God-hailed' albatross in Coleridge's "The Rime of the Ancient Mariner". This is the bird which 'made the breeze to blow!' but the sad and penitent mariner returns to pray at the kirk, accepting the old, dogmatic Christianity rather than:

> the glove-winged albatross. . .
> Scouring. . .the ashes of the sea.

The bird is 'glove-winged', both a reference to Love's disguise and its compassion, in contrast to the osprey's triggered claw. In the "Re-birth of Venus", the goddess,

> having failed
> To scoop out of horizons what birds herald:
> Tufts of fresh soil,

— the promise of a new land after the Flood — casts away the possibility of inspiration: 'shakes off an entire sea', and becomes a shark, prisoner of the old logic of competition, the 'kill-or-be-killed' of artistic fashion: 'Stayers, and searchers of the fanged pool'. In spite of the failures, water still offers its gifts of selfless immortality, especially in its extremity where it lies girded and surrounded by the earth of blood-rituals, in lakes and pools,

O Lakes, Lakes!

O sentiment upon the rocks!

In "Elegaic Stanzas" Hill fixes the rhetoric that he is using with the dull insult, 'As plain as spitting on a stick' and then bursts into an acknow-ledgement of the unfrozen 'Spirit', undercutting the grand storms and customs of Romantic diction, with 'O Lakes, Lakes!' This is accom-plished much as Rimbaud yearns after an unattainable grandeur with his poem "O Saisons, O Chateaux". The lake can be 'scummed' over by worldly purity as in "In Piam Memoriam", or can blaze a sudden glory as the aesthete of "To the (Supposed) Patron" dies his 'idyllic death'. But the lake and its lilies still remain symbols of a beauty void of excess of artistic trimmings.

Natural and fantastic creatures prey upon the plain of defenceless men from the air. Hawks, vultures, seraphs, owls, Harpies and the osprey are some of the hunters specified. The air shapes human deceit and guile:

Beware

The soft-voiced owl, the ferret's smile

bodies hooped in steel

Forever bent upon the kill.

(*Genesis*)

Perhaps echoes of the missile-race of the Cold War period reverberate through this set of images from the early 50s. Air is also the medium of vision, 'a region of pure force' where state-endorsed religions, once in-ternalised, stun and bind the intellect: 'Now I lack grace to tell what I have seen'. A new sensibility is given to those who have deserted the sea and been struck dumb by angels, and it is given through the medium of fire. Fire is a zealous egotism in Hill's work. In art or religion it may manifest itself with quite unselfish trappings, but it always devours and exhibits itself. Fire is connected with Lucifer, the Arch-Egotist, or the hermetics trying to refine themselves through an Alchemy of the Spirit. Fire acting upon human idealism or materialism, Spirit or Flesh, results in Steam; either the steam of water as in "In Memory of Jane Frazer", or the steam of blood in "The Emperor's New Clothes". The dream and instinct towards good become mentalised and a god is born. In fact, what has happened is that the ego has produced transcendent images of itself. The martyr has become the statue in the church. Jesus has be-come the Christ and the supposedly selfless poet has become the adorn-ed hero. The man is gone, but the 'blind-god', translated ego, lives on.

Man does, however, transcend this process in death. The dead stretch, dumb repositories of the past, ever-present, a solid stratum be-low the plain of men:

But the dead maintain their ground —

30

That there's no getting round —
Poetry is a pastime, a distraction from real suffering and death. Words
have to strain to their unaccomplished task, and are always in danger of
becoming merely fashionable. Tombs and shrines throng the landscape;
even between the tombs 'Tombs still extrude'. Myths too are conventions. They contain traditions and archetypes, (mainly those of the
Bible and Greek lore in Hill's case) which evoke and generate certain
patterns of belief. As conventions they run as much risk of simplifying
and falsifying man's actual position as do historical formulae. In some
cases they are one and the same thing. For example, the Fall might not
only be a clumsy metaphor for what actually happened in time, it might
also be a bad explication of human action generally, with the notion of
original sin. Additionally, since there is no definitive interpretation of
the myth, it can be used for different causes and reasons. "Funeral
Music" and a poem like "Locust Songs" show the danger of this.

But, as Coleridge says in the ninth chapter of his *Biographia*
> An idea, in the highest sense of that word, cannot be
> conveyed but by a symbol; and, in geometry, all sym-
> bols of necessity involve an apparent contradiction

The borders and nature of this 'contradiction' are fully explored in
Hill's work. He precipitates such attention by juxtaposing the 'two-
edged' symbols. Mythical and natural move alongside, Greek deities or
figures from the Medieval Christian imagination are shown watching
and influencing mankind. The metaphysical beings are often inseperable
from the qualities they symbolise. Gods, confused, vengeful, blind, are
the constant companions of men. The universe and the psyche which
men have invented by their namings throng with gods and spirits. It is
here that Hill's sardonic humour and the distance between himself and
his work are important. In the Emperor's Clothes section of "Doctor
Faustus" he writes:

> . . .a god
> Spirals in the pure steam of blood
> And gods — as men — rise from shut tombs
> To a disturbance of small drums.

The implication is that where gods are prepared for they appear. They
come 'as men' and own, at times, a vindictiveness and sadism which,
one suspects, only men could contrive.

Hill has also shown an increasing tendency to make obvious his
harangue between myth and art. He seems obsessed with sacramental
art, Pentecostal tongues as opposed and related to poetry, and the artist's representation of religious motifs. The Word is of course one of the
concerns in this debate. In his commentary about his poem "Annunciations" he writes:

> By using an emotive cliche like the Word I try to
> believe in an idea that I want to believe in: that poetry
> makes its world from the known world; that it has

31

transcendence; that it is something other than the
conspicuous consumption (the banquet) that it seems
to be.
  What I am saying in the section is, I think, that I
don't believe in The Word. The fact that I make the
poem at all means that I still believe in words.

Poetry as a revealer or builder of a 'higher reality' is disavowed. Thus
Schopenhauer is wrong and Plato, as far as Hill is concerned, right. Like
the table-maker in *The Republic*, the poet can imitate, turn a mirror,
but not capture the form of the table or nature as a whole. The 'highest
philosophy', as D.R.Dudley comments, cannot be communicated in
writing. Plato is guilty on other grounds in Hill's eyes. His reliance on
rhetoric to propound 'the common good' is one example. His 'academic'
distance and founding of the Academy exclusively devoted to research
could be others. But where logic and reason gave out, Plato inserted a
'myth'. Augustine was not to allow this kind of mythic gap in his examination of the Universe. But the 'myth' is Hill's medium. Even in
examining tension between integrity of belief and State-held religions
which mask brutal actions or complacency, Hill is to show figures wandering in mythical settings, grappling with the gods that are themselves.

  Perhaps Hill was to reach the nub of his alarming and strident
imagery with his interest in the Crucifixion. In "Lachrimae" the Cross
is almost tilted back on itself — total immolation of Self seen as the
grossest and grandest of Egotistical conceits.

II

Wallace Martin writes:
  Christianity, history, the sea, love and death, most
  of Hill's early poems are constituted from permu-
  tations of these few themes.

It is Christianity that Hill takes to be the central myth of Europe:
history continually flows away from and towards Christ's sacrificial act.
For nearly two thousand years, cults, evangelical churches, missionaries,
and the vast machinery of State and State-endorsed religion have prom-
ulgated the doctrines of Salvation and Election. This has not only
affected the way in which we think but has profoundly altered the language which we inherit. For the boy in "The Stone Man", words seem to
have 'smelt Revelation's flesh' — they seem to grasp after a vision as
compulsive and extreme as Christ's message. There is also the lure of
'The Word' which 'is the impulse that makes and comprehends' life: it
is, in fact, the Great Explorer. Language, at its best, can be sacramental
— that which transforms 'unredeemed' reality into a ceremony worthy
of the mind's full engagement.

  The idea of self-sacrifice is at the basis of Hill's conception of writing. T.S.Eliot wrote that if a poet wished to 'procure the consciousness

of the past' he must understand that:

> The progress of an artist is a continual self-sacrifice,
> a continual extinction of personality.

He was to write elsewhere that a moral and healthy poem could only be
written out of 'humility',

> ...the humility of man before the Tradition, and of the
> poet's conscious mind before his limited technical problems.

The emphases on, on one hand, poetic humility and sacrifice and, on
the other, the Tradition, especially of Christian literature, are greatly re-
spected by Hill. They are increasingly manifested in his work with that
intensity which Eliot said could only be gained through a process of
'saturation'. In Hill's later poetry this kind of 'saturation' in the Spanish
and English mystical traditions is obvious. In Christianity and in Christian literature as a whole, Hill finds that which Eliot hears in Dante:

> a complete scale of the depths and heights of the human
> emotion;...the *Purgatorio* and *Paradiso* are to be read as
> extensions of the ordinarily very limited human range.

Hill respects the Christian tradition not just because it contains this
'complete scale' but also because it is the only model which holds
enough cultural and spiritual weight to support his analogy of 'the
sanctity of the intellect'. As Milne has written:

> Hill's poem ["Lachrimae"] objectifies his private
> beliefs and unbeliefs by aligning itself with a strong
> tradition of English and European religious poetry.

In Christ and in those literatures, meditations, hymns and poems
which have gathered around his story, Hill finds the past and present of
the European imagination. He quotes Schneider in saying that Hopkins
in "The Wreck of the Deutschland" was 'to create the closest unity of
all human values in Christ'. This 'closest unity' is continually scrutinised
in his work, for Hill is by no means simply the devotee. In his poetry
the voices of scepticism, belief and outrage sound side by side. His verse
enacts a basic two-way process: it taps the great resources of lyricism
and intensity found in the Christian tradition and, simultaneously, within these forms, pursues that valid level of discourse which he calls 'the
drama of reason'. His verse also re-invests the Christian message with
those newer dramas and ironies which have become part of our modern
consciousness.

So much for the reason why Christianity occupies such a central
position in Hill's work, but how does this vast theme manifest itself in
tension with the other myths, histories and narrative voices in the early
poetry? Milne refers us to two extracts from "Dominae Public" in *King
Log* illustrating Hill's early attempts to 'meld poetry with prayer'. When
I mentioned voices sounding side by side I did not want to imply discrete modes of speech, but rather cross-rhythms, counter-pointings and
antiphonic echoes melded into one voice, rehearsing the 'drama of
reason'.

Ricks has called Hill

. . .a religious man without, it must seem, a religion; a
profoundly honest doubter. . .if we must suppose a
patron for Hill, it might be Thomas.

The doubts and impulses toward belief are mustered into total commitment to a melody and into a form which embodies 'simultaneous composition on several planes at once', where the poem, like Yeats' "Easter 1916" becomes a paradigm of the hard-won 'sanctity of the intellect'. This is achieved through pitch, rhythm, syntax and the modifications of the narrative voice. Ricks draws our attention to Hill's use of brackets and parentheses, and Hill has written of Coleridge's parentheses as antiphons of 'vital challenge'. Hill's own use of parentheses and antiphonal echoes are the results of his more central method of modification, of successive and varying formulation. But if a poem is to be 'a ceremonial, even a sacramental act' it must contain vital praise as well as 'vital challenge'. The 'praise' comes by way of the saturation which I have already mentioned, but this 'saturation' draws less attention to itself in the early work. "Canticle for Good Friday" shows a mind tenderly and yet mistrustfully examining Thomas, the poetic voice in some ways echoing Thomas's own examination of the scene. The spectrum of the disciples intentions, both conscious and unconscious, is evoked. The range of possibilities in the myth is drawn, from 'carrion-sustenance' to the aesthetical indulgence: 'choicest defiance'. In the early work, the gods, Christian and pagan, are shown occupying many roles which vary from the position of mere poetic 'furniture' to the flesh or 'Creation's issue'. They are statues and formulae, images and hieroglyphs. The 'drama of reason' is still to the foreground and heard more explicitly in the early work — the sceptic and the heckler are both present in the many layers of the narrative. The fact that Hill includes pagan motifs in his work at this stage shows that he has not yet decided exclusively to explore 'the closest unity of all human values in Christ'.

In the first poem of *For the Unfallen*, a book dedicated to the Elect, religious and artistic, we're presented with a brutal if invigorating view of Creation. The watcher deserts the 'unregenerate' clay for other myths, but they are soon lost on a 'pointless ocean'. (This possibly symbolises Humanism in man's intellectual development.) Despite the horror implicated in the decision, the watcher turns again,

To flesh and blood and the blood's pain.

For, and this idea permeates a whole range of Hill's work,

By blood we live, the hot, the cold,
To ravage and redeem the world:
There is no bloodless myth will hold.

Martin adds, as a gloss to the poem, that 'the violence of nature and history is not as surprising as the presumptuousness of one who assumes that man can transcend his natural condition'. But what is man's natural condition? Hill is interested in those who test the boundaries, either by choice like Faustus, or by force, like the Jewish victims. The martyr who shuns the whole world, living in death, is the central figure of "Lacrimae". The 'presumptuousness' is not as surprising in fact as those who consistently give way to the pull of tribal logic, inexorable as it seems to be. Yet the flight from 'the ancient troughs of blood' is obstructed by contradictions in the very nature of those who flee. As Wainwright suggests:

> The world is not so readily transcended or even evaded
> . . .such abnegation as the martyr seeks ('self-wounding')
> might yet be self-seeking.

A law of life: 'By blood we live, the hot, the cold', has been translated into myth repeatedly throughout history. Hill shows that the concepts have become a binary system in the speaker's mind: 'To ravage and redeem the world'. A clue is given in the line, 'And by Christ's blood are men made free', with its air of moralising and Biblical rhythm. The effect is one of merging and conflicting motifs beneath the surface of the words. Irony playing against despair, sinister *non sequiturs* complacently linked and, in the final couplet, a scepticism and outrage belying dogma. The bones cannot face such 'light'. As Martin points out, 'A myth based on blood can endure but if understood it may not be bearable'. The underlying shifts in meaning are emphasised all the more by the curiously fluid identity of the watcher. Is he God, the first man, man as a myth-maker for other men, or the unbridled ego imposing its inner dramas on the world?

But the myth of the need for regeneration is not as unanswerable as it at first seems. In 'Holy Thursday' the persona passes to the centre of his animality, to origins 'without fear'. This may well be an oblique narration of a sexual encounter in which the myth of darkness inherent in the act proves untrue: 'Lo, she lies gentle and innocent of desire'. In "The Bidden Guest" the theme of 'Pentecostal Tongues' which is to fascinate Hill in future work arises. The 'gift' can be used as a symbol for rhetoric, glib aplogetics or poetic expertise by Hill. The Christian ritual seems dull and cold beside the promise of Pentecostal fire:

> And suddenly a sound came from heaven like the rush
> of a mighty wind, and it filled all the house where they
> were sitting. And there appeared to them tongues as of
> fire. . .   (*Acts 2. 2-3*)

But the Communion suits those of 'leaner' hearts, wine, not fire:

> But one man lay beneath his vine
> And, waking, found that it was dead.

Christ the Vine has been ignored and in the next seven lines a dialogue emerges. One voice affirms inner darkness and one Christ's lordship: wounds confront and vie with wounds. But after all the other worshippers have left the servant remains, his 'heart's tough shell' uncracked. He has put out the blazing 'eyes that would compel'. The urge towards both a 'spurred speech' ruled by uncritical belief and a reliance on

Christ the denier of Self has been conquered. Jesus asserted that true life demanded a death of one's selfish existence, recalling fertility cults and the story of John Barleycorn. The logic of blood, (or its respectable and sacramental version, wine,) may be brutal but it is also impartial, no respecter of persons. The scene in this poem is formal. The candles are 'starched unbending' and the priest is 'stiffly linened'. The stasis of art can imply death and indeed the picture-within-a-picture of the dead vine reveals an inner decay. The Holy Spirit has 'passed through' this poem unreceived, but we find that the next poem, "The Turtle Dove", reveals how spirit and matter might be reconciled: 'She went to him, plied there; like a furious dove. . .'

But I pass now to "Picture of a Nativity", since in some ways it is involved with similar ideas of formalism and sanctified rigidity. It is enveloped between 'sea-poems': "Metamorphoses" on one side and "The Guardians", "White Ship" and "Wreaths" on the other. The first stanza deals with the damned, the drowned, floating in the remains of their own artistic endeavours which have fallen apart and decayed. The artistic process has failed. In Ariel's Song we find that Ferdinand's father's bones are now made of coral, but all that remains here are coral sores and detached faces. To rectify the sin of artistic pride,

A dumb child-king
Arrives at his right place;

The king's place is pre-ordained; each figure is frozen into its attitude. A Christ might see humans as demons 'buttered over' with flesh. Perhaps there is a hint here of those artists who intended their paintings to possess a higher reality. But is the child not also a banished Satan surrounded by slack serpents (slack because aesthetically drained of moral status), and worshipped by artists? It is in believing 'their own eyes' that men are condemned – Christ alone has true insight. Angels freeze above the scene. In attempting to convey a transcendent life-form some Renaissance artists did show angels affecting rigor mortis. How can one philosophically reach further than death in acquiring symbols for a supernatural reality? There are hints that the poem might be about the growth of Naturalism; at last men will begin to recognise 'Familiar tokens' among the common and bestial life around them, as Caravaggio found "Supper at Emmaeus" in peasants drinking wine.

In the next poem too the whole scene has an arranged and formal quality. Each drop of blood is deliberate, in that it is both 'intended' or intelligent and purposeful. The role manipulates the man – it is the wood (dulled because of its artistic usage) which spits blood, not But it is 'the Doubter' who bears the cross at the cliff-top of decision. He suffers himself to remain, 'At such near distance'. He smells the tangible realities of vinegar and blood, and sees the issue of one woman bleeding as well as the Christ. For the 'silent miracle' has not cleansed his brain of all earthly attachments. 'claw-roots of sense'. The flesh is here again bestial and Thomas stands at the cross-roads of experience.

If he stands apart he runs the risk of being called an artistic voyeur savouring tastes and smells, but if he accepts the marriage of mortal and Immortal he also accepts the atrocious blood-ritual.

In "Metamorphoses" pagan motifs loom larger. Martin writes that they are 'protean; they are a collage of 5 sections related to one another through overlapping themes and allusions to animals associated with Venus'. For example, in the second section, an advised poet is called an 'unlyrical scapegoat', (a he-goat being sacred to Venus). In the third section Venus changes to a shark 'hurricaned to estuary water'. Martin concludes:

> She (Venus) remains goddess, archetypal and powerful, but in her association with the sea acquires its destructive as well as its generative potential. Life originated in the sea, yet in the story of the Flood is destroyed by it; the love that arises with Venus springs from the castration of Uranus. The meaning of the poem is created through juxtaposition of archetypes that are referentially associated but traditionally segregated because when combined they tend to negate one another.

At first glance this may appear to be so. Each of the five sections holds a change within itself, as each of Ovid's chapters involves a mythical transformation. Hill is not the only artist to see Fear as a primary impulse of mankind. Heaney too is convinced of its potency as a formative as well as a decreative force. The first section of the poem captures the complete fear of infancy, the birth of consciousness. It is also a subconscious fear 'of a furred kind' such as animals may possess. Man has made his myths to control fear, a god to placate or a demon to serve, but in turn these have enslaved man. Hill takes us back and firmly asserts:

> No manner of address will do;
> Eloquence is not in that look.

Whatever Aristotle and the codifiers say about the uses of rhetoric, it has no place here. The central quatrain, by 'cutting back' through negatives displays another kind of fear which is to come to the fore in "Funeral Music" and *Mercian Hymns*. This stanza is using the very linguistic mechanisms of reason and qualification which cannot deal with the other fear. Odysseus waits to catch Proteus on the seashore – his fear is of the shape-shifter and therefore the Unknown. It is a fear which can be recognised anywhere by anyone and which can even be used creatively.

The second section opens with a rather effete scholarly cry. It depicts the birth of the artist, the word-maker. The race for critical acclaim is seen. Even the dead are a threat. But the balance of energy and tact is achieved and the poet becomes fashionable. The scapegoat has become one of the 'groomed optimi'.

From what could be taken to be a late Classical Roman setting we move to a conscious re-working of myth. Love personified has failed to find a new world: Art has failed her so the world is cast off and she infests the seas with a deadlier myth. She herself is foam-born, a product, – not like the dove, of the Spirit – of the Imaginative faculty. She becomes a shark, a competitor with other hunters. Art has become a competition: the pool, well of creativity and life, is now 'fanged'. Love has not converted the 'fear of a furred kind', merely transposed it.

In poems like "Little Apocalypse" and "The Bibliographers" fire and light are associated with the artistic process and also the transmutation of the soul. In "Drake's Drum" we find the sea burning spray and bodies – this synaesthesia cannot be reduced to direct correspondences. Hill confesses that he is fond of 'double-takes'. Newbolt's patriotic stanzas echo ironically behind these couplets. Nationality is unimportant in death; the sea cannot be owned though England in its show of Masculine militarism remains 'erect'; the dead have become the sea. Neither art nor rhetoric, wreaths not words reach the dead or those 'victims' of artistic endeavour. The 'padding' of the tide, thickened with their dissolved bodies, echoes the continual surges of artists towards fame. The poem "Wreaths" also relates heat and water; it speaks of a 'phosphorus tide' and dead men,

> Uttering love, that outlasts or outwastes
> Time's attrition

The dead of "Drake's Drum" have been melted down by their own egotism and no fashioned phrase or work can redeem their memory.

An example of the use of mythological archetypes is seen in "Orpheus and Eurydice". Hill writes about Love's struggle to appear in his poetry. The genuine love, this, not love as 'habit' or 'militant conformity' but the kind that shuns 'safe' dogmas and yet does not relapse into contrived rebellion. The narrator is a collector, a connoisseur:

> We have recitals, catalogues
> Of protected birds;
>
> And the rare pale sun,

This may refer to Orpheus's power to enchant wild animals, rocks and trees. In fact, it is the 'rare pale sun's' harp that he uses to do this. However, something jars in the last stanza. Love's pose is adopted far too self-consciously. The ambiguity of the last line shows how dubious Hill is about elevating compassion, even in relation to the 'rawly-difficult'. Eurydice literally means 'wide justice' and if Love in this context is searching for such an abstract sophism the vague ending is justified.

In "After Cumae" the artists become their own finished work. The whole landscape is anthropomorphised, much as men transfigured landscapes into spirits. But the scene with its perennial changes of hue and forgotten gods is not threaded by actual lines of energy that Heaney might delineate. Gods, 'sometimes-abandoned', are seen to perpetuate the idea that men's souls are eternal, whilst others become mere obsessions. Cumae, the ruins and the memory of an oracular centre, is resurrected once again — it becomes the ideal landscape for whole schools of Classical poets who leave behind them 'Fragments of marine decay. . .' The age-old crown of laurels is still sought, and the ancient questions of speech or silence, '. . .mouthy cave, the dumb grottoes' are forgotten.

"Little Apocalypse" and "The Bibliographers" crystallise the motif of fire which has been glimpsed but not explored before.

Concerning Holderlin, W.A.Coupe writes:

> With Goethe and Schiller, he shows the post-Winckelmann
> view of Greece as an ideal golden age in the development
> of mankind. . .; it is in his case quickened by an intense
> religious fervour, and in his later poetry expresses itself
> in a mystical belief in the spiritual rebirth of mankind and
> the second coming of Christ, the latter being seen in his
> private Neo-Classical mythology as the brother of Dionysus
> and the intermediary between classical antiquity and
> occidental mythology.

This may seem far removed from the traditional notion of sin, but Holderlin also held the Christian view that man has destroyed the possibility of his own harmony. It is only selfless love which can bring back 'the golden age'. Both Holderlin and the speaker of "Little Apocalypse" are tempters, tempting simultaneously towards a religion of art and a Humanist paradise with strong Hellenic overtones. 'Abrupt' means 'sudden' or 'broken from' and, though discrete, these temptations still contain elements of Christianity. The writers are close to the 'sun' of their own mythic patterns — the satire itself becomes 'scorching': 'Man's common radiance suddenly too rare'. The 'purifying' of humans towards a golden future is surely doubtful for Hill, as in any collective ethic. A 'new god' is manufactured among his own creative fires.

The cold, objective science of bibliography and, by implication, any recording, is the subject of "The Bibliographers". Lucifer, by another of Hill's deft inversions, is now a heaven-sent gift, showing how religious appreciation of the arts can turn back on itself in one lifetime. Different European councils influenced the ideological viewpoints in art. The bibliographer's amorality is stressed; they are engaged in measurement, not evaluation. Even Lucifer is not too much for their efforts: 'can estimate/ Your not unnatural height.'

Is then the 'feel' of archaic beauty properly an aesthetic or moral consideration? Or, as with the bibliographers, is this 'feel' merely a way of filing and classification? Hill has set up a whole web of ideological strands here, but a new voice intervenes with the fourth stanza. The dead still maintain their ground and the tombs still extrude. A world obsessed with light and truth in art lies at the mercy of the kind of shadow which this kind of art casts. The cold and unfeeling forces of the Universe 'envisaged in no cloud' or human brain, loom: a more threatening version of the framed Lucifers.

Though Hill is content, like David Jones, to include aspects of myth
and pagan ritual, which at times seems cryptic and obscured, his intentions seem entirely different. There was a particular type of formalism
exhibited by academic poets of the 30s and 40s which is very characteristically presented in these lines by Auden:

> Nothing your strength, your skill, could do
> Can alter their embrace
> Or dispersuade the furies who
> At the appointed place
> With claw and dreadful brow
> Wait for them now.
>> (*Song*)

In finishing the second of "Three Baroque Meditations" Hill writes of,

> Scent of a further country where worse
> Furies promenade and bask their claws.

Or as another example, take Auden's 'plain without a feature' where an
'unintelligible multitude' wait for a sign in "The Shield of Achilles'.
The poets of the 30s, in different ways, denuded the motifs of their
topographical and cultural particularity in a way David Jones would
despise, whereas Hill has built on the anonymity of these symbols till
the face value of a name like 'Christ' is borne under by other tensions in
the poem. Is Christ the Arch-Ego in disguise as a suppliant? Is He the
artistic conscience or Morality as a whole, or a particularly blind god?
The faceless narrator (also reminiscent of Auden) 'thickens the plot' of
the poem further. Hill at this stage seems to show in his work the culmination of a particular kind of oblique and many-faceted rendering of
symbolic thought – indeed the Shield of Perseus would be a good emblem of this method. However Hill is to 'side-step' and regain a certain
degree of particularity in the 'found' objects and fragments of *Mercian
Hymns*.

The whole of history seems 'engrossed in the cold blood of sacrifice'.
The 'self-healing' gods in "Of Commerce and Society" may destroy to
save, but such a ruthless heritage of sacrifice undercuts their ostensible
aims. They become psychic mechanisms, part of an inescapable system
of thought; they are self-perpetuating and blindly rehearse their repertoire of gestures. Sounds echo and re-echo and antiphonic voices ring in
history as generations pass. The terse description of the Apostles juxtaposed with the military leaders at Versailles in 1919 anticipates the
perfunctory, inattentive officials of Mercia:

> They sat.   They stood about.
> They were estranged.   The air
> ...fleshed with silence...
>> (*Of Commerce and Society*)

The gods of coin and salt and 'worked vessels' seem to be reminders of
former developments in trade – possibly the Hanseatic League. The
second part of the poem pictures the generations still using skeletons of

trade, not having learned from the 'much-scarred terrain'. In the "Death of Shelley" the field of history is strewn with previously submerged artifacts. The dead, like the myths, are historical presences: 'some of us have heard the dead speak'.

The archetype of the hero, Perseus, now has a
> clogged sword, clear, aimless mirror –
> With nothing to strike at. . .

The way in which men fog and obscure history is recalled in the name 'Auschwitz': the unbelievable becomes a fable. Biblical names are used to explain Nature: Jehovah, Babel, provide a perspective through which we can view the 'Archaic earth-shaker'. The line, 'By all means let us appease the terse gods', poised against the sinking of the Titanic, questions the changes and validity of belief.

America detecting 'the daystar' (again Lucifer) in a muddling and critical Europe is obviously ironical. The cliches and overlapping arguments of the section suggest that Hill embodies Europe's scholastic muddlings and voices in the verse (just as "Funeral Music" embodies 'a florid grim music broken by grunts and shrieks'). Nothing has made history bearable – Auschwitz and the Titanic and the pain connected with each underlie modern consciousness and everyday speech. Commerce and trade have increased in size and competitiveness since these disasters. The position has, we acknowledge as we are led through these poles of human endeavour, grown more de-humanised.

Throughout this first book the presence of the past is being gradually and exclusively attributed to the dead and their cultural remains. "Solomon's Mines" shows Hill's fascination with archaeology: 'spadework and symbol', which becomes more noticable in *Mercian Hymns.* Time is under constant scrutiny; the processes and storms of fashion vie with an artistic timelessness. Different life-styles move through Dove Cottage and in "Two Sonnets to the Jews in Europe" the Judaic ideas about succession and sacrifice stand in stark relief against those of their oppressors. The dead mean renewal in Jewish conception:
> . . .we grasp, roughly, the song.
> Arrogant acceptance from which song derives
> Is bedded with their blood, makes flourish young
> Roots in ashes.

Finally, "Asmodeus" exhibits how Hill seeks to probe chronologies with his poetic forms. It is written in a style reminiscent of a translation from Old Norse or Saxon. There are juxtapositions which defy neat ordering here: details of a modern house such as lightning conductors exist alongside belief in spirits, 'propitious things' that nest in darkness. Here we again find the 'Guide-book' martyr who believes his own transcendent vision,
> You, doubtless, hear wings,
> Too sheer for cover, swift; the scattered noise
> Of darkness looming with propitious things.

He sees a richness in death, but this kind of yearning is a 'lone journey out of mind'. The Christian cycle of threat and forgiveness is satirised:

A tax on man to seventy-times-seven
A busy vigilance of goose and hound,

The final lines create the impression of a medieval diagram of the body, illustrating the positions of humours and internal organs alongside each other. But, in this conceit, we do not forget the demon of the title and evil powers, obsessions and egocentric manias that inhabit some metabolisms: 'Hobbies of serious lust and indoor sin'. Asmodeus looms in to the present as much as the sardonic 'Warning to Bathers' sign seems to merge into the Harpy-feast in "Doctor Faustus". The lovers, a familiar motif in this book, are ejected from the house, marriage and Eden. Perhaps the doors of the head which they have passed through make this poem one of Hill's more optimistic works.

III

In *King Log* the Word becomes the pivot of Christianity. In "Annunciations" we are told,

The Word has been abroad, is back, with a tanned
[look
From its subsistence in the stiffening-mire.
Cleansing has become killing.

Hill glosses this:

The Word (line 1) is the impulse that makes and comprehends. Poetry before the poetry-banquet. The Word is an explorer (cf. *Four Quartets* passim.) By using an emotive cliche like 'The Word' I try to believe an idea that I want to believe in.

There is more than a little of the formal exercise and the desire for the definitive (informed) debate in this rhetoric. The anagoge works against itself — we begin to mistrust any voice, any emblem. Perhaps this is the desired effect. Wainwright writes of how Hill sees the danger of linguistic glibness — 'The Word becomes fashionable'. In writing of "Locust Songs", another poem concerning the Word, he concludes that it depicts the

early American vision of the New World as a New Eden. . .
the destruction of this ideal in a locust-like falling upon
the land is compounded by the tortuous Calvinistic confusion of worldly greed and lust for the wrath of an implacable God 'writhing over the rich scene.' So that
Shiloh is:

God in this
His natural filth, voyeur of sacrifice, a slow
Bloody unearthing of the God-in-us.
. . .seeking evidence of their own election, they (the

Calvinists) created Hell.

The two poems are about 'the damned'. The first, Hill says, embodies,
a prayer for contact. OR: Love, look to yourself, you
know the drill, among your friends some are non-elect;
keep a sharp look-out for these (and I hope to imply,
when you do find them, look quickly the other way.)

The second shows what happens when Love does not. The Word was in
the Beginning, but, within the bounds of rhetoric or a linguistic system,
there is no promise of a 'new world'. That philosophy, in the work of
Liebnitz and others, posited a range of possible worlds is a mere mental
abstraction for Hill. The Calvinist's whole world view is coloured by the
concept of an immutable deity: 'Bland vistas milky with Jehovah's
calm — '. Hill weights the third section with a specific name, date, and
place, but the action seems timeless and the last line seems balladic in
style.

"Four Poems Regarding the Endurance of Poets" also bear dedica-
tions, and two are dated. Tommaso Campanella, sufferer for both the
Divine and artistic word, finds that his cries are first 'mine' (his and
Hill's) and then 'God's'. Campanella (1568–1639) was imprisoned for
three long periods and wrote many of his most important works in captivity. He was always careful to distinguish between the realms of science and theology. Wainwright discusses the images of 'men mocked by
doubtful divine gifts' and, just as Campanella has composed his speech,
his torturers approach. The world is not easy to transcend — torment
only sleeps 'for a time'.

The shadow of the Roman Catholic belief in the corruption of the
Flesh, suppression of 'improper' speech and the Judgement lie heavily
over the memory of Robert Desnos. Days have become pits:

Look,
Seigneur, again we
resurrect and the judges come.

Desnos was interested in automatic writing and his love of dream and
oneiric eroticism has made him famous. The poet is a victim of words
which 'claw' his brain and of private and official expectations. But
Desnos' imagination is loud with 'dream-voices'. The mystic and the
rationalist compete in his verse and, finally, in Hill's poem he reverts
to the voice of a Catholic clergyman. The temptation is as much that
of his own garrulity and the desire to select one voice to give it utterance as it is the wish to give in to oppression.

We encounter the twin subjects of martyrdom and renunciation in
"Funeral Music". John Tiptoft defiantly preferred to be executed in
three axe strokes in honour of the Trinity. "Funeral Music" is centred
upon a consideration of versions of death. In the first sonnet God and
his Church are identified with the executioners:

So these dispose themselves to receive each
Pentecostal blow from axe or seraph,

The indecision between 'axe or seraph' rivals the kingly assumption of Divine Right but also continues the analogy between martyrdom and inspiration: 'Psalteries whine through the empyrean'. All eternity bears upon these events. Although they might seem unjust, they might be part of that 'blind' supernatural logic. Yet it is not that simple; the martyrs, despite their ambiguous temperaments, are Christians:

> The voice fragrant with mannered humility,
> With an equable contempt for this World,

'World' is capitalised for it means not just a world of objects but one of Platonic thought and attatchments. The final four lines of the poem consider the mortals, 'creatures of such rampant state', from another angle. Here hell-fire 'ghosts' upon these beings, locked into their 'vacuous ceremony of possession'. Both martyrs and executioners are 'rampant'. They indulge their lust for transcendence under the guise of selfless holiness. As "An Order of Service" intimates:

> Let a man sacrifice himself, concede
> His mortality and have done with it;
> There is no end to that sublime appeal.

The first sonnet finally comments 'no man's dwelling-place', both hinting at the inhumanity of the personae, and indicating the inhospitality of such ceremonies of possession.

Sonnet 2 reveals a mind trying to reconcile half-cynically blood and pain and the Universal plan. Towton (ironically enough fought on Palm Sunday) is enough to show the grim, arbitrary nature of human suffering. The ritual king, figurehead of state and God's puppet, draws 'our tribute of pain', echoing the hymn-phrase 'this our sacrifice of praise'. Instead of palm leaves and Hosannas we are shown 'fastidious trumpets' and the 'strange-postured' dead. The curiosity attending death seems to attend a sane point of view in Hill's work. No reconciliation is possible.

The first line of the third sonnet is as ambiguous as the last:

> They bespoke doomsday and they meant it by
> God...

The lack of pause before 'by/God' makes what might be a simple oath into a statement that each army sees itself as God's instrument, or that they see Doomsday and God as the same force. Doomsday is an imminent threat — a halt to linear time. But, posed against this, is the notion that once every five centuries one might see the scene for what it really is without the bias of religious dogma or idealism. The sound of battle, 'Which is like nothing on earth, but is earth' reminds us of our homely and bloody histories — such slaughter seems alien but is in fact an indelible part of our heritage. Like mole and snail we are vulnerable and blind. Earth, or rather 'earth-dwellers', have always demanded blood to maintain illusions and myths. Even the most delicate souls blaspheme; or do they? They, as the church, are Christ's bride, and their death anticipates union with their Lord. One recognises the dubious nature of Christian indoctrination — it has contributed to the soldiers' deaths and to their martial self-righteousness. The grimmest irony is that the victims of such framework cherish the symbols which have proved their downfall.

This conceptual captivity is stressed in sonnet 4. The persona speculates but finally, enmeshed as he is in Christian dogma, he must acknowledge that Averroes is wrong, that our lives are not a mythic but a real captivity. The primacy of the soul, (bringing the ghosts of Plato and Faustus into the poem) and its compulsion ('with tears and sweat') so often ending in sacrifice, are stressed. The primacy of mind and the stasis of time it affords are not acceptable.

The torches of ' Wild Christmas ' in the fifth sonnet recall hell-fire and burnings, but also Yule and the Norse fire-festivals. Wainwright notices that there is no silence for contemplation:

> At every turn the whining psalteries, the trumpets,
> Wild Christmas and its revel of atonement.

The festivities are seen as 'thirty feasts of unction and slaughter', 'the soul's winter sleep'. Men revel in the Christ-child's birth whilst slaughtering animals to gorge themselves. Trumpets cannot drown the scene — neither can they purify God's law of blood which inhabits every area of the believers' lives. The seraphs are instruments of this law, not pity. When men sing of the babe who has led them to their torture, the tortured pity them. They know that the singers too are victims. The damned show a greater tenderness than the 'righteous'. Martyrs wracked 'on inarticulate looms' of eloquent religious condemnation know the toil of glib speech.

The sixth sonnet, a speech between father and son, falls broadly in two directions. It could refer to Christ communicating with a man, perhaps Adam:

> A stranger well-received in your kingdom.
> On those pristine fields I saw humankind
> As it was named by the Father

It might also refer to one who was well-received in Heaven but was later abandoned — Satan. Some wish for their old Innocence; others are like zealous believers:

> Blind to all but one vision, their necessity
> To be reconciled.

The way of rejection endowed Christ with a potency too. But this man has composed his own 'Abandonment'. On another level the sonnet is about a father re-entering a child's view of the world ('your kingdom') before self-consciousness and fear have entered his perception. Yet even here 'the world's real cries' reach the father. Finally, estranged from a retrospective idealism or primitive Christianity, the father embraces his estrangement.

Sonnet 7 deals with human goals which finally fall through to 'the stark ground, Of this pain'. The man's conscience is averted. The incongruity between the Christian ideal of Agape and that of chivalry is glaring. Bright armies caught in a mutually sustained and opposing ideal cancel each other out, like the abstractions which they represent: prowess, vanity, mutual regard. All that remains is the pitiful slaughter of men deluded and deserted by those abstractions. Even so, the soldier thinks he hears his name called in praise, or summoned for the Last Judgement. 'It was nothing. . .' and predators gather totally oblivious of the idealistic conflict.

The final sonnet examines the way in which men and society manipulate the individual. Are they blind to the insignificance to their lives? Do they create a harmony in spheres beyond their senses? No myth or code is adequate to grasp the external reality of the Universe. That men should adopt an aggressive posture to bear witness to a distant 'unanswerable' order is terrible. Desnos' comment returns: 'Christ, what a pantomime!' But finally, no rationalisation, no nihilism, and no consolation renders death acceptable, especially such bloody and pointless deaths. The humans, unlike the composed Biblical Christ, are not finished.

Like *Mercian Hymns*, "Funeral Music" is disposed on a field of historical events: the lives of certain mystics and poets, the Wars of the Roses — and it also takes into account the 'ornate heartlessness of mid-15th century architecture'. Two historical motifs are used to further the narrative. Firstly, Hill's familiar 'plain'; whether 'pristine fields', the array of mankind, or the human mire. Secondly, there is the moment or the image that echoes (often apparently arbitrarily) in history. At several of these moments, attended by certain of these images, the subjects can withdraw from time. From the conjunction of these two methods we are offered different versions of history. In sonnet 7 we find the 'mirrored armies' on the stark plain. There is a moment of painful timelessness and clarity:

> I stiffened as though a remote cry
> Had heralded my name. It was nothing. . .

But it is a sharply-defined instant in nature too:

> Reddish ice tinged the reeds; dislodged, a few
> Feathers drifted across; carrion birds
> Strutted upon the armour of the dead.

This is the quiet aftermath of any battlefield, captured in an almost painterly way, but, as we are told in the eighth sonnet, it is an echo in eternity like the cry 'I have not finished' and blows from axes of men gasping 'Jesus'. All echoes 'are the same in such eternity' and the reader is thrown against his or her own conceptions of history. Is the cry, 'I have not finished' a mockery of Christ's cry? Surely passion and pain matter? Hill's stone monsters and the stone jaws of 'Caritas' outlast the generations, but there is the stillness apart from time; that of the mystic or the philosopher:

> . . .a palace blazing
> With perpetual silence as with torches.

Even here 'real cries' intrude. Despite the meditation, the realms of

thought are inadequate if undercut by unreasoning dogma:
> What I dare not is a waste history.

In recollecting a poet's history in "The Stone Man", the memories:
> The nettle-clump and the rank elder tree

prefigure Offa's and Hill's memories of crab-apple trees. There is always another half-glimpsed 'other-kingdom' seen in childhood, whether it is seen in half-finished grave-stones, in the eyes of a mystic or in a deeper kingdom altogether apart from time. Time can be obliterated physically. At the site of Lowood School in "Cowan Bridge", the narrator confronts 'A lost storm'. The child or the ghost of the child absorbs the turning seasons. The history of the school lives on inside the man too, but the openness and receptivity of the child are gone. This also anticipates the position of the child in relation to time in *Mercian Hymns*.

"Three Baroque Meditations" are an example of Hill using mythological figures culled from quite different backgrounds — Minerva, demons, Furies — to examine poetry and sacrifice. In the first meditation the demons both of eloquence and silence are exorcised but perversely thrive. The deathly aspect of Minerva, goddess of the night and lunar power, is praised; the poet becomes a priest of necessity — the necessity which urges man to reconcile himself with blood-laws also rules owl and field-mouse. The poet recognises that he is implicated in the lust and power of such killings: 'My fire squeals and lies still'. In the act of writing, Hill is aware that to sleep is to kill. Yet sleeping and killing are necessary sequences in the chain of life and the characteristically nervous wakefulness of both the 'baroque' mystic and his shadow (the hunter) is no refuge.

The second meditation could deal with the artist's obsession with an extreme art and his impatience with anything less, but using 'tact' he refrains from embarassing other writers. This 'tact' can be deadly under certain circumstances:
> Scent of a further country where worse
> Furies promenade and bask their claws.

Some further countries have desperately needed politically-committed poets revealing the brutality of the ruling 'furies'. Hill is aware of the price Lorca, Neruda and others paid. The 'Dead Bride' of the third section could be the Church or a writer addressing Christ. Christ is both a demanding Saviour and a mode of language:
> (By day he professed languages —
> Disciplines of languages)

The poet's tongue, like the owl, has a nightly prowl, its 'vixen skill' which must be cleansed for the light of day. This prowl is perhaps a skilful but obsessive morbidity, untamed and blasphemous. The addressed poet is 'the poet of a people's Love' and he has 'a sacramental mouth' The unclean poet or dead bride is offered the approved languages and clean words yet refuses and Christ weeps: 'I hated him' — yet His monumental dignity does not desert Him in His loss.

In the "Songbook of Sebastian Arrurruz" we enter into a poet's sensibility and his supposedly historical book. Here time is measured in a man's desolation — 'true sequences of pain' are established and undercut for this naming. But once experienced the pain can be metamorphosed into 'fortuitous amber'. Aesthetically and objectively it can become a thing of beauty. Imagination works upon the past and stylises and details it lovingly. The fragments of time are self-consciously falsified, but also loaned a softness, transcendence and bearable quality in the very act of 'piecing together'. Real memories of pain are crystallised and numbed as in several paintings of St.Anthony and St.Sebastian. Degrees of pain, real and imaginary, are weighed:

> I turn my mind
> towards delicate pillage, the provenance
> of shards glazed and unglazed, the three
> kinds of surviving grain. I hesitate amid
> circumstantial disasters. I gaze at the
> authentic dead.
>
> (*A Letter from Armenia*)

The fastidious 'eye' of the imagined poet will not allow him to find comfort in the words — not even Hill's usual indulgence in horrific imagery.

In his essay "Myth and History in Recent Poetry" Terry Eagleton writes
> Myth provides a measure of freedom, transcendence,
> representativeness, a sense of totality; and it seems no
> accident that it is serving these purposes in a society
> where those qualities are largely lacking.

He goes on to say:
> History, as Louis Althusser has reminded us, is a com-
> plex rather than a monistic reality; we should talk of
> histories, and one of the conflicting unities they form.

Both these statements are particularly apt in relation to Hill's presentation of a 'genius loci'. Offa is deeply implicated in myth and legend. His life and roles are bound up with perpetuating certain, often conflicting, mythologies. In a wider sense he is a myth: of Hill, of the Mercian landscape and of a certain human sensibility and habit of mind. The achievement of *Mercian Hymns* is that it provides a 'representativeness, a sense of totality', without foisting a neat moral framework upon the reader. History, its very fabric and addenda, is continually revealed in the *Hymns*. Versions of personal, of intimate and of public histories are explored. The perceptions of a Saxon despot keenly vie with those of a nameless child. Personae overlap and patterns of generation, settlement and fertility are considered. Actual events are manipulated by heralds, embroiderers, masons and court-witnesses. Words are parasitic, especially in the public context: they 'prey' upon emotion and circumstance to create an altered account of that which has passed. Our attention is drawn into swift correspondences between times. Actions become ambiguous and elusive. History is a dream of a childhood one cannot re-enter, of a past too violent for the 'luxury' of poetry and of sounds, objects and figures which recur, baffling chronological propriety. Since, as Wallace Martin writes, history offers continual testimony to the incoherence of reality, we find unresolved tensions, nameless faces who continually shuffle in the periphery of the poet's gaze. Then, suddenly, in a gesture, stance or child's toy, one recognises a valid and illuminating correspondence between times. We are all 'implicated' in history but we are also exiles from it. There is no way in which we can find Offa, but, in another way, because he is our ancestor, prey to human emotions, part of our earth, there is no way in which we can escape him. The post-war years with their preoccupation with housing and materialism clearly mirror Offa's lifetime. Democracy, or its debased equivalant has, in some ways, watered down the Saxon heroic ideals with safety and humane-ness, just as Humanism and Existentialism have contributed to the invalidating of extant outlets for man's sense of ritual. However, one has only to read of Watergate and the Stonehouse affair to realise that the manipulative power of Offa survives. In his essay, "The True Conduct of Human Judgement", Hill states that if *Cymbeline* is 'enchanted ground' then that ground is

> drenched in flesh and blood, civil history, morality,
> policy, about the which men's affections, praises,
> fortunes do turn and are conversant...

It is steeped, that is, in those knowledges which men generally 'taste well'. This is Offa's Mercia too. But Hill's sense of literary and 'real' time is more sophisticated than this rather vague delineation of general ground gives credit for (as his references to time as commodity and 'mechanical time' versus organic time in the work of Meyerhoff and Pearlman in "Redeeming the Time" might indicate). Add to this distinctly modern school of heuristic thought, Platonic and Christian versions of history, and the Neo-Platonic schools of thought which influenced Pound, Eliot and Yeats so much, and one begins to see the complexity of the basis for the *Hymns*.

Hill has set out *Mercian Hymns* on a field of historical and literary precedence. The very title leads us back to an Anglo-Saxon translation of the Psalms, Isaiah, Habakkuk, Deuteronomy, the Benedictus and the Magnificat from Luke. We must not be over-eager to draw close correspondences here. As Silkin points out,

> these texts are interlineally placed with the Latin taken
> from the Latin of which these are literal and not always
> accurate translations. Moreover these translations embody
> no sense of the Anglo-Saxon world at large. That is, they
> were probably intended as instructional texts for teaching
> Latin. Moreover the two Vulgates are themselves, of course,
> translations from the Hebrew...

And as Silkin goes on to imply, we must allow Hill a sensitivity to the differing overlays and analogues which accumulate around an often translated work.

The levels of the Biblical passages are however important as a long tradition of righteousness and vengeance of which the Saxons were aware. As Brooke writes in relation to the Merovingian 'farce' up to 751 AD.,

> It was natural for men in the Middle Ages and espec-
> ially churchmen of the 8th century to look back into
> the Old Testament for precedents for what they were
> doing.

The Biblical passages are both mythologically and historically relevant to the *Hymns*. They tell us not only about the Saxons in relation to the Jewish prophets, but also about the Saxon blend of Christianity and ruthlessness — a kind of amalgamation of the ideas of Christ and Yahweh. Briefly then, Isaiah 38, v.10-20, stresses the torment of a king who

reaffirms his faith in a seemingly pitiless god. The singer, afflicted by
fear of Sheol, asks God to be a father to him and asks to be allowed to
live in his Lord's house. Habakkuk 3 speaks of the approach of a direful
God who makes the earth tremble. The annointed are to be saved but
the wicked are shattered — the chapter ends in trust. Deuteronomy 32,
v.1-43 is Moses' song denouncing a people. It tells of the Lord's loving
kindness, and of how many turned to idolatry throughout Hebrew history. It is God's decision to take a bloody revenge and mock the false
gods:

> I will make my arrows drunk with
> blood, my sword shall devour flesh. . .

and the final assertion,

> he will punish those who hate him
> And make expiation for his
> people's land.

The two passages from Luke embody praise to the Lord for keeping his
promises throughout generations, and for his mercy. The terrible beauty, zeal and inhumanity reinforced·by absolute power in these *Hymns*
tell us something about Offa. The references to the different generations, the need to restore the land and the splendour of the Lord also
provide valuable precedents for certain of Hill's Hymns. But by far the
most important hymn for consideration in the light of Hill's work is one
of David's Psalms not included in the 150 found in the Bible, but only
in the *Septuagint*. Offa is a 'staggeringly-gifted' child, 'A boy at odds in
the house', lonely among brothers; he possesses a 'strangeness' and
grows up to behead men. Both Offa and Hill are taken to be a King of
some kind, 'a prodigy, a maimed one'. The man in the Psalm (probably
King David) 'was small among brothers and set apart by his musical ability'. God also set him apart and annointed him,

> I went out against foreign people. They cursed me in
> their temple. I took from him his sword and cut off
> his head and went on my way, having cleared the re-
> proach of Israel.

There are many echoes of these events and attitudes in Hill's hymns.
Offa is so convinced of his own status as supreme ruler of the English
that any challenge to his position is seen as simply 'A novel heresy'. But
like David and Jehovah: 'Forewarned I have thwarted their imminent
devices.' These echoes compose some of the most ancient of Offa's
histories.

R.H.Hodgkin in his *A History of the Anglo-Saxons* writes of Offa,

> We have the sense of his long shadow falling over
> England but we cannot discern the man himself.

Hill must be aware of the fragmentary sources from which we piece together a rather hazy impression of Offa. He ordered the building of his
Dyke, built a beautiful church at Glastonbury, gave birth to English
foreign policy, and was a friend of Charlemagne. He was called King of

all England, executed King Aethelbert and instituted the silver penny and many beautiful coins as a basis for currency. It is this 'long shadow' delineated by such facts which provides a historical setting in which the objects, personae and emotions of *Mercian Hymns* exist.

Martin Dodsworth writes,

> In Offa many men and ages meet: the author of the
> *Chanson de Roland*, Ruskin, the wielder of sword and
> the driver of a maroon GT. These are the translations
> of his universal form into the particular languages of
> time and place.

Hill provides the information,

> The Offa who figures in this sequence might perhaps
> most usefully be regarded as the presiding genius of
> the West Midlands, his dominion enduring from the
> middle of the eighth century until the middle of the
> twentieth (and possibly beyond).

It is this genius and its quality which is reserved for the most extensive and searching criticism in the sequence.

As Hill writes, by Medieaval times Offa 'was already becoming a creature of legend'. Hill has either traced or created the enlarging of this legend-weaving in his own lifetime. As Brooke writes,

> Whether on his [Offa's] parents' initiative or (as is
> quite possible) on his own, he was the one ruler of
> Mercia to bear the name of the great king of contin-
> ental 'Angel' from whom the Mercian kings claimed
> descent.

Widsid mentions this first Offa:

> Offa ruled Angel, Alewith the Danes: he was the brav-
> est of these men, yet he did not perform mighty deeds
> beyond Offa; but Offa, first of men, while still a youth
> gained the greatest of kingdoms; no one of the same age
> achieved greater deeds of battle; with his single sword
> he fixed the boundary against the Myrgings at Fifeldor.

Often such histories are shot through with superstition or mythological motifs. Offa of Mercia's lineage is traced back through Offa of Angel to Woden in an early genealogy. It is interesting also that Wat's Dyke, built in Ethelbald's reign ('A mere dress rehearsal for Offa's Dyke') was soon associated with the legendary Wade — 'an antique figure from the days of Teutonic paganism'. References to 'The Stag's Head', holly boughs, bonfires, mother-earth, elves, fire-dragons and rune-stones abound in *Mercian Hymns*. We are made conscious of the way in which activities and objects around us often recall or reconstitute a legend or mythical theme. At one point the narrator actually becomes 'Cernunnos, the branched god'. The references to mistletoe, crabapple trees, thorn-trees, oak forests, apple orchards, the blaze of chestnut boughs and Adam scrumping through leaves, are a little too insistent to pass over as simply descriptive background. The shire tree drips red 'in the arena of its own uprooting'. Groves of 'legendary holly' recall the Druidic listing and reverence for trees. Robert Graves, in *The White Goddess*, makes some important remarks on these motifs. 'The Stag's Head', merely a pub-sign in the *Hymns*, has always been a symbol of royalty. Mistletoe is a sexual symbol associated with Hercules (see Heaney's "Antaeus" poems), and sacred to Druids. It is a plant revered for its power in battle (a mistletoe spear pierced Balder's side). The apple tree mentioned in relation to the young Offa is a 'chieftan-tree' like oak and holly. Apples, of course, are an image which both Christian and pagan religions have used as symbols of temptation, choice, and fruitfulness. Holly is correctly accorded the title 'legendary' in the *Hymns*. Graves links pagan and Christian ideas concerning the tree-

> Since in Medieval practice St.John the Baptist who
> lost his head on St.John's day took over the oak-king's
> titles and customs, it was natural to let Jesus as John's
> merciful successor, take over the holly king's.

Hill does not enlarge upon these motifs but allows the echoes and figures which lie behind them to play upon the reader's mind. He often hints at profundity in his use of plant and animal life but allows the allusion to pass as a simple reminiscence. For example, at one point he refers to the princes of Mercia as 'badger and raven', but does not go on to tell us that the raven was regarded as a prophetic bird, Bran's crow — mistrusted and revered. Or, again, in the reference to boars 'worming' in the crepitant oak-forest, we are given as succinct and meaningful a microcosm of England as in the image of Offa's derelict sandlorry, but the reference is not expanded. Myths of branched men (dating back to Palaeolithic times), the Tree of Life, the personalities and powers associated with certain trees and animals are important in this context. But these are only elements of a larger idea — that of the earth cult in *Mercian Hymns*. The land is, with Offa, the most important single force in the work. "Hymn IV" tells us,

> I was invested in mother-earth, the crypt of roots
> and endings. I abode there. . .

and in "Hymn V":

> I wormed my way heavenward for
> ages amid barbaric ivy, scrollwork of fern.

The narrator is intimately concerned with the ground he walks on. He digs. hoards. and drinks from 'honeycombs of chill sandstone'. He has a sandlorry 'named Albion', and finds comfort in the sunlight with his cat. The burial and marriage ceremonies are confused at one point recalling rites of an earth-based cult. The detailed descriptions of marshes, heathland and Midland forests remind us that Offa, like Hill, has a care for 'natural minutiae'. Worms become 'red-helmeted warriors', 'a wasp's nest', a reliquary; fungi are 'soft shields', and bees make provision mantling the inner walls of their burh'. This is, of course, the eye of a medieval despot indulging in anthropomorphism. However, on another level, the analogies are apt. Insect as human life does have its feudal and belligerent aspects and these touches reveal a deft and light ironic twist in Hill's writing. We are shown a land seething with life: eel-swarms, coagulations of frogs, trout fry simmering, but this life is brutalised. The child batters frogs and workmen 'ransack ephiphanies, vertebrae of the chimera, armour of wild bees' larvae'. This kind of detail is interleaved with references to dragons and elves, and one recalls Heaney's landscapes connected with the Nerthus cults. As Heaney has found 'a tongue of the land' in his Sweeney poems, so Hill is approaching that which he admires in George Eliot, 'the speech of the landscape'. Many echoes are set up by the brunt of Hill's terse words. The buried dragons of Hymn XII remind one not only of the saurian guardians of treasure mounds but also of the story of Lludd and Llefelys where subterranean dragons fight and serve as protective spirits. Offa could be a maimed one because of the identification of great intellect or magical power with a crippled or weak person. Odin often appeared as an old man who had sacrificed one eye for the gift of knowledge. The 'wrapped head' of Hymn XV could be a reference to King Aethelbert's beheading, a reminder of Offa's sense of guilt. However, 'wrapped heads' were the centre of a Celtic cult in Britain, and Bran's buried head was another guardian of the land. 'England's well' could simply be a formulaic phrase for the sea, but the well is also the source of inspiration and knowledge in both Celtic and Norse mythology.

A vast, shadowy outline emerges from the associations with telluric cults: 'baleful night soil tetanus', rampart and ditch, and the underkingdom of 'crinoid and crayfish'. Offa takes possession of these contours. However, though he draws authority and strength from both pagan and Biblical traditions Offa is never only Cernunnos or the holly-king or Yahweh's representative. He is always prey to the kind of wry humour, pettiness and materialism of a human being. He is the spirit of the land and its most unscrupulous exploiter. Not only does Hill mention the 'mystique of status' in his essay on *Cymbeline*, but in "The Conscious Mind's Intelligible Structure", writing of Yeats and Burke he concludes:

. . .one would hazard the suggestion that the revocation
is the outcome of acute historical intelligence drawing
its energy from the struggle with that obtuseness which
is the dark side of its own selfhood.

Offa too possesses an acute historical sense and certainly holds to a brutal obtuseness. Much of his energy is drawn from his darker side but Hill's wording is significant — the word is 'selfhood' not 'self'. It is not his actual being but that which his Ego has laid hold upon which lends him his sinister energy. He is the entrencher, the builder of dykes and cleaver of sandstone. Even these roles are open to degeneration. It seems a 'falling off' when he is named as 'contractor to the desirable new estates', when battles become house-names and 'cohorts of charabancs fanfare' through Offa's province. The land is abused through 'deeds of settlement', ironworks and industrialisation. There is the satirical gift of 'dead crysanths' to an England 'coiled' and 'entrenched' by brickwork and paintwork — product of the very processes Offa set in motion. The 'hacked marl' reminds of the dyke — even the worms make 'ramparts of compost'. The first hymn leaves us in no doubt of Offa's involvement with the impulse to settle. As Brooke writes:

> Offa's charters make grants of land in many different
> parts of the country and so reveal the development
> and spread of his power.

He disposed of land in Kent without reference to the local monarchs, and though his structures were often beautiful and awe-inspiring, his tactics remind one more of a dubious property surveyor than a king. Settlement becomes the ruling passion of Post-war Britain. New estates spread, and Hill's relation had 'lived long enough to see things nicely-settled'. This England of settlement, 'brickwork and paintwork', reminds one of "East Coker":

> Houses rise and fall, crumble, are extended
> Are removed, destroyed, restored, or in their place
> Is an open field, or a factory, or a by-pass.

Hill's land is 'coiled', also echoing the fire-serpent or dragon, and a good deal of the historical and mythological interest in the *Hymns* is linked to the land. Even the child's sandlorry recalls this: its Blakean and originally Graeco-French name 'Albion' symbolises the accruing of linguistic and cultural deposits. The subject of settlement is linked to the third major strand which stretches through the *Hymns*: that is, the manufactured object or signa: art.

However, before considering this, it is necessary to look to some other mythological aspects of the *Hymns*. Donald Davie recognises Hill's creation of a king who spans history and, to a certain extent, metaphysics, as a myth in itself. The act of myth-making is revealed as a sinister activity in Hill's art. Offa was ostensibly a Christian king. He ingratiated himself with the West Saxons by building a very picturesque church at Glastonbury, and with the Northumbrians by embellishing the tomb of St.Oswald at York with silver, jewels and gold. In return we know that the monks at St.Albans 'shuffled' the deeds of the king onto his queen as a way of exonerating their benefactor. Offa is described as 'a martyr-ologist' (perhaps a wry inverted joke in relation to "Funeral Music") in the first hymn, not just because of Boethius, but also because he made the shrine of a Christian Roman soldier beheaded during religious persecution in the year 303 the nucleus of his monastery at St.Albans. Alcuin, a staunch church-father, wrote of Offa, 'You are the glory of Britain. . .a sword against its enemies'. He made Mercia for a long time seat of an Archbishopric, and the Pope recognised the enhanced power of the Mercian king by naming him 'Rex Anglorum'. But the marriage of Church and State is seldom comfortable. To the child Offa (and also, possibly, to Hill) nurtured in the sandstone and natural 'crypt of roots', the church and curate are both 'strange' at first appearance. In Hymn X we find the marked juxtaposition of a devotional language: 'What should a man make of remorse that it might profit his soul', with the glib if tender 'God bless' drowned by 'the death-howls of his rival'. The child is not at home with ecclesiastics schooling him in Latin. Indeed 'ancilla' and 'servus' remind us that such a child would find the virtue of a Christian king — service of a community — difficult to master. The Old Testament God, the kings of child-play and ritual are concerned with dominance not service. The pagan past is glimpsed everywhere. All challengers are innately mad and merely constitute 'novel heresies',

> I am the King of Mercia, and
> I know.

The assertion is as autocratic and ruthless as it is childish and pitiful. As law-maker, thwarter of hostile devices, namer and destroyer combined, Offa often reflects Yahweh:

> Today I name them, tomorrow I shall express the
> [new law
> dedicate my awakening to this matter.

Offa mirrors the decisively tyrannical image of the Jewish god as Lear relates himself to Zeus. The 'crux' is not the cross in Mercia but Charlemagne's gift of an Avar sword. This is what 'pilgrims' carry over the Channel; there is a savage irony as the beauty of the sword is des-scribed as 'a variety of balm' and the paragraph continues 'And other miracles. . .' Outside the world is predatory. Shafts from the winter sun home in upon the horizon at Christ's Mass. Conventions of giving and Christian fellowship are revealed to reflect ambitions and unspoken priorities. The wine of Christian ambassadors, possibly that of the Sacrament, reverts to 'urine and ashes' like the plumber's tea in Hymn XII.

The visit to Pavia is significant as this city lay on the main route of pilgrimage to Rome. There might be an irony in the fact that Offa's daughter, after expulsion to a nunnery, was seen begging bread on the streets of Pavia. Writing in 747 St.Boniface notes that there were 'a great many women of bad morals in the city'.

Hymn XXIV shows how ecclesiastical architecture with its often pagan and military motifs can be altered by the 'moody testament' of an itinerant mason. Agape is lost somewhere in the warriors and dragon-coils. The question, 'Where best to stand?', though perhaps simply an observer's query, also reminds us of the choice between faiths or versions of reality. The Anglo-Saxon Kings often changed religion; some remained secret pagans long after conversion to Christianity. Heaney, in "Now and In England", comments on the wording and images of this Hymn:

> The mannered rhetoric of these pieces is a kind of verbal
> architecture, a grave and sturdy English Romanesque. The
> native undergrowth, both vegetative and verbal, that bar-

56

baric scrollwork of fern and ivy, is set against the tympanum and chancel-arch, against the weighty elegance
of imperial Latin. . .the occasion, the engendering moment seems to involve the contemplation of a carved
pediment — a tympanum is the cubical head of a pediment — which exhibits a set of scenes: one of Eden, one
of a kind of harrowing of hell; and the scenes are super-
vised by images of the evangelists. . .this. . .mode of
presentation. . .resembles the compression of the piece
itself. The carving reminds him of the carver, a master
mason. . .this mason is itinerant — a word used in its
precise Latin sense, yet when applied to a travelling
craftsman, that pristine sense seems to foreshadow its
present narrowed meaning of a tinker, a travelling tin-
smith, a white-smith. . .Tympanum, of course, is also a
drum, and the verb 'pester' manages a rich synaesthetic
effect, the stone is made to cackle like a kettle-drum as
the chisel hits it. But 'pester' is more interesting still. Its
primary meaning, from the original Latin root, pastorium,
means to hobble a horse, and it was used in 1685 to mean
'crowding persons in or into'. So the mason hobbles and
herds and crowds in warrior and lion, dragon coils, tendrils of the stony vine; and this interlacing and entangle-
ment of motifs is also the method of the poem.

One can but praise Heaney's etymological and onomatopoeic senses
here. He accurately traces the overlap between verbal and descriptive
wording whilst also applying the kind of 'envisaging' which the verse
demands. In the passage above, an Irish Latinist recognises an English
one, and the whole essay is remarkable for the light which it throws
back onto Heaney's own linguistic undergrowths and graftings.

The second paragraph of the Hymn does indeed offer a compressed
if odd picture. The Christian message becomes popularised and assimi-
lated into local and traditional ideas. Christ becomes a pagan mummer
in saving Adam and, in a characteristically blunt but delightful pun, is
called 'a cross Christ'. The 'disjointed' music of Messiaen may run
through the final paragraph of Hymn XXIV but this fact does not serve
to emphasise the contrast between Resurrection hope and the dust
blanketing ecclesiastical architecture and the entombed dead. The dead
have 'clawing wings' for the mason 'dresses' the stone with beastly
forms; perhaps Heaney is right to assume that the mason holds the central viewpoint in *Mercian Hymns*. The disparity between these grotesques
and church interiors mirrors the incongruity between private and public
areas of belief and the distance between doctrinal consistency and the
untamed imagination. The ritual and personnel of the church surround
Offa but somehow the old Yuletide spirit survives the mottoes of peace
and goodwill. There is a wry invocation of the troll-wives, tooth-be-

witchers, who become, in time, merely inane old ladies taken up with wedding preparations. Behind these women lurk the shadows of the 'sigewifs' or victory women who were held responsible for pain and disease in Saxon times.

Finally the seasons rotate in the same steady, but often brutal, way. Earth lies 'the ghost bride of livid Thor' and the shire-tree drips. The sky-god's lightning has torn up the totemic tree recalling the elemental conflict which Heaney makes much of in *North*. The departure of Offa is accompanied by a ludo game, itself a struggle for survival and security, recalling the casting of twigs or bones of divination. (Ludo comes from the Latin meaning 'to play'; we must not underestimate Hill's capacity to contrive word-games.)

The most persistent pagan image in the *Hymns* is the dragon. Offa's photograph is 'horned'; he 'wormed' his way upwards ('wurm' meaning dragon); and he 'hoards'. The earth becomes the 'fire-dragon's facetted skin' recalling Fafnir, the world-serpent. England itself is 'coiled' and cars spout 'plumes' of smoke. Airships are 'dragon-tailed' and the mason 'pesters' 'dragon-coils' and 'clawing wings'. Offa seems to possess a hot humour. The fire imagery of the *Hymns* allies him with Milton's Satan. Bonfires whistle, leaves are inflamed and Offa accrues a 'stinking blaze'. He threatens with ash, and trout fry 'simmer' in the pond as he passes. Wattle smoulders, children incinerate rubbish and the narrator ponders over coin-makers and forge-workers. Even lullabies are charred, and the last dream of Offa starts as Gran lights the gas. Hill has used fire and metal to convey extremeties before: we remember "The Assisi Fragments" dedicated to Wilson Knight, which contain references to fire and a serpent. Offa, like Shakespeare's Cleopatra, is an 'old snake' radiating in the luxuriant heat of the land and a domineering sexuality. Sexuality is submerged in the *Hymns* and only emerges in a fit of mentalised sadism in Hymn XVIII.

II

As well as Christian and pagan elements in the *Hymns* we also find an interest in legend, popular folklore and belief. C.H.Sisson writes, 'This is a world of metamorphoses where Offa King of Mercia assumes a variety of shapes with a life stretching over 12 centuries'. Offa is, in many ways, the confluence of hints and seemingly chance remarks in the *Hymns*, but we are also made aware of the danger of drawing strands together, of legend-weaving. Those who name, translate or live out roles are often creating false, and, in Saxon England, bloody fictions. On a more obvious level, we are told of elves, eldorados, a chimera and dragons. Offa is 'cushioned' on a legend (the word is doubly apt here) of his own self-possession and genius. In the first hymn the 'ritual king' is created by naming his territories and, in the second, a wider legend is created with less distinct boundaries. We have already seen how Offa cannot perceive without reference to his store of fantastic tales. In the chancel arch and subterranean dragon these stories gain a concrete and conceptual reality respectively. By Hymn XXI some heroic legend is marred beyond recovery. The 'real Camelot' and 'carillons' are surely ironic. In the rush of newly-mobile suburban dwellers, commerce, and local legends made accessible for tourists, the old tales die. There are, however, survivals. In Hymn XXII 'dragon-tailed' airships and winged warriors reveal how certain images are too deeply ingrained in the popular imagination to be blotted out. The old heroes assume new shapes. The re-entry of beings '. . .im/mortal as phantoms.' into this 'sublunary world' can happen through many mediums, not just through the minds of knights or saints but through a vision of the common working man, nameless and reliable —

> They trudged out of the dark, scraping their boots
> free from lime-splodges and phlegm. They munched
> cold bacon.

They seem as timeless and anonymous as Heaney's mummers. The child's mind is particularly receptive to tale and legend. Hill's narrator as a boy is most 'open' to the stories 'in the earthy shelter', echoing rituals of subterranean initiation. The eldorado, false vision of a consumer society, concludes in a headstone of washstand marble. There is a wealth of archaeological, mythological and biological material gathered from the Mercian soil, but the rhetoric of hero-making is both splendid (Hymn XXII) and threatening (Hymns VII, VIII, X and XVIII). However, there are glimpses of Hill's humour in the 'tooth-bewitchers' and 'fortified' warriors of Hymn XXVI.

Offa's position in relation to the Romans is arguably more important that references to Ruskin, Boethius and Edwardian England. Sir Cyril Fox writes of Offa's Dyke that it was designed by a man of military genius and exceptional engineering skill and was 'carried out with such precision that it reminds one forcibly of Roman genius and Roman energy'. 'Roman flues' lie under the earth in Hill's Mercia; they are 'the long-unlooked-for mansions of our tribe'. 'Flue' can also mean to open outwards or inwards and is additionally a word for a fishing-net. There is a sense of extending borders here, of collecting more and more people under a single head. Offa recognised the Romans as a symbol of tribal unity — mansion-builders for a people. They bear witness to a strength and discipline which left great architecture, administration and statecraft. Offa makes a journey to Italy, is praised by the Pope and is educated in Latin. Charlemagne, Holy Roman Emperor, is Offa's friend. But if English ditches are sometimes strewn with forgers' corpses, the Tiber can foam bloodily. The religious language, Latin of officialdom and court rhetoric do not obscure these facts. The King at the crowning seems foreign and imposed upon the people. In a similar way Offa is raised in deference to a foreign power and, for his part, inherits Roman ruthlessness, military strength and architectural skill. It is intriguing that a man so 'embedded' and and nurtured by his own soil should accede so readily to the model of Roman autocracy. Offa extends a massive offer (the pun is surely conscious), a more comfortable and efficient society for the sacrifice of moral qualms. An 'offer' is also an act of worship and, literally, a presentation of two forces ready to engage in battle. 'Ofer' from Old English means 'above', hence someone of high rank, but can also mean 'a bank', and one notes Hill's insistence on ridges and mounds. The most telling interpretation is found in the fact that if a Roman said 'offa' he would mean a ball of meat, cutlet, a tumour, an abortion, or a shapeless mass.

Hill's technique in the Hymns has obvious links with Anglo-Saxon formulaic verse, Latin ecclesiastical verse and song, and Biblical expression. So, for example, 'Troll-wives', 'tooth-bewitchers', 'wergild' and the decisive almost bluff tone recall early English prose and poetry. Often, disguised or modified phrases, even cliches, add to the allusiveness of the verse. For example, two Biblical echoes which appear more unconscious than deliberate are the mole shouldering 'the clogged wheel, his gold solidus' in IV, recalling Isaiah 2,v.20, and in X, the first sentence of the third paragraph seems to recall Christ's injunction about gaining a whole world.

History, or histories, in these *Hymns* is, as we shall see, very much a matter of echoes in a confusing and, to a larger extent, unassimilable continuum. Hill grapples not only with the shadow of an entity but also with a location throughout time. Hence, in Hymn II, 'a specious gift, A syndicate'. These fragments and scraps create an overall impression of the mode which the author wishes to stress. The 'specious gift' is also the Word which cannot capture emotion or actuality with any precision, and which has contributed to the fragmentation of modern life. Hill uses precise and compacted images: often one feels that one is seeking significance in quite ordinary events giving an insight into the processes of 'making history'.

On a purely technical level one can see at least two ways in which the *Hymns* operate. The *Times Literary Supplement* called them: 'Trimmed, interlocking units, polished without glossiness. . .tense but unstrained'. They can be taken as autonomous units, some of which assert their individual concentration and power:

> Shafts from the winter sun homing upon
> earth's rim.   Christ's mass : in the thick
> of a snowy forest the flickering evergreen
> fissured with light.

or,

> It is autumn.   Chestnut-boughs clash their
> inflamed leaves.   The garden festers for
> attention: telluric cultures enriched with
> shards, corms, nodules, the sunk solids
> of gravity.   I have accrued a golden
> and stinking blaze.

The words are shot through with correspondences and associations with the other Hymns. Perhaps, like the 'house carls' and Offa's actions, the

Hymns and history itself can be shuffled. This feeling of an arbitrary order is increased by the disjointed seasonal shifts of the Hymns. They move from a 'false' Easter to Spring, Summer and Autumn, but then back to Spring with 'simmering trout-fry'. We then return to Autumn and Winter with 'Christ's mass' and to Summer weekends (XXI), but suddenly we have to re-trace our steps to a real Easter and skip many months to Yule-tide. In *Waiting for Godot* Pozzo's speeches mix tenses and ignore great lapses of time just as Caliban's remarks make it clear that linear chronology is not the norm on Prospero's island. The jumbled timescale of the Hymns is a more muted but crucial factor in their structure. Offa seems lord of this chaotic history, decisively pulling the year from its wheel whilst also affirming seasonal and orderly values.

III

The greatest triumph of the book is Offa himself. The brief references, insights and obliquely-recorded incidents surrounding him define a psychological perception, an analysis of familial, social and emotional pressures which create Offa as a man in time without indulging in the fallacy of historical knowledge. Hill's earlier concerns are implicitly involved here the intractable nature of words refusing to 'grasp' events, the luxury of poetry in the face of suffering and the irrecoverable past. The Hymns are themselves 'legend' in Eagleton's sense of the word. This legend is acted out in a literary landscape torn from the ease of the Pastoral mode. Mercia is glimpsed in a degraded eclogue: curt injunctions have replaced the bucolic dialogue and the land is quarried, mined, settled and roamed by tourists. Offa rules as the unchallenged tyrant of this territory. In his 'person' we find a close study of the ideas of talent, tyranny, kingship and their effects. The role of the King, the brutality that he has inherited, the fact that he is 'staggeringly-gifted' but sadistic in a violent age, all play against each other. Additionally, we find an interest in the relations between king and people, workmen, plumbers and modern humans. Hill alludes to the tensions and complexities of government but is aware of the illusion of a definitive historical viewpoint. As Blackstone writes in Sisson's epigraph, our laws are subject to a total dependence on the laws of Nature governing human activity and the natural world. In addition, it is the 'law of revelation' by which we gradually accumulate general principles. One might say the 'law of revelation' includes the general corpus of myths, legends and 'lessons' by which the human race acquires moral laws. Neither lessons or laws are simple and one cannot blame previous societies for the brutal laws they endorsed unless one supplies contemporary evidence. Hill stresses the violence of Offa, but he also appreciates the processes which engender policies. Ruskin, in the eightieth letter of *Fors Clavigera* (literally 'Chance is the Key-bearer' or 'key') points out the necessity for all levels of commerce to be intimately concerned with the 'life of the workman'. 'The Lord, the King' is 'only an instrument' to that end and this concern is the only basis of royal or other social power. This is, of course, in stark contrast to Offa's policy, the fate of Hill's grandmother and Ruskin's "Matron and Maid". Ruskin quotes Plato;

> there was an ancient polity amongst us and ancient
> divisions of rank founded on possession.

He goes on to write of the Guardian Law of Life, in the perception and obedience of which all the life of states forever consists — 'The Laws of the Fatherland', or, as Ruskin adds, 'the earth'. Ruskin uses this linkage to support his argument about human considerations being the only bases for authority. However, Offa is 'invested in mother-earth', the very spirit of the soil, yet his state is hardly built upon the conceptions of humaneness and service. Yet Offa is talented, does unite the people, import foreign craftsmen and reveal great tenacity. Part of the dilemma is realised in the lack of Coleridge's 'moral copula' from Ruskin's sentence which links 'Fatherland' and 'earth'. One is a geographical concept and the other ideological, and they are drawn together in a way conducive to the ruler or rulers.

Heaney comments on Hymn XXV:

> Ruskin's eightieth letter reflects eloquently and plan-
> gently on the injustice of the master and servant situa-
> tion, on the exploitation of labour, on the demeaning
> work in a nail forge. . . He goes on to compute that the
> woman and the husband earn altogether £55 a year with
> which to feed and clothe themselves and their six child-
> ren, to reproach the luxury of the mill-owning class, and
> to compare the wives of industrialists contemplating
> Burne-Jones' picture of Venus' mirror with these, their
> sisters, who had only, for Venus' mirror, a heap of
> ashes. . . .
>
> It seems to me here that Hill is celebrating his own
> indomitable Englishry, casting his mind on other days,
> singing a clan beaten into the clay and ashes, and link-
> ing their patience, their sustaining energy, with the glory
> of England. The 'quick forge', after all, may be what its
> origin in Shakespeare's *Henry V* declares it to be, 'the
> quick forge and working house of thought', but it is
> surely also the 'random grim forge' of "Felix Randall
> the Farrier".

Heaney is at once too textually optimistic and too Yeatsian here. Hill has not sung and does not here sing of 'lovers and dancers. . .beaten into the clay' or of a 'clan'. His tone is infinitely more menacing than the Irish writer concedes:

> It is one
> thing to celebrate the 'quick forge', another
> to cradle a face hare-lipped by the
> searing wire.

The forge does not appear as a proof of indomitable will-power but of the bludgeoning tedium and danger of Industrialism. One remembers Blake as much, if not more, than Shakespeare:

> Cheshire & Lancashire & Westmoreland groan in anguish:
> As they cut the fibres from the rivers he sears them with hot
> Iron of his forge & fixes them into bones of chalk & rock.
>
> **("Jerusalem, Emanation of the Giant Albion")**

One might ask does Hill poise the worth of terraced housing and chara-bancs against the nailer's darg and crippling work-rates, and this question again brings the figure of Offa into focus. His authority is not based upon the people but on the land and on his binary 'genius'. How-ever, the pressures of office, government, childhood arrogance and his position in the family all take their toll of Offa. His gaze is 'foreign'; his sarcasm and pilgrimage seem lonely. An exile, he treads the land of his childhood — a ritual figure estranged from humanity by his ruth-lessness. Such a 'genius loci' blurring with the outline of a King who half-believed in divine right does not fade easily from the fabric of time or the popular imagination. If there is something of Hamlet in every man then there is also something of Offa.

> I am the King of Mercia, and
> I know

Hill, aware of the power of echoes, has let the inner mass of his main character be 'filled out' by other forms, other voices. King Leontes, the tyrant of *The Winter's Tale* holds a great fondness for his son and sees him as an embodiment of his own youth:

> 'I fecks!
> Why, that's my bawcock. What! hast
> smutch'd thy nose?
> They say it is a copy out of mine. Come,
> Captain....!
> *(Act 1 Sc.2)*

Offa too seeks his childhood and remembers smeared hands. 'Smutch'd' recalls Offa's cat Smut, and both words reveal a legalism, a Puritanism of mind. The figures of Lear and Cymbeline also lurk behind Offa — both mythical or semi-mythical Kings of England who reveal sadistic undersides to their personalities. Lear particularly is echoed in refer-ences to heathland, and in Offa's strange departure where the tyrant passes from this world rather like Lear's ghost in Act 5 Sc.3. The child's sudden violence to frogs in Hymn VII recalls young Marcius, the son of Coriolanus, 'mammocking' a butterfly. There are more recent parallels: Offa binding the English together and threatening enemies with a cigar remind one of the famous caricatures of Winston Churchill.

In "History as Poetry" Hill writes:

> Poetry
> Unearths from among the speechless dead

> Lazarus mystified, common man
> Of death.

There is a sense in which history is mystery. The dead themselves are 'speechless' and all men are 'common' in death. The crash of Hymn XVII seems to be a personal reminiscence, but it also reminds of the elusive nature of the past. Words are clumsy, often dangerous 'tools' and a poet's eloquence can be 'damning' and 'damnable'. Even the most precise verse approaches a knack of tongues. Yet, as the first two Hymns illustrate, the effort of grappling with shadows and words that 'claw' the brain can be a strident reminder of vanished life.

Is Offa a presence or an absence surrounded by artifacts? We are given no physical details, and he is only defined by objects and people who surround him. Even his sensuality seems ritualistic, isolated and ponderous. This figure is in marked contrast with the 'common man', plumber or weaver, the anonymous 'they' of the Hymns who converge as the sequence closes.

David Jones writes in the Preface to *The Anathemata* that he has allowed himself 'to be directed by motifs gathered together from such sources as have by accident been available to me, and to make a work out of such data.' He goes on to write, 'The artist deals wholly in signs . . .but there is a time factor effecting these signs.' In relation to these statements one immediately remembers Offa's coins, the irony of his kingship and properties in modern terms and the ceremony that surrounds him. His personality is gradually illuminated by personal signs:

> A pet name, a common name...

> private derelict sandlorry named Albion
> a biplane, already
> obsolete and irreplaceable.

> He adored the desk, its brown oak inlaid with ebony,
> assorted prize pens, the seals of gold, and base
> metal into which he had sunk his name.

> Offa Rex, resonant in silver. . .

> his noon cigar. . .

These signs are effective because they deal with objects which we have all seen or owned - not just swords and maces but aeroplanes and lorries. We have all seen the fool's gold, the harp-shaped brooches, confetti, hundreds and thousands, radios, charabancs and GT's. These signs and figures are juxtaposed: fire-dragons with plumbers, gleemen with car-dealers. The form of the sequence reinforces the idea of objects and artifacts used to manifest history and personality. Hill could be said to create a tapestry-like effect in the hymns. The silver veining of Augustan prose, gold-leaf of Old English sounds and voluted grape-vine of polysyllabic Latin words. Heaney provides a metaphor of carving but the juxtapositions often leave us the impression of a fluid, changing

historical perspective more akin to the loom than the chisel. The third
part of Offa's death hymn:

> . . .he left behind coins, for his lodgings, and
> traces of red mud.

remind us that a single thread from the poem can illuminate the whole
weave. The coins and lodgings recall the Saxon world and the sandstone
Offa's telluric associations. Yet this could be a motorist leaving a motel
having scraped mud off his boots. The texture of the poem has been so
well built up that this ending 'ties up' several threads in a powerful and
poignant vision, hinting finally at the way we all leave life, alone and
penniless.

> We cannot hope to measure the sum of these (modern)
> developments. . .Our ethics, our central habits of conscious-
> ness, the immediate and environmental membrane we in-
> habit, our relations to age and to remembrance, to the
> children whose gender we may select and whose herditity
> we may programme, are being transformed. As in the twi-
> lit times of Ovid's fables of mutant being, we are in
> metamorphosis. To be ignorant of these scientific and
> technological phenomena, to opt out of their effects on
> our mental and physical appearance, is to opt out of
> reason. . . .Today our dialectics are binary.

Hill, in looking for the 'drama of reason' in his criticism of Eliot and
Arnold, must be aware of these binary dialectics'. There is no definitive
view in his work. Industry, the automobile, research into the nature of
time and psychology, have all contributed to the shifting perspectives
of the Hymns. Not only dialectic but also visual image depend on these
considerations in Hill's writing. In "The True Conduct of Human
Judgement" he writes

> It could be said that *Cymbeline* involves the realisation of
> double images, not as Donne's visualisation of the spirit
> of mutual regard ('My face in thine eye, thine in mine
> appeares') but as we might refer to double exposures in
> photography: accidental or contrived palimpsests that
> come from one view having been superimposed on another.

This is as evident in Hymn XV as anywhere in Shakespeare's play. A
man gardening, Hill's narrative voice, Offa dividing a realm and Cernunnos wagging in the brances of a dead tree, are connected in a single
humourous line:

> In brief cavort he was
> Cernunnos, the branched god, lightly concussed.

Images flash before the reader's eyes and at the periphery of his
attention. The action itself is an unwitting celebration of older gestures
— a half stunned recognition. This process can be said to operate in the
work as a whole — sounds and meanings are superimposed on one
another. Two critical statements that Hill has made are crucial here. In

"The Conscious Mind's Intelligible Structure" he writes of Yeats'
"Second Coming",

> The poet is hearing words in depth and is therefore
> hearing, or sounding, history and morality in depth. It
> is as though the very recalcitrance of language – and
> we know that Yeats found the process of composition
> arduous – stood for the primary objective world in one
> of its forms of cruelty and indifference.

Secondly, this statement from his essay on rhythm: 'Language
gravitates and exerts a gravitational pull'. Offa is a creature made of
soundings and gravities inherited from different linguistic traditions.
The words are attempted probes of history, morality and personality.
Heaney likens Hill's delectation for savouring words and the whole
gamut of meanings, sounds and histories associated with them to that
of Joyce:

> There is in Hill something of Stephen Dedalus's hyper-
> consciousness of words as physical sensations, as sounds
> to be plumbed, as weights on the tongue. Words in his
> poetry fall slowly and singly, like molten solder, and
> accumulate to a dull glowing nub.

Hill's work is not fragmentary in the sense that it uses clipped or unfinished references. However, the organisation of the Hymns is such that
each section is deposited as a fragment, often with an autonomous
weight of meaning. These are by no means just scraps of the life of Offa
but tantalisingly offer themselves as glimpses of biography, even docu-
mentary. The second Hymn is a pertinent example. Both form and
content seem to be fragments or shards:

> A pet-name, a common name.   Best-selling brand, curt
> graffito.   A laugh, a cough.   A syndicate.   A specious
> gift.   Scoffed-at horned phonograph.

There are elements of Imagism here. The image of the phonograph hints
at memories of the early 20th century: it is mocked by the young and
horned like Cernunnos and Satan. It is familiar and laughable but also
something of a relic – phallic, almost part of a warrior's accoutrements.
It records history but can never reproduce the event. Like Offa it is de-
funct but also splendid. History is a jumble of significant and extraneous
matter. The order of sounds is similarly confused as in listening to an
old record. 'Best selling brand' could be Omo, and the 'curt graffito'
could be 'fuck' or 'piss off'. A laugh or cough also contains the essential
vowel sound. A syndicate could be the O.F.C. (Overseas Food Corpor-
ation) and a 'specious gift' could bring us back to 'offer' or 'offertory'.
The 'starting cry of a race' is, of course, 'They're off!' There are many
suggestions and echoes of Offa's name in these lines.

Hill, like Jones, uses ceremony: marriage, funeral, namings, crown-
ings to organise and to give his work an impetus and tension. We have
seen previously in *King Log* how this poet can construct literary

'envelopes' around his work. We are reminded again of Jones' ideas about signs, the valuable artifacts of civilisation in reading the contents list:

IX	Offa's Book of the Dead
X	Offa's Laws
XI	Offa's Coins
XIV	Offa's Laws
XV	Offa's Bestiary

All of which constitute substantial conventions, forms in history, ways of recording. Offa's Laws are genuine as far as can be ascertained, but Hill does not use the Laws accorded to Offa. He writes rather with the laws in mind or in reaction to those laws, commenting wryly from time to time. The 'signs' are an organisational device — points of departure for Hill. Moreover, they are still points in the vortex of time.

Offa is influenced by his position in his family and, in a wider context, by his lineage. The process of generation, children linked to the earth, remains and archaeology, are quite evident in the Hymns. Men turn to ash or dust, wine to urine, sinking into the same earth. The kitchen garden is 'riddled with toy-shards, splinters of habitation'. The prevailing irreversible patterns are 'Processes of generation; deeds of settlement'. The second of Offa's death-hymns deals with tracks of ancient occupation — 'Hearthstones; charred lullabies'. History holds a personal gravity. 'Our children and our children's children, o my masters'. Offa, 'a boy at odds in the house...who fostered a strangeness', finds

> 'Not strangeness, but strange likeness. Obstinate,
> outclassed forefathers, I too concede, I am your
> staggeringly gifted child'.

The processes of generation are as inescapable as the seasons — we are reminded of Yahweh's covenant with Abraham 'from generation to generation'. Michael Alexander remarks on the humerous quality of the passage, especially the word 'child'. In fact the question of the rights of genius is connected to the fascination with mystery in the book. The reference to 'child' could be Hill's urbane mockery of the pompous rhetoric that tempts him when comparing his own life to that of Offa. Can man obtain a transcendance through the work, literary or monarchic, which lives after him? Both the writer and Offa are part of a process however much they strive for an independent, somewhat solitary excellence. The double irony in these lines — a viewpoint in history both mocks and is mocked — reveals, as Sisson says, a mind of 'extraordinary justness'. There is a sense in which modern man, the poet, self-conciously 'contains' a good deal of history. Hill has always had an almost Jacobean taste for 'black comedy' — the narrator is fully aware of the irony inherent in the stance he must take and in the texture of the words he is made to use. Art is a sacrifice, especially for a keen literary sensibility, of the most extreme of critical faculties or else the poem would remain unwritten. This kind of humour is perhaps compensation.

Finally, there is a layer of fantasy to the Hymns – an appeal to the otherworldly. History is a dream, a recession into unknown realms in which echoes, memories and lost sounds stir. The real King recurs in child's play, a chief or a village 'King'. Sounds linger in 'charred lullabies', a solitary axe blow that is 'the echo of a lost sound', a 'protective bellow' or the 'haleine' of a car exhaust. There are promises of rebirth in sacrifice – that blood creates a redemptive myth and 'uprootings' leave room for growth. The only method by which man can enter history without the demands of logical authenticity excercising their own kind of blurring is in a dream where the irrational and fantastic are part of the textures of life. Offa is dreamy and 'gives' himself to unattainable toys. He is shown swaying in mild dream; his realm, England, his childhood, genius and ground lie before him like a dream. He shuts his eyes and wills a tower out of the earth (again a masculine, assertive, even sadistic power is glimpsed.) Mysterious, transcendent beings, (recurring also in *King Log* or *For the Unfallen*), gather in tapestries and dreams. Offa recedes into 'the last dream of Offa the King'. This oneiric recession draws from a wide selection of sources: Shakespeare, the dream convention in the writings of the Romantics, and the dream in Anglo-Saxon and Celtic literature. Offa's literary nature has become dream-like, half-forgotten. The legend-weavers have not been able to make a good King Richard or Arthur of him. A remorseless darkness lies at his core.

In childhood fear Offa and Hill's protagonist find 'the landscape flowed away, back to its source'. At the last Offa is 'murmurous'; like any ancient legend he remains resonant but incompletely defined and complex. Is man a static ego, a cluster of voices striving for supremacy or an emptiness, an unmarked, malleable 'nothing' which is shaped by socialisation? Offa finally eludes explanation as does time: 'he withdrew from them', leaving only hints of his existence. In Hymn XXVIII even the tumult of generation 'recedes as though into the long rain' and finally, even in walking towards the people and land which moulded his genius, 'he vanished'.

The bitter beauty of the still-points in time reminds one of Eliot. A damson-bloom of dust floats in the dawn light – a dense image of the beauty but transcience of existence. In the heart of the 'snowy forest the flickering evergreen' is fissured with light. Groves of legendary holly remain 'silverdark, the ridged gleam' – a light, inhuman, dazzling, has pierced to the very pith of being. For a time, in the first paragraph of Hymn XIX the narrator is confronted by 'the thorn-trees thin smoke' and wonders, 'At this distance it is hard to tell'. A timeless fear is realised: is the wattle burning? Are the far cries and iron tinklings sounds of slaughter or martyrdom? For a moment he is one with the insecure husbandman or farmer. Behind generations, the dream and still points in that dream remain. The light in the forest, the dust-bloom and flicker of holly are Hill's images for this — points of reference and stasis outside human activity. They are hints of that Platonic sublimity which Coleridge writes of in *Animae Poetae*. The moment of Offa's departure is both his end and his beginning (echoing the end of "Burnt Norton"). It seems to be a keenly sad yet lyrical ending — the last dream, Gran lighting the gas, the child's game and the remaining 'signs'. In the last analysis, history always eludes us even if glimmers, sounds and images remain to fascinate and baffle with the power, charisma and brutality which is the English past. To explain away the metamorphoses and fragments would be a mistaken concern but would also tell us relatively little about the success of the Hymns.

Alcuin, after the death of Offa's son, wrote:

> You know how much blood his father shed in order
> to establish the kingdom for his son and this has been the
> destruction not the establishment of the Kingdom.

Alcuin too had lost faith in 'the glory of Britain'. In his eightieth letter of *Fors Clavigera* Ruskin accused the fashionable ladies who wielded so much power yet did so little good: That their beauty and virtue is used as an excuse 'for all the iniquity of our days'.

One might conclude that Offa's genius should not have been indulged so bloodily. The argument of 'revelation' as expounded by Blackstone does not alter the condemnations of Alcuin and other contemporaries. Such equivocation is not really embodied in the text. The words plumb moral depths but do not furnish the reader with a frame of judgement. Coleridge wrote, 'For language is the armoury of the human mind; and at once contains the trophies of its past, and the weapons of its future conquests.' The buried mind, the fire-dragon's 'facetted skin' is here given an imperialistic impulse. It is because Hill is aware of the linguistic changes around us, of our inability to scrutinise with any exactitude the history we find ourselves involved in and of the mystery of human personality that he creates such a literary structure as Offa. It is a consideration of this range of involvement which helps us to realise some of the cultural impetus which lies behind Offa's history and myths, which are so elusive, so varied and cryptic and yet also so compelling.

"Lachrimae" are based on "Seven teares figured in Seven Passionate Pavanes" by John Dowland and the words of Quevedo, Lope de Vega and Robert Southwell. They seek the unity and authority of an authentic and historical ms but contain undercurrents which are quite modern and sceptical. Lines from the original work are quoted and amended and sometimes the beauty of the original devotional tone is caught and sustained.

Though *Mercian Hymns* contains the names of artifacts and details such as the motto on a coin or tapestry, modern phraseology often intrudes, or is indeed the basis of the hymn. "Lachrimae" are based more substantially on and are more greatly imbued with the sentiment and language of their sources.

The teares are organised around the Crucifixion — for Southwell and the others, the focal-point of martyrdom in a suffering universe:

> You are the castaway of drowned remorse
> You are the world's atonement on the hill.

"Lachrimae Verae" with its picture of Christ's body twisted by 'human skill' into its 'proper' posture shows the appeal of sensuousness and man's readiness to compose pain. The voice is one of stock devotional response — that of unworthiness, of total separation. It is a sinner's confessio. The first stanzas with their marine metaphors remind us of St. Sebastian in "Of Commerce and Society" 'naked as if for swimming'. Both martyrs are pioneers of an unknown element. Additionally, once dead, their legend becomes fluid and infiltrates subtly into the minds of men.

Milne writes:

> In "Lachrimae" the brutality and sardonic humour of
> his earlier poetry is transfigured in seven rhymed sonnets
> which create a close 'unity of all human values in Christ',
> through the correlation of the martyr's life with that of
> the poet. . .through the co-existence of belief and scepticism
> . . .and through the connected rhythms of eternity and time. .

Milne continues in Notes:

> Both the Elizabethan martyr, Southwell, and the modern
> poet, Hill, enact their own 'deaths' or 'decreations' for
> something beyond selfhood . . .

An analogy can be laboured, and I think it tenuous to assume that Hill's search for a 'chaste' diction takes him to such an extreme and unchaste application of the Eliotic dictum of sacrifice: a linking of the obliquity of what Milne calls, his 'real' self in the poems with Southwell or the other martyrs' deaths. The analogy is no doubt borne in mind but Hill's poetic stance gives rise to a persona or personae who are both attracted and repulsed by such formulation. The 'real mask' for the 'conscious mind's intelligible structure' is formed in a layering or complex of versions of devotion here. Each sonnet is spoken by voices which fuse at some times and separate at others, some of which speak for all kinds of sacrifice, some of which speak for none at all.

In "Pavana Dolorosa", the quest for martyrdom becomes an art in itself, aside from heavenly considerations. Martyrdom is the truest art compared with the other creative equivalents:

> Self-wounding martyrdom, what joys you have,
> true-torn among this fictive consonance.

The preparation for death becomes the ultimate consonance, a musical microcosm of the Pavana as a whole. The extremity of music suggests that which is beyond sound:

> music's creation of the moveless dance,
> the decreation to which all must move.

and,

> Your silence is an ecstasy of sound.

This also implies that in this world the martyr cannot escape aesthetic considerations. Art, like God, once created, attends us constantly, even if it is denied, ('your nocturnals blaze upon the day'). Wainwright remarks on this use of paradoxes and how the symmetry of martyrdom may be deceptive: 'I stay amid the things which will not stay.'

In "Funeral Music" the opposites of the fatalistic meditation:

> . . .if it is without
> Consequence when we vaunt or suffer, or
> if it is not. . .

are not allowed to dominate the poem as a whole. Paradox is no real escape for the mind. "Martyrium" explores the boundary where material suffering stops and art takes over:

> . . .brooches of crimson tears where no eyes
> > weep.

To the martyr the purity and sufficiency of art are delusions in a suffering world. The stark juxtapositions of the Jesus-faced man crowned with flies, swatting grass and the streaked gibbet, the real and ideal Christs, recall Offa, Cernunnos, and the coins bearing the king's image. The day is peaceful and the heat from the earth possibly symbolises the earth's desire for transcendence. The wheat calls to mind Christ, Bread of Life, and the hissing shadows, the sacrifice which enables each harvest to rise. The gibbet is the focus of attention as in *The Dream of the Rood* — the tool of sacrifice gains reverence. Money, the viaticum of the Roman soldiers, their 'throwing lots' and Judas's silver, transform desire into an airy presence.

"Lachrimae Coactae" (felt or forced tear) is narrated by a perceptive persona who finds a neat dandyism in the composed stance of Christ:

71

> . . .your trim-plugged body, wreath
> of rakish thorn.

The disciple's progress is again between paradoxes: 'harsh grace and hurtful scorn', crucified who 'crucifies' and 'what grips me then, or what does my soul grasp?' He finally makes the mystic's presumption:

> You are beyond me, innermost true light

Obliquity, holiness and intimacy are married in this line. Christ's hidden 'quiet' underlying matter indicates that all 'bright shows' are void. Christ's silence is only a semblance in any case.

Wainwright sees "The Masque of Blackness" as a parody of the study of the flux and attractions of the material world. Here Christ's rival is Amor, 'Self-love, the slavish master of this trade.' The speaker pays 'lip-service' to the scriptures but one wonders what layers of meaning lie under the assumption that the greed of all men springs from the Fall? Instead of seeking the god-given answer, men here seek to create their own false Eden. The effort is fruitless — a Midas-Feast which turns sour. But the poet savours the rich imagery and lingers over the sumptuous personifications, even the final 'starry' work that vanishes in chaos. The tone of condemnation and exhortation is quite lost. This may be a 'parody of the exaggerated deliberation of the theorist organising experience'. It may also be a parody of a poet ensnared by his own images which are themselves products of the 'conquistador of fashion and remark'. 'This trade' could be in fashion; it is also poetry which creates its own heavens quite independent of doctrinal models.

"Lachrimae Antiquae Novae" (Old Tears New) shows how the true sorrow 'lives' on beneath the ikons. Indeed 'lacrimo' also means to distill. Men who have not cultivated a worldless sensibility, whose observances are 'wild and objectless', cannot grasp the distilled, true Christ. The whole ecclesiastical carnival — penances, retrospection, bogus saints and golden paraphernalia — pose one immense 'judas-kiss' to the true spirit of Christ. In the lines of the fourth stanza:

> fulfilling triumphs of the festal year.
> We find you wounded by the token spear.

are recalled the 'thirty feasts of unction and slaughter' in "Funeral Music". Christianity becomes either license to dominate or sanction to submit to that dominance. Christ is 'imprisoned' in the gestures and rhetoric of his earthly representatives: his only representatives. One feels that the poet recognises his own poem as being as much a stab in Christ's side as the hypocrisies which he exposes.

Wainwright sees "Lachrimae Amantis" as the fine culmination of the theme of artifice in expression. It is the plea of a 'half-faithful' one sick of his own unworthiness, laziness and repetitive hypocrisy in the face of Christ's sufferings. The whole picture, angel, house, stranger at the door and the return of the unwelcome master is culled from devotional literature and the Bible. It is pathetic and intensely lyrical at the same time. In the 'ws' sound and repeated 'v', 'th' and 'f' sounds we almost feel the tempting slumber: 'that I have drowsed half-faithful for a time'.

However, the angel is not without a sinister touch, for it embodies the internalised and ineluctable nagging of the conscience endorsed by religion. The writer relishes the conventional yet efficacious repentance of the sonnet. The tender image of Christ is as seductive as the identification between the reader and the persona. But such images and myths, though attractively poised, can be deadly beneath the voice of compassion. They not only order and label experience but seek to absolve men of their responsibilities for their actions. Both Quevedo and Lope de Vega wrote repentances after leading racy, sometimes heretical lives. (Quevedo had cartooned 'hellfire' scenes in his youth.) How seriously should one take this conventional repentance? Yet the sonnet is the finest of the eight. A gentle inner flaring is felt in the words:

> At this dark solstice filled with frost and fire,

and the sufferings of Christ are sensitively linked to the thaw and spring of the natural world:

> your passion's ancient wounds must bleed
>
> anew.

"Songs from Pentecost Castle" re-examine the bonds of the mystic's self with God and ought to be considered alongside "Lachrimae". They rely on old Spanish songs and the work of Jacopone da Todi as sources. Echoing these sources, Hill achieves the compactness and density he desires. Is this, as Sisson suggests, a mind in search of artifice 'to seek indirect utterances'. Possibly, but many of these 'utterances' and their attendant ironies are far from indirect. As poems they no longer comment internally upon history; they are living versions of history. Maybe at the loss of the width and fine, if at first difficult, clarity of *Mercian Hymns*, Hill has gained a new strength in the ambiguous power of these approaches. Certainly these quatrains are less expansive. The bulk of the words are monosyllables; each vowel is heavy with sacramental associations.

In the first three quatrains we find St.James and St.John — the recital of their names changes into a rosary and that in turn becomes 'child-beads of fingered bread'. In this Communion of suffering the child-victims of Hill's earlier poetry are poetically resurrected. The Bread is never broken and, in poetry and song, the 'love-runes' never uttered; there is only the

> scrolled effigy of a cry
>
> our passion its display.

The passion only represents a stereotype of pain: a social gesture. The second song is a simple questioning. To many the act of complete devotion has been a step into the dark. The persona fears total abnegation, the mystic merging with God and the death of man's selfish ego. The song finally restates the transitory and painful nature of life — the speaker addresses himself: 'why do you not break/O my heart'.

It is both a command and a query. The heart must be conquered before God can act, but the third song centres upon a marriage built around two paradoxes concerning desire and possession. A suitor presses that he will be faithful to his bride, but the beloved is also

> you of all women
> my soul's darling my love,

Is this a search for a Muse, that higher reality which was Plato's ideal, or the Holy Virgin? The tone, plain yet intense, seems to reveal these songs as meditations, devotions or spiritual exercises of the kind Loyola encouraged. The devotee is lost 'in the dream's grasp' but his desire is unworthy of 'its object'. The marriage was not for love so the speaker considers both lovers 'dispossessed' in his sleep. His very sadness is a possession like the humility of the mystic. Dream is a force that dispossesses, but a 'resurrection' out of sleep produces a new kind of ownership in the last stanza. The two last songs take up the theme of holy woundings. The close suffering relationship between Christ and the worshipper is summoned up in the fourth song. The apparent simplicity of the stanza:

> As he is wounded
> I am hurt
> he bleeds from pride
> I from my heart.

conceals a density of thought — Christ composed his own victimisation and therefore 'bleeds from pride', but He also bleeds for the sinner's ambition. The dying Christ gives life but one composed of acts of denial. The disciple needs Christ's life-giving example, but how much are these devotional gestures resented by the devotee? Finally, the wounded lover goes down to the well; the mystic will eventually see,

> nothing at all
> yet eye to eye

recalling the Biblical suggestion that we see 'through a glass darkly' but will one day see the divine reality 'face to face'. There is a hint of fulfilment, the resolution of paradoxes and achievement of mystical unity. The clarity of 'non-being' is juxtaposed against the unsanctified water which cannot assuage the wounds. The heavenly water gives back no reflection of the soul for it has already merge with God.

The foci of these songs shift at re-reading. For example, one realises that the fourth song passes from a wounding through death to life with a gentle, almost catechetical repeating of 'As he is. . .'. They also move from a comparison: 'As he is wounded/I am hurt. . .' through a paradox: 'as he is dying I shall live', to a strange reversal of sentiment, a 'sting in the tail' of the last stanza: 'sick of forgiving/such honesty.'

Yet the words are not as blasphemous as they seem if one re-interprets the subject of 'honesty'. The 'point' of the songs therefore shifts and changes, becomes unclear and then transparent like the reflection in the well. Hill is commenting on the rhetoric and mode of allegory, of the kind that might be exemplified by *The Song of Solomon*. This sparse setting allows him to portray the pitfalls and 'betrayals' of the Word in a very telling and basic way. Stripped of all the baroque 'furniture' of Furies and shoals of corpses, these disembodied voices show how language can pressurise and undercut itself in a medium which seems as simple as a nursery rhyme.

Hill's achievement in *Mercian Hymns* is not merely the reconsideration of natural speech but also the use of a historical structure arising from the 'matter' of Britain. Medals, coins, workers, myths and 'luminous' moments all build an idea of Britain as a psychic and geographical entity. Heaney writes of the book:

> It seems to me here that Hill is celebrating his own indomitable Englishry, casting his mind on other days, singing a clan beaten into the clay and ashes, and linking their patience, their sustaining energy, with the glory of England.

Here Heaney is referring to a specific Hymn, but the moods he discusses are evident in the book as a whole (even if Heaney has simplified their import). There is also a half-acknowledged intent to celebrate in the eight sonnets which we have, of "On the Death of Mr.Shakespeare.'

Hill can grasp the 'phantoms of sublimity' at large on English heaths and estates better than any other contemporary poet. There is the flavour of Victorian retrospection tingeing the Arthurian dream in "Idylls of the King":

> The pigeon purrs in the wood; the wood has gone;
> dark leaves that flick to silver in the gust,
> and the marsh-orchids and the heron's nest,
> goldgrimy shafts and pillars of the sun.

The fecund and pagan shadows as well as the sub-strata of a people's laws and won compromises are felt presences, growing out away and down from the Christmas scene:

> ....essence of the year;
> the apple-branches musty with green fur.
> In the viridian darkness of its yews
> it is an enclave of perpetual vows
> ("The Herefordshire Carol")

Some of Hill's finest images of the suspiciously sublime moment are to be found here. With a deft hand he has cleansed the Romantic forms and draperies of their cumbrous language. At times this achieves a 'heart-breaking' purity:

> so that the dove takes flight,
> bursts through the leaves with an untidy sound,
> plunges its wings into the green twilight.
> ("Idylls of the King")

The 's's of 'bursts' thresh with the soft but firm 'th's and 'v's of that long middle line to give a sense of struggle, hissing shrubbery and obstruction, before the bird drops free into light. Or, for example, the ideal and its image becoming one – the Platonic Form and its copy merging in: 'how the rose-window blossoms with the sun!'

Few poets could command and yet also temper such a stream of aureate sensations with its sustained tone of hushed but fervent voice. In the same poem ("The Herefordshire Carol") we find the cottage girls rising from their beds to repair old braids – again the active pains-taking craftsmanship of a people. And in one stanza of "The Laurel Axe", a masterful microscosm:

> Platonic England, house of Solitudes,
> rests in its laurels. . .

The debit is heavily felt – the axe-blade emerging from the stock of triumphant and fashionable laurel reminds of the Roman and fascist emblem. Platonic England is a land of tenantries and 'a religion of the heart' where servitude and carnality are caught in the gleam of the 'rood blazing upon the green'. Child-souls still register for Christ's dole and some still find consolation in the theological proofs of their own 'dam-nation'. Two sections from "A Short History of British India" lay bare the monstrous greed of an Imperialist nation:

> fantasies of true destiny that kills
> 'under the sanction of the English name.'

'Law-books' are seen to over-rule the emperors. In some ways the them-atic patterning of India as a still bride and England as 'red-coat devotees', light, and images of cannons, is similar to Heaney's deployment of images in dealing with Anglo-Irish relations.

There are some beautifully rich pictures of Indian life: the wayside shrines, flame trees, ruins and endless roads. Hard-won optimism be-comes a tenuous naivete in a passage where ambiguity has become a language of feeling, delicately portrayed and equivocal as a passing mood:

> Vulnerable to each other
> the twin forms
> of sleep and waking touch the man
> who wakes
> to sudden light, who thinks that this
> becalms
> even the phantoms of untold mistakes.

This heartfelt wellbeing is indeed wishful, as Wainwright says, 'muddled' as Europe's dreaming in "The Martyrdom of Saint Sebastian", in the face of English history and the 'mazes' of thought, inescapable and vicious. What end does this perennial dreaming serve and how can men continually ally their social ideologies and subjective impulses with in-creasingly rarefied and seductive visions of English landscape? These are the 'affective myths' of an imperialist nation, thrown out as shad-ows, almost as direct consequences of material arrogance. The truth of this kingdom, as doubtful as all such formulations are, 'shows disrepair'. England here rests in its 'injured stone' and is still 'at ease' with obsolete observances and 'languid praise'. In the third sonnet of "A Short History of British India" the mannerly wheeling of 'flawless hubris of heroic guilt' and 'conclave of abiding injuries' has become the throw away statement, 'India's a peacock-shrine next to a shop'. And England, the dormant progenitor of the kind of energy which can leave in its wake such emptiness, settles into its own dynastic idolatries — those Platonic ideals which informed the writings of Coleridge, Pugin and Disraeli. If there is, as Peck writes, a certain tenderness in this vision, it is the self-abrading consideration of those cherished dreams tempered by a Coleridgean sense of wonder:

> . . .the nigh thatch
> Smokes in the sun-thaw; whether the eave-drops fall
> Heard only in trances of the blast
> Or if the secret ministry of frost
> Shall hang them up in silent icicles,
> Quietly shining to the quiet moon.
> ("Frost at Midnight")

These are miniatures, the poet's small worlds behind glass, under a crystal dome, crimsoned over in the rose-window, 'in cabinets of amethyst and frost'. All is distant, recorded, 'good bedside reading', trapped 'in sepia waterglass' or photo albums and, ultimately, open to manipulation. 'And, after all, it is to them we return'. In "Damon's Lament for his Clorinda, Yorkshire 1654", Hill wryly makes the poet turn upon himself, as if this 'man of words' recognises the irony of this literary occasion for the first time:

> ....And who is this clown
> doffing his mask at the masked threshold
> to selfless raptures that are all his own?

The anonymity is instructive. Caught in his own games the surrogate author has still performed deftly, incisively, even beautifully.

> Poetry lessons, in fact were rather like catechism lessons:
> official inculcations of hallowed formulae that were some-
> how expected to stand us in good stead in the adult life
> which stretched out ahead.

Verse and narrative have always held a profound, often hallowed sway, in the Irish consciousness. Alwyn and Brinley Rees relate how passages from *The Tain* used to be recited as if they contained supernatural power and how certain stories were accorded influences of good and evil by the people and their leaders. But Heaney's poetry is not written in praise of 'the glory of the days of Conchubar, Cuchulain or the burning hair of Caoilte'. He has left behind the kind of mythology that Yeats and AE dealt with. His poetry started with the hard, often brutal land, and the people who work on it. Any mythology which one might perceive in his work is bound up with these realities.

Just as Heaney chose to ignore the Heroic idiom, so his sense of language differs from the 'high' sentiments of the Celtic Twilight writers. He has, he tells us, always been fascinated by the forbidden: words like 'piss' and 'hell to your soul', and the repugnant, like the 'farting' frog mouths in "Death of a Naturalist". He has come to link this engagement with the covert and taboo aspects of life with a pagan sensibility.

As for his art and its development, he admits that he admired 'the sensuous brunt of the words and metre, the sturdy collision between nature and art, the poetry's direct appeal to the nervous system', found in Anglo-Saxon and Middle English. Ignoring for the time being the import of the nationality of Heaney's models, one notices the poet's interest in the overlapping of verse, nature as a whole and the consciousness of the writer.

These elements: the 'religious', the forbidden, and physicality, are finely embodied in Heaney's verse, and especially in that aspect of his writing which Edna Longley calls ' a search for new gods'. We shall deal later with the particular myth the poet gives voice to, but firstly we must see how Heaney's style and views are indebted to the most ancient Irish poets.

The oldest and perhaps most revered and accursed deity in Ireland is the land. In *The Hidden Ireland* Corkery writes of the different personifications and hymnings of the land, especially in Gaelic verse. Heaney has also made use of the 'Aisling' convention, but most of his poems start from a more elemental level. He writes of Patrick Kavanagh's poem "The Great Hunger":

> . . .its elements are water and earth rather than fire and
> air, its theme is consciousness moulded in and to the dark
> rather than opening to the light.

For Heaney the dark is possessed of a living and potent energy. One
might say that the pictorial symbol for his early verse could be a door
opening into darkness. This 'dark' symbolises both external mysteries
and psychological depths. Corkery tells of how poets would sit alone in
the dark with stones on their faces to versify, and links this practice
with pagan ritual. Alwyn and Brinley Rees write:

> . . .such priestly functions as divination and prophecy
> also came within the province of these early Irish poets
> who, it may be added, wore cloaks of bird feathers as do
> the shamans of Siberia, when , through ritual and trance
> they conduct their audiences on journeys to another world,

Whether consciously or otherwise, as Brown has returned to the method
and vision of the saga-makers, so Heaney has adopted a poetic stance
strikingly similar to the spirit of these old Irish poets. Like them he
views the dark, vegetable and animal life, and dreams, as inspirational.
His narrator walks abroad in search of a vision. His language reveals an
obsessive, at times frightening, earthiness echoing Synge's statement:
'Before verse can be human again it must learn to be brutal'.

Chadwick and Dillon write that the most important class in ancient
Irish society was that of the poet (fili) who,

> . . . seems to have inherited much of the prestige of the
> druid of pagan times. . .(he was) honoured and feared
> like the brahmin in India. He was no longer a priest in
> this Christian society, but he had means of divination
> akin to magic. Or at any rate, he had them in the pagan
> past, and the tradition of his magical power had survived.

The druid, or more accurately, the shaman figure, is very useful in an
examination of Heaney's poetry. As Piggott points out, save for the
doctrines of Immortality and human sacrifice recorded in Roman writings, we know very little of the actual practices of these pagans. However, due to the writings of Eliade and others, we know a good deal
about shamanic ritual and belief. Shamans are honoured members of
'primitive' societies – the guardians of ancestral secrets, healing powers,
ritual magic and legends, and they undergo sacred dramas, acting out
the fantasies and fears of their people. They were supposed to talk with
animals and 'shift' their shapes into trees, rivers, or any natural object,
living or dead. Their souls were often 'given' into the keeping of animals
and they firmly believed that every object had its corresponding spirit
or soul. The central persona (or personae) in Heaney's poems often
assume the guise of an animal or object: tree, eel, trout or earth. There
are poems concerned with the bridging of the gulf between the human
and non-human world. A little boy is caught in a net in "Limbo", a

79

mermaid mixes with humans in "Maighdean Mara", and a child is brought up by hens in "Bye Child". These are not just strange events, examinations of semi-mythic stories or biological hybrids. They are also 'myths' of particular facets, often hidden, of the human consciousness and Unconscious. Heaney's metaphors also connect man to the land and woman to the sea; gods are embodies in worldly events such as famines. He dwells on pagan ritual, ("The Last Mummer"), old oracular customs and the influences of celestial bodies. He has said that Fear is his Muse and this fear stems from modern Ireland as much as from Pre-Christian superstition, as much from oneiric and sexual tensions as from external threat. Heaney's imagination is essentially empathic and conducts a 'raid on the inarticulate' when confronted by nature; his narrator's mind is allowed to push through roots and earth, to flow with sea and watercourse, to ferment in dark wells among that which gathers lichen and that which is preserved. His concern with the dead, 'deranged' or rejected subjects of the poems also links him with his shamanistic narrator.

Are we, however, justified in using this figure as a critical model? In "Tollund Man" and extracts of the Sweeney poems the narrator assumes the shape of an estranged priest, a man of the woods. In "Funeral Rites" he advocates a public ceremony involving a descent into the tombs of Boyne. Sitting Bull, a real shaman of his time, is mentioned as one of the dispossessed in "Hercules and Antaeus". Heaney sees the feminine tendency, the Marian devotions of Catholicism, as an immensely assuaging influence, but there are a number of indications in his work that this devotion will have to re-assimilate the native power that it only partly embodies or it will wither. My chapters on Heaney show a writer whose various narrators develop and blur from the workman or artisan with fatherly feelings for the land, and condense into the fílid, the wood-kerne with powers: the shaman.

Heaney's historical imagination which concentrates on the different overlays which created his environment is inseperable from his verbal and auditory senses. Words, their impacted literary and spoken histories, the physical fact of their interaction with palate and tongue, the very flow of the speaker's breath, build up the historical perspectives of each poem. In "Now and In England" he writes of T.S.Eliot's term, 'the auditory imagination',

> I presume Eliot was thinking here about the cultural
> depth charges latent in certain words and rhythms, that
> binding secret between words in poetry that delights
> not just the ear but the whole backward and abysm of
> mind and body; thinking of the energies beating in and
> between words that the poet brings into half deliberate
> play; thinking of the relationship between the word as
> pure vocable, as articulate noise, and the word as ety-
> mological occurence, as symptom of human history,

memory and attachments.

Heaney's 'presumption' here is best seen as his practice. In this respect he exercises a deliberation and energy which again summons up the shadow of magic and the shaman. In "The Seven Poets" Mackay Brown writes of the craft and belief of the Siberian poet:

> There was some kind of kinship it seemed between
> the speech of a people and their natural surround-
> ings. Birds, winds, waterfalls, the coil of a river, the
> shape of a hill, even the hush of falling snow, moulded
> speech. . . .Human speech can not be left to itself — it
> will wither — its roots are deep in the elements, our
> tongues take nourishment from the splash of the
> salmon in the river . . .

One need only turn to "Anahorish" to see the similarities:

> *Anahorish*, soft gradient
> of consonant, vowel-meadow. . .

or "Gifts of Rain":

> The tawny gutteral water
> spells itself: Moyola
> is its own score and consort,
> bedding the locale
>
> in the utterance,
> reed music, an old chanter. . .

He is finely aware of his own native tongue, 'our gutteral muse', in contrast to that of the contemporary English who find the 'gh' in Broagh 'difficult to manage'. This point is also borne out in his use of a quotation from Joyce:

> "How different are the words 'home'
> 'Christ', 'ale', 'master' on his
> lips and on mine." Stephen Dedalus.
>
> ("The Wool Trade")

He coins words like 'jobber' or 'mizzling' to evoke sounds in nature and also introduces words into new contexts: a river 'harping', a 'snout of flood', a prow 'sniffing the Liffey'. He uses archaic words and colioquialisms like 'glib', 'kesh', 'broagh', 'rath and bullaun', or, in this extract from "Belderg",

> So I talked of Mossbawn
> A bogland name. 'But *moss*?'
> He crossed my old home's music
> With older strains of Norse.
> I'd told how its foundation
>
> Was mutable as sound
> And how I could derive
> A forked root from that ground. . .

This tentative confession is a valuable statement, perhaps a step in the right direction towards modifying chauvinistic Irish literary opinion. The analysis of and sensitivity towards place-names is part of a larger issue: a keen attention to locale. His writing places a remarkable emphasis upon details of human custom, flora and fauna:

> like the coccyx
> or a Brigid's Cross
> yellowing in some outhouse. . .
> ("Traditions")

> a snipe's bleat is fleeing. . .

> *little goat of the air*
> *of the evening.*
> ("The Backward Look")

and the beautiful and delicate rendering of a mole in "Bone Dreams":

> I was told 'Blow,
> blow back the fur on his head.'
> Those little points
> Were the eyes.

It is not just this attention to natural minutiae which further reminds of the shaman or filid figure but also the ability to find gods in the strangest of places. Gods and goddesses in this poet's work seem freed from the abstract and purely symbolic positions which they have occupied so often. He does not make us ask, like Yeats' audience, 'Does Yeats actually see fairies?' Rather, he convinces the reader of psychic and spiritual forces latent in the landscape.

This poet's technique of identifying the first person singular with the land and nature generally led him eventually to recognisable deities, firstly to the Antaeus myth and then to Nerthus. In "Gifts of Rain" the swollen river recalls the shifting and flexing subject, Dives, 'hoarder of common ground' and reveals a need for 'antediluvian lore'. One remembers Lawrence's comments about an Atlantic people, an informed and skilled race, and indeed one often feels that Lawrence's and Heaney's myths hold a profound similarity. When Lawrence writes:

> Now it is time to invoke the Deity, who made man an
> adventurer into the everlasting unknown of consciousness.

one feels that this 'Deity' is the source of those forms which inhabit Heaney's poems. However, it took an Iron-Age myth located in a recognisable landscape to quicken Heaney's mythological imagination.

In 1965 P.V.Glob published his book *The Bog People*. It is a strange mixture of enthusiastic scholarship and awe. In introducing his subject Glob quotes Thoger Larsen who urges an identification with previous generations:

> Yet they were made of earth and fire as we,
> The selfsame forces set us in our mould:
> To life we woke from all that makes the past
> We grow on death's tree as ephemeral flowers.

Glob's book is pervaded by an awareness of, even a tendency towards, superstition:

> One of the helpers overstrained himself and collapsed
> with a heart attack. The bog claimed a life for a life; or,
> as some may prefer to think, the old gods took a modern
> man in place of the man from the past.

Both of these claims are highly presumptuous and not justified by any expansion. Larsen enjoys the reputation of a visionary poet and throughout the book Glob's objectivity seems to vary strikingly. Even after considering the brutal methods of sacrifice, Glob ends his book with an almost admiring look at the goddess that inspired the killings with a statement resembling belief:

> They were sacrificed and placed in the sacred bogs
> and consummated by their death the rites which en-
> sured for the peasant community luck and fertility
> in the coming year. At the same time, through their
> sacrificial deaths, they were themselves consecrated
> for all time to Nerthus, goddess of fertility — to
> Mother Earth, who in return so often gave their faces
> her blessing and preserved them through the millenia.

Glob has fallen 'between two posts' in his rhetoric. On one hand he has opted for a kind of semi-Romantic empathy with the Iron-Age people and, on the other, he is stating in very suspect terms his own vague feelings. Heaney deplores such a loose rhetoric and his "Bog Poems" are given over to a painstaking scrutiny of his own clusters of feeling towards the victims. However, Glob's admiring language and his sense of intimacy with the victims' former lives surely helped the Irishman to recognise the Bog people as 'befitting emblems of adversity'.

In defining these emblems Heaney also manages to clarify the outline of the previously blurred poetic narrator. In re-discovering the sacrificed dead the narrator develops a stronger and more convincing voice. In "Exposure" the persona considering the modern Irish poet's responsibilities refers to himself as 'An inner emigre' or a 'wood kerne', that is, a deserter or brigand. This sense of isolation, of a lonely existence in the woods, misunderstood by society, is part of the mystique surrounding the priestly narrator who has gradually emerged in *Wintering Out*. Recognition of the stratified dead, the culpability of religion and the ancient roles of poets also involves the narrator in 'weighing' responsibilities. "Exposure" shows a man trying to balance, however unsatisfactorily, the 'diamond absolutes'; it is a process the narrator is to return to again and again:

> As I sit weighing and weighing
> My responsible *tristia*
> > ("Exposure")
> . . .his nails
> hung in the scales

83

with beauty and atrocity
("The Grabaulle Man")
A loosening gravity,
Christ weighing by his hands.
("Westering")
This balancing action recalls the priestly and shamanistic functions of
settling tribal disputes and determining policy by recourse to divination.
Ritual observances and offerings were believed to balance natural and
supernatural forces in the environment. This 'weighing' and the burrow-
ing or leaping into nature are two of the most important stances adopted by the shaman figures in Heaney's poetry. The shamans of Siberia
believed in a process of stripping off their human bodies, bone after
bone, and then constructing themselves mentally. By this process they
thought they probed the very roots of nature and, after merging with
all forms on an elemental level, they re-lived their own creation, so
gaining magical power. The stripping off of human guise and merging
with earth, corpses, relics, and then the return to human emotion
happens too many times in Heaney's poems to make illustration necessary. Jung has written of similar activities as 'processes of individuation'
and John Haffenden, in talking about Roethke with Heaney, asks if 'a
Jungian idea of regression in order to reconstitute' one's 'own personality' could be related to the Irishman's work. Heaney's answer is non-
committal but, however one interprets these patterns in his work, by the
time of "The Tollund Man" and, again in "Kinship", the figure of the
shaman, priest and spokesman for the tribe has emerged. This stance
has profound implications in relation to Heaney's whole sense of myth
and history, as I will make clear in the next chapter.

The Irish influences on Heaney's poetry are too many and too
diverse to mention except in passing. However, there is profit in acknowledging the influence of Heaney's stay at Berkeley in California.
Heaney recalls that at the time 'nature mysticism stuff was hot on the
ground — everybody trying to be a Red Indian or whatever'. One must
not forget that Berkeley through the 1960s was a centre of unrest,
political activism and theories for an alternative society. Ten years after
the San Francisco 'Renaissance' of the Arts, Berkeley, Haight Ashbury
and the Bay became symbols of a 'new consciousness'. More importantly for Heaney's work, two parallel movements gained publicity.
Firstly there was the 'Back to the Land' and communard movement —
a new emphasis was placed on ecology, self sufficiency and conservation
of natural resources. Secondly, there was a situation of religious up-
heaval where charlatanry, Eastern cults, pagan traditions and mysticism
were active. At the same time in the Celtic countries a great surge of
interest in the native traditions and cultures arose. There has been a
barrage of books concerning megalithic monuments, ley lines, fairies,
the 'old' earth religions and the lost gods of Britain. When Pound and
Eliot wrote of the mystery religions and the Fisher King it is true that

their verse had a cultural context: that of the informed literati, the cult of Blavatsky and the readers of AE and Jessie Weston. However, Heaney's books have appeared in a social environment where Hesse, Tolkien and D.H.Lawrence have literally been read by millions. This interest in mythologies, the search for new gods and ecological concern has almost certainly marked Heaney's poetry. The very fact that he mentions Sitting Bull, the medicine-man and revivalist of Sioux religion, is significant; in "Hercules and Antaeus" the Irish dead have been aligned with the Red Indian, who, due to the new interest and translations of Indian texts in the 1960s, has become the last of the noble pagans, mindful of the natural balances which rule the Universe.

Heaney finds himself in a country at war with itself and with England:

>   The muzzle of a sten gun in my eye
>   "What's your name, driver?'
>   'Seamus. . .'
>   *'Seamus?'*
>   (The Ministry of Fear")

The myths that lie behind Republicanism and Unionism are at conflict and this sense of confrontation has allowed, in fact urged, Heaney to bring his own mythopeoia and perception of Irish history to the fore in his work. Not only is the narrator's own history recalled in metaphors of weaponry, but Heaney uses past examples of confrontations: the Croppy Rising, Smerwick and Vikings in Dublin, to convey his urgent myths. There is the need for a cosmic and feminine compassion to assuage old wounds and the necessity to face the forgotten dead, to let the victims of previous aggression germinate into creativity and peace instead of violence.

Heaney compels our attention to myth and history in his most consistent and powerful way by his use of words. The central metaphor for linguistics in his work is that of biological organisms. Words are never isolated or static; there are graftings, overlappings and analogies between different levels and kinds of language: geographical, historical and religious. One example is his use of the first person singular. He uses this not only in what we have called a 'shamanistic' way, where the subject becomes blended with a natural object, but he also lets the name of the subject drift across the poem suggesting new possibilities and resonances. For example, in "Servant Boy" we start with a person 'wintering out', both a statement of agricultural terms and the deployment of an emblem for an emotional state. The successive naming, 'Old workwhore, slave-/blood' re-defines the servant and the 'body' of the poem becomes a medium for metamorphosis. The gentle words of 'a jobber among shadows' become almost an analogue to the main poem, modifying its immediate focus to widen into a glimpse of figures working in semi-darkness. The trail of the servant-boy becomes itself personified and begins 'first footing'. Not only does this hint at a being moulded from motion and fodder but, also, it seems to be a trail which precedes

its maker, a track which goes on before. Are the 'little barons' landlords,
bidders or the cockerels? This term blurs distinctions which are already
shifting in the poem: the order of cause and effect is reversed. Confusing, illogical aspects of existence: dreams, psychic and other phenomena,
the syncretic power of words and the complex nature of human perceptions and impressions are fused in this poetic development. The central
being of the poem is both human and non-human, vegetative sustenance
and a representative of a spirit of Irish resistance — a force which embodies various historical and mythological tensions. These forces inter-
act with the processes of nature. For example, Anahorish is described
first in terms of a single attribute, a linguistic kenning: 'place of clear
water', then in terms of human retrospection, a faculty it helped to
form and influence: 'first hill in the world', with its Muiresque and
Christian undertones. Then various physical descriptions are given, followed by a metaphor between sonic and geographical lilting: 'soft grad-
ient', swiftly rounded into another metaphor of language as physical
feature: 'vowel-meadow'. The persona draws out a sharp visual image
formed within a consciously poetic stillness, almost a poem within a
poem:

> after-image of lamps
> swung through the yards
> on winter evenings.

Each metaphor verges on the next, each never allowing a fixed picture
to develop but building up shifting layers of impressions.

One does not want to falsify Heaney's mythos: the spirits and goddesses of his work are linked with a particular locale but he never plays
down the distance between man and nature. The separateness of man is
as much part of his heritage as his animality, his mammalian presence.
In "First Calf" the cow stands feeding her offspring after the act of
birth: 'Her wide eyes read nothing'. The human can only grasp after the
'semaphors of hurt'. He admits elsewhere that his persona is an 'inner
emigre' and that his own feelings about the bogs and Nerthus, all his
florid diction and taut phraseology cannot atone for the horror of the
Irish violence. He, like Yeats, knows that 'nothing will suffice'. The
admission is a starting-point for his continually renewed questioning.

A large part of Heaney's work deals with the Irish conflict directly;
for example, Part II of *North*. His use of myth and nature is not an
escape from 'clucking' gas and terrorism, but a way of addressing them:

> I could risk blasphemy,
> Consecrate the cauldron bog
> Our holy ground and pray
> Him to make germinate
>
> The scattered, ambushed
> Flesh of labourers,
> Stockinged corpses. . .
>
> ("The Tollund Man")

The medium of the poem, the narrator's stances and the projection of nature as a changing, independent, yet also interdependent plane of being, all enable the writer to bring his mythos to bear on the present bloody situation.

Heaney's use of form too is very varied. Within an apparently formal framework the poem seems to be allowed a life of its own, changing and restating its subjects like a living organism. For instance, the poem "Kinship" comprises six sections of verse with each section containing six quatrains. The symmetrical outline is partly deceptive for the syllabic content of the lines varies from two to nine syllables: (usually the lines operate round a 5—6 syllable unit which could be said to constitute the essential 'organs' of the poem set inside an outer 'membrane'). This central unit of the poem through which the material is conveyed as it changes, almost becomes an entity translating words as a body translates gases and foods through its system. In a schools broadcast Heaney said:

a poem is alive in an animal, mineral and vegetable way.
It comes out of a creature, out of a man's mind and
feelings, and it lives and is clothed in the substance of words.

In an interview for *London Magazine* he said that in 'pure poetry' the poem houses 'power of some kind'. This naturalistic metaphor embodied in form, narrative flow and the changing outline of the subject or subjects is the very quick of this poet's portrayal of myth and history. Words have their origin in ancient belief, namings, events, and a poem is a force, parallel to the forces of dreams or the supernatural which come to inhabit these terms. Each poem represents a living complex of historical and mythic associations and, as it is read, the melody and imagery bring these presences into light for the reader.

Whether or not the poems hold an internal cohesion and unity as well as this shifting sense of life will have to be considered elsewhere. It is arguable that Heaney's use of strong metrical patterns and sturdy overall and stanzaic structure are enough to hold the poems together. Certainly, some of his wordplay is so adventurous and colourful that they need 'bedding' in a strong rhythm and framework.

For Heaney both landscape and poetry resonate history and life. The energies which occupy both literary and experiential areas of life have a dark source which must be tapped to offset the sterility and bloodshed of the present. Often the sacrifices of the past have been forgotten. Much that is valuable is neglected or repressed — the latent resources of a people and the 'energies beating between words' and these must be marshalled in order to blanace the mind's, as well as the world's, ecology — to alter the structures of feeling. In relation to such beliefs Heaney has developed a vital and invigorating use of poetic form and words. He has also developed a changing but recognisable literary counterpart: the filid or shaman. It is out of this figure's quarrel with himself and that other 'man of words', Seamus Heaney, modern poet, that the significant and exciting poems emerge.

DEATH OF A NATURALIST / DOOR INTO THE DARK

Walking to school in Anahorish in southern Derry Seamus Heaney once met a herdsman or road worker who remarked to the boy, 'Aye, the pen's easily handled. It's a lot lighter than the spade.' The comparison remained with Heaney and surfaced with the poem "Digging" in *Death of a Naturalist*. The rhythms of the poem are those of a nursery rhyme but an image in the second line jars the reader's consciousness:

> Between my finger and my thumb
> The squat pen rests; snug as a gun.

We expect a shot, a literal and literary killing. Instead we descend with the narrator's father and suddenly we witness another dislocation, this time of linear chronology. The digger's back 'comes up twenty years away'. The jerking, tense rhythm of the poem and the shifts in imagery and thought mirror the actions of the digger. It is a significant figure to begin a book with: potato and peat diggers have become cliches of Irish life. The speaker, his father and grandfather are inextricably linked with generations of Irish labourers. The impetus of Heaney's poetic thrust is downwards into the soil and into the past. His poems are 'raids on the inarticulate', or passage-ways into the ruminant dark often symbolised by animal life or feminine sensitivity.

Beneath the wonder of "Digging" and the diction imitating work patterns there is the menace of the gun and the sniper. We are conscious that the smells of digging, the 'curt cuts' and the 'squelch and slap' are facts from both outer and inner landscapes. The poet, isolated as he is from these work patterns, finds his imagination rooted in the same soil. Heaney's protagonist is to dig with the pen beneath the surface of language, through concepts of Nature and history, and is to probe the deepest recesses of personality.

The poet has written:

> "Digging", in fact was the name of the first poem I
> wrote where I thought my feelings had got into words,
> or to put it more accurately, where I thought my feel
> had got into the words. . .I felt that I had let down a
> shaft into real life. I didn't care who thought what
> about it; somehow it had surprised me by coming out
> with a stance and an idea that I would stand over.

To Heaney the poem is a thing — a being of feeling and textures, sounds and sharply defined images. The movement of the narrative is from finger, thumb and pen and back to them in a circle. However, much as one might like to trace a kind of Freudian regression here — a journey through images which mirrors the wholeness of the child's first association of spade and pen, one must not forget that the atrocity of recent Irish history bears down upon these lines. Heaney obviously feels reservations about a commitment to this kind of stance. The digger is caught in a genealogy of manual labour — 'Just like his old man'. In spite of this Heaney will 'dig' with his pen and his alter ego will imaginatively 'follow into the mud'.

Many of the poems in *Death of a Naturalist* centre on patterns of initiation: initiation into the act of creation, which is always a telluric force into the poet's work, and also initiation into a life, lived in relation to a power which rises and spreads through Nature. The townland in "Death of a Naturalist" has a heart of festering flax:

> Daily it sweltered in the punishing sun.
> Bubbles gurgled delicately, bluebottles
> Wove a strong gauze of sound around the smell.

The subject of the 'centre' in Irish myth and history is too detailed to describe extensively here, but since it underlies so much of Heaney's work a few facts are relevant. In the Rees' book *Celtic Heritage* there is a discussion of the way in which the centre at Tara represented the Masculine, aggressive principle, and that at Uisnech represented the Female or passive principle. Tara was, for the four provincial Kings, a geographical and cosmic centre. Yet it was at Uisnech that Mide, chief druid to the people of Nemed, lit the 'first fire'. Both centres held great political and religious importance. The seething 'heart' of Heaney's townland seems the very matrix of life, the spawn-beds from which creatures emerged in the heat of prediluvian existence:

> There were dragon-flies, spotted butterflies,
> But best of all was the warm thick slobber
> of frogspawn. . .

The roll of the 'o's here, the lazy music of the soft 'b's in 'slobber' and the long 'awn' of 'spawn' leaves us with a fine impression of the ripe sacs and liquid, warm and coagulating. There are obvious sexual overtones. The child attracted by this spawn has a neat little sermon in the mating of frogs delivered to him by Miss Walls. 'Miss' sounds prim in this context; a woman devoid of carnal experience. Maybe the same 'Walls' refers to mental barriers or the to neat categorising of Nature, for the lesson is a fine example of storybook anthropomorphisation. It reveals a limited and blinkered sensibility; she has not only ignored the elemtnts of fright, awe and disgust in these living beings, but has also ignored the urgency of the sexual instinct. If this dam is a centre, it is one of male sexuality. The chorus of the frogs is 'bass' — they sit suggestively cocked on sods with 'loose' phallic necks, and their 'blunt heads' fart. These are the 'slime Kings' and their vengeance is a reptilian attack not simply on the encircling townland and human encroachment but also upon those neat consciousnesses which seek to reduce our responses to Nature. The Kings of the slime, or semen, are linked with the forbidden and hidden; farting, gross-bellied, sexually precocious, grenades, cocked (penes or guns), they pose an 'obscene threat'. They are parts of a human scope which civilisation has sought to cover up, part of a wildness that industrialism has damaged. The spawn is tacky and in a rush of childish, 'heart-thudding' words:

> I knew
> That if I dipped my hand the spawn would clutch it.

we experience the narrator's fear of his own sexuality and that of nature as a whole. It is seen as a purely human arrogance which imbues the frogs' natural functions with obscenity; they brood in the poem like long-ignored inhabitants of the dark side of the human psyche. Heaney excels at linking the different spheres we allocate to sexuality, vulgarity, dreams, the unconscious and madness.

The flax is decomposing around the frogspawn, providing a perfect 'womb' for the young amphibians, so the dam becomes a symbol of continuity and of life in death. The dam also throbs with inarticulate noise recalling the cacophony before speech began. It is a mandala of seething life and death: the pool out of which all spots, dots, freckles, colours and smells, the vast variety of animal and vegetable life arose and into which it may fall. Does the weather influence the frogskin or vice versa? It is impossible to say, for they are both set in a vast, mysterious organism. The dam is a microcosm of the universe with its cycles of creation and decreation. 'Dam' also means mother, usually of an animal, but has been used in popular folklore to refer to the devil's mother. The alternative meaning helps to fuse the menacing and fecund aspects of the poem. The dam brings to mind the Earth Mother, particularly the female mouth or vagina, symbolising both her voraciousness and bounty.

One wonders if this image of the centre is, at least in part, a reaction to the Eliotic image of light and radiance representing spirituality in "Burnt Norton",

> And the pool was filled with water out of sunlight,
> And the lotos rose, quietly, quietly,
> The surface glittered out of heart of light.

It is a passage filled with the light of cerebral and religious purity where the Hellenic and Dravidian ideal of radiance is blended with the lotos of perfection. The lotos is found as a symbol of truth in the Greek, Indian and Egyptian traditions. Heaney brings the myth back to earth and the senses. He has also brought together highly-coloured, fecund and muddy imagery reminiscent of Shakespeare's association of Cleopatra with the flood-plains, insects and snakes of the Nile. It is as if a pit containing the taboos and neuroses of Western culture were to open exposing the 'scales and slime' of forbidden thought, heresies and fantasies. But to Heaney this is not just an image of physicality but also of spirituality. The Celts believed in the world of Annwn buried under the ground where a faery folk lived in their palaces and fields. Hence, the Celts revered darkness, especially chthonic darkness, and the earth as much as the light. Heaney, like Patrick Kavanagh's ploughman, finds a 'star-love-ly art/In a dark sod'. Additionally, here Heaney has placed the frog, the Medieval image of ugliness and disease, at the threshold of the depths.

There was something in the Celt and in Neolithic man which drew him to construct dark buildings full of ritual objects — oratories, tombs and longhalls. The dark in these places was and is an experience: 'The dark gulfed like a roof-space'. The interior in "The Barn" is an area of realisation for the child. It enters his dreams like a dark hoard for his own submerged desires. It is literally a 'hell' which, in its original Germanic form, meant a dark hiding place. This dark is animate — bright eyes stare 'From piles of grain in corners, fierce, unblinking'. The sacks of corn become active. They are a people's hoarded wealth, perhaps little domestic deities or the incongruous faceless fears of a child's nightmare. The corn like 'grit of ivory' reminds one of the relentless 'grinding down' of animal life for money. Cement is an image of urban sprawl and the harness and plough socks implicitly image the end of the age of the horse and agrarian labourer. 'Bright objects' form, the darkness gulfs and 'great blind rats' move in upon the dreamer. It is a surreal picture containing references to nursery rhymes such as 'blind rats' and 'sackfuls' coming after little boys (though these are oddly distorted from their settings in "Baa Baa Black Sheep" and "Three Blind Mice".) Two shafts of golden motes remind one of a temple such as New Grange, and the farm implements recall the peasant risings. But the poem echoes on a subliminal level beneath the layers of association.

The theme of initiation also makes itself felt in "An Advancement of Learning". The river 'nosed' past, 'pliable, oil-skinned', like some strange marine creature. Before the rat is named we are aware of an un-wholesome, blood-chilling presence existing on the periphery of our intuition. The break in the line:

My throat sickened so quickly that

I turned down the path in cold sweat.

and the ejaculation, 'But God', enact the emotions and physical react-ions of the persona. 'My throat sickened so quickly', using the s, th, i and c sounds almost recalls the act of retching. The 'nimbling', 'sliming' and clockworking rat is well-pictured in the choice of words.

Ears plastered down on his knobbed skull,

Insidiously listening,

works so well as a swift portrait, the sibilants and 'i' sounds reinforcing the blunt tactile impression of the words 'knobbed skull'. We think of the other terrifying rat from Eliot's "The Fire Sermon". Eliot's rat takes the place of 'Time's winged chariot' in Marvell's poem. Heaney's rats also represent the challenge of time and of how a human must, at some stage, assume responsibility for his physical and mental projection. But Heaney is not one to name if the physical impressions of a creature can stand alone: 'This terror, cold, wet-furred, small-clawed'. The term 'rat' would be so much a diminuation of this encounter. The poem is

about self-realisation and power in a world which is a network of predatory and competing powers. Personal control over animals by staring or
other methods is a prized skill in tribal society and is often part of initiation into the mysteries of adulthood. In *The White Goddess* Graves
writes about Shakespeare mentioning the power of Irish poets to rhyme
'rats to death',

> having somewhere heard of the seventh century Seanchan
> Torpest, the master-ollave of Ireland, who, one day finding
> that rats had eaten his dinner, uttered the vindictive aer:
> 'Rats have sharp snouts
> Yet are poor fighters.'
> which killed ten of them on the spot.

The victory of the persona is followed by his crossing of the bridge
— achieving a new passage to adult sensibility. Heaney, like Robert
Frost, can use ordinary activities to suggest psychic or mythic achieve-
ments. The title of Heaney's poem echoes Bacon's *The Advancement of
Learning* (1605). Bacon theorised that education should be based upon
experiment rather than abstract thought, an emphasis which had been
displaced by Plato and Aristotle ignoring the 'wisdom' of primitive man.

The encounter with the rat is such a concrete experience — it places
the persona on a level with tribal man where fear of the wild must be
overcome. In writing of this experience in the way he does Heaney is
creating a fable or parable similar in some ways to those of the ancient
Greeks. The child-figure moves from the vulnerability of "The Barn" to
a new response to the initiatory experience.

In "Blackberry Picking" we find that Nature can confound assertive
and proprietorial gestures. The knots and meshings of the natural network are essential to its survival. Again, we are given a sense of the
quickly-multiplying, branching and spreading of organisms:

> At first, just one, a glossy purple clot
> Among others, red, green, hard as a knot....
> Then red ones inked up.

Vegetation and fruit are used as emblems of sexuality underlying all
parts of nature. The 'flesh' of the first berry is sweet, 'summer's blood
was in it'. There is a suggestive line spacing in the pause between, 'Leaving stains upon the tongue and lust for' and the word 'Picking'. The act
of plucking fruit has long been associated with sexual intercourse; we
need only bear in mind what de-flowering means in folk songs. The
picker's fervour, the blood stains and the lust — the references to wine,
pricks, and hayfields — re-awaken ideas of pagan fertility rites: Dion-
ysian or Irish rituals held at the height of Summer.

The dating 'Late August' at the start of the poem leads us to Robert
Graves's writing of the 'vintage season' in *The White Goddess.*

The wine in the poem is 'thickened'. Unlike the holly berry and
prickles associated with Christ and his blood, this juice is black and
purple. There is a feeling of over-ripeness and perversity. Instead of

92

Christ the Lover redeeming his Beloved we find that the genius of these plants is Bluebeard, sadist and murderer. This suggestion of sexual guilt: 'our palms sticky as Bluebeard's' linked with fertility ritual is continued in the Bog Poems. The goddess in "Come to the Bower" comes 'touched by sweetbriar' and in "Bog Queen" we find 'bruised berries' under vengeful victims' nails. The picking carries its penalties: 'Our hands were peppered/With thorn pricks'. The transitory nature of the fruit mirrors the child's realisation that human joys have a tendency to cloy and that the human body is subject to final decay. Even the byre, centre of farmyard existence and symbol of Nativity, and then the bath, like the dam or reservoir, cannot preserve the berries. The metaphor of rodent colouring is deliberate here:

> We found a fur,
> A rat — grey fungus, glutting our own cache.

The berries seem to be transforming into an animal nemesis like the rats or frogs taking revenge for the 'rape' of natural resources. The child's voice is desperate: 'I always felt like crying', but "Churning Day", the next poem, comes as a reassuring parable of human interaction with nature. It enacts a kind of natural alchemy in a domestic setting. The 'stink' of churning milk is 'wholesome' and the sexual overtones become 'lawful' connected to procreation; the communion of sperm, egg and the weaning milk within the family structure. It is as though the child-narrator has passed out of the nightmarish images of "The Barn" and "Blackberry-Picking" into a motionless and unconscious existence, surrounded by images of affirmation, motherhood and sustenance.

However, the initiatory rites of the early tribes were also concerned with confronting the imminence of death. "The Early Purges" and "Dawn Shoot" centre upon the ambiguous feelings of humans, especially children, exposed to and implicated in killings. In "Dawn Shoot" the persona's mind is full of martial metaphors: Bull's-eye, hoarse sentry, rocketed, reconnaissance, parachutists, reveille and all-clear. There seems to be a Beckett-like anonymity to this setting and at times the scape seems to be an interior, the sky an unfinished ceiling: 'Clouds ran their wet mortar, plastered the daybreak'. Of course 'mortar' and 'plaster' hold their military meanings too. Heaney's 'poetic eye' is sensitive to movements of creatures around the hunters. It is a moving, cudding, watching, catapulting and whinneying world. The hunters' minds anticipate the snipe's movements:

> Loping under ferns in dry drains, flashing
> Brown orbits across ploughlands and grazing.

Empathy, imagined or real, between hunters and hunted is, of course, as old as the Palaeolithic era. Australian aborigines and bushmen of the Kalahari use songs, spells and costume to try to enter a mystical communion with their victims. Heaney has written already of his squat pen 'snug as a gun' and some, including Ted Hughes, have written of poetry as a hunt for animals, and Heaney himself has said 'A poem is alive. . . .'.

Thus a simultaneous 'hunt' is on; not just for the animal subject of a poem as in Hughes' case, but also for the living creature which is the poem itself. If the poem is successful both will have crystallised in the words.

The gods of Celtic mythology loved a good hunt. There is the Great Hunt of Irish myth, the hunt in "Culhwch and Olwen" and Arawn, King of Annwn, riding with his hounds in *The Mabinogion*. There is another kind of hunt in the streets of Belfast and a desire to forget in the way that the boys of the poem 'miss' the 'sleepers'. The images are consistently phallic: rockets, bulls-eyes, roots and the cock. The paucity and greyness of the setting, the 'snipe' breaking from the corner and 'a playboy' trotting up to 'the hole' reveals the impoverishment of the boy's vision. Again, the brisk jokiness of the slang, echoing a folk song:

> 'Wild rover no more',
> Said Donnelly and emptied two barrels
> And got him. I finished him off.

supports the feeling of brusque guilt and casual phrases used to conceal this. To 'dander' in American slang means to show one's temper. It is a significant shift of meaning from the Irish slang which presumably means to dawdle or walk confidently away. The poem lays bare the dangers of initiation to this kind of life and rhetoric; like the kittens of "The Early Purges", these snipes could easily be human, especially in the final lines of the poem. It also condemns art as masturbation for there is a mental thrill in the trajectory of slugs and an abstract pleasure in the staunch efficiency of 'I finished him off'. However, the force is masculine and is opposed to Nature — hence the sterility of the language. The Female is frightened and distant.

> A mare whinnied and shivered her haunches
> Up on a hill.

The boys who have come and gone on the railway line, symbol of industrial commerce in the Irish landscape, have failed to 'connect' with the land. Consequently they must beware in case they become the simple unquestioning men of "The Betrothal of Cavehill" in *North*. It is a country where childhood snipings have too often ended in manslaughter.

"At a Potato Digging" draws a familiar scene, recurring,

> . . .mindlessly as autumn. Centuries
> Of fear and homage to the famine god
> Toughen the muscles behind their humbled knees,
> Make a seasonal altar of the sod.

'Seasonal altar' sounds like a phrase from *As You Like It* or one of Dafydd ap Gwilym's poems, but there is nothing gay or light-hearted about this 'religious' homage. Mother Earth here is 'the black mother', possibly one of the Macha; the faithless ground whose 'rough bark' is the humus. Vegetable and human growth merge. The knots of potatoes (a clean birth), are like a twined umbilicus and the piled potatoes are 'live skulls, blind-eyed'. These skulls 'balanced on wild higgledy skele-

tons' become the starving labourers of forty-five. J.C.Becket in his
Short History of Ireland remarks in his very plain style:
> The influence of the famine was so tremendous
> that it touched every department of life. Its most
> spectacular result was a rapid and permanent decline
> in the population, to six and a half million in 1851
> and five and a half million in 1871.

Famine is characterised with bird metaphors:
> Faces chilled to a plucked bird
> In a million wicker huts
> beaks of famine snipped at guts.

The poet is undertaking to address perhaps the worst event in the history of his nation. We remember Kavanagh's mechanised scarecrows in "The Great Hunger" (1942). In his essay on Kavanagh, Heaney writes that there is,
> an artesian quality about his best work because for the
> first time since Brian Merriman's poetry in Irish at the
> end of the eighteenth century and William Carleton's
> novels in the nineteenth, a hard buried life that subsisted
> beyond the feel of middle-class novelists and romantic
> nationalist poets, a life denuded of 'folk' and picturesque
> elements, found its expression.'

Further on he comments on "The Great Hunger",
> It is not about growing up and away but about growing
> down and in. Its symbol is the potato rather than the
> potato blossom. Its elements are water and earth rather
> than fire and air, its theme is consciousness moulded in
> and to the dark rather than opening to the light.

It is to the dark and earth that the pickers tend in "At a Potato Digging", 'Processional stooping through the turf'. But the 'black hutch of clay' with its hard 'tch' sound admirably echoing the texture of the clay turns into huts of famine. The 'skin' of this earth pitted with pus-filled holes makes this a bitter and angry poem that shows the earth, both the bitch and Hope of established religion, lying 'rotted like a marrow'. However one regards the soil we are all ruled by its influence. Even the most careless farmworkers spill 'libations of cold tead, scatter crusts'. 'Good smells' as well as the stench of putrefaction 'exude from crumbled earth' and Heaney relishes describing the white interiors and earthy taste of the potatoes. As ever, he 'weighs' the properties of earth — his own memories and the heritage of his people are compared. The rotting potatoes like the scum-covered blackberries remind us of the need to treat Nature with respect and of thwarted sexuality turning sour on a person like Maguire in "The Great Hunger". Pickers and skeletons are sexless and the digger is mechanical. Hearts are petrified — 'cream' and seed are found in the earth and split vegetables. It is possible that the bird imagery suggests a resolution of the sexual tensions.

The pickers are 'like crows' on 'crow-black fields'.

The crow or raven was associated with the Morrigan, goddess of destruction and, certainly, the role of the crows on the battlefield has
long associated them with disease and pestilence as in Anglo-Saxon
verse. The fourth section of the poem starts with 'a gay flotilla of gulls',
as the workers, as if convinced of the deadly repetition of their task,
start to eat. The long fast, like a celibacy, is broken and 'libations'
scatter as they 'take their fill'. 'Flotilla' borrows a metaphor from the
sea and water, a nourishing element for the hard land. Graves associates
gulls with the period March 19— April 15 since this is when 'Gulls congregate on the ploughed fields'. The white of the gulls is a welcome sight
after the bleak crow-black, reminding one of ecclesiastical censure on
sexual activity.

The reader has 'moved through' poems of initiation, warnings of
decay and a description of a hunt to the confrontation with hard human
history in "At a Potato Digging". "The Diviner" is the first poem in this
collection which hints at a mystic perspective on reality. Divining is a
very old form of magic, but it is feasible that it relies upon natural
powers we have not yet learnt to describe scientifically. In "The Diviner" a man taps this mysterious power:

> Spring water suddenly broadcasting
> Through a green aerial its secret stations.

In a lecture delivered to the Royal Society of Literature in 1974,
Heaney said this of poetic technique:

> Technique involves not only a poet's way with words,
> his management of metre, rhythm and verbal texture;
> it involves also a definition of his stance towards life, a
> definition of his own reality. Technique is what turns,
> in Yeats' phrase, 'the bundle of accident and incoherence
> that sits down to breakfast' into 'an idea, something
> intended, complete', and if I were asked for a figure who
> represents pure technique, I would say a water diviner.
> You can't learn the craft of dowsing or divining — it's a
> gift for being in touch with what is there, hidden and
> real, a gift for mediating between the latent resource and
> the community that wants it current or released. The
> diviner resembles the poet in his function of making
> contact with what lies hidden, and in his ability to make
> palpable what was sensed or raised.

Anthony Bailey, in his article on Heaney, mentions the poet's finding in Sir Philip Sidney's *Apologie for Poetry* the statement: 'Among
the Romans a Poet was called Vates, which is as much as a Diviner'.
Bailey comments,

> Heaney comes on things in a similar way, by that
> sonambulist process of search and surrender that is
> perhaps the one big pleasure of poetry that the

96

reader of it misses.

Heaney shows his reservations towards Latin culture in "Freedman" and obviously his ideas of Nature and the poet differ from those of Sidney. In this alliance of poet and diviner they do however agree; the link between divination and poetry is ancient in Ireland. The filid was a seer who, as well as composing songs, foretold the future by augury and sacrifice. By the time of the thirteenth century not only had the filid inherited something of the druid's role, he had also become a composer and singer like the bard.

The 'call' of the water in this poem is linked with the sexual urge. The diviner is an anonymous male whose 'rod' jerks down 'with precise convulsions'. The reliable and uncompromising qualities of the erectile sexual organ are mainfest here, pointing out the object of desire. There is a mystery in the fact that the water will only summon the 'gifted one' — or the chosen lover if we continue the analogy. The rod points downward, anticipating Antaeus's love for Mother Earth, her caves and streams like arteries. The poem is permeated by the 'primitive' idea that the earth is shot through by a mesh of unseen forces. It is obvious that Heaney, in writing this poem, was grappling for some kind of mystical counterpart as poet; this figure is not only to become more well-defined and powerful as the verse develops but it is eventually given the narrator's first person singular. This growing apprehension of the poet's gift to 'see through' and into the natural world is startlingly realised in 'Cow and Calf", "Turkeys Observed" and "Trout".

"Trout" recalls the fish poems of Ted Hughes and D.H.Lawrence, but the Heaney poem is more direct — his metaphors are less qualified and the movements more graphic. The Irish poet is not distanced from his subject by the workings of his memory. Instead we are confronted by the instant menace and skidding trajectory of a 'fat gun barrel'. The military emphases cannot be forgotten: torpedoes, bull's eye, fired, reporting, tracer-bullets, volley and ramrodding are all possibly culled from memories of the last war or current bloodshed in Ireland.

The Salmon of Knowledge, after it had eaten of nuts falling from the nine hazels of Poetic Art, was caught in Ireland. Finn, on tasting the salmon, was given the gift of inspiration. Heaney's trout is a cipher for acquisitive knowledge and the fervour of the poetic process. As opposed to the ancient ιχϑὑς symbol of Christianity the trout in Heaney's poem indicates menace — a tracer that never burns out. This can suggest terrorism, or perhaps there is a fleeting glance of the lightening flash of poetic inspiration. Graves writes of rituals where the Devil's intended lover changes herself into a trout, among other forms, in order to escape him. He also mentions that the fish was considered famous for its sexual indifference but this is not the temper of Heaney's trout.

The poem consists of four quatrains and a final isolated line, and the trout image operates through lines of six syllables. The first stanza, starting with an anonymous verb, 'Hangs', and then switching to the image of the fat gun barrel, evokes a sensual vision. The gun barrel 'deep under arched bridges' and the butter down the river's throat reinforce the sexual tone. In the second stanza we are not sure whether the 'depths' or 'muzzle' are 'smooth-skinned'. The drama of the trout's identity continues into the third stanza where the fish seems to be controlled from the outside: '. . . .fired from the shadows'. The diction of the fourth stanza displays how Heaney can compress words connoting movement in order to disrupt the flow of words and how, on another level, he can truncate a phrase to imitate a jolt of movement:

> . . . .darts like a tracer
> bullet back between stones
> and in never burnt out.

The phrase 'in never burnt out' is a particularly adept statement. It is both a pun in itself and also a kind of 'double exposure', an image which is blurred back onto itself, due to the lack of commas. The two final lines restate vitality from another perspective. The trout seems minus his skin: 'A volley of cold blood' and becomes a rush of liquid within another pouring mass. Such a precise Kenning-like construction is almost a poem within the poem. The 'o's in volley, cold and ramrodding press the image home, suggesting the round shape of a lateral cross-section of the fish. The last line is a ramrod in itself; set apart, the insistent 'r's and hard 'd's and 't's build up a strong tactile sensation. We can see the fish pushing against the water as the line itself offsets and nudges an end to the poem.

Joseph L.Henderson, in his essay "Ancient Myths and Modern Man", writes that sometimes a fish is a 'transcendent symbol of the depths'. They are 'symbolic denizens of the collective unconscious' and 'bring into the field of consciousness a special chthonic (underworld) message'. Heaney's trout seems to be such a creature. At first the hanging fish in the arch reminds one of Christ and the gun metaphor takes us back to "Digging". Heaney is beginning to thread and re-thread strings of related sexual, numinous and artistic images in his work. This fish recalls a motif from the zoomorphic patterns in *The Book of Kells* and yet also remains a biological fact stripped to its barest essentials. The trout brings with it a psychic shock; this mixture of threat and exhilarating wildness and its implications for the human consciousness are to become an obsession in Heaney's work.

"Poor Women in a City Church" involves the reader in a scene informed by the element of fire. It is important to realise that the book as a whole is organised around 'element' poems. We start with "Digging", "Follower" and "At a Potato Digging", all earthy subjects. "Waterfall" and "Personal Helicon" are concerned with freshwater and "Diviner" links earth and subterranean streams. There are two poems of the land meeting the sea, "Valediction" and "Lovers on Aran". Air and fire in Heaney's work are stranger, frightening and almost supernatural forces. "Honeymoon Flight" and "Storm on the Island" reveal the impact and eerie vacancy of air. "St.Francis and the Birds" is perhaps an attempt to be more light-hearted and appreciative when considering flight.

"Poor Women in a City Church" focusses on candles: wax, bright asterisks, blue flames, candle tongues and blue mincing flames are mentioned. As in Brown's descriptions of female reverence there is a depth of ancient worship contained within this poem, but there is also an element of mockery

> . . . .blue flame
> Mince and caper as whispered calls
> Take wing up to the Holy Name

Hill has used candleflames and religious awe as metaphors for poetic 'tongues'. The air of mixed irony and child-like awe in Heaney's poem recalls Stephen Dedalus's 'Above the flame the smoke of praise' in *Portrait of the Artist*. Heaney's wonder is finally centered upon the women. They change from being 'dough-faced' and 'beeswax browed', providers of food and domestic harmony, and become transfigured, outshining gold, altar lace and marble. The material wealth of the Catholic Church is, of course, commented upon. This is a religion of the sky — the flames are blue like the sky and Mary's robe. They are also yellow like the sun and the gold of shrines. In *North* Heaney's developing mistrust of the solar religions involving violence and materialism comes to a head.

In the *London Magazine* Heaney remarked:

> My sensibility was formed by the dolorous murmurings
> of the rosary, and the generally Marian quality of devo-
> tion. The reality that was addressed was maternal, and
> the picture was one of supplication. The attitude to life
> that was inculcated in me — not by the priests, but by
> the active, lived thing of prayers and so on, in my house,
> through my mother was really patience. At the bottom
> I think that probably patience is the best virtue....In
> practice the shrines, the rosary beads, lots of devotions,
> were centered towards a feminine presence, which I think
> is terrific for the sensibility.

There is a muted version of this liberating Marian patience in the poem, but if Heaney has tried to distil these or similar feelings into the poem he has not succeeded. We are left with hints — a poem which one feels is at best only half realised.

"Twice Shy" succeeds where "Gravities" fails. The swift flourishes of description in the second stanza are immediately impressive. The casual tone of the talk and stroll is interrupted:

> Traffic holding its breath
> Sky a tense diaphragm:
> Dusk hung like a backcloth
> That shook where a swan swam,
> Tremulous as a hawk
> Hanging deadly, calm.

The metaphors are blunt and theatrical. Style is under scrutiny: 'Her scarf *a la* Bardot,/In suede flats for the walk.' The magazine glossiness and theatrical scenery quiver at the edges and finally disperse as the swan is likened to a hawk. The image flickers on the 'inward-eye', revealing firstly the swan and the hawk laying bare the nervousness beneath the calm. The image also hints at the watcher's physical and psychic sight. The swan symbolises purity of motive, perhaps vulnerability in love. The hawk is the hunter, voracious and sexually destructive. Both lovers recognise themselves in the double image and this shifts the poem into a portrayal of inner needs.

Love is also a metaphor for art here, 'juvenilia' referring both to adolescent affairs and early writing. The lovers, unable to rely upon deep bursts of emotion (associated with earth and mushrooms), are forced to engage in aesthetic, mentally pleasing and thrilling aerobatics. It is the image of themselves that they play with '. . . .a thrush linked to a hawk'. So the talk is, they both know, ultimately childish. If the couple cannot rely upon deep-rooted passions they can perhaps rely on 'still waters running deep' like David in Psalm 34. This means trusting in the Unconscious — deeper levels of their being — in order to find a common source for communion.

> Finding a voice means that you can get your
> own feeling into your own words and that your
> words have the feel of you about them.

They in fact comprise 'a shaft into real life'.

We have already encountered the embankment in "An Advancement of Learning". It does in fact present a clearly defined borderline between two elements; it also shows the ability of men to channel water. In both the earlier poem and "Twice Shy" the narrator learns to trust the inner strengths — unconscious and conscious — which the river and enbankment respectively symbolise.

Swans were emblems of ageless mastery of passion and will for Yeats in his "Wild Swans at Coole". Graves writes that in Gaelic the pagan goddess Brigid was identified with the White Swan. The hawk was usually a sun symbol descending 'on the Pharaohs at their coronation from their father, the Sun god Ra. . .' The conflation of the hawk-swan image thus compunds the obvious confusion and agitation of the lovers.

Another pair of lovers in "Lovers on Aran" prepare the reader for the same metaphor Heaney is to use in "Ocean's Love to Ireland". **"Shoreline" and "Shorewoman". It is, of course, an anthropomorphism,** ancient in its power, echoing myths of creation. It also asks the kind of directional question that "Waterfall" asks, 'Did sea define the land or land the sea?' This is a challenge to myths of polarity to accomodate the view that sea and land, man and woman, are co-existent and mutually defining. Unlike Brown with his images of the ploughed waves and seas of corn, Heaney does not seek to unite the different natural forces. They may define each other but do not finally merge their identities.

100

The sea 'sifting from the Americas' seems exotic and is compared to 'broken glass' as if the fixities of art cannot contain it. It is as though through the interaction, the 'collision' of art, sexuality and the unknown, a true psychic shock of words words is awoken. The action of natural forces upon themselves and upon the human mind have raised a poetic presence just as the 'salvo' of space upon a rock can raise a frightening 'huge nothing' in "Storm on the Island".

"Personal Helicon" is the finest poem in the latter part of this collection. The startling and strange tricks of perception one experiences on looking into wells are gathered:

> . . . .the trapped sky
> A white face hovered over the bottom
> gave back your own call
> with a clean new music in it.
> . . . .a rat slapped across my reflection.

The textures, smells and echoes of the wells are here and also the associations of a child's mind: for the wells are scaresome, aquariums, and on a purely physical level, dark drops, 'doors into the dark'.Helicon refers to a mountain in North Boetia where the muses are supposed to reside, but the name is generally used in reference to a source of inspiration. Wells occupy a unique place in Irish belief. The well of Segais or Connla's well, which nobody could visit save Nechtan and his three cup-bearers, was the source of inspiration and knowledge for the ancient Irish. Over it grew the nine hazels of wisdom. Oisin in search of water for the ' Colloquy of the Ancients ' went to the white-rimmed well of Uisnech, which nobody had found since the battle of Gahbra. John Sharkey writes of the connection with the Mother Goddess in *Celtic Mysteries*:

> The custom of hanging clooties on trees or bushes by
> a secret well was once widespread through Scotland,
> Wales and Ireland. It is also common in the Middle
> East. The symbolism connected with the Mother
> Goddess has been largely forgotten since the change
> to church-based Christian ritual.

There is a well of St.Brigid in Liscanor, County Clare, where the trappings of Christianity barely conceal an ancient pagan heritage. Of course, as a pit in the ground filled with water, source and sustainer of life, the Mother Goddess analogy might be more important than is at first apparent. The smells from the centre of Heaney's childhood are of 'waterweed, fungus and dank moss'. The book has turned full circle, or almost: 'All year the flax dam festered in the heart'.

It is the darknesses that Heaney desires to set echoing and these darknesses, full of slime and growth, seem indicative of the vast generative power of life itself. As when Pound's hero enters the cave with his torch and there is a cry of 'Io, Io', these dark recesses seem to be as womb-like as any cave or underground maze. However, Heaney's wells are those he knew intimately as a child – their history stretches back through the Irish Christian and pagan well-cults to the Neolithic world of local spirits or genii. Pound's caves are culled from Greek mythology and are not necessarily part of his experience. Heaney's child is trapped in the well; his sky is encapsulated by it. The reference to Narcissus is not a casual one. It is not merely the reflection which is part of himself but the ferns, well-water and roots. Heaney talks of a 'seminal impulse', a level of life 'lying beneath the very floor of memory'. Here we find a ghostly retribution for uprooted plants, intimations of fear and wonder and fairy tales and legends about wells. The well is a medium which translates the boy's image and constitutes a drop into a lower, more ancient and subconscious level of biology and geology. Most important is the well in the boy's being and the echoes which the echoes of the actual well have set sounding in that 'backward abysm'.

II

In his lecture delivered to the Royal Society of Literature in 1974, Heaney said:

> When I called my second book of poems *Door Into the Dark* I intended to gesture towards the idea of poetry as a point of entry into the buried life of feelings or as a point of exit for it. Words themselves are doors; Janus is to a certain extent their deity, looking back to a ramification of roots and associations and forward to a clarification of sense and meaning. So here are a number of poems that arise out of the almost unnameable energies that, for me, hovered over certain bits of language and landscape.

Such a statement alerts the reader to the dual and often reciprocal energies in Heaney's poems. It is a statement of belief too: a belief in 'almost un-nameable energies' at times inhabiting the land and the language.

Door Into the Dark opens with darkness, with "Night-Piece" and a question; 'Must you know it again?' Heaney seems to test the silence. Some poems in *Death of a Naturalist* examined the overlapping areas of geography, psychology and aesthetics rather dryly. They do not seem to 'cover enough ground' either thematically or verbally and poems such as "Gravities" and "Docker" are disappointing because they rely upon quite simple metaphors to hold the main emotional thrust. It is left to *Wintering Out* to explore the rich strata of linguistic deposits. *Door Into the Dark* is a book opening like a door onto the expanses of darkness, finding new areas to illuminate, and exploring, above all, the flexings of the human, animal, and vegetable worlds.

Immediately the curious and mysterious noises and impulses of life are thrust on the reader. The question is from an anonymous darkness to an anonymous subject – it remains unanswered. Instead we are

quickly given enlarged segments of a picture. Is the horse ill or frightened or has she given birth? Stories of spirits tormenting farm animals
or horses sensing hidden presences are aroused here. The strange use of
synecdoche means that the horse becomes obscured — a thing of textures. At first the vulnerable mouth lifting from 'each separate tooth'
(the small 'hammering' of the vowels creates a swift picture of a line of
shining teeth). Then with a soft rushing of sound we are given two
French forms of Latin words: 'Opalescent haunch'. The words are visual
as well as linguistic hieroglyphs. Because of the lapidary metaphor we
see a muscle carved in a gleaming quartz-like stone. The milky colour of
opals makes one think of moonlight, and the sibilants of 'lascent' help
us envisage a nervous sweat. Haunch, also a cut of meat, reinforced by
the details of 'muscle and hoof' awakens sinister associations of knackers'
yards and the horsemeat the Irish prize so much. The 'piece' of the title
could refer to the poem itself or to a slice of meat or even to a gun that
killed the horse.

We pass naturally to "Gone". 'Gone' literally means lost or hopeless,
but in a Southern Irish accent it could well refer to a gun. We start with
a remarkably microscopic and sensitive image: 'a cobweb of grass-dust',
an image of neglect and a passing order. Accoutrements betray signs of
death as if by a quick trick of 'sympathetic magic' they inherit the fate
of their wearers. The movement down the trappings to 'Droop in a
tangle', recalls the swift glance ending in the hooves in the present
poem. The horse has 'made' his home, conditioned it to his living
presence, and 'must'. The stable, now unmade, is no longer meaningful.
The horse's 'must' recalls its durability, strength and stubborn affirmation of an age which stretches back nearly 6,000 years. "Gone", with
its numbed half-rhymes ('blinkers', 'ticking', 'lost', 'must'), and infre-
quent full rhymes ('band', 'hand', 'dust', 'must'), is a sonnet mourning
the passing of an era. Both poems possess an almost haiku-like quality
and reveal a new power and compression, an awareness of dramatic
possibilities and an appreciation of verbal and visual strategies.

The Celts revered their horses and often attributed supernatural
powers to them. As Alwyn and Brinley Rees write:

> In mythology, animals are not mere brutes; they are
> possessed of a supernatural intelligence and power. Their
> association with the birth and infancy of heroes is world-
> wide, and in many cases they befriend or serve their
> heroic 'kinsmen' beyond the days of childhood.

Later we will cover the importance of the ploughman's societies in the
work of Brown. Ross talks of the dependence of nomadic cultures upon
the horse in war and peace. Graves writes of the 'Three Eponae', the
mare goddesses who were worshipped among the Gallic Celts, 'and there
is a strange account in Giraldus Cambrensis' *Topography of Ireland*
which shows that relics of the same cult survived in Ireland until the
twelfth century'. Heaney must at least be aware of the great Celtic

103

tribes of Ireland who relied so heavily upon the horse.

In "The Forge" the central role of the Smith in the ancient and modern world is examined. Many tales are told of heroes gifted with Smithcraft and Graves mentions these mysteries in *The White Goddess*. The Rees write of the sexual connotations of craft initiation and quote as an example that the smith was considered 'husband of his forge'. The fervour surrounding and mystery attached to the forge are startling: 'All I know is a door into the dark.' The anvil itself, though unclear, 'must be somewhere in the centre'. It is likened to the fabulous unicorn and called 'immoveable, an altar'. The mysterious persona who watches the traffic is also a strange, shadowy figure, guardian of craft for a community. The irony of 'To beat real iron out' is evident in a country whose metal-working industries have become massive concerns and whose crafts have been largely replaced by production lines. The poet too 'expends himself in shape and music'. He too strives to create a lasting commodity while remaining aware of the flux of life out of which he draws his material.

These three poems 'place' the collection. Both man and horse move and depart in darkness. The figure of the Smith is crucial because, like the dancing figure of the stag sorcerer from the Trois Freres caves, the Smith is part animal himself: 'Sometimes, leather-aproned, hairs in his nose'. But he is also god of fire — Hephaestus, artificer and craftsman for the other gods. As guardian of Promethean fire he stands at the threshold between animals and men, men and gods. His altar is 'horned', revealing the masculine power which first 'broke' and tamed horses.

This phallic power is found in an intensified form in "Dream"; the pole seems to be representative of an industrial culture and we remember the impact of the Telegraph system upon modern culture. The terror of the final section hints at a blow against social and psychic oppression and the billhook is, of course, traditionally the weapon of the agrarian peasant. The weapon is hand-forged, harking back to the days of the craftsman. There are many echoes in this scene: the figure hacking at the phallic pillar could be an Oedipal manifestation taking revenge against paternal authority. This could be Cronus the emasculator destroying his father or an advocate of the oak cult in North Greece gaining power over the Pelagasian farmers and wielding a golden sickle. Apollo and Perseus both wielded sickles against tyrants. The Druidic 'emasculation' of the sacred oak by the lopping of the mistletoe, the procreative principle, is another version of this chain of myths. The poem also holds echoes of the Druidic cult of skulls and the practice of beheading so popular amongst Irish warriors.

Heaney's work in his last two books will grow increasingly engaged with nations and individuals who have conquered or oppressed the Irish people. This 'pole' might represent the Vikings, the Normans, the tyranny of Catholic Christianity, Protestantism and the English, or all of these forces. According to Jung, Campbell and others, it is a particular facet of dreams that they contain many composite figures or images. This is a dream after all; the billhook may be Heaney's art, a distorted version of the pen or spade, which he is tempted to use as a weapon. This may have been in fact a repressed desire which has surfaced in this shocking image. In "Now and In England" Heaney discusses the fact that Irish writers will have to use the weapon the English have given them — that of the English language.

The poem, however, has the texture of a real dream. The quick descriptive flourishes and spare brutality of the vision give it an authentic feel and the transformation of an object into a man is a palpable shock. Visually it reminds one of a propagandist poster from Eastern Europe or China, or even one of Goya's 'dark' lithographs. Heaney has forged a scene of compelling power from the archetypal figure of the hero supplanting evil.

"In Gallarus Oratory" starts with the 'community pack' in 'a core of old dark'. Each word is laid down like the very stones of the eighth century building: 'A core of old dark walled up with stone/A yard thick'. Like a diving bell the oratory becomes a vehicle, but in this case a spiritual vessel, and drops to the centre of the earth.

There is a growing opinion that the Celts and Neolithic peoples believed in an occult and potent earth energy which could be channelled through the use of stone circles and sanctuaries. Heaney definitely believes in 'the dark centre', and in a radio broadcast he called it:

> . . .the blurred and irrational storehouse of insight and
> instincts, the hidden core of the self — this notion is the
> foundation of what viewpoint I might articulate for
> myself as a poet.

The vision of 'The sea a censer, and the grass a flame' indicates a fiery enlightenment after a magical initiation. The last line reveals a whole world as a spiritual offering, conversely referring also to the all-pervasive presence of deity. The king like the blacksmith stands at the threshold to the depths. This is an 'oratory' and we must not forget Heaney's view of utterance as a shaft into real life.

The 'sterner myth' of a pirate queen in battle dress in "Girls Bathing, Galway 1965" is possibly the Morrigan, Celtic goddess of the sea, posing a stark contrast to a 'milk-limbed Venus'. She is an unpleasant, vengeful deity who is heard laughing as men drown and who preys upon battlefields. But one must not forget Anne Bonney, the Irish woman who left the West of Ireland to become the most famous female pirate of all time. Her exploits were extraordinary and a huge bounty was placed on her head. The pagan myths 'melt' into the tide of history and Christianity arrives on the scene:

> And generations sighing in...
> Labour in fear of flesh and sin

Christ's acknowledgement of his destiny gains a new irony: 'For the time has been accomplished'. The writer's persona cannot even escape the fractious history of his home on this beach. There is a glint of hope in the fact that Venus, symbolising another realm of love and vitality, becomes an everyday manifestation here, but the overall impression of the girls is mixed. The 'sterner myth' and shuttling of the years are inescapable and the horror of Ulster in the late 60s is about to erupt. One also remembers Stephen Dedalus' vision of a girl on a beach and how much his description in *Portrait* owed to the very church which he was rejecting.

We might see "Rite of Spring", which begins a sequence of six poems, five of which deal broadly with female sexuality and fecundity, as a companion poem to "Girls Bathing, Galway 1965". Women for Heaney, as for the old Celts and many tribal nations, were 'doors into the dark', whether they lived in matriarchies or not. They are the guardians of the Other World, sometimes, as the Rees write, exclusively so.

> In the delectable Other World of "The Adventure of
> Conle", 'there is no race there but women and maidens
> alone'. The fairies are known as 'The Mothers' or 'The
> Mother's Blessing' in parts of Wales, and they are some-
> times thought of as being exclusively female.

In Ireland the native gods, the Tuatha de Danaan, are thought of as 'Tribes of the Goddess Danaan'. The Morrigan is the 'great queen'. Especially relevant to Heaney's poems is Sharkey's short chapter on the Triple Goddess:

> The recognition of water as the first principle and
> source of all life to those who move over the land,
> dependent on its bounty for food and sustenance, is
> reflected in the dedication of the main river sources of
> Western Europe as sanctuaries to the Celtic fertility
> goddess. . . .The goddess is bountiful but also merciless.

After "Rite of Spring" stressing the themes of frigidity and feminine sexuality related to the seasons, "Undine" takes us back to the most basic of sexual metaphors. In talking of Undine Heaney remembered that as a child the ground seemed much closer to him and the watercourses seemed to stretch as far as he could see. Muir expresses the same feeling in *The Story and the Fable*:

> (a child) is much closer to things since his eyes are only
> two or three feet from the ground, not five and six....I
> lived my life in a small separate underworld, while the
> grown-ups walked on their long legs several feet above my
> head on a stage where every relation was different.

"Undine" is spoken by the feminine persona, a personification of the water itself; one feels that one's eye level is literally as low as the waterline. Undine was the nymph whose song beguiled sailors on the Rhine and here the myth of the mermaid who lives on land is given a new setting:

> He explored me so completely, each limb
> Lost its cold freedom. Human warmed to him.

106

It is a statement of unity just as much as Brown's drawing our attention to the common origins of earth, bread, sun and man. The poem anticipates "Maighdean Mara" in *Wintering Out* and some of the images are crudely suggestive: 'I swallowed his trench'. The myth of the workman as 'husband' of his materials is enacted again. Undine is transient and uncontrolled feeling — she personifies illogical emotions which sweep through the metabolism like underground currents: 'Then he walked by me. I rippled and/I churned'. Medieval ideas about the hot and cold wet humours of the body are conjured up, as well as superstitions about the holy nature of crossroads or the confluence of streams:

> I churned
> Where ditches intersected near the river.
> Until he dug a spade deep in my flank.

Both "Rite of Spring" and "Mother" use the image of the pump for a woman. In the first the farm-pump is a nameless symbol of womanhood where the shape of a simple device echoes the shape of the female genitals. In the second the female persona identified herself with the plunger and spout. The 'spirit' in "Undine" shifts between being an ordinary woman, a watercourse and the Great Goddess in her aspect as young lover. In the last two stanzas the man becomes the land whose seed is 'brassy grain' and in reaction the water becomes human. The sexual act is responsible for this transmutation. The workman 'lying in the furrow' with the water recalls various cult practices such as the King of May prostrating himself on the glebe or sacrificial bodies being scattered into the ploughed land to make it fertile. But these rituals, these qualities of earth and water are also part of the emotional repertoire of a human couple. They operate on a level of cliche in everyday speech: 'I was swamped by her presence', or 'I was all at sea'. Heaney does not think any of these echoes too obvious or commonplace to utilize.

Door into the Dark is essentially a transitional book. In his search for a fitting narrator or main character for the poems Heaney has conceived the epic hero of "Dream" and yet still wishes to include the darkness and fervour of mystical initiation ("In Gallarus' Oratory"). Additionally, he is grappling with the ambiguous and potentially self-destructive force of the Male creator embodied in the figure of the Smith in "The Forge". In the next two books of poetry we will see how this figure, that of the brutal emasculator and dark King, will split into two. On one side we will find 'earth-starred denizens': Antaeus, an inner emigre or a grave-haunting Hamlet who often assumes an alternately assuaging or outraged voice. On the other side we will find Hercules, the sky heroes, the Protestant Jesus, the men of Cavehill, Vikings and policemen. But *Door into the Dark* has also insisted upon the prevailing need to give voice to the feminine side of the human psyche. The two poems which pose, on one hand, resolution, and on the other, a promise of future development in relation to this collection are "The Plantation" and "Bogland".

For the ancient Irish the concept of the centre was the basis for all mysteries and they organised their courts, counties and views of the Universe around the idea. "The Plantation" is full of charmed rings: toadstools, the black char of a fire, and the circular progress of the narrative itself:

> . . .toadstools and stumps
> Always repeating themselves

> Or did you re-pass them?

> . .And having found them once
> You were sure to find them again.

The Western mode of linear thought is baffled by the circle. The insistence upon diamond absolutes, polar opposites such as good and evil, cannot survive in a circle where points on opposite sides of the circumference eventually pass through one another. "The Plantation" depicts a mystical line passing through all aspects of human life and sensibility and enacts this in its running together of paradoxical statements:

> Someone had always been there
> Though always you were alone

> Though you walked a straight line
> It might be a circle you travelled.

> ...pilot and stray — witch,
> Hansel and Gretel in one.

Even male, female, oppressed and oppressor are linked by this line which is as vital and undeniable as man's own humanity; it is the 'world's live girdle' in "Vision". Ignored or rejected peoples open to the influence of Nature are found here. Campers, gypsies and tramps, like the Croppies, Woodkerne and Sweeney sleeping wild. Stories and legends of fairies and the sidhe and banshees might be recalled: 'Tales of fog on the mountains'. The moral impulse which is strictly confined to one direction — the 'straight and narrow' road — is here subordinated to a collective or encompassing impulse which is multi-directional. Once inside the Plantation the centre is limitless even though geographically it borders on a road. Simultaneously, this 'centre' unlocks the doors of words with the result that vowels impinge and lilt on the tongue: 'bleyberries quilting the floor', and sibilants, 'a's and 'r's create cells of plangent and glowing sounds: 'black char of fire'. Or, with a quick flourish, a line of muted and sounded 'e's tails off a stanza and a description: 'or their excrement'. Words implying textures are pushed into conjunction for their complementary sounds: 'To the hush and the mush/Of its whispering treadmill'. Plantations are a byword for exploitation, robbery and the presumptuous actions of English landlords to the Irish. However, this plantation is overgrown and has once again become hospitable to all comers, a magical place. The poem ends with the assertion that the ego is not static but itself contains a circle running through apparently opposed qualities.

Contrasted with the clay of "Bann Clay" which 'holds and gluts', we find the peat of 'Bogland', which melts and opens underfoot. Heaney writes:

> The best moments are those when your mind seems to
> implode and words and images rush of their own accord
> into the vortex which happened to me once when the
> line 'We have no prairies' drifted into my head at bed-
> time, and loosened a fall of images that constitute the
> poem "Bogland".
>
> I had been vaguely wishing to write a poem about
> Bogland chiefly because it is a landscape that has a
> strange assuaging effect on me, one with associations
> reaching back into early childhood. We used to hear
> about bog butter, butter kept fresh for a great number
> of years under the peat. Then when I was at school the
> skeleton of an elk had been taken out of a bog nearby
> and a few of our neighbours had got their photographs
> in the paper, peering out across the antlers. So I began
> to get an idea of bog as the memory of a landscape or as
> a landscape that remembered everything that happened
> in or near to it. In fact, if you go round the National
> Museum in Dublin, you will realise that a great propor-
> tion of the most cherished heritage of Ireland was
> 'found in a bog...' At that time I had been reading
> about the frontier and the West as an important myth
> in the American consciousness, so I set up — or rather,
> laid down — the bog as an answering Irish myth. I
> wrote it quickly on the next morning, having slept on
> my excitement, and revised it on the hoof, from line
> to line as it came.

Heaney stresses the relation between physical excitement, sleep and spontaneous writing here, and elsewhere he has said, 'I only write when I am in the trance'. This is the scape which he is to elevate or 'bed down' into a 'befitting emblem of adversity'. The Western prairies, vast and flat, replete with memories of shoot-outs, rustlings and violence, seem to represent an aggressive male power of expansion; a power which threatens to slice at the sun. But here 'the cyclop's eye,/Of a tarn' seems to be a symbol of the vagina and Feminine principle, especially caught as it is in the retentive womb of the bogs. This land is victim of the sun's aim or, in mythological shorthand, the influence of the Sky-father who trains his rays on the earth, crusting it over with a dry surface. The following four stanzas stress the preservative nature of the soil: its inability to mould hard matter through chemical changes or produce an 'ikon' like the "Relic of Memory". The key word is 'assuaging' in Heaney's description of his ideas of the bogs; it is a word he uses elsewhere to describe the mollifying and healing influence of the Marian tradition. The words 'bottom' or 'end' cease to have a meaning in this poem. Like the inexhaustible loving aspect of the Pauline God of 1 Corinthians 13 this concept of infinite provision is a mystery. The search into the bog is also a search into the psyche: 'Our pioneers keep striking/Inwards and downwards'. Psychology seems to be in its infancy here, still probing an expansive darkness. 'Every layer' has been camped on before and, in a way, every man contains the history of the human race — his consciousness has been moulded by historical processes. 'The wet centre' brings us back to the flax-dam, reservoir and well as images of the fecund but inexplicable human self. The layers of the bog are like the strata of socialisation and conditioning, of roles and responses which surround the human entity.

The movement of this poem is centrifugal; 'the horizon encroaches toward the female centre which is composed of substances which simultaneously awaken sexual and decreative associations: 'salty and white', 'black butter', 'soft as pulp'. This is not a unifying centre like that of "The Plantation" — it is in constant confrontation with the masculine energy of the sun: 'bog that keeps scrusting/Between the sights of the sun'. It is in this image of the bog that various strings of female motifs: 'empty creel', 'bone-hooped womb', 'the pump', the wife's 'linen cloth' and the piratical energies of "Girls Bathing, Galway 1965", are finally resolved in a recognizable landscape. In the 'bottomless' bogland with its seepage, tarn and cultural deposits, we find the virgin, the aggressive lover and the mother, beneficent or hag-like, merging into a composite ground.

As a whole the book does not reveal the linguistic invention or sensitivity of *Wintering Out*; neither does it possess the kind of historical insight and foci which are to make *North* so memorable. The clean and finely-honed pictures of the early poems in *Door into the Dark* with their painstaking accuracy and sculptural quality are quite unique in Heaney's writing, and he does not really follow this method up in the next two books. But what *Door into the Dark* does reveal is a man examining layers of psychic awareness and continually drawing on chains of images and words to give shape to his preoccupations with a new power. It reveals a sharp focussing of the poetic eye upon routes to that 'otherworld' of darkness and creation and upon the archetypes which guard doors to that world. Heaney has by no means finished his struggle with the initiator, King or 'Smith' figure and will not reach a satisfactory expression of all the tensions which he feels are involved in this character till *North*. However, *Door into the Dark* expands his poetic vision of the feminine side of conscious and unconscious life which he, as a person, finds so crucial and assuaging. It is for these reasons and for the fact that this book gives the reader so moving and immediate a vision of 'the Dark' that it is a transitional collection, one in which we find Heaney's sense of myth deepening and gaining greater unity and his dramatic use of mythological character gaining greater skill and clarity of definition.

'Terror was present in Seamus Heaney's apprehension of the forces of
nature from the start', writes Jeremy Hooker in his review of *North*,
and in reply to a question from John Haffenden Heaney said that he
works from: 'Any amount of dread. Fear is the emotion that my muse
thrives on. That's always there.' When asked if he could redefine this
fear in terms of awe he replied that no complete person should be without fear. Fear of frogs, of policemen, of bombs, of unseen forces and of
the 'three nets' which Stephen Dedalus attempted to avoid. Fear is a
key concept in *Wintering Out* — it is the mother of curiosity and
wonder, and not vice versa. Fear moulds each word and lodges it as a
historical 'gravity' exerting pressure within the structure of the poem.
Fear influences the rhythm and form of the poem since Heaney adapts
each stanza to the flexings and, at times, jolts, of emotion which rule
the writing.

Because of its anonymous subject "Fodder", the first poem in
Wintering Out, seems to operate at a subhuman level. The voice embodies the desire of land and animals for 'fodder' and that desire is
imaged in the stall, cradle of Jesus and the centre for farmyard life:

> These long nights
> I would pull hay
> For comfort, anything
> to bed the stall.

This hunger is also human: the need for fulfilment and vision. 'Fother',
a trick of local pronunciation, is near enough to the child's lisp of
'father' to summon up a mythic child, born of the earth, seeking his
parent again: 'I open/My arms for it/again.' The stack itself is a store of
preserved nourishment ready to fall 'at your feet' — a miracle 'multiple
as loaves and fishes'. The haystack is elevated to the position of an altar,
to an image of supernatural sustenance. The words are full of the shud-
der and pour of rushing sheaves:

> a bundle
> tossed over half-doors
> or into mucky gaps.

One notices the clump-like quality of 'a bundle' dispersing like falling
grass into the 's's and soft 'lf' of the next line. There is the effect of
tackiness and wedged hay achieved in the simple words 'or into mucky
gaps'. In the second stanza Heaney creates a swift metaphor (that of a
vice and a house) to voice a double entendre — the eaves of the stack
are what is taken from the stack. Heaney lingers over this for the sound
of the words and the tactile impression of hay being eased from a tight
wedge. The final lines hint at the need for animal comfort and for a

111

power to assuage sexual and mental conflict.

From images of man's common animality and vulnerability we emerge into the world of human atavism – a search for historical recognition. The 'long seasoned' rib of oak brought back from the bog to the carter's thatch conjures up the generations of Irish Gaels: 'the moustached/dead, the creel-fillers'. Here in "Bog Oak" the mood is one of resignation after long striving. The forbears' wisdom and the images mirror this inpotence:

> as a blow-down of smoke
> struggles over the half-door
>
> and mizzling rain
> blurs the far end
> of the cart track.

The fact that these ruts lead back to no 'oak groves' hints either at the bleakness and centreless existence in modern Ireland or at Heaney's inability to reach back through history to racial resources – the creative genius of the tribe. The narrator can only travel back as far as the language of Spenser and the picture of the foreigner 'dreaming sunlight'. The geniuses who creep from 'woodes and glinnes' afford us our first glimpse of the wood-kernes, the inner exiles who take 'protective colouring, from bole and bark' ("Exposure"). These were the pathetic survivors of the harrowing war in Munster recorded by Spenser in his "A Vewe of the Present State of Irelande":

> Out of everie Corner of the woodes and glinnes they
> came Crepinge uppon theire handes for theire leggs
> could not beare them, they loked like Anatomies of
> deathe, they spake like ghostes Cryinge out of theire
> graves, they did eate the dead Carrions, wheare they
> Coulde find them...

It is in defining the role of the Elizabethan English landowners in Ireland that Heaney arrives at a clearer definition of his own culture. By 1598 the Plantation Policy was well under way and 400,000 acres of land were confiscated after the Munster rising to be granted to English families. The handling of the whole situation was incompetent and slow. The Gaelic way of life which was, as Becket writes, 'so closely bound up with personal services and with family rather than territorial titles', was seriously undermined.

For Heaney Spenser represents the writer as foreign administrator. In an article for the *Guardian* he writes accusingly of the Englishman: 'From his castle in Cork he watched the effects of a campaign designed to settle the Irish question'. He and the silver poet Sir John Davies watched the demise of a civilisation 'whose lifeline was bitten off when the squared-off walls of bawn and demesne dropped on the country like the jaws of a man trap.'

The search for 'oak groves' in the poem is significant for, as Heaney writes in the same article, 'Grove is a word that I associate with the classics, a sunlit symmetrical tree-line'. The grove he mentions here is Grove Hill as viewed from his childhood home of Mossbawn. He goes on to say that the Englished version of 'oak-grove' does not satisfy his auditory imagination, as does another name: 'The Dirraghs, from doire as in Derry'.

In relation to this schism of linguistic history it is interesting to note that the oak was the tree of the Dagda and other Thunder gods — the prime symbol of the Druidic religion. Heaney is allying the Irish tribes of sky worshippers with both the Druid wielding a golden sickle and the 'white-robed priests' of the Classics. He is disavowing the sky-cults, the 'cutters of mistletoe', and identifying with the disinherited geniuses who, in "Bog Oak", have lost their impotent and crippled status as recorded by Spenser and have assumed a distinctly menacing stance, encroaching upon the Englishman's sunlight. Moreover, the clash of myths is being portrayed as active on the poet's own ground and in his language.

"The Last Mummer" is difficult to disentangle from its mysterious narrative; is the dreamer of the third part the retired mummer or a different person? Is the terrace that of a rich family, and is that the reason for his apparent rage, or is it merely a line of houses and the gate-beating an obscure ritual? The mummer seems to be an emblem for a particular kind of personality and the straw mask and hump could be psychic rather than physical. Heaney is, of course, qualified to talk of country taboos and 'the long toils of blood'. He has mentioned to Robert Buttel that the poem might be about Ian Paisley or, alternatively, poetry, or both. The last mummer with a hunch, stick and stone could be one of a number of 'mummer' figures. Both Beelzebub and Little Man Jack have humps. However, different figures often overlap from district to district. The last mummer left upon the stage is often the Clown who can also be said to represent all the mummers because in some plays they all address each other as 'jack'. Of course an ancient pagan tradition lies behind the mumming, which might have originated as mock drama mumming the death and resurrection of the Divine Priest-King. There are hints that the mummer of Heaney's poem is the wood-kerne, the disinherited filid in another form. There is a mummer called the Wild Man or Jack-in-Green who, as Gascoigne points out, is very ancient indeed:

> A line has been suggested, convincingly, that goes all
> the way from Hercules (a leading character in Dorian
> mimes in pre-Athenian days...) down to the devils in
> medieval mystery plays and the Wild Man in pageants
> and finally to Harlequin.

The ash-plant and stone could, when seen in this tradition, represent a fertility-giving power. Jack-the-Fool, though, is a likely candidate to fill the 'role' in Heaney's poem because he represents an area of chaos and illogical strength which has been largely ignored by modern civilisation. E.K.Chambers writes that not only did mumming help to initiate and participate in the festivals of the rustic calendar, but it also gave prestige to the omnipresent Fool: 'the Man-Woman, that unquiet spirit, for whom there is no obvious function, but for whom a place always has to be found...' The word 'mummer' is derived from the French verb meaning 'to utter or murmur', and with the passing of the old rites and even their mock equivalents comes that 'luminous screen' which takes the burden of utterance away from the people. The mummer yearns for cockroach and cricket, a life open to many levels of reverence and difficulty. The old year dying again takes us back to the dramas depicting the death of the Sun God and the Goddess in her hag-like or austere aspect. We glimpse the passing of a whole age as the mummer recedes into the dreamer's memory and the moon, no longer a great goddess but the Christian Host, rises from the holly grove which resembles a sacred vessel. Graves writes extensively of the holiness of the holly tree and the holly king, and here we remember Hill's use of holly in *Mercian Hymns* as representative of a deep and mythic past and Christ's mass. The link with Christ is, of course, emphasised in the carol where Mary bears Jesus just as the holly bears its berry. The departing mummer making 'dark tracks' strangely echoes the last dream of Offa, and the line of mummers seems akin to Hill's anonymous workmen. Both embody a vanished spirit and a life in rhythm with the environment.

The speaker in "Land" is concerned with a sensitive intimacy and balance. He raises small cairns to serve as altar or landmark and 'composed habits for those acres'. The ambiguity of 'habits' means that, not only do we imagine the worker giving the land a different schedule of growth, but also we imagine him clothing his bride (the ground) with crops. As a result he achieves balance — neither raping nor neglecting the land. His reward is 'free passage' and 'in place' of his intended gift he leaves: 'a woman of old wet leaves'. 'Dollies' made of corn and hay are well-known through the whole of Europe and are often left as offerings to the spirits after harvest. This 'woman' seems an effigy of the Earth Mother in her hag aspect. In Ireland the last sheaf of corn cut was known as the cailleach (hag). Perhaps this portion was meant to assuage the destructive temper of the hag spirit after the spirit of the Biblical injunction for husbandmen to leave some of the crop for poor gleaners. This 'woman' gazes out past 'shifting hares', reminding us that witches were supposed to 'shift' their shape into hares and that the hare was sacred. These animals add to the fecundity in the scene.

With the third section the figure of the shaman comes to mind. His prostration against the 'phantom ground' images the priest representing the Sky Father mating with the earth and the Red Indian listening to distant movement. In this move downwards and the silence the man not only holds a realisation of the interpenetration of matter and spirit, but also enters into the life of rabbit, vole and mole. The explosive trajectory to the surface from underground and the shock of the snare reveal how intimately the poet's persona has learned to 'inhabit' nature. The snare could be that of his human perception and self-consciousness. The snare is merely a painful ornament for him but would mean death for a small mammal: barriers between human and animal are not easily transcended. The effort of empathy and then return to human consciousness identifies the persona with the Celtic past. Lewis Spence writes of the Milesian hero Amergin, who can change his 'shape into an eagle, a herb, a lake'. Remarking on the quality which enabled Amergin to accomplish these metamorphoses, M.D'Arbois Jubainville declares that according to the tenets of Celtic philosophy it consisted in 'making oneself identical with those forces of nature which the magician desired to wield. To possess this science was to possess nature in her entirety'.

Man is the language-maker, victim of his own Babels and diverse lexical patterns, but he is also 'still mammal', and there is a base to his utterance and verbal play which is, at times, inarticulate and incoherent. The soundings of "Gifts of Rain" mean the ability to 'sound out' depths but also simply to make a noise. Underwater technology, especially sonar, has alerted humans to the importance of soundings: the transmission of sounds and charting of depth by echo. We live by 'sounding out' the silence and the capitalisation in the twelfth line emphasises the mysterious quality of a verbal and audible pattern made in air.

The gifts of rain are lyrical images: 'a flower of mud', and can consist of liquid vowels: 'reed music, an old chanter' (the double 'e', lift of the 'usic' sound and muted ring of the French 'a' in 'chanter' summon up the roll, ebb and lap of waters). The gifts are difficult to assimilate. The ache to interpret history, to gain 'antediluvian lore' and to perceive a vision 'for my children's sake' are most keenly felt in a time of drought when the baked river floor images the deserts of prehistory before water brought fertility. There have been various and long-lived scholastic debates about the origins of language: whether it originated in imitation of nature or from innate mental structure in man. Heaney's persona finds his need for lore answered by the river itself: 'The tawny gutteral water/spells itself', and then we are given the gorgeous roll, the mixture (to an English ear) of 'royal' and 'yolk' in Moyola, its 'own score and consort'. The Elizabethan detail emphasises the regal and active aspects of the river. 'Moy' means plain, but P.W.Joyce thinks that there is a case for inferring that any river called 'Moy' may be known as a river of 'virtue'. Anne Ross has written that river names often reflected the names of goddesses, such as the Boyne and the Shannon named after Boand and Sinann. Here the farmer finds his goddess again: 'A swollen river,/a mating call of sound/ rises to pleasure me.'

In Heaney's work Nature has a habit of spelling itself. The locale is bedded 'in the utterance' (itself a sexual metaphor) and its sound passes eventually into language. The mutterings of the river are an affirmation of the most ancient links between Nature and human speech and this reciprocity is given an amorous turn as the 'calling of the blood' is answered. The narrator takes the name of the Biblical beggar who gained heaven ('Dives' is also a watery pun) and in hoarding 'common ground' assumes responsibility for the speech of a tribe. It is significant that the central filid or mystical narrator is being used also simultaneously to explore the rhythms and music of speech and also to discover common values, loves and burdens of a heritage.

"Toome" is an exercise in the onomatopoeic archaeology of language. In speaking of the place-name poems in *Wintering Out* Heaney has said:

the pleasure of the poem for me and I think for anyone
who gets anything out of them is in the rustle of the
language itself, the way it unfolds and plays, and that
was the actual feel of writing them.

The mouth of the narrator changes to a hollow under a slab and the act of speech becomes a forage downwards into the physical strata of cultures, notably warlike cultures: 'flints, musket-balls' and torcs. 'Toom' in Cork and Wexford is a place-name derived from 'Taim', a burial mound. In 1951 Mitchell investigated an old sandy spit near Toome Bay north of Lough Neagh. He found scrapers, hammer stones, and remains of what could have been a harpoon indicating the presence of hunters and fishers. The place-name is a 'door into the dark' of pre-history and the psyche of the speaker. The 'soft blastings' have remained through time, and take the narrator's mind back to the source of life where, according to some myths, strange conjurations of animals and men existed: 'elvers tail my hair'. One remembers the boy in "Lough Neagh Sequence" who believed he could be dragged into the water by eels. Elvers and eels seem to be symbols both of literary and mythological quest. In "Viking Dublin:Trial Pieces" we find the lines:

a child's tongue
following the toils

of his calligraphy,
like an eel swallowed
in a basket of eels,
the line amazes itself.

The eels' shape here mimics the Celtic mind brooding and meandering over Norse art, but also provides a fitting emblem of the self-contained, self-referential mystery of art. Ó Suilleabháin says that eels were associated with the devil and that there were many stories of them coming to life after they had died. They seemed to have inherited some of the serpent's power in the Celtic mind. To Heaney the eel represents an arbiter, messenger between land and water and, by analogy, the Otherworld. The eel represents not only the strong, phallic earth-based power of the Horned God and the power of sexual attraction generally, but also the magical fluidity of liquid reflecting the convolutions of mental and artistic processes and stories of shape-shifting. The eel is the world's 'live girdle' which binds man to sperm and salt – his biological origins.

The poem begins with the mouth, agent of communication and magical power in Celtic tradition (a person's 'other-self' or 'soul' was said to be able to leave the body by the mouth). 'Blastings' make one think of spells and curses for they can mean 'withering or shrivelling up caused by atmospheric, electric or unseen agency'. The personae becomes a microcosm for the world itself. As the tongue is 'dislodged' the 'hero' descends into an underworld to seek a remedy for the language. He finds himself in bogwater, and the elvers, keepers of mystery and art, attend him.

In "The Backward Look" a concern for language, namings, speech and physical movement blur together as if caught in the wavering trajectory of a snipe. The seven quatrains are bound together by the corkscrewing flight; the snipe is a creature both literally and metaphorically of the element that makes life bearable: 'he corkscrews away/ into the vaults/that we live off'. This is both air and the store of poetics and accumulated speech still alive around us. This bird is a catalogue of sounds:

> its nesting ground
> into dialect
> into variants,
>
> transliterations whirr,
> on the nature reserves –

We may detect an image of transcendence for the modern Irish poet. The bird flits through the 'sniper's eyrie' and 'twilit earthworks', conjuring up not only the rifleman and scarred roads of Northern Ireland today but also the forts and warriors of the troubled Irish past. In popular folklore the snipe is a hardy and wise bird. Diodorus Siculus expressly states that Druids predicted the future from the flight of birds and the Irish are known to divine future events from bird-calls. The Celts wrote of supernatural birds of various natures: some enchanted and brilliantly plumed flocks, and others malevolent and monstrous, winged creatures. The crane and other marsh birds were worshipped, but the snipe, a less obvious choice for deification, is not found in this retinue, perhaps because it is a March bird associated with the wind and madcap antics. One feels that the snipe here performs a similar function to the eel except that it unites sky and earth instead of water. The strangely part-bird, part-mammalian reputation of the snipe ('little goat of the air', 'bleat') make it a compound emblem for art and human potential. The Viking carving in "Viking Dublin" is 'a bill in flight', part of 'the craft's mystery'. The birds in "Saint Francis and the Birds" flutter up 'like a flock of words' and are 'the best poem Francis made'. These references remind one of the bird motifs in *The Book of Kells*, where birds, humans, decorative emblems and lines all find new unity in the interlacings and patternings. These patterns which bewitch the eye which tries to find linear connections seem to have evolved from the idea of the maze, which itself is a way to the Otherworld. This link between the snipe's flight and the maze is very instructive as far as Heaney's poem is concerned. The snipe in "The Backward Look" performs a 'sleight' of wing, an act of craft or wisdom, and 'it corkscrews away' describing its own spiral. George Bain thinks that 'The Chronology of the ornamental symbols commences with spirals'. He continues:

The circle may be considered as man's first step in art...
The spiral is an application of its constructional methods
that rapidly become magical.

The maze and spiral are brought to mind again in linguistic trade-routes and in the 'fieldworker's archive' — crop-patterns, rotations of grains, another type of ancient design. The snipes in "The Backward Look" (a look into personal and linguistic history as well as the Orphic gaze toward the artist's beloved) are in complete contrast to the rocketing and catapulting snipes in "Dawn Shoot", where the rhetoric and the bird's military and abrupt flight betray the limited perceptions of the personae.

"Oracle" starts with an injunction echoing ritual directions: 'Hide in the hollow trunk/of the willow tree'. The basis of the sonnet is a simple game of hide-and-seek, but it shows a sensibility literally encased in nature. The seekers 'cuckoo' the hidden person's name and this has a startling correspondence in Professor Ifor William's work. He writes:

it is because the cuckoo utters its 'where?' so
constantly that it is represented in early Welsh poetry
as a Kill-joy; for 'cw-cw' pronounced 'ku ku' means
'where, where?'

But the cuckooing here entails more than this, for the children's voices enter the medium of pure sound where all cries, twitterings and songs merge; they too are immersed deeply in nature. The oracle has complete hearing: 'You can hear them/draw the poles of stiles'. It is as though the whole range of experience has become accessible, compressed into this moment of childish ritual. The willow tree too is a vital part of the mystery. As Culpepper says succinctly, 'The moon owns it'. Its connection with witches is so strong in Northern Europe that the words 'witch' and 'wicked' are derived from the same root of 'willow'. It inspires eloquence and is sacred to poets since it endowed Orpheus with his musical gift in the grove of Persephone. The tree listens: it possesses lobe and larynx and the childish words 'mossy places' link its interior with the birth of sexuality.

"The Other Side" anticipates poems (particularly in *North*) which deal with the rival traditions, matriarchal Catholicism and patriarchal Protestantism. The division could have been presented in a simplistic way, but there is a distinct irony in the description of the Catholic family: its 'mournful' rosary, lack of Biblical teaching and untidy acres are as much part of the farm as its fertile homeliness: 'our fallow,/nested on moss and rushes'. The Protestant farmer swatting weeds recalls the sky-worshipping invaders conquering the ancient tillers of the land. Like

118

David or Moses he represents Yahweh, a foreign god 'too big for our small lanes'. He is shown as an isolated figure, well-schooled in the Old Testament, but scared of sexuality, faltering 'on a rut'. The rosary is a 'lovemaking' to his ears and the final desire to communicate the price of seed shows the persona recognising the cost of family life, the community as opposed to the individual. The poem is strong because it reveals the vulnerability hidden inside the farmer's aggressive stance and does not indulge in simple dichotomies as some of the poems in *North* are apt to do.

In "Linen Town" a civic print is unfrozen; pen and ink reveal the clearly-defined scene down to the last detail: 'It's twenty to four/by the public clock'. The picture is suspended, almost a de Chirico plaza: 'Under bracketed tavern signs,/The edged gloom of arcades.' The poem recalls a time when possibilities were running out for Ireland. J.C. Becket writes:

> In spite of these weaknesses and dangers the constitutional experiment of 1782 might have succeeded but for the French revolution. For Ireland the effects of this were fatal. All the elements of unrest were encouraged, and it became more and more difficult to maintain the authority of government.

The date Heaney probably refers to in "In Twelve Year's Time" is the start of the rising on 24 May 1798. It was put down in a very cruel manner, especially in Wexford, but it had established:

> a tradition of revolutionary violence which, from that time onwards, has exercised an influence, varying in strength but never negligible, on Irish politics.

The 'young McCracken' of the third stanza is Henry Joy McCracken, a supporter of Wolfe Tone, who encouraged an uprising in Ulster after the real impetus of the rebellion had already subsided. His fate was typical of those of other minor leaders. In 1799 the Act of Union was passed, disenfranchising eighty Irish boroughs and limiting thirty-two others to one member each.

The unusual suspension of the line: 'This lownecked belle and tricorned fop's' could refer us either to the tongues of the observers or to the fashionable 'tongue' of the time. The inversion of the phrase makes us wait for the possessive 'fop's' to find an object in the words 'swinging tongue', admirably imaging the waving of the hanged corpse and the eloquence of the executed leader. The water-tint both 'fetches' and 'fences' us in. Such prints have become greatly valued but in spite of the quiet streets it depicts, it also anticipates the rise of sectarian hatred and so 'fences' North and South, Catholic and Protestant, from each other. Like those who gathered to watch the hanging, the art enthusiasts miss the savagery of the scene and the historical events which succeeded it.

"A Northern Hoard" opens with lines asserting the power of dream and sidereal rule over a woman's body. The love-act is displaced as the

119

narrator locates the opening 'fault' which is both a geological fissure and the cause of 'siren and clucking gas'. The alternative to the 'pale sniper' isolated in his anaemic and obsessively phallic hostility is an act of conjuration where the flaw or fault of a tribe is 'dreamed' and transmitted into a plant and the plant then uprooted. The shrub is soaked with the blood of previous generations and the mandrake with its human-shaped root and human shriek seems an ideal repository for a nation's guilt. The 'Earth-sac' must be uprooted or the centre-tree, the Tree of Life of Ireland, will petrify or become the stump of the third section.

In "No Man's Land" the persona is a deserter, abhorring complicity in and responsibility for the suffering. But Ireland is still 'my smeared doorstep', a single building with its 'lumpy dead'. The palms like streaming webs are both shattered tropical trees recalling Hiroshima and hands blown to a horrible gauze-like consistency. Spirochete is a spirally undulating bacteria which causes syphillis and severe fever. The Irish troubles have escalated to germ-warfare and even the dreamer, the filid, is powerless to avert false healings. With "Stump" we switch to a Bosch-like scene where the 'plague' has become a ghastly witch's sabbat and the persona is a carrier, a spirit as destructive as the riders of the Apocalypse. Yet he is also the victim, the 'cauterized stump'. Is this the genius of the uprooted mandrake or the Irish consciousness which is implicated in and victim of its own violence? The question is loaded: 'What do I say...?' The narrator both asserts desolation and yet insists upon his need to translate the disaster by turning it into words: 'Hallowe'en finds man and nature amputated again:/The turnip-man's topped head'. Anne Ross writes at length about the Celtic cults of the head and concludes: 'The human head was regarded by the Celts as being symbolic of divinity and otherworld powers'. Therefore headhunting was an effort to exorcise the temporal and spiritual powers of rivals. In *The Mabinogion* Pwll's head possesses powers of prophecy but in "No Sanctuary" we find no hospitable well or spring temple protected by skulls. The ancient festival, the Samain of the Celts, here symbolises the death of a culture – Christian belief is nullified by the death mask's stare. Harvest is inverted to a death-rite. The successive denigration of the people and their return to and reliance upon pagan customs remind one of the final passage in *Fishermen with Ploughs*. In both works there is a suggestion that man needs to return and look into the undifferentiated energy, the chaos at the heart of the unhallowed light.

"Tinder" goes back to the Stone to 'tinder, charred linen and iron'. Man is stripped of his accoutrements and Heaney's question is the same as Brown's:

> Huddled at dusk in a ring,
> Our fists shut, our hope shrunken?
> What could strike a blaze
> From our dead igneous days?

The motif of flames repeated here has replaced the vegetative centre and, though 'flame-pollen' seems to anticipate the growth of a new energy, the fire dies. The ground has been razed for the possibility of new histories and fertility, but also for new self-destructive 'Gomorrahs'.

Heaney has written:

> I have always listened for poems, they come some-
> times like bodies come out of a bog, almost complete,
> seeming to have been laid down a long time ago,
> surfacing with a touch of mystery.

In a similar way, when Heaney first saw Glob's photographs of the sacrificed bog victims, the images of his dead grandfathers and the faces in coffins during his childhood 'surfaced' into his mind. "The Tollund Man" is Heaney's first real attempt to use an emblem capable of containing a common adversity and averting threats of cultural amputation and loss. As always, it is a linguistic quest as much as an intellectual one. The names 'Tollund, Grabaulle, Nebelgard' become almost like words whispered over a rosary – they are at once ciphers of common imaginative ground and of racial memories. Killings for an Iron Age Goddess of the boglands are recorded throughout Northern Europe, including Ireland. But, as Heaney is to infer in *North*, these Jutlanders and their language are related to the Vikings who settled in Ireland.

In the first section Heaney's gentle description echoes Glob's writing:

> his peat-brown head,
> The mild pods of his eye-lids,
> His pointed skin cap...

Heaney draws upon metaphors of honey, treasure and vegetable life to describe this man – almost an offgrowth of the peat – he seems to be a compression of a fairy or peat-spirit, a changeling and a sacrificed king-priest: 'Bridegroom to the goddess'. The fourth stanza realises a masterful combination of sexual, geological and religious power in the image of the tightening torc. Cernunnos was supposed to possess an ornament with this power, but we also remember the myths of strangulation associated with the female sexual organ. The purity of the 'saint's kept body' is seductive for a poet, intent on describing complete empathy with nature.

With the second section, the voice fills out with fervour and the figure of the Iron Age priest is finally realised. The Christian and hallow-ed is defied: 'I could risk blasphemy'. In a swift flourish Heaney's persistent image for ritual fullness – a cup, monstrance or stoup – is presented in its ancient Celtic form and located in his heartland: 'consecrate the cauldron bog'. Then there is the sudden profession of a shared and re-awakened 'centre' of power: 'Our holy ground', and a plea for fertility to an anonymous pagan deity, the dead and the transfigured Tolland Man: '...pray/Him to make germinate/The scattered, ambushed/ Flesh of labourers'. These lumpy corpses and horribly spattered young brothers contrast violently with the mild picture of the Tollund Man. The enemy seems a nemesis, trailing the brothers for miles along the rails like the hunters in "Dawn Shoot". This poem seems to have 'arrived' so easily — there is no straining or uncertainty of image as there is in "A Northern Hoard" which basically deals with similar needs. It is this ease (in spite of the narrator's outrage) which makes the poem beautiful, but which almost finally negates the horror of the brothers' deaths by making them acceptable in juxtaposition with ritual.

The 'sad freedom' of the third section shows the victim's total trust in the Goddess, his acceptance of his sacrificial role. Beyond thoughts of violence and savagery, these emotions forestall any immediate judgement from the reader. His death was at least part of a framework of belief and it held a meaning within the seasonal and agricultural rhythms of a people. The seeds in his stomach are 'winter' ones and his triumph in death was the dream of high-standing summer corn. The violence remains as a tension beneath the surface of the poem — perhaps the man was an unwilling victim and his was an unsuccessful sacrifice; the narrator is a prisoner of his own formulations and mythic idealism. He is left 'Unhappy and at home'. The 'man-killing parishes' (such incongruent words when juxtaposed) are too much like his own. The second section remains a threat but one feels that the myth will not actually support the narrator. The passionate outburst is startling and impressive and despite the qualifying 'could' of the first line it is a speech which is recalled again and again in Heaney's later work.

In "Nerthus" there is a confluence of movements in weather, wood, grain and peat. The wood takes the moulding of weather but also provides a signpost for the landscape and heat for men. There is a photograph of a stick representing the goddess Nerthus at Foerlav Nymolle in Glob's book: it is long, thick, and split into two branches about half way down. Glob says:

> The branch in itself possessed natural 'feminine' form —
> suggesting a slender body, rounded hips and long legs
> and only the most distinctive features had been added
> by working or carving it. The sex was shown by a strong
> incision where the fork began... Head, arms and feet were
> all lacking, and it is perhaps just because of this that the
> female character of the figure is so apparent.

But the ash-fork staked in peat is also strongly phallic, especially as it suggests an 'unsleeved' limb. Cleft ashes have long been known as objects of fertility and reverence. It is the tree sacred to Woden and there is another link between Nerthus and the lord of the Norse gods. There is a goddess called Nerthus occupying a minor position in the Norse spectrum of deities, but as Glob writes, she was a great goddess and inferior to none in her own cult-areas:

> this goddess was being worshipped as far back as the
> Neolithic period, as we know from depictions of her on

122

pottery vessels. She was carried in amulet form at the
end of the Stone Age, although it is only the indicating
necklaces that tell us she is concealed in the slender
forms of these pendant ornaments...

The fork in "Nerthus" is aesthetically beautiful and deeply resonant on
a totemic level, seemingly reminiscent of Tantric lingam-yoni symbols
depicting the interpretation of the two cosmic principles. The fork is a
'found object' and a 'spoken' object, a word — 'Nerthus': 'For beauty,
say an ash-fork staked in peat'. I would stress the 'say'. It is a human
utensil like a word that has been let sink and grown back into the
elements. A 'Kesh' is a causeway and a 'loaning' is a space between un-
cultivated fields; the unusual wording heightens our sense of the poem
as an object, a statement cut from the silence with precise and sensuous
words tapering off with the soft feminine 'er' endings.

"Cairn-maker" is a poem which draws off those unconscious creative
impulses which are inseperably linked with a reverence for Nature. The
persona may rob the stone's nest but only to 'betroth' rock to rock and
to preserve a balance. Heaney has what Snyder would deem a proper
respect for his natural materials: 'And dressed some stones with his own
mark./Which he tells of with almost fear'. Nature reciprocates his care
by honouring the small cairns with flowers and plants. This man seems
allied with the stoneworkers of the Mesolithic and Neolithic ages with
their fascinating drystone craft, corbelling and balancing huge capstones
and dolmens. Ireland is rich in Neolithic structures; it is estimated there
are over a thousand megalithic tombs on the island. The Burren mentioned in the poem is an area of County Clare where there is a great
concentration of small-chambered cairns. They were used for communal
burial, but do not form a cemetery complex. The Burren, with its fine
pastoral landscape, must have attracted these people for its farming and
grazing potential, though arrow-heads indicate hunting was practised.

The poem is about a congruence of instincts; the idea of erecting
stones as a covenant with the gods seems to have permeated most cultures. The man is 'strangely' affiliated to the ground, to that which he
touches and handles. After the act the fecund flower imagery blossoms
with suggestive names: 'ladystock', 'heather-bells'. The 'male' power of
ordering and initiating the relationship of rock to rock, the prerogative
of Adam, has been exercised with a care and attention which has been
rewarded. The persona, following an urge familiar to the disciples of
Jung, has participated in a 'love-act' with Nature and the 'fruit' of this
relationship thrives as the land relaxes after contact and artistic climax:
'Blowing in each aftermath of wind'.

The first three poems in the second part of the book deal sensitively
with intimate emotion and the real stress underlying contact between
the sexes. Heaney's grasp of detail is remarkable: the slightly sick effect
of the 'demented bride' in "Wedding Day", the mother's heartbroken
memory of 'glistening back', 'small boots' and the vague inkling of

something unwholesome 'dogging us' in "Summer Home" reveal the poet as a master of the apparently simple but keenly-weighed scene.

From considerations of a wider national and personal mythos we move to immediate and frank emotion. The first line of "Wedding Day" initiates the reader into the current of feeling: 'I am afraid'. There is pain and panic behind the ritual – the finality of marriage becomes horrifying. Only the half pitiful, lowly graffiti of hopeful love and the wife's bodily presence help the speaker out of fear. The swift emblem of the 'skewered heart' and the ambiguity of 'legend of love' show that sexual relationships are tenuous but also reach back to the origins of romance as we know it, to the world of the troubadour and courtly love.

The presence of spirits and unseen pressures fill the air in "Summer Home" as it starts with a question, an intimation of something gone wrong. The wind off the dumps recalls Ó Suilleabháin writing that a sudden change of wind could kill and the verb 'dogging' gives us a sense of an underworld, of the hounds of Annwn, Cerberus and Anubis. The mat is an ancient symbol of the female sexual organ and the taboos which surrounded it, but, of course, here it becomes an image of a covering hiding the rot of a relationship. The very air is 'possessed'.

The scene of the narrator 'bushing the door' and the small 'lost weeping' hold profound mystic significance. Cherry was connected with the Nativity in a version of the story written by, as Graves calls him, a pseudo-Matthew. These are blooms for a goddess – the rhododendron, noted for its evergreen leaves and opulent flower, is a fitting emblem of undying fecundity. The figure entering the door arrives like a disguised visitor from faeryland; half-flower, half-man, another reference to the shapes in Celtic border-work. The weeping figure seems to conjure up any number of myths about human lovers pining after their supernatural consorts – the 'belling' cry on one level recalls fairies, pleas for supernatural attention, and, on another, echoes the death-cries of Actaeon transformed into a hunted stag by Diana. The line 'on my name, my name' holds the music of gathering despair and confusion and modifies the rhythm for the 'fall' into the gentle elegaic: 'O love, here is the blame'. The desire to externalise pain and compact it into a concrete image is felt again. Heaney uses his persona as the parabalist and maker of ceremonies re-aligning old and efficacious emblems of power, marrying them with a new intensity to offset fear. The blooms become 'frank', plainly bespeaking their new role. May is the month of the greatest of purification ceremonies and for the Celts meant the wearing of greenery instead of the straw of winter. It was the dawn of a new and orderly day when doubtful forces could easily be averted by certain herbs and flowers placed over the door. But May marriages (and hence altars) were also perilous affairs, a fact embodied in the sexual tension of the poem. Captured in the dainty music of 'taint', 'sweet', 'chrism', we find the flower-offering decaying into an oil for annointing. We are led to the admonitions of a priest.

The third section reveals the persona's awareness of the limits of his ceremonies, his readiness to posit healings, and the fourth couplet, in a splendid small flourish, catches him in the act of postulation. To 'tent' means to attend to, but also to probe, anticipating the 'blade' image which in turn swiftly embodies the May combatant. 'Tent' is also a word for a red wine used in the sacrament. The wound is both healed and opened by the annointing. Human formulation does not necessarily lead to peace – wine transubstantiates in the Mass but the persona remains doubtful. The poet's healing is a manipulation of vision: pictures and words like:

> as you bend in the shower
> water lives down the tilting stoups
> of your breasts.

In the bathing female we have the Goddess of Love, Aphrodite, the foam-born. The images of life – breasts, woman, water – are seductive and perhaps deceptively so. In "Aisling", a poem from *North*, the artist is Actaeon, victim of the Muse's temptation, the exhausting search for the effective and meaningful word or phrase. In "Summer Home" the poet is tempted anew by the goddess bathing. 'Stoup' in itself is a precise and evocative metaphor for the breasts, continuing the cup and chalice imagery.

The line changes to an irregular unit of four syllables, and we realise that this splitting grain refers us back to the ash-fork in "Nerthus". The poem becomes a series of referential statements. It is as though an illuminator of a Celtic scroll is working and re-working certain key images and patterns into the texture of the work. This splitting is 'unmusical' in contrast to the verbal and visual harmony attending the vision of the bathing female. However, it prefigures a real healing. The path to the heart of all growth is taken, but only after a painful crisis, a splitting.

The hot foreign night and children weeping bring the poem to a sudden grim and matter-of-fact impasse. The short words and decasyllabic hard line, the curt Anglo-Saxon roots: 'We walk the floor, my foul mouth takes it out', stress the already uncomfortable images, but the maize and vine speak of a potential fullness and fertility. The grapes, unlike the stoups, are filling slowly and surely even though their weight is a 'burden' hinting at Christ's sacrifice, the seed that must die. The pillow is a symbol of unity displacing the lice-infested mat and the dawn attends obeying the priest's instructions. The shift of scene to the cave's dripping dark calls to mind the subconscious world of the couple. Mircea Eliade writes of old stream-thronged caves being considered 'mothers' of mythical generations and, of course, some experts think of the Spanish caves at Altamira as the wombs of civilisation. Here love exists microscopically but certainly. The poem follows a centrifugal course – from the air possessed by spirits, through the flowers and vegetation myths, through the wound and possibilities of healing to Nature, sap

125

and the dark underground. The white path of sap and the moist caves also summon up the basic healing qualities of sexual union.

In the wake of poems hinting at widespread female hurt – the pain of individuals collectively constituting the wounded Earth Mother – come poems of hybrids, changelings, nature spirits and unfortunates. Heaney was born into a land where the traditions of fairy abduction, fairies mating with men and fairy children born into human families are both ancient and yet 'close to the surface'. Lewis Spence tells of being taken to see a thin and curiously formed child with the air of a wise, old man. His parents assured him that the child was a fairy. It was popularly believed that fairies left behind a substitute for a person or animal they had taken. Often these substitutes risked exile from the community. These stories suggest two basic and complementary trends. Firstly, that these people tried to explain physical or mental abnormalities, psychic reverberations, strange sights and psychological quirks by creating a realm for them. Secondly, that this realm was given access to every aspect of the life of the individual and the community. A mad child was 'moonstruck', advice was always available from consulting the millions of omens around one, and the Otherworld, often existing parallel to this one, was a force to be reckoned with.

In the image of the girl stirring 'as from a winter sleep', uncradling her breasts, and wandering among cattle beyond the range of the headlights in "A Winter's Tale", we find another manifestation of the Great Goddess. She is cut from hedges and wires, restrictions of the dogmatic and narrow-minded people – the borders and barricades which divide the Irish consciousness. She is a 'maiden', a virgin of the hearth or Vestal who seems partly merged with the landscape: 'dewy roundings and folds'. There is, of course, the element of humour. The country people, exuding neighbourly courtesies and kindness, still greet the girl in the normal way when they find her naked in their hearths. In Shakespeare's *The Winter's Tale* Perdita is 'Most goddess-like prank'd up', and speaks at length of the desirability of lawful birth, sexual communion and 'an art, which does mend nature'. The girl in Heaney's poetry is unsocialised and wild, and yet she is also the symptom of a society which is increasingly involved with cars and wires, mechanisation generally, at the expense of human contact.

"Shorewoman" introduces the reader to three poems about the sea, The Gaelic proverb stresses natural and sexual bondings and sets up a network of tensions which come to bear on each word. Metaphors of weaving, machinery and geography are used to create an awareness of parallel realities and the actions of the poem shift between these planes. In the image of the dolphin 'hooped from tail to snout' we find a concealed poetic trigger which sends the reader's mind back over Heaney's verse to Yeats. In "Cana Revisited" a woman's womb is called 'bonehooped', and in "The Forge" we find hoops lying rusting among the other paraphernalia which, by implication, is the hoard of the artist's

126

symbols. It is the 'golden smithies' of the Emperor which 'break the flood', that 'dolphin-torn' sea in Yeats' "Byzantium". Heaney is well aware of the Celtic symbols of Yeats, the close weave of image-begetting images reminding us again of the thronging margins of illuminated scrolls and what Chadwick and Dillon call the artist's 'horror vacui'. Heaney has attested a similar horror:

> We are bombarded by the empty air.
> Strange, it is a huge nothing that
> we fear
> ("Storm on the Island")

"Shorewoman" is a poem consciously exhibiting itself as a 'new world', a created scene examining its own origins and delighting in the intricacy of its literary machinery. Anything 'hooped' might not just be ribbed but also man-made. The 'cold eyes, and bodies hooped in steel' in Hill's "Genesis" seem to be emblems of extreme ideologies in art and elsewhere. In Heaney's poem the porpoises and dolphins cartwheel like 'flywheels of the tide'; their backs are 'oily' and they are 'propelled'. Tightly wound into the images of machinery are sexual meanings, especially those to do with female sexuality. The small hill and 'viscous muscle' and sickness of the character 'beyond the head' need little comment. It is an image both of the hugeness of unknown psychic forces and of ignored female sexuality that we find in the whales 'collapsed' on the dunes. The shells — cockle, clam and oyster — are drawn in contrast to 'moving sinewed dreams' and are scrubbed hoards of moonlight. They are perhaps safe, manageable dreams and more assimilable female roles, the female body being ruled by the moon and drawn by the tides.

Paradoxically, in this poem which is extremely conscious of its artificial nature alongside its compelling physicality (even the sand 'riddles' the air) there is a real affirmation of the actual essence of fear. The old fisherman is described as 'all business'; he is taciturn and 'copes' with the fish, and his words are sparing but adequate. Yeats' "The Fisherman" shows a man who stands apart from his prey but Heaney's salmon fisher is 'annihilated on the fly'. Like the narrator in "Shorewoman" he is implicated in Nature: 'I go, like you, by gleam and drag'. If the figures in "Shorewoman" are male, the older man could be the impassive 'smithy' of his craft and the younger one alive to the flux of horrifying life outside the fixities of art. If, however, the narrator is in fact a shorewoman and the older man is her father the poem takes on a different air. There is the fear of a girl's own repressed sexuality and the line 'loaded against me' which fattens up 'towards the light' is obviously phallic. One must not forget the ancient nature of the patterns used here. Brown has used the weaving metaphor for the sea and Eliade has suggested that some of the oldest tribes on earth believed in the connection between the moon, woman, and the art of weaving. Both the sea and weaving can be seen as a mesh, and, to Heaney, poetry 'lies in the

127

summoning and meshing of the subconscious and semantic energies of words'. The writer of "Shorewoman" has involved us in a mesh where the strands of literary creation, mental and subconscious associations and ancient mythic patterns interrelate.

"Limbo" reveals a conflict of myths. The netted infant is a real child but bears a resemblance to the strange aquatic babies of Kingsley's *Water Babies*. Water is regarded as the primordial fluid of origin and the 'small one' is thrown 'back to the waters'. Once he is there he becomes an illegitimate spawning, a minnow. The woman's cross is not only the Christian disapproval of bastardy but also her own pain. Christ, perhaps in the tradition of the Fisher-King, is a fisher of souls and was himself imaged in the form of a fish,ιχθυς ,by early disciples. Christ cannot reach the child because this limbo of the unbaptised is an unlawful realm — 'some briny zone'. The reader is encouraged to infer that different moral perspectives exist outside the circumference of Church and respectability.

The statement at the beginning of "Bye-Child" prepares us for the tale of a voiceless mental cripple. Instead we discover someone more beautiful and terrible. The narrator confesses his perplexed uneasiness when confronted by the memory: 'a rodent/On the floor of my mind'. We remember the mouse-grey floor of "The Barn" and the two sacks moving in 'like great blind rats'. The child seems to be an inhabitant of the Unconscious — a lost human faculty. He is 'frail', luminous, weightless, and like the subject of "Shorewoman", he has been reduced to the bare grounds of his psychic presence. The Shorewoman, convinced of her right to lie 'fallow', becomes a 'membrane' like a protective hymen, 'between moonlight and my shadow'. The child has become a spirit, a little void, deprived of all human socialisation and development of personality. He 'stirs the dust' because he inhabits the 'outhouse' at the back of the human mind. The 'clue' to the final stanza lies in the words 'After those footsteps, silence;/Vigils, solitudes, fasts'. This child has been forced to explore territories quite familiar to the mystic — the sense of ego is beyond him, a yolk in the window outside.

The presence of the moon hangs over these poems. Artemis, the Moon-Goddess, presided over birth and the tree of life in Northern Europe. The moon rules dreams and poesy. She is the 'inconstant constant' Goddess who presides over faery and fluctuating moods and is associated with great mystery in the Celtic mind. The passive and female lunar power poses an alternative to the phallic and aggressive strength of the solar deities and heroes.

Heaney has sought after distances and unknown qualities: dreamworlds, the line between sanity and madness, the darknesses outside Christianity and recorded history. Here we enter a mind which has been forced to explore 'lunar distances/Travelled beyond love'. The distance is psychic too. The moon influences the laying cycles of hens but this 'henhouse' boy is all spirit. His love of light seems to suggest a growth towards physicality but he has already survived human stupidity and has tested heights 'beyond love', the furthest reaches of the soul's drift towards the unknown. The poetic implications are obvious too. The boy's wordlessness is eloquent. This is not just the stammering 'o' of a mouth but a restatement of the strength of inarticulate noise, breath and sounding in Nature. These can convey 'truths' which a system of evolved signals and ciphers cannot.

The mania to map and chart has resulted in the discovery of the life of atoms and molecules. It has, to a certain extent, resulted in a more complex and ultimately mysterious version of the Universe, but often it has stripped man of his reverence for the subject of his studies. California is a centre of the greatest probe into distant space which has ever taken place, but it was here also that scientists began to realise the limitations of strictly scientific observation. The map at the beginning of "Westering" is 'official', a damning term in Heaney's verse. Here is the heavenly body which has presided over these poems revealed in close-up: 'The colour of frogskin,/Its enlarged pores held/Open'. It is alive, conscious and receptive. More importantly, it is the same hue as the frogs who leap from the timeless slime in "Death of a Naturalist". Europe too has its craters at the Somme and Normandy and in the streets of Derry. But the cradle of civilisation has become an 'empty amphitheatre', (significantly shaped as if to receive a planetary sphere.) On the day of the Crucifixion the journey to the 'New World' starts, ostensibly leaving symbols of capitalism (shopblinds) and religion (still churches) behind. Roads 'unreel' as the metaphor of fishing from the previous poems continues. Each stanza is ravelled in its own coils of thought and we rediscover tightly-wound images that Heaney has used elsewhere. The moon's bony shine takes us back to the moonlit membrane in "Shorewoman" and cobbles like eggs seem to reawaken the idea of the Moon as a Great Mother/Hen, recalling "Bye-Child". The moon's stigmata show the Great Mother as the repository and carrier of the world's collective pain, but also reveals how the moon has been 'afflicted' by the attention of minds tinged by centuries of an exclusive Christianity. The final stanza can be interpreted as an ominous and humorous vision. For Heaney, the moon's dust is 'untroubled' and men's efforts to provide themselves with exhaustive knowledge are as presumptuous as an evangelising mission to the moon. As America witnessed the horror and power of a religion intent on converting the world, might not outer space? There is some real dread behind the playful logic. Perhaps the persona feels trapped — the myths of his past breed in his mind and prove inescapable. But organic life — 'frogskin', 'pores' and all — is also inescapable and is ignored at our risk.

The moon becomes a spherical image of eternity, the finished circle resolving the meshing of symbols and thought. Jacobsthal, in his essay "Imagery in Early Celtic Art", writes:

To the Greeks a spiral is a spiral and a face a face, and it

129

is always clear where the one ends and the other begins, whereas the Celts 'see' the faces 'into' the spirals or tendrils: ambiguity is a characteristic of Celtic art...it is the mechanism of dreams, where things have floating contours and pass into other things.

This tendency is particularly displayed in the poems in the latter part of this collection. The basic mysteries and concerns remain, but Heaney continually remoulds and redistributes his images until many layers of life and art are bound together and threaded with symbols. The first section of *Wintering Out* shows Heaney involved in enlarging the 'fetch' of his words, invoking issues of origin, speech, breath and mythic identifications with the environment. He has found a unique way to 'weigh' and balance these elements in his work whilst also invigorating them by recourse to the physical existence of words and their roots. His handling of psychological and supernatural motifs has grown subtler as he has 'fallen back' on delicate imagery and exciting rhythms of speech. In the manner of the great Celtic artists he has 'wedded' the different tensions in his work, the various allusions and elliptical references, into a single mesh where the line of narrative and detail becomes a single thread which crosses and recrosses itself as it scribes continually complex patterns:

> his calligraphy,
> like an eel swallowed
> in a basket of eels,
> the line amazes itself.

NORTH

The word 'north' rings with an un-Irish music. The Old-Saxon term is derived from Old High German, 'nort', or the Old Norse 'northr'. The boglands are soft and the culture is 'a congruence of lives', where houses stand rooted in a tribal totem of quernstones and relics that sinks away into the ground..Here, in this heartland, delving into the living past is easy. Even the roots of words lie revealed for the most casual etymologist. There is, however, a Gap that lies to the North; an entrance for the English and the Norse with their Sky-gods, Odin and Thor. The North is where the cliches and propaganda of TV men and journalists vie, and where a nation lies charred and divided. Out of the 'mother bog' and into the North, both the North of the mind and the real Belfast, emerges the narrator of these poems:

> Hughes' sensibility is pagan in the original sense: he is a
> haunter of the pagus, a heath dweller; he....appeared like
> Poor Tom on the heath, a civilised man, tasting and test-
> ing the primitive facts; he appeared as Wodwo, a nosing
> wild man of the woods... Hughes' art is one of clear out-
> line and inner richness. His diction is consonantal, and it
> snicks through the air like an efficient blade, marking
> and carving out fast definite shapes; but within those
> shapes, mysteries and rituals are hinted at. They are
> circles within which he conjures up presences.

This is Heaney writing of Hughes, but one feels tempted to provide a substitute: Heaney is the haunter of the boglands and riverside woods. He too tastes 'the primitive facts' and his verse sounds like a peatblade at times: 'Nicking and slicing neatly, heaving sods/Over his shoulder, going down and down.' He has used the persona of the filid and hermit, the isolated half-animal, half-man:

> I am...
> An inner emigre, grown long-haired
> And thoughtful; a wood-kerne
> Escaped from the massacre,
>
> Taking protective colouring
> From bole and bark, feeling
> Every wind that blows.

This figure operates from what he regards as the 'centre', the reservoir or the source. The consonants in his poetry are not the 'watchdogs' of the fluid life of the vowels. They are, as in the speech of his neighbours, the slight 'natural' impetuses which give full flight to the deep and resonant earthy sounds, 'Moyola/is its own score and consort'. Heaney has written: 'I think of the personal and Irish pieties as vowels and the

131

literary awarenesses nourished on English as consonants....'

Each line of unfurling and sensual vowels celebrates Heaney's Irishry, his 'gutteral muse'. Unlike Hughes, whose art is 'one of clear outline and inner richness', Heaney's craft is fully lodged in the various colourations, glintings and textures of the inner mass, whether it be vegetable, animal or mineral. The outer lights and darknesses are defined as the persona works outward from the centre. Hence the importance of the digger in his work, digging to get 'inside things' – to cut open turnips, to delve into circles of bones, to break into skulls to find 'compounded history' and to feel the music burst outwards from the gentle uvulations of his forbear's speech. His whole landscape tends to inherit this probing quality: stones and trees sink to become embedded and preserved.

He clearly feels the imposition of the English language. Rounding off his essay "Now and in England" he writes:

> I have simply presumed to share in that exploration
> through the medium which England has, for better or
> worse, impressed upon us all, the English language
> itself.

His persona recognises himself as an 'inner emigre'. The exile is imposed both internally and externally. He feels an alien, a poet distanced from the work-rhythms of his ancestors and from the streets ruled by the 'Ministry of Fear'. Yet his birthplace, and what one might call his 'ghost' tongue, are both Irish. He finds himself in the strange position of being at the centre and yet, simultaneously, digging to find it. Seamus Deane writes that Heaney belongs to Ireland 'as though his body temperature and that of the atmosphere coincided'. Deane's analysis seems a classic example of an enthusiastic reader confusing the real poet with the narrator. This mistake is unconsciously revealed in Deane's essay; for, if Heaney is already the genius of the Irish bogs, a guardian of the centre, why is poem after poem 'an act of recovery, then of hoarding?' One part of Heaney agrees that 'Description is revelation' and another part that Revelation is already available in place names, speech and buried treasures of bone and coin. The Irishman in the narrator is thrilled as he acquires the gift of poetry:

> Those hobnailed boots from beyond the mountain
> Were walking, by God, all over the fine
> Lawns of elocution.

But his name revealed another music already in his veins which would influence his newer poetic acquisitions,

> 'What's you name, Heaney?'
> 'Heaney, father'.
> 'Fair
Enough.'

One can hear the enthusiasm in the Catholic priest's entirely superfluous question as much as one can hear the disapproval and mistrust in the soldier's queries:

'What's your name, driver?

'Seamus....'

'Seamus?'

The name is as much a cultural hieroglyphic as the letters they find. Heaney feels an organic link with this music, a theme echoed in "Traditions":

Our guttural muse
was bulled long ago
by the alliterative tradition
her uvula grows

vestigial, forgotten

This tongue is in danger of being 'leashed'; it is wild, ancient and often concealed. Heaney can trace the 'living tradition' to the writers Daniel Corkery describes, and it even manifests itself in the work of an essayist like William Carleton.

Attitudes held towards the Irish peasant and his language are crucial for Heaney. He discusses Joyce's battle to retain integrity in his use of words, translated through the narrative of Stephen Dedalus. Stephen's attitude to the old Irish peasant in *Portrait* is very different from those views which Yeats, Lady Gregory, Synge and Douglas Hyde held. Heaney writes of how these other artists might have admired the old man's words, and goes on to say:

But, within the Joycean context, it is presented as a
parody, as stark ridicule. The cultivated, elaborate and
ironical Dedalus will not make a provincial dialect the
basis of a style, nor will he finally make the historical
wound of a language-shift, from Irish to English, the
basis of cultural politics.

This language-shift has made itself felt in the work of every major Irish writer in some way or other. In his lecture at Aberystwyth Heaney talked of how contemporary Irish writers had learned how the English language could be 'subdued' to the Irish experience. In fact it has become a 'native weapon'.

How does Heaney use this 'weapon'? This question is linked to both his sense of myth and history. How, additionally and importantly for *North*, does he use other languages? In writing of Hymn XXIII of Hill's *Mercian Hymns*, Heaney discusses

the liturgical and the Latinate of the first paragraph
abraded and rebutted by the literal and local weight of
'scraping their boots free from lime-splodges and phlegm...'

In "Bone Dreams" Heaney explores the depth and variety, the rich body of his own vocabulary:

Bone – house:
a skeleton
in the tongue's
old dungeons.

I push back
through dictions,
Elizabethan canopies.
Norman devices,
the erotic mayflowers

of Provence
and the ivied latins
of churchmen

to the scop's
twang,.....

Both of these examples show how Heaney is able to write in the very linguistic terms he is describing. However, neither passage is a good example of the full subtlety of his etymological attention. To Heaney as to Emerson, every word is a fossil poem. I have chosen "Strange Fruits", an unrhymed sonnet, to lay bare some of the traditions that have captivated this poet.

The roots of the words in the first line are evenly spread. There is the Germanic shortness of 'Here is the girl's head', the clinical Latin of 'exhumed', and the French construction 'gourd'. Then come the blunt Latin dissections: 'Oval-faced, prune-skinned, prune-stones...' Then to add a feeling of lightness and femininity there is the mixture of Old German and Middle English in the motions and airiness of: 'unswaddled the wet fern of her hair'. Again, as if balancing the words, we find the colder 'exhibition of its coil', which is, in turn, offset by the 'ai', 'ea', 'eai', 'th' and 'ty' sounds of the next line. The words 'perishable treasure' bring together a Roman scrupulosity and sense of mortality and a Greek awe, touched by the gentleness of old French consonants. The splendid, rough and earthy texture of the scene is never forgotten as we hear the Old Saxon and German sounds: 'Her broken nose is dark as a turf clod'. The fruit is 'strange', not just because it is human, buried and ancient, but also because it is described in a foreign tongue. The foreigner here speaks English, but the quoted authority is a Greek, representative of another martial culture. The contrast between the fastidious historian and geographer writing his confession and experiencing 'gradual ease' (words with the courtly feeling of Medieval Latin and French) and the barbarian victims, starkly recorded in Old Saxon and Norse words: 'Murdered, forgotten, nameless', is obvious. To give the poem a sense of unity we return to the mixture of Latin and Germanic forms found in the first lines. The beatification, though presumably German in realisation, is a Latin term. The final line reaches up through common Germanic to Latin 'reverence'. The flatness of the phrasing emphasises how the barbarian sacrifice has historically 'outstared' the Latinate awe. For Heaney, words are compounded historical weights — correctly used they can unlock cells of past thought and feeling. Myth is inextricably linked with the evolution of words. Kennings and old expressions often provide linguistic ties with ancient myth; the names connected with myth — Antaeus, Nerthus, Diana, Actaeon (to recall a few that Heaney uses) — are often clues to the function of the myths. Further, once 'interpreted', the name of a god might reveal a long-neglected figure or image that recurs compulsively in the human psyche. Thus Heaney might re-discover:

> Our holy ground and pray
> Him to make germinate
>
>   ....ambushed
> Flesh of labourers

in the Tollund man.

What of Heaney's use of Latin and other quotations? In "Whatever You Say say Nothing" we find the lines:

> I believe any of us
> Could draw the line through bigotry and sham
> Given the right line, *aere perennius*.

These words, meaning 'more lasting than bronze', drawn from the thirtieth ode in Horace's third book of Odes, reinforce the general linguistic tension of the verse. Desire for order may have brought these solemn Horatian lines to Heaney's mind but there is also a glance towards posterity here, towards the lines which have outlasted centuries. In the following poem "Freedman" we find the Latin phrase '*Memento homo quia pulvis es*', or, 'Remember man what dust you are', in the centre of a scene which connects Belfast and Rome. In fact, the original text of this poem was called "Romanist Poem". Heaney is using his knowledge of the Classics as a subtle weapon exposing the tracings and linkings between language and ideology. By analogy we can imagine how his acquaintanceship with Shakespeare, Keats and Hopkins is being drawn on in his work.

One might recall the 'rift', a stylistic and thematic gap between the first and second section of *North*. Hooker writes:

> Part II consists of poems that confront the tragedy of
> Ulster more personally than anything which this poet has
> published before. In my view, it is, for this reason, less
> effective than Part I, although parts 4 and 6 of the em-
> phatically non-Byzantine "Singing School" belie this
> opinion. It seems to me that, even in Part II, where he
> writes of the divided north and of his own self-division
> metaphorically, using his primary imaginative sources,
> he writes both more powerfully and with more effective
> directness. The tragedy is far too deeply rooted in his
> Ireland, in himself, for it to be expressible in either
> purely political or self-consciously personal terms.

I partly disagree with this evaluation for reasons I shall discuss. What is made clear in this passage is the linguistic gap between the dense quatrains of "Hercules and Antaeus" on one hand, and the semi-prose of "The Unacknowledged Legislator's Dream" coupled with the conversational narrative of "Whatever You Say Say Nothing" on the other. In the first section of the book Hercules triumphs over 'earth-starred denizens' and the second section finds us inside the war-scarred North. This, of course, has its literary implications. The rhetoric is modern, ironic and swift. Words have become blunted and 'journalese' has contributed to this idiom:

> Who proved upon their pulses 'escalate';
> 'Backlash' and 'crack down'; 'the provisional wing',
> 'Polarization' and 'long-standing hate'.
> Yet I live here, I live here too, I sing.
>
> ("Whatever You Say Say Nothing")

The poet cannot and, if he is to communicate with a large audience, must not, ignore the changes in the written and spoken word. Heaney therefore includes the very slang of the media which he always mistrusts and sometimes hates.

* * *

The First Part of *North* is enveloped between evocations of the life and death of Antaeus. In "The Municipal Gallery Revisited" Yeats has written that he and two contemporaries relied on 'contact with the soil' for inspiration and that from this contact '....everything Antaeus-like grew strong'. According to Diodorus Siculus, on his trip to fulfil his tenth labour Hercules sailed to Libya where he killed Antaeus – a monster who had constructed a temple of skulls. The name Antaeus literally means 'besought with prayers' and Heaney's details reveal an old deity of the earth:

> I rise flushed as a rose in the morning
> ...rub myself with sand....
> Girdered with root and rock.

Heaney is well-versed in notions of mythological history – the old struggles between Catholic and Protestant possibly necessitate this. The personification of the Earth turns the reader again to the Earth Mother. Mircea Eliade writes

> One might say that the Earth Mother constitutes a form
> that is 'open' to, or susceptible of, indefinite enrichment,
> and that is why it takes in all the myths dealing with Life
> and Death, with Creation and generation, with sexuality and
> voluntary sacrifice.

The conflict here is between a culture reared on such a responsive and inclusive myth, that of an ancient earth divinity, possessing strength but reliant on vital connections with the soil, 'the cradling dark', reverence for animal life and an attention to rights of indigenous peoples and an invading clan of sky-worshippers. This solar cult is based on hero worship. Hercules (in his aggressive Latin form) long known for acts of

136

savagery, embarked on his tasks in expiation for killing eight youths in a fit of madness. He was armed by the Olympians and sent out to kill lions, hydras and to prove his mastery over monsters and animals in general. His principal allegiance is to Zeus, the sky and thunder god, and as Heaney writes, the hero's future is 'hung with trophies'. He represents a masculine, aggressive power, not just of brute, but of intellectual proportions: 'the challengers intelligence / is a spur of light'. He brings with him the concept of measuring: distance and time, embodying the dissection of the Universe into manageable units in contrast to the cosmic ideas of Pre-Socratic philsophers like Parmenides and Heraclitus, who saw the world as an indivisible entity. His second power is to feed 'off the territory'': both the foreign soil and the very notion of territory, the ethic of personal possession. Finally, he succeeds with 'banks' (in a capitalist flourish): 'Antaeus/high as a profiled ridge'.

Hercules is the son of Zeus and a mortal woman (if one likes, he is the first mortal to 'rise'). His quest for fame is ultimately crowned with his achievement of Immortality. Up has been heaven and down hell for centuries. Christians worshipping another 'sky-born' son of God and a woman beat back Sitting Bull and his 'pagan' followers and fenced off their lands. However, certain speeches by Indian leaders show that they had no concept of owning the land. The Danes massacred forces led by Byrthnoth at Maldon. The Northmen were worshippers of Odin and Thor, also sky-gods. Balor, the one-eyed robber god and King of the Fomors was blinded by Lugh, the sun-god, in another great battle. Balor, also a giant, champion of the mysterious old race, was defeated by the Tuatha de Danaan, powerful invaders who were to dominate all Ireland. These examples provided in the poem, accumulate to create the impression of a collective myth: the patriarchal peoples' worship of an omniscient sky god takes precedence over previous cults (often previously tolerant of one another) in a violent rupture of the social fabric.

However historically accurate this process is (and one is tempted to regard it as another concealed 'golden age') it is a myth which has importantly affected the work of Heaney and Brown. Heaney has said

.....and it suddenly struck me that Antaeus is beaten, that Hercules comes along, lifts him off the ground and sweeps him out of the way. The Hercules-Antaeus thing came to seem to me as the myth of colonisation almost, that Antaeus is a native, an earth-grubber, in touch with the ground, and you get this intelligent and superior interloper who debilitates the native by raising him, taking him out of his culture, his element, and leaving him without force. You could think about Ireland in those terms; it's almost rudderless, culturally.

The ground of the 'poem' is Ireland too, running with the inland waters that Heaney has written of in many poems. Antaeus lives among 'her river veins, every artery, secret gullies'. Eliade writes at length about the subterranean world, considered as the womb of the Earth Mother and the rites connected with these beliefs. Water blending with earth creates the basis of fecindity.

The 'v' of Hercules' arms could be the Roman or Italian 'Fascisti' 'V' or that of Victoria Regina or, of course, Churchill's famous gesture supposedly signalling victory for Western democracy. At an equally threatening level it could be the widely-known overtly sexual sign of the vulgar aggressor.

With these two poems we are given the idea of a central conflict of culture and belief in *North*. However, one feels that even Hercules is preferable to the looming bulk of Chaos which follows in his wake ("Summer 1969"). The next four poems: "Belderg", "Funeral Rites", "North" and "Viking Dublin:Trial Pieces", have at their axis the idea of the continuity of Irish history (glimpsed in the reference to Breughel in "The Seed Cutters") and its interruption by Vikings. At another level the raiders are part of that continuity. Have there not been waves of invaders since the dawn of Irish memory: the Cessair, the Partholon, the Nemed, the Fir Bolg and the Tuatha da Danaan among others? However, these peoples were supposedly of a different ideology from the Viking invaders. The early 'proto-Irish' fought in order to settle the land, but the Vikings sought booty and knowledge, 'geography and trade'. In "North" Heaney recalls the Danes: 'hatred and behindhands' and in "Viking Dublin" their

> scoretaking
> Killers, haggers
> and hagglers, gombeen-men,
> hoarders of grudges and gain.

None of the 'Thor's hammer-blow' of their violence is forgotten:

> With a butcher's aplomb
> they spread out your lungs
> and made you warm wings

In "Belderg" a friend of the narrator views history purely in terms of cultural deposits and challenges the poet's exclusive recourse to the Irish language in the study of place-names: 'But the Norse ring on your tree?' Suddenly, all the alienation and bitter memories of the Norse, the human enmity, are like 'marrow crushed to grounds' between the quernstones of successive cultures, forming one 'world tree'. This tree is underground, a spine of quernstones stretching downwards towards 'the first plough-marks/the stone-age fields, the tomb'. The terror as well as the mystery of these cultural strata is felt. The speaker cannot allow himself the luxury of ignoring a foreign culture which has influenced the Irish landscape and consciousness.

Part of Heaney's concern has been to relocate and make efficacious the assuaging ceremony, and in "Funeral Rites" he juxtaposes an actual funeral against a private vision of public ritual. The cupmarks in the stones at Boyne have been interpreted in various ways but Heaney has used the cup or stoup as a sign of fertility. The 'serpent' formed by the cortege is an old symbol of fecundity. The crowd descends into the 'healing' dark which is tomb, womb and symbol of the mystery which surrounds them. This descent from the streets of Belfast, the bloodshed of 'each neighbourly murder' into the neolithic tombs, is endowed with the sense of pagan vision. Entry into and re-emergence from the dark are perhaps the most ancient of all human metaphors for death and re-birth. Like a funeral, the poem has three parts, and the third turns to another feud. In his reading at Aberystwyth Heaney talked of forgive-ness displacing a welter of blood revenge in *Njal's Saga* when Gunnar dies. In fact, in the Saga, the writer, although acknowledging Gunnar's mercy, shows his ghost extolling his own honour and strength. It is this stance which determines Hogni and Skarp-Hedin on a trail of brutal revenge. Although Flossi and Karri, the surviving protagonists, finally forgive each other, Heaney does seem to read a forbearance into Gunnar's thoughts which is not there. In some ways this parallels his and Glob's Romantic treatment of the bog-sacrifices. Heaney uses Gunnar as Brown uses Magnus, but with considerably less justification to do so. Gunnar fits somewhat uneasily into the idea of arbitration. For Heaney, Gunnar is beautiful here because, 'though dead by violence', he seemed to see outside the vicious circle of death and oath-killings for a second. The poet strains to make a ceremony at the heart of the Irish troubles — the Boyne area — and in the hope that this burial could be a sufficient arbitration for all the Irish dead. The Viking names could, at last, rest easily upon Irish landmarks.

Heaney's narrator is to learn from the Norse sagamen and court poets, and to school himself in their word-hoards which are part of his own mind and history. Myles Dillon and Nora Chadwick write:

> The fiercest impact of the Viking attacks on Celtic lands
> was on Ireland...two Norwegian leaders together made
> Dublin the chief centre in Ireland, and the base for their
> fleet operating against the coasts of the surrounding
> countries.

We move to the 'nubbed treasure', the trial pieces which follow the course of man's attempt to carve the record of his physical and imagin-ative life. David Jones would be at home in these delicate pictures of 'found objects':

                    a small outline

> was incised, a cage
> or trellis to conjure in.
> Like a child's tongue
> following the toils
> of his calligraphy...

> ...interlacings elaborate
> as the netted routes
> of ancestry and trade.

The features of the artifacts and those of their makers overlap. The line is a child's tongue, a bill in flight or a swimming nostril.The poet turns his pen from a child's line mimicking a ship into the mud of time, aware of the apparently specious nature of his efforts: 'jumping in graves,/dithering, blathering'.Hamlet, descendant of Saxo's Amleth, in his turn a fossil-figure descended from the folk literature of Iceland, Ireland and Denmark, enters the poem as the poet's surrogate, as he kight have been for Shakespeare: 'skull-handler, parabalist,/smeller of rot' (the pause here suggests vegetative and animal decay but the meaning is compounded as we read): 'in the state, infused/with its poisons,/pinioned by ghosts/and affections'.

In Section 5 we find ourselves inside the Viking tradition. The first line echoing a popular song and the rhythms set up in the second stanza prepare us for the strange appeal; the Vikings are as much Heaney's fathers as the native Gaelic speakers: 'Old fathers, be with us'. The call upon the wisdom of ancestors is a tribal convention. The longship becomes a womb; it bears a child and has 'mother-wet caches'. Yet it threatens to fulminate and is bristling with concealed violence. Its shape is also phallic, sword-like and it cuts into the soil as much as the horror of contemporary bomb-blasts. But when the human vitriol has evaporated, the bones lie mutely and the hull becomes a trove for the curious, like deposits in bog-loam.

Dublin becomes a vast tribal House of the Dead, a landscape of skulls, a print by Dore or Goya. The skulls are both symptom and cure of the Irish problems. The persona sees 'compounded history/in the pan of 'an old Dane', and sends his words hunting; words that dig, uncover lost causes and old quarrels in the conviction that the key to dissension lies, not solely in belief or language, history or the land, but in all of them. Jimmy Farrell in Synge's *Playboy of the Western World* is quoted at length in the final passage. his speech spliced with echoes of the Graveyard scene in *Hamlet*. The wild man, the 'failed Oedipus' questioning after his supposedly dead father, clumsily trespasses on the diction of Hamlet's courtly conceits. The 'trouble' in the State is exposed for all to examine.

In "Bone Dreams" we turn to another invading ship — the first discovery: 'White bone found'. Metaphors take flight, and the ship, likened to a stone, is wound into the narrator's 'sling of mind'. The tongue flickers into what becomes the body of the English language: 'strange fields'. Groping past other influences the Saxon longhouse is reached. The hall is seen to frame the horizons of Old English life; it is here that Heaney, echoing Bede, discovers a metaphor for the transitory nature of life — a bird flitting between windows, caught in the light for an instant. The Saxon language seems implicitly governed and limited by these horizons.

The ship in the grass becomes a 'love-nest' of the memory and the sailor's minds are full Britain, their goddess and lover. The speaker becomes glaciers, screes and a chalk giant, shifting his shape round the memory of a chalk pebble. The whole process of the physical transformation: '..ossify myself/by gazing:' recalls the shamanic techniques. There are many levels to this language and the link between sexuality and the land is not least among them. But the male entity, the aggressive chalk giant, begins to dominate the land and his stance becomes actively martial: 'I have begun to pace/the Hadrian's Wall/of her shoulder'. The successive invasions of metal bearing patristic peoples led, eventually, to the Roman Conquest and the Maiden is finally 'castled'. In the mole the speaker finds another symbol of England. The cameo of the dead creature is touching, but is this not, partly, English material power that Heaney describes in the words 'a big-boned coulter'? The little points of eyes are pitiful and sinister, indicating the blindness of England's imperial expansion. Finally, the whole of England becomes 'a play of grass and grain/running South'. A land preying on other lands. Like the persona, the mole is a digger, but here the animal is a microcosm of a much more acquisitive and merciless nature (glimpsed in the 'thick of a chisel') than that embodied in the peat-digger.

The main foci of the six following poems are the bog, its murdered and preserved victims, and clusters of sexual and pagan themes seen in the context of history and the land. The bower of "Come to the Bower" is another threshold of the dark and the past. The 'dark-bowered' queen waits to rise in "Bog Queen":'..from the dark,/hacked bone, skull-ware,/frayed stitches, tufts,/small gleams on the bank'. She is, at once, a buried victim and the mighty goddess, Nerthus or Danaan, in her darkest aspect. In "Punishment" her sexual proclivity is to the fore: 'the wind/on her naked front. / It blows her nipples'. In "Bog Queen" the female entity is older; her sash is a 'black glacier' and 'phoenician stitchwork' covers her breasts. The 'queen' in "Come to the Bower" seems the epitome of fertility:

> My hands come, touched
> By sweetbriar and tangled vetch....
>
> ...spring water
> Starts to rise around her.
>
> I reach past
> The riverbed's washed
> Dream of gold to the bullion
> Of her Venus bone.

Even the beheaded girl of "Strange Fruit" is described in terms of fecundity: her head is a gourd and her skin is the texture of prunes. The narrator has become an artful voyeur, creating his own object of sexual indulgence from the skull, and the ground is the 'insatiable bride'.

The narrator of these poems is and is not Heaney. That is to say, often the narrator could refer to Heaney and his experiences and feelings are analogous with those of the poet. However, obviously, there are times when, although the figure of the poem is a projection of Heaney's mind, a physical identification is impossible. For example, in "The Unacknowledged Legislator's Dream", a strange heroic, almost cartoon, figure emerges, and, in "Act of Union" the first person singular seems to be England speaking. It seems best to posit a character somewhere between the real poet and the totally discrete narrator. This figure might be called 'Heaney as narrator' since the poet is the first to acknowledge that his life and art intermingle. Where other entities are stressed in the first person our interpretation of them will necessarily vary from poem to poem. At a basic level, of course, the narrator is a cluster of words, an artifact, not a man.

If the 'woman' of the Bog Poems possesses interwoven sexual and mystical motifs, so the narrator emerges as a definitely-formed figure. He is the seeker, the weigher of 'beauty and atrocity':

> Who will say 'corpse'
> to his vivid cast?
> Who will say 'body'
> to his opaque repose?

He is the observer and recorder of history:

> I almost love you
> but would have cast, I know,
> the stones of silence.
> I am the artful voyeur.

He is instinctively a pagan disguised by a veneer of civilised responses. After the sacrifice he would

> ...connive
> in civilised outrage
> yet understand the exact
> and tribal, intimate revenge.

In "Kinship" he becomes an offgrowth of the peat itself, 'Kinned by hieroglyphic, peat'. He does not seem to have to 'reach past' or push through to his origins:

> I step through origins
> like a dog turning
> its memories of wilderness
> on the kitchen mat

His progress is easy and the ground receptive. For example, as he raises a turfspade

> the soft lips of the the growth
> muttered and split,
> a tawny rut

The bog is both mother and lover for him. It is a love implicated in the soft ground's more treacherous aspects; Heaney even recalls the forbidden thrill, the mysterious attractions of the deadly:

> I love this turf-face,
> its black incisions,
> the cooped secrets
> of process and ritual.

Seasonal shifts and human ritual are intimately related on this ground.

Section III of "Kinship" stresses the sexual role of the goddess very emphatically. The steam and sun, rich images of fecundity, are mentioned as a 'cloven oak-limb' is raised to twin that 'obelisk', the wettish shaft embedded in the soil. The phallic nature of these objects, the pagan significance of the love-nest disturbed by the limb and also the dual lengths of wood (possibly horns), compound the mystic depth of the poem. Love for the goddess, loves of dead individuals and the general fertility of the land are simultaneously expressed. The oak's use in druidical ceremony, and the 'trembling' bog cotton recalling the female principle, also heighten the sense of polarities in the poem. The narrator is aware of timelessness again as he faces a 'goddess' in an oak-limb, the 'they' who raise the oak could as well be ancient devotees as peat-diggers.

In Section IV Heaney restates the Yeatsian line with a decisive assertion: 'This centre holds/and spreads'. This modifies the 'bottomless' and wet centre of "Bogland" and the spawn-filled flax-dam of "Death of a Naturalist". Here the life is contained and the phrase 'bag of waters' reminds us of the cosmologies of early peoples who considered, like the early Norse, that the seas were bounded by a simple cup or vessel:

> each open pool
> the unstopped mouth
>
> of an urn, a moon-drinker,
> not to be sounded
> by the naked eye.

The 'bag of waters' and 'urn' images are, most obviously, microcosms of the bog, 'the melting grave', which is both a process and a preservative. Heaney is addicted to anthropomorphisms: the mothers of autumn, another pagan Triad emerges. The seasonal cycle disposes each plant, moss and heather to deposit its own propitiation (their bronze echoing the tribute of men). This 'bronze', the humus — chemical base of peat and the matrix for other growth — is the 'vowel of earth' that dreams of its present and past 'root' in its creations. Such wording has poetic and theological implications. It is possible that Heaney is referring to the mud and primeval slime out of which Homo Sapiens and speech eventually came. The vowel, common denominator of speech, becomes allied with humus, matrix of life. Nature is not, of course, simply orderly, and strange mutations occur, even in the weather, but, generally, there is the interaction of elements which create the environment: 'a windfall composing/the floor it rots into'. Out of these strange, sometimes arbitrary forces the persona 'grew', 'like a weeping willow/inclined to/the appetites of gravity'. Did the persona wish this elevation? The hunger of gravity sounds even more crippling than the 'insatiable bride' and 'the hungry soil' with their dark pressures. He might, like Antaeus, fear 'my fall', but all growth entails this fear. The 'fall' is part of the suffering which has been a constant feature of Irish rural life. Man also must return to the soil before he can possess the bronze of humus; he must eke out his own richness in life but with a respect for the natural processes.

As a devotee of the Nature gods might list the attributes of his deities

143

so the Speaker in Section V calls to mind an old acquaintance: '...god of the waggon,/the hearth-feeder'. The Peat-Digger is Prometheus, bringer of warmth and light to a community. The man is deified because of his archetypal function and because the narrator recalls his own childish awe for a skilled and indispensable worker. The speaker feels privileged to be this man's 'attendant', bearer of bread and drink, a veritable cup-bearer. The titles move from attendant to squire, stressing a range of cultural association and the passage of history casting our attention back to the first two stanzas. The Celtic circle is glimpsed in the 'hand-carved felloes' and the waggon-parts buried 'in a litter of turf mould' are again 'made flesh': the 'socketed lips of the cribs' and 'cupid's bow of the tail-board'. Most of all, as we read of the waggon-god, saluted, given right of way, whose word inspired the speaker's esteem, we think of those Celtic chieftains and charioteers of heroic legend and especially *The Tain*. Just as the nature gods are realised in seasonal shifts, as 'summer dies' and winter is born, the peat-digger assumes his full stature.

In part VI the poet turns to Tacitus, historian and geographer of Imperial Rome. There exists in Tacitus' work, at least in the *Germania*, a conflict between the Roman recorder intent to describe the superiority of the Imperium in contrast to the barbarian kingdoms, and the man who sought to judge the foreigners fairly. D.R.Dudley writes:

> Though aware of the defects of the Germans, Tacitus
> accords them something of the colouring of the Noble
> Savage in contrast to the corrupt Roman world.

One must, however, remember the context. Dillon and Chadwick write:

> ...from the time of Vergil to the 5th century AD, the
> proud Romans looked to the Celtic peoples as living
> 'beyond our world'.

The Romans never reached Ireland, but there were plans for its invasion, and Tacitus recorded these in chapter XXIV of *The Agricola*. The first stanza rings with a violent indignation and a macabre pride which would sound inflated were it not for the actual dead of Ireland. We find the grove in a lake dwelling banked with corpses. The dead are 'fearful', anticipating a growth of bloodshed. The pagan mind makes another centre. Dillon and Chadwick write:

> One of the fundamental features of Celtic religions is
> the wide prevalence of sanctuaries connected with
> natural features, especially, springs, rivers, lakes and
> forests.

The sacred grove was the central sanctuary of Druidic religion. Heaney has assembled, in one image, ideas of a composite centre which drops down through wood, water, flesh, and history: the occult focal-point of Celtic religion. The narrator in "Punishment" senses a hidden equilibrium behind the savage acts. From the 'sacred grove' of his art Heaney faces outward to the English culture. The English (like Julius Caesar, observing druidic rites) stand aghast at the slaughter:

...they lie gargling
in her sacred heart
as the legions stare
from the ramparts.

In spite of the blockades of Belfast Ireland is still a 'sacred heart'. The irony, awe and keenness of the voice are so forcefully compounded here that it is difficult to disentangle them. The narrator invites Tacitus, the civilised man divided against himself, the faithful and yet biased 'scriptor', back to Ireland. He had written

I have often heard Agricola say that Ireland could be
reduced and held by a single legion with a fair-sized
force of auxiliaries.

But the narrator replies to the Romans, to the English soldiers, politicians, Irish terrorists, sympathisers and perhaps, most despairingly, to himself '....where nothing will suffice'.

The statement 'We slaughter for the common good' is full of dark irony. In spite of the fact that primitive tribes do practice euthanasia for the benefit of the community and human sacrifice was regarded as efficacious, does anyone profit from slaughter? The prospect of political and social schism makes us examine the words 'common good' very carefully. There is a horror of the professed eloquence and bland surety of these lines admirably 'rounded off' with the ambiguous aside: '...report us fairly,...'. The narrator is trapped within his own admiration of the beautifully-preserved dead and his recognition of the patterns of 'casualty and victim' which attempt to 'pacify' the earth. There is more than a hint of the old John Barleycorn message here, but Heaney's persona is more implicated in the Celtic past, its skull cults, ceremonies and beliefs than Brown's characters. The complex of aesthetic, spiritual and social ideas contained in this voice threatens to tear it apart. The goddess is the focus of these ambiguities and keenly-felt dilemmas. She '...swallows/our love and terror'. This goddess is clearly representative of, among other things, Irish chauvinism in its many forms. Heaney is quoted as saying that in the Iron Age of Northern Europe there was:

a society where girls' heads were shaved for adultery...
a religion centering on the territory, on a goddess of the
ground and of the land and associated with sacrifice. In
many ways the fury of Irish republicanism is associated
with a religion like this, with a female goddess who has
appeared in various guises. She appears as Cathleen ni
Houlihan in Yeats' plays; she appears as Mother Ireland
... I think the republican ethos is a feminine religion in
a way.

One feels that Heaney is so close here to saying that republican violence is the dark side of Catholicism, the destructive aspects of the pre-Marian Goddesses which have not found a 'home' in Christian doctrine. This goddess recalls a world outside the narrator's knowledge and yet

145

she reflects the mysterious, irreconcilable elements in his own nature, towards which he reacts with love and terror. Finally, the speaker mingles with the devotees or drops into the impersonal language and doctrine of the faceless crowd where the response is 'love and terror'; there is no middle ground. This poem does not achieve the resolution of "Funeral Rites", yet it is a much more powerful work. The poet's dilemma is strikingly conveyed in the final anonymous and grim tone; it is a response we are to remember at the book's close:

> As I sit weighing and weighing
> My responsible *tristia*.
> For what? For the ear? For the people?

"Ocean's Love to Ireland" is a poem swept along by waves of memory, from the picture of physical rape framed against the ancient thought-patterns: 'He is water, he is ocean...' to the ground 'possessed and repossessed'. Ralegh's poem, "The Ocean to Cynthia" speaks of the 'powerful empery of sorrow in loss'. The 'empery' of Ireland is well founded in loss, in dispossession and invasion. Elizabeth called Ralegh 'The Shepherd of the Oceans', but he replied that even the oceans were ruled by the moon. Ralegh's poem was conceived with Cynthia (Propertius' literary name for Hostia) serving as a mask for a queen. In the work Ralegh adopts the pose of a wronged lover; a deeply ironic stance when we realise that he was responsible for a number of colonial experiments throughout Ireland, and that in 1580 he helped to put down the Irish rebellion. Colonel San Joseph, despatched by the Pope, landed at Smerwick Harbour. Ralegh, under the command of Ormond, beseiged the fort and massacred over 500 of San Joseph's soldiers. The irony of the poem is convincing. Ralegh abuses one land, personified as a maid, whilst worshipping a fiercer matriarch. Spenser's *Faerie Queene* lauds Elizabeth as a holy and supernatural monarch, and as Hughes writes:

> The Queen of England was already, automatically, the
> representative of the old goddess — the real deity of
> Medieval England, the Celtic pre-Christian goddess with
> her tail wound round those still very much alive pre-
> Christian and non-Christian worlds.

The Irish loss is simultaneously linguistic, sexual and national, but the 'ruined maid' cannot, unlike the land, be possessed. She is the central muse of a long tradition of "Aisling". The very essence of Irishness, she recedes into the heart of Nature, into the centre, 'ringlet-breath and dew'.

In "The Betrothal of Cavehill" gunfire 'barks' questions but cannot answer them. Heaney outlines the differences between north and south:

> And the profiled basalt maintains its stare
> South: proud, protestant and northern, and male,
> Adam untouched....

The associations of 'guns' pointing upwards, aggression, the menacing 'they' and the groom's car set against the hideouts and vegetation linked with 'my love' seem over-stressed. One recalls D.H.Lawrence's fine descriptions of the feminine part of the most determinedly male souls, or Brown's lines about Viking women and their concealed but dominant roles in the preying and killing. Heaney's formulation seems crude in comparison. The probabilities that these gunmen are not virginal Adams 'before the shock of gender', and that they have learned to suppress those emotions they regard as feminine, are left unexplored. The gunmen could, however, be Southerners, their guns challenging the Northern male-oriented power. They could be gunmen for the goddess, recalling the Tuatha and the charioteers fighting for Danaan. One feels though that if these layers are present the reader has to supply too much. The 'parable' remains a stark outline, a relief cut from intractable igneous rock.

The second section of *North* starts with a dream of fabulous strivings – a hero feeling out known weak spots. It is a dream of failure. It is as though Heaney is facing himself through his previous work and con- cludes that his attempts to communicate the terrorism, wounds and possible cures in Ireland have been as fabulous as this cartoon hero from a TV serial. Even this caricature, endowed with impossible strength, is captured and gaoled. The technique alters; the narrator turns to the reader mouthing Heaney's succulent word music, savouring the textures of rich description. Just as the 'hero' finds himself trapped, the narrator suddenly speaks and his tone is accusatory, personal and unavoidable, trapping the reader in his detached role of aesthete: 'Were those your eyes just now at the hatch?'

"Whatever You Say, Say Nothing" could be Heaney's first attempt to use the language of the English, 'journalese' and new verse forms as a weapon. Where can the conscientious, socially-concerned poet go from 'I'm cauterised, a black stump of home'? One of the major ascendants in British poetry Heaney has also, in writing of his homeland, come to a dead end. The public await his new 'fashionable' collection and expect to find the narrator going through his bag of wordy 'circus tricks' in an attempt to convey the horror of Ireland. Heaney has found that he has had to write himself into a 'new history'. This history must be recorded in a new way. In Bailey's article, Heaney takes issue with Yeats' remark that the artistic intellect is forced to choose between the perfection of the life or the work:

> He thinks life must be intertwined, a continuum. He is
> anxious to keep 'a gift for being in touch with what is
> there, hidden and real, a gift for mediating between the
> latent resource and the community that wants it,
> current and released.'

However, he is careful not to respond too directly to what Bailey calls 'the compulsions of the times'. Yet Heaney does seek for the 'chink', or 'a small leak' – the way through to communicate the horrors in a compassionate and responsible way. As is proper, he remains tenta- tive over the direct influence poetry has on a situation but does discuss the need for a solution: 'changing the structures of feeling'.

147

"Whatever You Say, Say Nothing" consists of four sections of alternatively rhymed quatrains. The tone is direct and personal and the diction consciously the language Heaney hears around him: 'Oh, it's disgraceful, surely, I agree,'/'Where's it going to end?'"It's getting worse.' Such rhetoric is a betrayal, not a redemption of popular sanity, as it reduces pain to a few stock phrases. Even the vitriolic voice of the dissident has been hushed: '...the heretic/Has come at last to heel and to the stake'. The conviction is steadily pushed home as each layer of excuses is ripped away. The very modes of speech and thought have been blunted and although 'I believe any of us/could draw the line through bigotry and sham...' the right line is not given: 'I am incapable'. The title of the poem is given a sinister twist: 'And whatever you say, say nothing'. Heaney draws from Horace and from *The Aeneid* and street-lore, but the reader is left with the bare human necessities: 'a bite and sup,/We hug our little destinty again'. Hooker adheres to the opinion that Heaney writes more effectively when he brings his 'primary imaginative resources' to bear upon the troubles. Heaney is grasping for a different kind of 'resource' and effectiveness in these poems. I find "Exposure" a convincing and powerful poem precisely because it contains both 'self-consciously personal terms' and 'his primary imaginative sources'. The strident voice of "Whatever You Say...." has been modified and Heaney has found a valid way of combining everyday personal awareness: 'How did I end up like this..../For what? For the ear? For the people?' and the figures springing from an imagination feeding off Irish history, landscapes and legends: 'a wood-kerne..../Taking protective colouring/From bole....'

"Freedman" tends to serve as an introduction to the six 'Singing School' poems. Originally, a prose poem entitled "Romanist", the last paragraph read:

> Caste marked annually, I went among the Freemen of the city for their inspection. In forum and theatre I felt their gaze bend to my mouldy brow and fasten like a lamprey on the mark. In vain I sought it myself on the groomed optimi, on the hammer heads of lictor and praetorian. I was estimated and enumerated with my own, indelibly one with the earth-starred denizens of catacomb and campagna.

The original obviously holds echoes of *Mercian Hymns*; the use of Latin and natural detail is similar. Hill, however, has left Roman remains underground much as Heaney finds Norse relics under Dublin. But Rome never conquered Ireland (at least not by invasion) and to this poet it represents a power, both foreign and repressive. The English and Northern Irish Protestant cultures represent one aspect of this Roman stranglehold. Another aspect of the Roman influence is, of course, the Roman Catholic Church, especially in its more negative and dogmatic form: 'I was under that thumb too, like all my caste'. Heaney has added a verse to the original; he tells of a salvation by poetry that even Stephen Dedalus might find naively idealistic. Heaney juxtaposes the two views well; the idea of a slave rising above himself and attacking his cultivated 'saviours', and that of a repressed victim hitting back within the culture of his enemies. The writing also apes the Latinate English of academic institutions and the Churches of England and Rome.

> ...Manumitted by parchments and degrees,
> My murex was the purple dye of Lents
> On calendars all fast and abstinence.

The poem, as it stands, is a less cohesive picture of the 'slave in Rome'. but in a series of abrupt glimpses it conveys a cluster of ironies and recalls a chain of images running through the book. The gazes like lampreys, and the hammer heads (of the prose poem) take us back to the phallic influx of seaborne forces of the Viking and Ralegh. The mouldy brow and earth-starred crowds recall Antaeus and the power of the soil. They are lines spoken by a 'man of the earth' submerged in an aquatic and predatory environment.

The transplant that Wordsworth suffered as a child serves as a foreword to poems mirroring a much greater cultural shock. Bailey writes that Heaney's family

> moved from Mossbawn when Heaney was 14, and though
> the new farm was not distant the effect was to seal off
> his childhood, almost hermetically.

We can only imagine what the move to Bogside meant —

> I was so homesick I couldn't even eat
> The biscuits left to sweeten my exile.

Heaney knows what it is like to be fostered by 'beauty and by fear'.

The quotation from Yeats speaks of a friendship between a stable-boy and a lad from the land-owning classes allied only in their mutual zeal at a time of a war which would help create the present situation in Ireland. The title "Ministry of Fear" holds at least three layers of meaning. A 'Ministry' can be a department of government, a supernatural office or ordinance, or a 'fostering', an exercise of care on behalf of a person or persons. Heaney's old life follows him through the lines with the images of mountains and ivy — a scent of hay. Words, particularly names, had already acquired that 'hieroglyphic' effect for the aspiring author threatened at gunpoint. Fear here is institutionalised, but Heaney recognises almost wryly that such terror and inquisition helped speed and intensify his art.

The dark, threatening figure obsessed with 'census-taking' and arithmetic and associated with machinery and the phallic fire-arm in contrast to the organic lines of turnips and potatoes, looms into the boy's life in "A Constable Calls". The helmet of officialdom has left a bevel in his head suggesting machinery again, and the 'domesday book' under his arms refers us to the 'arch-helmeted' Norman invaders. The ticking of his bicycle fades into the drums of Tyrone in 1966. The drummer seems

149

the very personification of the crude anonymity of Irish internecine violence. There is the sky imagery (thunder, raised up, air) and the phallus ('balloons at his belly', 'between his chin and his knees', 'seasoned rod', 'He parades behind it'). The drums almost become vast diseased phalli. The skin is scourged and the human 'buckles under' his message. The stethoscope is possibly the probing phallus of modern science testing the sway of aggression; the imagery of this poem is blurred and strained as if the noise and hatred have misted the artist's vision.

Heaney finds it difficult to forget his centres: '...stinks from the fish-market/Rose like the reek off a flax-dam'. As the festering flax symbolises overweening human pride and nature's revenge in "Death of a Naturalist", so the fishmarket, full of revolutionary gossip, conjures up dissent under Franco's rule. Here another culture with strong ties with Catholicism and old matriarchal values: 'Old women in black shawls near open windows', is submerged in poisoned waters thronged with uniforms. The centrality of Heaney's sense of responsibility and of his admiration of Goya are obvious. Goya's nightmarish visions recall the sky gods, cannibalistic and tyrannical. Saturn is the Latin counterpart of Cronus who led the Titans against their father Uranus and castrated him. Another sky-god, Zeus, was responsible for the death of the child-eating Cronus who had become a tyrant in his own right. To the Greeks Chaos was the first flux of matter out of which every god and living thing emerged.

Goya concentrated on the darker aspects of Chaos, linking it with the violence and corruption of the Spanish court and professional soldiers of his time. The narrator's excitement is evident as the poem returns to the jerkiness of a semi-prose:

>...Gigantic Chaos turning his brute hips
>Over the world. Also, that holmgang
>Where two berserks club each other to death
>For honour's sake, greaved in a bog, and sinking.

The identification is deeply felt as the Irish artist is forcibly made aware of historical and personal crises.

Hooker writes of *North*:

>...Breughel is the presiding genius of the first half, while
>the horror of Goya's "Shooting's of the Third of May"
>dominates the second. Seamus Heaney refers to both
>artists, but I do not mean to imply that his ways of see-
>ing are other than his own; only that he moves from a
>realism that is capable of depicting both the enduring
>values and hard facts of a particular social pattern, and
>works through historical and mythical elements, to a
>sense of appalled but helpless implication in a commun-
>al experience of terror; and from this to a consciousness
>of unheroic escape 'from the massacre', as 'an inner emigre'.

Heaney's 'choice' of Goya's paintings reveals his appreciation of, not just a local terror, but of metaphysical and cosmic schism realised in existence as a whole, and focussing back upon Heaney's particular landscapes.

"Summer 1969" poises a counterpoint to "Fosterage", a poem written so as to be stylistically opposed to itself. "Fosterage" is at once a history, an excuse and a denial. There are no words 'imposing on my tongue like obols'; rather, these are the bold flourishes and passionate gestures attributed to Goya:

> ...Me, newly cubbed in language, he gripped
> My elbow. 'Listen. Go your own way.
> Do your own work. Remember...'

The interjections are swift, clamorous and almost desperate. There seems little attention to the pressures of words and the real richness of Heaney's vocabulary. The two berserks clasped in combat and sinking – a microcosm of the Irish disasters – are offset by the two literary friends grasping at mutual encouragement. Bailey writes:

> By way of Glob and bogland, Heaney (till then the poet
> of a vivid personal landscape) began to find an answer to
> the question of what images and symbols might be
> adequate to the Irish predicament, now he could offer
> what Yeats called 'befitting emblems of adversity'.

In Goya's picture there is no break from the stranglehold. Often, Heaney's language has belied or at least undercut the bleakness of what he has described. It seems that in this section he has not allowed himself this luxury.

We are left with "Exposure". Alders and birches inherit 'the last light'. According to Graves, the alder marks the emergence of the solar year from the tutelage of night. Heaney is to write of 'protective colouring', and the green alder-dye is associated with fairies' clothes in British folklore. Graves adds:

> in so far as the fairies may be regarded as survivals of
> dispossessed early tribes, forced to take to hills and woods,
> the green of the clothes is explainable as protective colour-
> ing: foresters and outlaws also adopted it in medieval times
> ...Principally the alder is the tree of the power of fire to
> free the earth from water.

The wording 'protective colouring', details of nature spirits and the 'dispossessed', the emergence of the solar year and the connection between fire overcoming water, like the comet overcoming poisoned waters, all suggest that Heaney is familiar with Graves' book. Why then, if we credit Heaney with a knowledge of these correspondences, is the 'ash tree cold to look at'? The ash tree is the sacred tree of the god Gwydion, whose followers, according to Graves, seized supremacy of the national shrine in England from Bran's worshippers. We can add the name Bran to Heaney's list, 'Balor, Byrthnoth and Sitting Bull'. Graves goes on to write that in Ireland, the tree of Tortu, the tree of Dathi and the branching tree of Usnech, three of the Five Magic Trees, whose fall

in the year 665 AD symbolised the triumph of Christianity over paganism, were ash trees. In British folklore the ash is a tree of rebirth; it is
also the tree of sea power or of the powers resident in water. It is no
wonder that a tree that signifies knowledge to the Norse, rebirth to the
English, a violent seizure of a national shrine, and seapower, should be
cold for an 'earth-starred' Irishman to look at.

Birch-rods are used in rustic ritual for driving out the spirit of the old
year. The birch is the tree of inception. It is no surprise that Heaney
shows them inheriting the 'last light' on a December evening.

The persona seeks a cosmic sign. Those million tons of light remind
him of the light of haws and hips and his childhood. Instead, the earth
draws him again and he imagines a mud-lodged hero, kinned by mould
— a more substantial alternative to the Tarzan or liberator of "The Unacknowledged Legislator's Dream" or a David fighting against Philistinian
Sky-worshippers.

A meteor inspired Mohammed, but the narrator here is simply a
despairing human. A voice, at once intimate and self-conscious, yet
powerful, breaks through the imaginings:

> How did I end up like this?
> I often think of my friends'
> Beautiful prismatic counselling...

The apparent simplicity of these lines impresses one as the words unfold
in a flow of Middle French and Greek sounds. The following line holds
a strange resonance echoing the metaphors of some of the politically
committed writers of Eastern Europe or the harsher songs of a balladeer
or his modern equivalent. Heaney's line holds a compelling force if
simply because of its closeness to impulsive and unsoftened thought:
'And the anvil brains of some who hate me'. The 'anvil brains' are the
'hammer heads' of "Romanist" but we also recall the phallic anvil-horn,
flattening of iron for hostilities and Thor's hammer.

The question about weighing brings back all the questions of the Second
section: 'Have our accents/changed?', 'What's your name, Heaney?',
'What's your name, driver?', 'Any other root crops?'. We are led into the
ambiguous section:

> Rain comes down through the alders,
> Its low conducive voices
> Mutter about let-downs and erosions
> And yet each drop recalls
> The diamond absolutes.

Heaney has loved the let downs and erosions: '...each bank a gallows
drop,/each open pool'. Yet in each raindrop he finds the very 'diamond
absolutes': law, nationalism, religion, intractable politics, which cut like
diamond points through all he has written. "Plantation" revealed the
circle where absolutes do not exist, but the ideologies of his time are
fixed and abrasive. On another level, Heaney hates the 'let downs': the
lying and killing, the erosion of friendship, customs, speech and trad-

itions, and the breakdown of trust; the reduction of men's lives: 'Coherent miseries, a bite and sup/We hug our little destiny again'. The 'absolutes' become the stasis of art away from the rain whispering of decay and away from human fallibility and hatred. That artistic distance is to be admired and yet distrusted.

Despite the artistic permanence and the inflexible beliefs of his countrymen the central persona has become:

> ...neither internee nor informer;
> An inner emigre, grown long-haired
> And thoughtful; a wood-kerne.

Unlike Joyce, Heaney did not stay abroad but has accepted an inner exile. In taking the role of 'inner emigre' Heaney is courageously admitting his own particularly tenuous and isolated position. 'Kerne' comes from the Irish 'ceithern', and literally means a lightly-armed Irish foot-soldier, a peasant, or a boor. This hermit taking on protective colouring reminds one of Sweeney, the genius of woods, a wanderer of seashores and scrublands, who runs with the wolves and deer. Bailey writes:

> At Glanmore, Heaney began work on a modern version
> of a long medieval Irish poem, usually called the Frenzy
> of Sweeney, which he calls Sweeney Astray. Sweeney is
> an Irish King (in other words, a warlord) in County An-
> trim who is cursed by a local Saint, and, with the ground
> cut out from under him, goes flying round the country-
> side nesting in trees and hiding in ditches. For a green-
> fingered poet, Sweeney is a splendid mouthpiece — as
> Heaney realises — 'a man who lives in intimacy with the
> animal and vegetable world; a tongue almost of the land
> itself, a voice that utters its bleakness and beauty'....

Sweeney is sundered by dualities too.

His saga arises from:

> a culture that precedes the Norman and English invasions
> of Ulster...[it is] a work that allows two mythologies a
> home in its story. So, in one way, Sweeney represents a
> fallen establishment east of the Bann, tormented by
> hindsight; and yet in another way, he is a genius of places
> and cultures associated with West of the Bann. His story
> is like a prism but can refract different psychologies and
> break the hard light of opposing minds into a beautiful
> elegaic spectrum.

His is, in fact, a story which reconciles the 'diamond absolutes' in a circle of coloured lights. Heaney's statement about Sweeney being nearly 'a tongue of the land itself' is an emphasis upon ties between man and Nature which have not been stressed in popular life since Christianity, teaching, not man's partnership with Nature, but his separate soul and duty to be a 'good steward', overran the Irish pagan peoples.

The Sweeney-figure and the wood-kerne are intimately connected with that figure I have called the Shaman or filid. Both outlawed King and Shaman take the guise of animals, are 'tongues for the land', speak poems of power and are considered to be mad. Both speak of and to animals; both criticise certain rulers or politicians and both enumerate trees, plants and their properties. Their shapes underlie much of Heaney's verse:

> geniuses who creep
> 'out of every corner
> of the woodes and glennes.'

> small mouth and ear
> in a woody cleft,
> lobe and larynx
> of the mossy places.

> Nestrobber's hands
> and a face in its net of gossamer.

This is Dives, hoarder of common ground, or a last fabulous mummer, It is a man split between the poorland — the inheritance of Lazarus — and the 'old Gomorrah' of the city. With "Exposure" the stridencies of the Iron Age priest and the tribal Celt, accusing Roman invaders, are lost. After the charicature of the "Unacknowledged Legislator's Dream',' where the narrator speaks of 'muzzles' pointed at 'the butt of my ear' (the wording recalling Synge's Jimmy Farrell yet again), the folksy pseudo-Hamlet of "Viking Dublin" and the fervent writer of "Freedman", we are left with the voice of a humane and doubtful filid: doubtful of his responsibilites and of his abilities to fulfil them. The comet's omen is missed but perhaps 'these sparks' of words, this figure of the gifted hermit (part animal, vegetable and mineral) and the sympathetic stance that Heaney shows in this last poem will contribute towards altering the 'structures of thought'. It is no longer heroic to stay in the battle.

Heaney's 'parables' contain images of the centre which does hold, of the reconciliation of opposites and of the rituals which suffice. Heaney seeks to make men realise that they need not choose between internee and informer. He is continually 'overhauling' and revivifying his language in order to press home this point. The poem is his weapon — a touchstone with which he and others can sense out the physical and psychic territory which surrounds us: 'A poem is alive in an animal, mineral, and vegetable way.' The power of being a poet '...lies in the summoning and meshing of the subconscious and semantic energies of words'.

Contrary to the stated opinion, it is no 'meagre heat' he has found in such ideas and practices. The narrator has missed the comet, but, as usual, this poet has discovered the richest and most useful treasure by looking down: in his refusal to ignore previous failures; in the earth at his feet.

LOAVES AND FISHES / THE YEAR OF THE
WHALE / NEW POEMS

...it is more the look of the islands that suggests heraldic
stillness and a hoarded symbolism – quarterings on the
hill, pasture and meadow and cornfield, a slow change
throughout the year; and, older still, the great shield of
the sky swarming with azure and gule, and clouds like
fabulous beasts rampant.... Heraldry is the mysterious
signs, deeper than art or language, by which a family or
a tribe pass on their most precious secrets, their love of
a kingdom lost.

These words do not just help us to appreciate some of George Mackay
Brown's stylistic devices, they reveal a habit of mind – an art that
thrives on patterns. Like the quernstones under Pentland Firth which
grind out sea-salt, Brown's writing continuously hones down the bare
matter of human experience in order to reveal the significant signs. In
writing of the work of John Firth he comments: 'Labour in the fields
was seen as a ritual, a ceremony, a dance of bread'. The common and
backbreaking work of men is elevated to the level of religious observ-
ance quickened by the pangs of their hunger and poverty. Exactly the
same process is enacted in the tradition of the Ballad form itself where,
for instance, the seasonal round of sowing, tilling and harvesting becomes the Ballad of John Barleycorn. The basic unit of power and
meaning within this context is the word:

It is a word blossoming as legend, poem, story, secret,
that holds a community together and gives a meaning
to its life. If words become functional ciphers merely, as
they are in white papers and business letters, they lose
their 'ghosts' – the rich aura that has grown about them
since the start, and grows infinitesimally richer each
time they are spoken.

Mythical and cultural deposits are latent in words themselves but in
Brown's poetry there is the continuing demand for utility:

'Art must be of use', says Storm Kolson, the old blind
Orkney fiddler – 'a coercive rhyme, to strand a whale
in the rock, a scratch on stone to make the corn grow.'

Brown is not merely recording or using the patterns of Old Orkney
in his verse; he is reinstating their power in a modern idiom. They are
patterns in what he regards above all as a potent weave (and the metaphor of fabric is a favourite for this poet). However, there are mysteries
in the work. No attempts to render the word effective will succeed if
the 'ghost' of the word's evolution is not present. A poem seeks the
silence – the 'beyond words' and Brown's poetic personae are shown

beset with this difficulty. To Brown as to Hill the result can sometimes seem like a series of cryptic images rather than a poem; there is a desire manifest in both these poets' work to grasp for an alternative language 'rinsed' of shallow usage.

"The Masque of Bread" from *Loaves and Fishes* contains a ritual, but also a sense of doubt. It finds a resolution in the verse itself as the 'first steeple' shakes out its petals, 'Circled in order round the man that died'. It is a poem of a timeless scape. The archetypal street of doors (each door a year), the 'bakehouse' and masks of animals reveal a vivid ability to intensify and abstract detail:

> The loaf the bakers laid on the long shelf
> Was bearded, thewed, goldcrusted like a god.

> Each drew a mask over his gentle eyes
> — Masks of the wolf, the boar, the hawk, the reaper —

The poem makes use of a wide variety of legends. There are of course Christ, the Bread of Life, Everyman and the theme of Resurrection. There are also John Barleycorn, the Stations of the Cross, the convention of the masque, and older ceremonies of bread-making. The 'slum' of old age might be industrial but the setting for the rest of the poem seems to be allegorical, almost theatrical, reminiscent of Ben Jonson and Inigo Jones' elaborate masques. Even the poet is found 'seeking past a swarm of symbols'. The poem illustrates Brown's taste for strictly visual motif: masks, symbols, stations and heraldic signs. These conventions absorb vast areas of experience and reduce them to metaphors, patterns and archetypal, but nonetheless meaningful, stories. The tension between the archetype and the individual, the symbol and the experience, relevance and formlessness, is crucial in Brown's work. It is his determination to create a mythos which is large and far-reaching enough to embody contradictory elements which makes his work so powerful.

In "Gregory Hero" we see how a man is remembered in symbol. The very act of legend-making is being used and commented upon here:

> Five suns lit his dust.
> They're out, and for his death
> We yield him images; he was
> A Viking ship, a white stallion.

> Twelve winds knit his strength

The images are colourful and seductive, but the reader remains aware of the after-image of the actual man who lived. To Brown all art reduces experience to patterns:

> Poetry, art, music, thrive on these constants. They
> gather into themselves a huge scattered diversity of
> experience and reduce them to patterns; so that, for
> example, in a poem all voyages — past, present and
> future — become The Voyage, and all battles The
> Battle, and all feasts The Feast. This is to look at all

156

those events of time which resemble one another, yet
are never quite the same, in a symbolical way.

But, as he goes on to admit, 'the symbol remains an abstraction'.
It is the word 'again' in the third stanza which informs us that
this is the deathless 'Hero of a Thousand Faces', the subject of Joseph
Campbell's famous study. Finally, the poet addressing 'Tall virgins'
speaks of a Gregory who never dies and who will always pursue 'you
round the world'.

"Port of Venus" is, at first glance, a poem about the 'holy earl'
Rognvald at Narbonne, where he meets the Countess Ermengarde and
experiences the ideals of courtly love at first hand. But it is a relationship not a particular time and place which is described. Narbonne is a
'strange port' and Ermengarde is 'a girl with snooded hair, and shy cold
breasts'. It is the confrontation of a hawk and doves and the characters
seem to be 'types':

Events are never the same, but they have enough
similarity for one to say tentatively that there are
constants in human nature, and constants in the
human situation, and that men in similar circumstances
will behave roughly in the same fashion.

Brown's use of historical setting and narrative is coloured accordingly
with the emphasis on recurrence and similarity which at one extreme
folds history from the phenomenon of time. Hill in contrast would mistrust such parallels in history. He feels that events elude words and
human judgement, but to Brown the word is primal and contains a sacramental power as palpable as its accumulated historical meanings. The
Nativity in "The Lodging" and the synthesis of modes of writing in
which it is decribed are at the centre of Brown's art. The language is
sumptuous and finely-woven, rich in metaphor:

The stones of the desert town
Flush; and, a star-filled wave,
Night steeples down.

A ribald song, the tired Roman, the innkeeper, drunken shepherds
and 'queer pair' below — it is almost as if we are seeing a gilded, two-
dimensional painting by Simone Martini. The 'relevant' figures attend
their stations. The event is again popularised — we have the unspecified
'strange land', 'the desert town'. Drunken shepherds dance and the
inn-keeper rummages in the till. The impact of the poem is in its understatement; the Christian mystery has been folded back into ordinary
events and words, and the 'queer pair' below remain offstage.

The rhythm of traditional folk song and ballad informs "The Heavenly Stones". The setting is doctrinaire, part of traditional Christianity,
but the whole weight of the poem rests upon the mysticism of the signs:
the disc of gold, the perfume and the earthen bottle. The 'lightsome lad'
is obviously a Christ figure but, in his position as first person narrator in
the poem, he also seems any child, anywhere. The scene is the farm of a

patriarch, a comfortable if ordinary existence – perhaps a Utopia in Muir's sense or a state of pre-existence. Unlike Christ, the lad throws two of the gifts away, though, in ultimately choosing the cross, perhaps Christ did too. The use of number and colour connected with spiritual affairs is an old folk and balladic motif:

> ...three, three the Rivals
> two, two the lily white boys
> clothed all in green oh...

or another example is this verse from the ballad "The Royal Fisherman":

> Then he pulled off his morning gown
> And threw it over the sea,
> And there he spied three robes of gold
> All hanging down his knee.

Brown has written that 'the Reformation killed the songs and ballads of the people.

"The Heavenly Stones" is a conscious attempt to render new images and immediacy of vision in the convention of the apocryphal ballad of Christ's childhood. The 'Bread of Life' is here too, but the child remains oddly objective about the decisions. The crib and cross that his father makes are not compulsive or inescapable. The transcience of empires is mocked but it is still a shock when we realise that the decisions, the profound significances lurking behind the sprightly quatrains, are the whims of a child. There is something of Blake's shrewd naivete in that last stanza:

> I flung away the heavenly stones
> Yellow and black and red
> That I had played with all day long
> and, laughing, crept to bed.

The hallowed earth-and-life rituals dissolve into a child's laughter. It is a child's game which has made such knowledge bearable, just as some dances absorbed the rhythms of ploughing, scything, cooking and redeemed them from drudgery.

In *Magnus* Brown writes

> The body-spirit dichotomy, or the body-intellect
> dichotomy is a prideful cleaving of a man's nature.
> Earth and man and sun and bread are one substance...

This is not a colloquy on strictly Christian lines: to the Biblical Christ and Apostles a man's body was not one with his soul. But as Corbishley points out, it is a Catholic's belief:

> For the Catholic, all that is at all, because it shares in the
> good of existence is, so to put it, on the side of God. And
> man, half-intelligent, half-matter, stands in the centre of
> the created scale. Flesh and spirit combine to form one
> entity, flesh the instrument and not the enemy of spirit,
> spirit the master but not the slave-owner of flesh.

But this pre-supposes the dichotomy in the first place and Brown's view of history with its masks, costumes, patterns and redeeming laughter of a child seems to have more in common with mysticism and eastern religion. In such traditions all history would dissolve in a laugh for the child is God, and the whole epic has merely been God, in many forms, playing a game with Himself. Spirit and flesh are really one in such a belief, but Brown has compared the 'horrible goddess of plenty' to a 'vast and bland' Buddha and, in his stories, he seems to have little time for the Hindu cycles of reincarnation and the gradual erasure of Karmic fault. If we seek for a clue outside orthodox Catholicism to inform of Brown's view of mythic reality, it is to be found in mysticism. The Indian beggar in *Greenvoe* believes in the 'omnipotent life-giving Word' but, of course, he is conversant with the dark sonnets of G.M. Hopkins. The Sikh boy in "The Seller of Shirts" is studying 'The Topography of the Mystical Books of William Blake'. Both salesmen stress the legend of Krishna and his song which is Peace. Orthodox Catholicism stresses the unity of spirit and matter but does not really admit its realisation on earth. Mystics experience, or claim they experience, this one-ness here and now, often following a 'dark night of the soul'. Rolle, Juliana of Norwich, Meister Eckhart and Traherne (significantly writing of 'Orient wheat'), are nearer, in premise, to what Brown is saying. G.M.Hopkins' theory of 'inscape' reinforces his religious beliefs and the doctrine of God infusing earthly matter is, one suspects, a peculiarly attractive notion for Brown. In the Middle Ages the ordered hierarchy of earthly kingdoms was supposed to mirror the order of Heaven. In such a world there can be representatives of Christ, Mary and Judas, and as in *Pilgrim's Progress* or *Piers Ploughman* an Everyman lives out his spiritual quest on earth. Additionally, the gold, dark oil, bitters, tears, blood and wine of "The Heavenly Stones" enact a kind of alchemy whereby the child drifts through mortality. The symbolism takes on a Yeatsian density: 'The shaken branch, The Voice, the draped/Whispering coil of flame'. The child is tempted by the 'Flesh'; one of the beauties of the poem is that it can be read on one level as the story of a child playing at growing up.

What of the Marian aspects of true Catholic devotion in Brown's work? Effigies of holy virgins are linked by a succession of splendid images with seasonal shifts and rhythms in "Daffodils". The Marys are island women on the rocks, long candles on the altar, and , finally, three daffodils, 'shawled in radiance'. The rose 'bleeding' on the solstice stone reminds one of older beliefs:

> Surely no house on earth could be as desolate as Maeshowe
> on a midwinter day, so dark and drained of the sweetness
> of existence. But in the midst of this ultimate blackness a
> small miracle takes place, when the sun sets over Hoy on
> the afternoon of the solstice about 3 o'clock, a single
> finger of light seeks through the long corridor that leads
> into the heart of the chamber and touches the opposite

wall with a fugitive splash of gold....It is as if a seed of
promise has been sown into the womb of death itself.

Between the alignment of the 'corn tides' it is such events which
draw faith from men. To Brown the first 'centre' and essence of all
vital sacrifices is found at Christ's cross. The world's whole circle of
sorrow and deprivation,

> ....shudders
> down to one bleeding point
> Mary Mary and Mary
> triangle of grief.

All women, obeying the call of their nature like the Holy Triad, attend
the life and death of men. The images of "Daffodils" are extraordinarily
beautiful — the Marys are suffused with the pale radiance of devotion.
The Female Principle in Brown's work is an enduring force for reconciliation and peace. Women are the long-suffering, stable and fruit-bearing
figures, mindful of the rhythms of life and death and making life bearable. In "Culloden: The Last Battle" God is distant, baffling and largely
forgotten, but the action winds to a hushed calm in the weaving and
singing of Morag. This reverence for the life-giving Female energy is
married admirably to the nostalgia for a lost kingdom, the fascination
with the holy and self-sacrificing Magnus (noticeably celibate), and the
orderly stations in the life of Everyman. Progress is seen in terms of
another goddess: 'a synthetic goddess, vast and bland as Buddha, but
without love or tenderness or compassion'. Only another goddess, all-
encompassing, lavish in material reward, could pose a threat in Brown's
world.

Brown protests against the myth of the Orcadians being of Viking
lineage, 'blood of their blood, a pure stock', for the Vikings as the
Protestants are representatives of a patristic culture, often aggressive,
and the gentle monks attending their old rituals must passively endure
both. These brothers make the Lady of the Headland in "Our Lady of
the Waves". They affirm unity and are strongly associated with the
feminine aspects of their goddess:

> Brother wind, gentle sister raindrops —
> That's what they call this black whirl
> of Storm.
> They haven't a sword between them.
> Here they come in procession
> Demure and harmless as girls.
> ("Norse Lyrics of Earl Rognvald Kolson")

The monks at Eynhallow were members of a Celtic Christian monastery,
probably Columbans. This emphasis on the Female Principle continues
in the poems about 'Our Lady' in *New Poems* and *Fishermen with
Ploughs*. The 'artisan' poet labouring in the 'Kingdom of the ear of corn',
serving his Holy Lady, is stressed again and again. But the link between
Pagan and Christian within the matristic tradition is not smooth. Faith

is difficult, and meaninglessness hems us in, as Brown shows in so many of his stories. As a writer he himself can find chaos (flames and dark-nesses), the Universe without ruler or hierarchy, exhilarating. This ten-sion informs his work but essentially he leaves the random swirls of water and describes, rather, the patterns which they make. As a wor-shipper, as a Catholic in Orkney, he finds himself in a feudal tradition but it is a feudalism which remembers the Catholic kings and holy earls, not the Protestant lairds, as its rulers.

The poem which provides us with the fullest picture of Brown's framework of thought at this time is "The Seven Houses". Mother, midwife, friend, lover: 'Seventy thousand ordered days/Lay ravelled in the arms of a woman.' Life is an avenue of images; man walks past various doors to the 'Seven houses'. The poet's firm structuring rein-forces the separate reality of each house:

> The nine candles are burning.
> Here with reptile and fish and beast
> You dance in silence.

Such is the beauty and compression of the third stanza that a host of associations rise up. No animal can enter the state of human child-hood, but this could be merely a remembered yard with 'No dogs allowed' chalked on the door. How many childhood memories and archetypal stories are recalled in the lines:

> ...A tree in a gray courtyard,
> Here the animals dare not enter,
> The tree is loaded with apples,
> Three women stand at the tree.

Yet there is no apparent strain in the gentle progression of image. Brown has adopted a tone comparable with that of Eliot in *Four Quartets*. It operates at many levels: a gentle voice as if talking to a child, a visionary voice calling up images of spiritual and psychological depth and a historical voice taking the reader back to the 'axile tree' of the Medieval mystics. Bill in *A Time to Keep* reads *The Martyrdom of Man*. The cross in this story is the insignia and essence of all human suffering and the cross in the third house of the poem inherits this weight. The three women are the three Marys again, reminiscent of the old triple goddesses (eg. Brigid), but are also mother, midwife and lover-wife who look on as man is tied to the Tree of Life. The layers of legend and motif are complex beneath the apparent simplicity of the verse. The Fourth House is strangely medieval, though 'engineer' is included in a list of occupa-tions. Each role is portrayed as an interlocking unit in a co-operative whole but the problems of the Machine Age are ignored here and the reader senses the strain of retrospection. In the fifth stanza we draw to a climax as, 'Under the seven stars you watch and wait./Inside, flames twist and untwist their hair.' The dangerous 'fall' into middle age and policy is marked by a confusion of images. It is as if we are looking at a Bosch or reading a Hermetic text:

161

The hungry sit at a narrow table
And the Golden Man
Summons another beast from the flames.
The negro hangs on his tree:

This is a dangerous 'board': whilst people starve those in power are
seduced by an array of vanities. The challenge is to light one lamp in
growing darkness. Finally, the darkness 'staggered' as we learn of the
all-embracing compassion of a woman. The women who accompany the
male here are all different manifestations of the Great Mother – 'The
woman receives you./The woman takes you in.' Even Christ, Son of the
Omnipotent Creator, chose the way of life through a woman's womb as
David Jones has so movingly written. But this truth does not free us
from the pain and conflict of 'the dance'; the enemies can only lay aside
their masks temporarily 'And later resumed them'.

However, Brown is not a blind adherent to the Feminine Principle;
he can see the darker aspects of the Goddess, as he reveals in writing
of the women of the Norse:

These women had a stony patience that men found
fascinating and frightening. They were the sea watchers,
they stood at the rock before dawn, after sunset when
the ships and the fishing boats were out, their eyes cold
as kittiwakes. They hovered like priestesses about the
mysteries of birth and love and death, swaddling the
infant, shrouding the corpse, permitting men to lie with
them in the fecund darkness so that a new generation of
providers might inherit the islands. Their instincts told
them too that a family is only strong and thrusting so
long as it is locked in dangerous conflict with the
farmers over the hill, with the seaport along the coast,
with the neighbouring kingdom. The secret promptings
of women are behind much of the heroism and tragedy
of the Iceland sagas....

However, generally, the female side of the human personality is
praised in in Brown's work. "The Image in the Hills", another poem in
the collection, probably refers to the Lady of Rackwick, a statue of
Mary placed 'between field and sea' on Hoy. This Mary is much older
than Christianity though – she is representative of the Image in Art:

Build an arch of hard words,
April flows from her wounded hands,
The gentle beasts and legends gather.

She guards fields, river and birds, preserving their lives in art as well as
mothering them in a physical sense with the sun, rain and food. This
relating of Word and Image is almost tantamount to a religion of Art
but is not quite; for Brown there is an ultimate distinction between the
aesthetic and the religious sides of life. However, the tradition of the
poet or balladeer as a servant of a lady or Love (in the courtly sense), is

so strong in Brown's work as to suggest that aesthetic and spiritual lover
overlap. The Universal Mother of Orcadian myth merging with the
figure of Mary is implied in such ideas. In his story "Hawkfall" Brown
shows a Neolithic chieftain going to be with his dark bride (he often
uses nuptial terms to convey spiritual states), but in *Magnus* God, at
least the god of the early peoples, is masculine. There is no doubt however that Brown is aware of the ancient 'Mothers' of Sea and Land.

One must not forget that Brown's vision is a balanced one. The last
stanza of "The Seven Houses" is crucial, as it reveals the male refusing
to accept his mask and 'kicking against the traces' for fundamental individuality. He will strive to control his destiny or rebel in a Promethean
or Faustian way. The Viking, the Protestant and, strangely enough, the
atheist, are part of this tradition. The Orcadians of old believed in the
'Mither o'the Sea', a benign spirit of the summer, who stilled the storms
and brought warmth and life to the waters. Teran was her enemy, the
implacable winter spirit, but the 'Mother' would always triumph. Later,
when these beliefs either merged with Christian motifs, or faded to
superstition, the islanders thought that even if God was all-powerful,
'His world was infested by ill-disposed and dangerous creatures'. The
world was 'in fact' believed to be a controlled chaos. The Vikings brought
belief in Fate, 'Wyrd'. Not believing in an omnipotent deity, they knew
that Odin, their battle-captain, would have to face Fafnir and Gotter-
dammerung. They therefore prized individuality and staunch heroism in
the face of a distant but inevitable triumph of Chaos. In Orkney the
World-serpent became the Stoor Worm who was killed by a humorous
character called Assipattle, who, significantly enough threw a burning
peat on the worm's liver. Peat was the centre of light in festivals like
Johnsmas held by the Orcadians. For Brown, the Protestant and the
existentialist, though ostensibly from very different camps, are rootless,
jealous and scornful of tradition. They seek a constant deliberation, one
with logic and the other with the doctrine of Biblical salvation, to assert
their individuality. This is why lines like: 'Through the arrogance of
atom and planet/May the lamp still burn' are so crucial. Each particle of
existing energy strives for survival, but even this, as vital as it seems, is
not as basic as the underlying unity, the ever-present one-ness.

The poet too can be a saviour of a kind, and in "Hamnavoe" Brown
sets out to save the day for his father. It is an exercise in personal history. The tinker, the crofter girl and fisher lasses recur in this familiar
landscape where the essential substances pour outwards to invest the
scene with a new richness. Beards are 'spumy' with porter, a lass dreams
of 'cornstalks and milk' and the 'amber day' ebbs out. The ninth stanza
takes on a distinctly Symbolist tone when: 'The Kirk, in a gale of psalms,
went heaving through/A tumult of roofs, freighted for heaven...' But it
is also Brown's childish conceit which informs the lines. The rhythms
of the community are increasingly to occupy Brown's verse and we cannot talk of his sense of history or myth divorced from the Orcadian

people.

> The boats drove furrows homewards, like ploughmen
> In blizzards of gulls. Gaelic fisher girls
> Flashed knife and dirge
> Over drifts of herring.

But there is a new opposition to these patterns: '...because, under equality's sun,/All things wear now to a common soiling'. This may seem a simplistic Yeatsian and reactionary judgement, but we must remember that to Brown such egalitarianism means the fading of patterns and the reduction of local variety. In *An Orkney Tapestry* he writes:

> Nowadays there is a distinct trimming and levelling up; a
> man is ashamed to be different from his neighbour. The
> old stories have vanished with the horses and the tinkers;
> instead of the yarn at the pier head or the pub, you are
> increasingly troubled with bores who insist on telling
> you what they think about Vietnam or the bank rate or
> heart transplants, and you may be sure it isn't their own
> thought-out opinion at all...

There is no room here for speculating upon the political connotations of such views. We have already seen where a desire to recall feudal artistry and order took Pound, but *Magnus* reveals Brown to be virulently opposed to fascism, and one suspects that the Liberal traditions of Orkney with their emphasis on individual expression are nearer Brown's opinions. *The Year of the Whale*, taken as a whole, provides us with deeper excursions into, and more searching statements of, the mind of a community. Poems like "The Funeral of Ally Flett", "Shipwreck" and "Farm Labourer" penetrate to the core of the hard existence, often with a sombre but lyrical austerity:

> 'God, am I not dead yet?' said Ward,
> > > > his ear
> > Meeting another dawn.
> > A blackbird, lost in leaves, began to throb.

Simultaneously, in this collection, Brown's treatment of the past grows fuller and greater in detail, anticipating the better Viking poems. "Culloden:The Last Battle" is not a great poem — the central metaphors of men as hogsheads and fighting as reading texts, seem distanced and forced. But there is a definite ability to capture not only the sardonic, terrifying grimness of battle. but the whole accent of awed speakers after fighting:

> > We had hastened
> Faithful as brothers from the sixth cry of God
> To play this game of ghost on the long moor.
> His eyes were hard as dice, his cheek was cropped
> For the far tryst, his Saxon bayonet
> Bright as a wolf's tooth.

Two poems, "The Abbot" and "Horseman and Seals", deal with the

lonely monastic life in the islands. "The Abbot" is by far the more
effective poem, revealing a greater integration of narrative and image. It
also employs a style reminiscent of the mnemonic catalogues in ancient
literatures as each monk is examined:

> At Rinansay, Einar was a butterfly
> Over a tangled harp,
> The girls miss him in that low island.
> Now when candles are lit
> For matins, in the warp of winter,
> He drifts our gray moth
> Among the woven monotonies of God.

They are evocative words musically summoning up the scene. The
Abbot's creed is again that of the fields and earthly processes: 'Christ,
crofter, lay kindly on this white beard/Thy sickle, flail, millstone, key,
oven'. The transformation into Christ's image, the Bread of Life, for the
sustenance and comfort of man is described here. The figure of Christ as
crofter reinforces the idea of masks and also the story of Everyman,
who is capable of redeeming and making holy his own sphere of life.
There is little hint here of the religious persecutions and the schism between man and Nature that some Christian fathers stressed. To this
father, Labour and Religion are one. Storm Kolson said to the astonish-
ed harvesters,

> The dance is a rising and falling of feet like unto your
> labour, a good circling, and from this pure source, the
> Dance (that was in the beginning with God) issue all the
> slow laborious necessary diurnal rounds whereby men
> earn their bread.

The pace of the poem is slow, intimate but decisive, matching the
considerate ruminations of an old cleric:

> From the timbers we made a new door
> And the Swedish boy
> Has Latin enough to answer the priest now.

One can see that, before we enter upon *New Poems*, Brown has developed a complex and coherent social and metaphysical vision. This vision is
drawn from two main traditions: that of the Medieval Kingdom with its
orderly hierarchy and Catholic dogma, and secondly that of folk belief
and creativity. This second tradition had at its centre the 'pure source'
of 'DEATH, BREAD, BREATH' and the cosmic Dance, and we find its
fullest expression in the Ballad and the ceremonies of poor people.

II

The *New Poems* were composed over a period of eleven years, (1959
– 70), and exhibit all the main dramatic elements which Brown is to
continue into his poems of the 1970s. In the *Orkneyinga Saga* the story
of Earl Rognvald is interspersed with skaldic verse:

Now our good ship, land forsaking,
Laves her breast in limpid waters
Long ere he who sings these verses,
Sees again the northern islands;
With the sharp prow I the yielding
Earth-surrounding sea am carving
Far-off Spain – land, sweeping southward.

The lyrics and runes of the Norsemen have had a profound influence on Brown's writing. He has returned to the old writings equipped with the terseness and concision of Pound and Eliot. He gives an illustration of how this has affected his versions of the lyric in *An Orkney Tapestry*: I juxtapose his version of Armod's poem about the night-watch with the translation of A.B.Taylor:

We watch o'er the sea steed   Night. Sheets of salt
While o'er the stout gun-whale   Armod on watch
The billow breaks wildly   A heave of lights from the island
  Thus duty is done   The lads of Crete
While the lazy land lubber   Toss in hot tumbled linen
Sleeps by some maiden   The poet on watch
Over my shoulder   Cold burning unkissed.
I gaze towards Crete.   [Brown]

One can see how Brown has rendered the moment more immediate and made the sailor's emotions more tangible. The scene is set quickly and Brown's imagery (the linen, the wash of lights), heightens the impact of the final line. Perhaps this series of sharply-defined impressions is nearer to the spirit of old Norse verse, but it is clear that the medium which has had most influence on Brown's writing is the prose of the sagas. A typical quotation can be taken from the first part of the *Orkneyinga Saga*:

> After Sigurd his son Guttorm ruled one year. Torf
> Einar, son of Earl Rognvald, succeeded him. He was a
> man of great power, and was a long time. Halfdan Halegg
> (high-legs) made an expedition against Torf Einar and
> drove him from the Orkneys.

This can be compared with "The Five Voyages of Arnor":

> I, Arnor the red poet, made
> Four voyages out of Orkney.
> The first was to Ireland.
>
> That was a Viking cruise
> Thorleif came home with one leg.

In *Winterfold* Brown has begun to use a more compressed Norse lyric form, but in *New Poems* and *Fishermen with Ploughs* he relies heavily upon the Norse narratives with their genealogies, accounts of voyages and deaths. "The Five Voyages of Arnor" and "Viking Testament" show that Brown is developing a dextrous variation of moods: from almost trivial detail to humour to beauty,

166

I won the girl Ragnhild
From Paul her brother, after
I beat him at draughts, three games to two.
Out of Bergen, the waves made her sick.
She was uglier than I expected, still
I made five poems about her,
That men sing round the benches at Yule.
She filled my quiet house with words.

That quality which Wiggin has called Brown's 'prismatic eye' is evident:
'Women in black stood all about me/There were lilies and snow on the
hill above Broadfirth...' The importance of direction, colour (white
waves, blue road, black cough, red poet), the stylisation of their language
('A hundred swords were broken', 'Prayer on a hundred white wings'),
and the routes (Dublin, Micklegarth, Narbonne), of these people are
convincingly conveyed. Religious emotions are also accepted and recorded simply: 'We saw the hills where God walked'. "Viking Testament" is closer to a list of attributes and symbols and the narrator is a
rune-maker. Here, in the 'Ox' section, a man is made legend (recalling
Hymn I of *Mercian Hymns*):

His father sang to the curious seals.
His father had fair dust to lie with
Ingibiorg, tallest of women.

The richness of common speech and simple statements offset by glowing
superlatives is revealed in these gentle cadences. In "Dove" the affec-
tionate mockery of a Viking for a monk is mimicked. Their hymns are
viewed as incantations: 'their tongues/Compel corn and oil/From the
seven ox-dragged seasons'; their god as. 'a scarecrow with five red tatters';
and their philosophy is mocked, 'Who call the codling 'little silver
brothers'/Even as they suck the bones clean'. But it is in the wistful
yearnings of the 'Rose' section where we find an old man's affection for
his daughter captured in a swift series of images which is the finest part
of this poem:

What can I leave thee? Thou hast
Horizons of whale and mermaid
Far in the west, a hall,
Three ships in Cornwall and Ulster, trading,
A young son with black curls
And five horses in the meadow.

The same eye for local historical detail and vibrant image, and a fervent
elegaic voice are found in "Our Lady of the Waves".

The rune form is re-examined in "Runes from a Holy Island" and
"Runes from the Island of Horses". They have elements of jokiness

An island without roads
Ikey the tinker
Stood throat-deep in the bog.
("Lost")

popular tale,

> A man-of-war enchanted
> Three boys away
> Pinleg, Windbag, Lord Rum returned.
> ("Press-gang")

and riddle,

> Sigurd lay with three women,
> Reckoning his mother
> and thwart twin sister.
> ("Respectability")

In such a mixture it is difficult to pick out the stern modern metaphor from the folk ditty, saying, or snippet of gossip. The past lies clenched in these words; they have been honed down to an area of commonalty in language where popular phrase and exalted lyric are inextricably linked. The tongues of poor women gossiping wear words down till they become hieroglyphics, dense in implicit meanings. One must not forget the Viking runes in Maeshowe inscibed there by visiting warriors; the short cryptic rune-form has become part of the Orcadian habit of mind.

"Sea Orpheus" is the unusual poem in the collection. It is an attempt to link nature myth, folk tale, popular story and modern urban life. The 'Salt One' seems less a 'Sea Orpheus' loving his Eurydice than a Poseidon or Teran, a great elemental god:

> The Salt one
> Turned the wave round. He gathered
> The Song of the Five Seas
> Into his loom...

The 'tide-raped' girl also seems part of an older world like the looms and quernstones which old Orcadians heard shuttling and grinding beneath the spume. The swift progress through myth, the picture of the 'old salts', Eurydice, Ahab and Jonah, to the gull over Glasgow is unlike anything in modern verse except sections of Hart Crane's *The Bridge*, as he moves from the Indian goddess, to Columbus, to Brooklyn Bridge. Significantly perhaps, the American also uses a gull to link time and place. While it illustrates the different levels of narrative that Brown attempts (most easily seen in the drowning girl, Eurydice, a cold mermaid, one mortal cornstalk, and the buttercup girl) the poem should either be longer and sectional, or less ambitious in its sweep. The narrative tone is light, not strident, but there are too many different strands and the theme of metamorphosis does not finally help the poem to cohere.

There are four poems in the book associated with particular times and events. The event is always submerged to a varying extent in an artistic convention. "The Masque of the Princes" is a song of the skald Arkol in the Yuletide of 1015. One notices the reduction of detail inherent in the use of skaldic verse and Brown, of course, utilises this:

We commandeered fields round the city
And cattle, barns, horses, women, wells.
They threw down fire from the wall.
A skull was charred.
Roofbeams hissed in the Seine.
We circled the wall with dice and wineskin.

The lines about the merchants and priests seem almost inevitable — the poet of the attackers is forced to strain for an effective image: 'The city rotted slowly/Like a spotted corpse in a charnel'; or to squeeze a black humour from the event: 'When the wind lay towards the city/We turned the sputtering ox on the spit'. Then comes the skald's confession

I put the seige in a set of formal verses.
The skippers did not praise that poem.
(This is for blacksmiths and poachers.)

and in the list of spoils the last item is 'foreign rats'. The skald is more honest and incisive than most; he has not belittled the bravery of men or glorified it. He has not lessened the horror of the seige (a convention in its own sense), or his own implication in the collective guilt. If his superiors cannot accept his poem, and one can sense his knowledge and resentment of the feudal system here, he will present it to those who are forced to rely upon wars and stealing for their bread.

"Lord of the Mirrors" is 'A dance Bernard of Ventadour made, with masks and lutes and ladies, for the investiture of Philip, Count of Narbonne in April 1130'. The three sections are organised as follows: in the first the Prince, mindful of the tradition which he joins, gains answers from the coats-of-arms on a shield. It is possibly the most stylised of Brown's statements — the heraldic symbols actually speaking:

It,[heraldry] is a stillness into which the torrents of
history are gathered, like an unflawed mill pool. In the
silence an image out of the past stirs, and illuminates
things in our present circumstances, as individuals or as
citizens of a country or as members of the human race,
but we do not understand. Heraldry is the fury of history
made wise and formal; from its hands we take at last the
wholesome images — the heart's bread — that our ancestors sowed for us in passion and blindness. That quiet pool
turns the mill stones of religion, and of art, and of the
simple graces and courtesies of daily living.

These images are the burnished symbols which inhabit the collective and individual subconscious. Poets, like the Prince, question the silence; finally the Prince meets with the mystery of essential one-ness. He, the images, the shield and all that is gathered there are one: 'A breath, surge of cloud,/through the bronze mirror'. His very breath becomes image as it enters the medium of the mirror.

The second section deals with various conceptions of love within the hierarchies of Nature and society. Love is the raison d'etre of life and each level must be imbued with its urgency. Bernard of Ventadorn, (1148-95) was the troubadour of self-abandonment, humility and rapture in love, and he captured an alternating vision of despair and ecstasy in his exhilarating 'canso' forms. Love is a religion, exalting and purifying in his work. Bernard's submission to the 'domna' or Lady is feudal and complete — she is almost synonymous with Amors and holds the power of happiness and sorrow, life and death. Bernard was of poor origin and, significantly enough in relation to Brown's mythic vision, he was the son of a servant who was a baker.

The final question to man bears an unsettling mystery and we are left with a strangely Eliotic vision: 'On the garden pool, breezes, a/caul of sackcloth'. Here in the pool in the garden, source of life, where man has created order, his death-wrapping and babyhood vestment float. The sackcloth is empty — it is merely the covering not the essence. If the answer to these cryptic images is given it is in the third section.

Here, the ancient story of the Hunt (bound up with aristocratic history) is combined with the story of the sacrifice and Christian Nativity. This results in an inversion of the story — Christ, the Stag, or mankind in general is hunted and dies; the earth is empty and then a star 'pierces the rafters' like 'a seed of promise'. Night's shroud lies on the hill but soon there will be a new birth. The 'breathings of ox and ass' break into the work not only as a welcome warmth but completing the redemption of all creatures and their desires. 'Men handle the jewel' (the story, symbol, song), 'and know themselves enriched'; and after the ritual questioning, the rood becomes fragrant with new hope and purity. The different sections with their symmetry, the reciprocal motions of the questions and the masked creatures remind us that this is an orderly dance for a twelfth century court. The royal stag becomes Bonnie Prince Charlie after Culloden in "Prince in the Heather". The association of the stag with a Divine King is an ancient one. In "The Killing" by Edwin Muir Christ's wreath-knot looks like 'the last stump left, of a death-wounded deer's great antlers'. However, the Stag or Hart is usually a divine messenger, especially of sky-gods. Its horns mark it as a creature of the sun. In the legend of St.Eustace a stag with a crucifix in its horns (revealing a link between the horns and the axile-tree) leads the saint from a hunt. In the ballad "The Three Ravens" a fallow doe kisses the red wounds of her lord and buries him.

The ballad is in marked contrast to the former poems. The indignation is soft in inflection — the sad lyricism is not 'pressed down' between tensed images:

> But it did not douche the terrible fire
>   of the English,
> Their spewings of flame.
> (I think it will rain a long time at Culloden
> And steel rot under the stone.)

The whole scene seems bathed with a misty light in which actions become sluggish and dreadful: 'Casually the cannonball burst those ribs,/Removed that leg' and Brown's usually well-defined images blur, 'A great shining thing is gone forever from the glens'. The prince fled, the stag did not bend 'obedient to the arrow'; there was no martyrdom and since the stag was 'frightened' there is nothing for the Bard to pledge his faith in.

The motifs of the Hunt and Christian Nativity and corn-myth are taken up again in "Carol". It follows the progress of the Creation, from the first star bleeding and the hills being born out of 'The war of cloud and summit' establishing the essential nature of suffering in the world. Priests abstract the 'sources' to give hope for the 'passionate and the dead'. Christ becomes the earth-tree bearing godwounds and the obedient deer which turns to the arrow. A consequence of the belief in unity is that the hunter and the farmer who kill and plough are not blamed for their implication in the cycle. Earl Haakon Paulson and Herr Lifolf from *Magnus*, Rognvald Kolson, the Calvinists at Rackwick, even Judas, the Nazis or Ulf Hreda who strung out the renegade Brodir's guts on a tree, are necessary parts of human cycles. It is only faith that can make such truth bearable, for, as the hunter breaks the grape and as the blacksmith uses his reaping blade, the cry that arises is: 'A child wailing,/A child's cry at the door of the House-of-Bread'. 'Our atom-and-planet night' shows how deeply this cry penetrates to man's inmost core.

Such a myth has enormous social implications in a world which has known Belsen and Babi-Yar. Were these martyrdoms necessary? "White Emperor" shows Brown confronting the 'shadow among the ashes' and attempting to apply his cosmology. The soldier's song echoes the work of Kovner and Holub; the images are reminiscent of Goya and the archetypes of the Tarot pack, but the skulls here are real ones. Both ideologies: the Church supporting the Old Emperor by appeasing the peasants with myth and the 'Red One' preaching comradeship, have proved no refuge for the soldiers. (There is perhaps a suggestion that the peasants were more comfortable under the old regime, but there is also a distinct cynicism in the line 'Children of the White King'.) The soldier's plea is that basically they are not soldiers or peasants:'We are the people.'

Natasha seems to be the expression of the people, their only hope: 'I measure the sun with lucent eyes'. A woman is given the final vision in a storm of rage and chaos — she is the promise of the future, leader of the song and repository of men's hopes and fears.

The 'Masque of Princes' poems, five in all, show Brown scrutinising his mythos. He is not blind to his attraction to the Medieval estates where all have their roles, but neither is he ignorant of the fact that such was the squalor, abuse and bloodiness of the times that only thieves were not, in some way, hyprocrites. Brown asks, does a knowledge of unity help men to rule, to love, or lay down their lives? Each narrator is at a crisis in his life and "White Emperor" is a fitting climax where old orders have collapsed and the popular strident chorus has taken over from the ballad. How can one live in and help build the 'Kingdom of the Ear of Corn'? The answers, if they are such, are, from the needs of the people, 'the heart's bread', the knowledge of underlying but unseen unity, and from the power of the Female Principle which receives man at his most desolate.

In *An Orkney Tapestry* Brown talks of three coats being woven in the Medieval Orkneys. First, the coat of the Estates, 'the warmth and comfort and well-being of the people, a symbol too of their identity and their ethos'. Then the coat-of-State, a mystical, hierarchic garment of rule. Then,

> there was the third coat; as yet only the monks in lonely
> islands wore it – the long white weave of innocence that
> they must have ready for the bridal-feast of Christ.

It is then no surprise when we find that "The Coat" deals with the 'Coat of Life', as recalled in the earth, harvest and making of bread. This links the poem with "The Ballad of John Barleycorn". The third stanza is clever and witty, suddenly bringing the Maker of the Coat, an old ploughman and the poet together: 'Lie after lie he stitched/Into a masterly tale'. But the tale is not so easy to 'swallow' as a cup of ale: 'The thread shore in his throat'. Life is not just a game to be decorated by the artist's fancies. There is a terrible beauty and earnestness in the wearing of the 'Coat of Life'.

"The Ballad of John Barleycorn, the Ploughman and the Furrow" is an example of how well Brown can give the already existing Barleycorn songs, with their hintings of older myth and folk humour, a new precision and colour. The unexpected turn of the ending reveals the dominant motif of the labourer who is able to win a bride from Nature. This bride is, of course, the Earth, but mermaids, selkies and fairy's daughters have all been lured from their habitat by ordinary menfolk. Part Two of the sequence, "The Tinker's Song", which is partly in dialect, deals with a tinker who is captured by men in gray, green and yellow. There could be a triad of vegetable deities (their colours are ones of growth) who have degenerated in the popular imagination to elves who need music under the hill. This echoes the story of the fiddler who was kidnapped to play at an elven ball. Music is often compared to a set of stylised gestures used normally in farming and fishing to render a harvest from the 'black furrow'.

"The Fiddler's Song", spoken by the old, blind fiddler to his Eurydice-figure: Freya in *A Spell for Green Corn*, is a fitting end to the sequence with its elegaic pleading. On a purely human level it could be taken as a plea to find new love, but the fiddler could be persuing his job, wooing the earth in winter, telling her not to mourn in a barren way for the harvest that died (the 'yellow hair' of the poem).

The "King of Kings" and "The Wedding Guest" are prose-poems concerned with nativity and the spirit of birth. In the former, the innkeeper at Bethlehem writes a series of letters to a security officer about his visitors. It is compelling to follow Brown as he marshals his characters. The flux of many races — Greeks, Parthians, Cypriots and Romans, representatives of a wide empire — establish the inn as a centrifugal point. The Magi tell of:

> *Blessings given to men in the beginning that have been*
> *wrongly spent on pomp, wars, usury, whoredoms, vain-*
> *glory: ill-used heavenly gifts... We are looking for the*
> *hands that first gave them... Let them shine now in the*
> *ceremonies of the poor... Perhaps this kingdom does not*
> *exist... Perhaps it is hidden so deep in love and birth and*
> *death that we will never find it... Perhaps the Kingdom is*
> *a very simple thing.*

There is a certain humour when 'Coalface' asks, 'What have you got for us in your cellar?' Perhaps he ought to have asked about the stable. The 'old treasures', essences of human existence gathered by wise men, come into their primary significance here. The tale is left remarkably 'open-ended' for Brown, who sometimes likes to press his message home too forcedly. The reader takes from it what he will: the options of chaos and order are left unresolved, but we have witnessed the gathering at Bethlehem. By leaving out the actual birth, Brown makes us judges of history. Did the wise men project the mystery which they needed so badly onto the birth of an ordinary child?

"The Wedding Guest" is a cryptic journey through 'signs' to the 'summons and the ceremony'. Tinkers, emblems of unthinking pagan lust, are passed; women watch the sea and each section closes with a surprising image of folded or opposed dualisms:

> ...the wind falling folded me in two huge dove-wings
> ...the naked tinker boy now held the shell
> of his ear, a colder sea mouth.
> ...their thin eyes prised at the oyster of the horizon.

If the journey is symbolical, the man has already passed the Cross when he comes to the 'body of Barleycorn'. The lure of the alehouses is potent and even lends a Biblical atmosphere, but the traveller goes on to 'a ghostly Bride cup'. He is now cut 'free of the Flesh' — 'a beast-bearing ghost' — and as the star glows and he enters the cowshed with the young lady, maker of butter and cheese, we begin to discern a procession through the elements again.

Brown, as much as Heaney, is a seeker of 'centres'. If 'Earth and man and sun and bread' are one then the energy which forms this one-ness must be Incarnate, present in matter. The heart of Maeshowe in the middle of the Mainland on the afternoon of the solstice at 3 o'clock is one such centre. The heart of the Mass in the Kirk on Egilsay is a 'centre' for Magnus:

> He felt secure then, like a guest in a lamp-splashed,
> jubilant castle.

173

Christ around me
Christ before me
Christ beside me
Christ above me.

Corbishley writes of the Catholic:

He takes very seriously his profession of faith in 'the
communion of saints', thinking of himself as a member
of that vast household of God, which reaches into
heaven where the Church triumphant enjoys the beatific
vision and stretches out to the furthermost limits of the
earth where he knows that the central act of worship,
the Mass, is being offered 'from the rising of the sun even
until its setting'. In that sacrifice annihilating space and
time, he believes that he draws near to, is indeed person-
ally associated with the Death of Christ himself, perpet-
ually offered for the salvation of the world.

I have quoted this passage at length because it seems to echo so
fully the spirit of "The Wedding Guest". It is at Christ's Kirk on Birsay
that the first miracle of Magnus for the tinkers is portrayed in *Magnus*.
The man in "The Wedding Guest" is going to early mass in Birsay with
the guardians of the single 'watch-lamp, like ruby or stigmata or rose'.
Brothers fish and till the land as the traveller enters through the 'parted
sea':

Here is your single cell, here all time is but the lucency
of a single morning, prepare here your distillings of the
Rose... Doves enfold him – a raven sail leans westward.

The symmetry of the scene is faultless. The Bridegroom within the
Sanctuary within the Kirk on the island in the arms of the ocean. The
boat, plough and westering sail, doves and roses, are all images of pene-
tration and interpenetration. The Bride in spun-gold is the setting sun
and the concentric circles quivering 'up and down' from the bells sound
backwards and forwards through history. The mixture of ceremonial,
Romantic and 'ordinary' language is striking – there are echoes of the
Medieval mystics, Dante and even Bunyan here. The man seeking his
'single cell' takes on an allegorical stature and the Tinker, symbolising
pre-Christian consciousness, is seen as the oldest level of human life.
The journey is a quest by stages through human history and the narrator changes as he travels. He starts with Youth and rockpools, goes
through the 'smithy' of his Flesh, drags his lusts 'a beast-bearing' ghost
and finally abides at the 'centre'. Some might find the urgency and
ecstatic 'ands' of the last passage a little overblown. However, this
vision of the Christ-like Everyman journeying to the place where Bride
and Bridegroom are one within the circles of life, is basic to Brown's
work. He uses the parable of the Wise and Foolish Virgins and the story
of the parting of the Red Sea with sensitivity.

In the first part of this chapter I have shown how Heraldry and the

174

Ballad are both important model's for Brown's writing. In the second part I have concentrated on the Christian story, Nature myths and motifs such as the Stag, the Coats and the essences which culminate in a vision of the Centre. Brown's steady examination of the wide traditions of devotion to a Goddess, who, beneath many masks, controls the lives of men, is perhaps the most remarkable reality in these poems. It is a devotion which folds all of history and belief into its radiance and which reaches its finest flowering in the Marian poems. As Brown's work progresses he becomes more interested in condensed lyrical and runic forms and these will eventually lead us to the most powerful poems he has ever written, in *Winterfold*.

The interaction of the world and the Image has, in Brown's eyes, brought forth art:

> Language, open the sacred quarry.
> Pagan in clouds, a stone image,
> She guards the field, the river, the birds.
> ...Build an arch of hard square words
> ...Stand in the poem, nude, cold girl,
> Till the Word wakes and all stones die.

The image in "The Image in the Hills" is the actual stone figure — repository of a people's beliefs — a pagan sign and also the vision grasped after by the poet. The quarry is a reminder of the image-making forbears, and of the imagination, sacred because of its life-enhancing potential, loaning form to pagan as well as explicitly Christian signa. In Edwin Muir's "Thought and Image" a view of Creation becomes also a metaphor for the creative act:

> Past time and space the shaping Thought
> Was born in freedom and in play;
> The Image then on earth was wrought
> Of water and of clay.

In both poems the Word or God in the form of the Christ-child is born to balance the formula. Thought and Image, the Created world and the preserving ordinance of Art are not enough. The Word is a human product but, unlike and transcending language, it holds within it a mystery, 'a ghost' which is distinct from and outlasts any of its local meanings or usages. All this is obvious enough when considered in relation to the first chapter of John's Gospel, but the Word in Brown is a cipher both for the poet's role and for his poetic cosmogony and, as such, provides a fundamental sense of unity and coherence to both. It is tempting to dismiss Brown as a writer who has found various patterns: heraldry, the Nativity, John Barleycorn tales, attractive, and has blended them together in writing which holds elements of mysticism, saga narrative and folk-tale. Philip Pacey has emphasised the medium of heraldry in Brown's work and then proceeded to point out how Brown selects, juxtaposes, but gives clear definition to his images on a 'new ground'. Pacey, like most critics on Brown, is content to isolate different strands of belief running through his work and investigate them without recourse to the overall 'weave' that they form. This process necessarily leads to a disjointed effect and, in Pacey's case, the different themes are left unrelated. This would not pose any problem if these elements always stood sharply delineated and existed as discrete parts in the work, but they do not. Brown's 'patterns' do seem, often because of his inclusion of contradictory and 'modern' material, partial glimpses of a wider mythos, strands which have not been woven into the 'one garment' of his work. However, it is precisely because Brown includes areas of chaos and formlessness in his work that a reader senses the scale of the poet's urge to fold and relate his material. Clues to the syncretic impulse in Brown's work are most clearly seen in comparing his poetry with that of Gerard Manley Hopkins and Edwin Muir.

> Myth comes bringing to our minds the realm of great
> powers, ceremonies of primal kings. Its persons are be
> yond our human condition... But folk and fairytale have
> their home in the gossip of old wives and little children,
> stories about the cooking-hearth and the nursery bedside.

This distinction between myth and folktale is relatively meaningless when applied to Brown's work. Often, John Barleycorn, the corn itself and Christ, are joined in the medium of his images. It is a step that Hopkins never desired to take in his poems. Like many Catholics, Hopkins believed in an underlying presence in matter: Heaven is 'astrew' even in the storm that wrecks the 'Deutschland'. In "As Kingfishers Catch Fire..." Christ plays

> ...in ten thousand places,
> Lovely in limbs, and lovely in eyes not his
> To the Father through the features of men's faces.

The idea of Christ as Everyman is commonly echoed in Brown's work and Hopkins' affection for the picture of the Nativity, likening it to any peasant birth is, at times, folded in a language which anticipates Brown's 'These are indeed the barn; withindoors house..../Christ home, Christ and his mother...' Compare this to the final lines of "From Stone to Thorn": 'Shepherd, angel, king are kneeling, look/In the door of the barn'. Despite the similarities, Hopkins' overall vision is very different from Brown's for precisely those reasons which distinguish Brown's themes from the mainstream of Catholic thought. Hopkins comes as near to identifying Mary with the old fertility goddesses in "The May Magnificat" as he ever does:

> Flesh and fleece, fur and feather,
> Grass and greenworld all together;
> Star-eyed strawberry-breasted
> Throstle above her nested.

However, the poem pivots around the last lines:

> This ecstasy all through mothering earth
> Tells Mary her mirth till Christ's birth
> To remember and exultation
> In God who was her salvation.

God redeems his Bride, the world, and, because this act is omnipresent, the beauty of nature is shown at its height, already realised. Yet however cohesive the poem is within its own precepts, a modern reader cannot help but feel a sense of ideological schism. It would have been no

177

use to indicate the pagan origins of the Great Mother to Hopkins because he regarded the patterns and signa of a pre-Christian world as irrelevent, false and 'unreal'. In a letter of May 17, 1885, to Robert Bridges, Hopkins wrote: 'Believe me, the Greek gods are a totally unworkable material; the merest frigidity, which must chill and kill every work of art they are brought into'. He had previously mentioned a play he had seen recently:

> But *Ulysses* is to act; and in earnest, not allegorically, you
> bring a goddess among the characters: it revolts me. Then,
> not unnaturally, as it seemed to me, her speech is the
> worst in the play: being an unreality she must talk unreal.

This presumption must seem critically, if not theologically, naive, but it is plain that Hopkins saw no division between belief in life and belief as expressed in art. This is a far cry from David Jones when he writes in "Art and Sacrament" of a man considering his beloved:

> So that what was Miss Flora Smith may turn out to be
> Flora Dea and Venus too and the first Eve and the
> second also and other and darker figures, among them,
> no doubt, Jocasta. One thing at least the psychologists
> make plain: there is always a recalling, a re-presenting
> again, anaphora, anamnesis.

But it is not to Jones but to another poet we must turn to find where Brown gained his poetic reconciliation of Catholic belief and universal myth.

The sheriff in Brown's story "Ballad Singer" fears that in poetry the mind is 'lost in a labyrinth of happy images'. Muir's labyrinths are 'dark' with accumulated associations, but the analogy with art is definitely among them. There are, of course, other correspondences. Muir has a fondness for Medieval imagery, heraldic carvings in stone and a hostility towards the Calvinists forcing their faith on the peasants: '...Knox and Melville clapped their preaching palms/And bundled all the harvesters away...' Like Brown, he betrays a fear of materialism: 'our only enemy was gold'. But perhaps Muir's main contribution to Brown's sense of myth is his religion of (what we shall call) Everyman. In his poem "The Myth" Muir writes:

> My childhood all a myth
> Enacted in a distant isle;
> Time with his hourglass and his scythe
> Stood dreaming on the dial...

As his life nears its ends the narrator sees

> ...at each border of the land,
> Like monuments a deluge leaves,
> Guarding the invisible sheaves
> The risen watchers stand.

Muir writes in *An Autobiography* of his childhood and the importance of his rural infancy when viewed with the hindsight of urban experience.

The child to Muir seems to stand in a mythic setting outside time and immune to the cataclysms of the adult world. Often, as in "Day and Night", Muir gives the child an innate knowledge of primeval truths: 'Shapes too simple for a place/In the day's shrill complexity'; and a direct role in the shaping of the world: 'Upon the sixth or the seventh day'. Here a father seems God and God any father.

Brown's ideas of the 'Kingdom of the Ear of Corn', the interaction of the Barleycorn myth, the Christian story, the lives of farmers and mysticism generally, also have their counterparts in Muir's verse. In "The Journey Back", the Image of Man embodied in Everyman pursues a course of exploration. He becomes a dancer in many masks:

> So I...
> Body on body, am both father and child,
> Causer and actor, spoiler and despoiled,
> Robbing myself, myself, grinding the face
> Of the poor, I poorest, who am both rich and poor,
> Victor and victim, hapless in One.

The poem which anticipates Brown's visions of cornfields, flailing, the 'self-begotten cycles' of agrarian life, is "The Island". The arts here are seen as utile, necessary for sanity, and we are told of the common substance of men and matter: 'Men are made of what is made,/The meat, the drink, the life, the corn...' This statement is very similar to Brown's emphasis on the unity of origins in *Magnus*. The pictures of grain gatherers, 'golden hills of corn', the generations of 'man, dog and flock', all pervaded with a Sicilian atmosphere, resemble Brown's descriptions of Christ's village and the Nativity. The 'tongue is transmuted' for it is the Word which has brought about this unity and made 'indigenous art' and 'simple spells' effective.

These few details culled from Muir's work do not in any way prove that Brown has an integrated cosmology, but they do reveal landscapes: a timeless island or the fields after harvest guarded by 'watchers' where man's fundamental nature is realised and the various potent myths are reconciled. These peaceful scenes pervaded by a sense of plenitude and eternal innocence enabled Brown to make his Orkney of the mind and spirit.

At the centre of Brown's cosmology is the actual world, and superimposed over what he considers to be a seemingly chaotic and formless environment are the patterns which men make and the images they produce. All objects and substances of this world are derived from the same essence: 'Earth and man and sun and bread are one substance; they are made out of the original breath-smitten dust'. The order which men have imposed and the forms in which matter has resolved itself have emerged from chaos: 'Men must never despise the flames and darknesses they have come from'. Chaos and Order, for Brown, like sea and land, night and day, arrogance and acceptance, death and life, are opposites, but are also complementary parts of a whole. Man is a pattern-maker;

179

his labour and art, his whole conception of the Universe is a process of ordering. Conversely, he is subject to patterning. Though every atom strives for individuality, man falls victim to larger correspondences: 'Events are never the same, but they have enough similarity for one to say tentatively that there are constants'. The doubt about constants is part of Brown's scheme. Rather as in the Chinese concept of Yin and Yang there are no areas of human life where just one presiding reality exists. There are 'constants', but there are also differences, elements of complete individuality which, in an extreme form, constitute Chaos. Men create symbols out of 'a huge scattered diversity of experience': '...all voyages past, present and future – become the Voyage'. It is a process of 'pattern-within-flux' which causes Magnus to wonder before his death.

Men extract 'significant' substances from matter. The Magi selected gold, frankincense and myrrh, and alchemists isolated the five elements. These become invested with hope and faith to bridge that other schism between opposites: the gulf between the natural and supernatural. But Brown does not separate sacramental and profane matter. The crushed grape in a peasant's village, the crofter's corn and the loaf of a poor family are as holy as the elements of the Mass in his eyes. They too are part of the circle of growth: death, resurrection, harvest, sustenance and death. Everyman, by his very humanity, is Christ crucified on the staggering fact of his own mortality. Each babe in a poor woman's arms conveys a Nativity, a seed of hope in the pain of poverty. The world is shot through by such correspondences: a babe in a womb, seeds in a glebe, solstice sunshine pinpointing the heart of Maeshowe. Just as men select certain substances to symbolise a transcendant significance informing life, so they choose geographical centres like Maeshowe or the kirk on Birsay, where sometimes, almost paradoxically, the human and divine meet.

Man's life can be conveyed imagistically: a procession of masks, a series of doors or streets, stations of a pilgrimage or the Houses of Life. The central image of this repertoire is the life of Christ. Each cornstalk re-lives this story as does each mouthful of bread. Christ is folded within the Great Mother. She signifies love as obedience, most easily seen in Brown's presentation of the monks. She is embodied in the early Earth Mothers, the Statue in the Hills, the Triad of Marys, the shore-watchers, and those women who give birth to, mate with, and sew man into his last garment. She is an image of unity, but often the Male Element, insisting on material gain and violence, wars against reconciliation.

Brown takes Orkney to be a microcosm of human life where he can view the array of different 'types' at first hand. In *Magnus* he defines how the 'three coats' of human life determine men's lives on the islands. The coat of State, of the feudal hierarchy which binds its members together, is particularly interesting. Brown has an ambivalent attitude to the old order: the laird, the abbot and the king. He understands Mans, the peasant in *Magnus*, and the young socialists in his stories who rail against their rulers, but in "The House of Man" he gives a strangely Medieval picture of an idealised society where all trades and all layers of society have their place. He abhors the loss of the 'ghost' of words and the dehumanising aspects of a machine-orientated life, but admits his debt to modern science. As Pacey says, Brown is forced to accept elements of 'progress' and chaotic change whilst remaining attached to the images and orders which prevailed for centuries and survived, in part, due to the concepts of privilege and obedience. At either extreme of the 'types' present in humanity we find two figures that Brown turns to in order to elaborate his ideas of chaos and order.

Pacey has written that Brown seems to use the tinker figure to represent the poet's eye, and the eye of his imagination. He quotes Brown's statement: 'The old stories have vanished with the horses and tinkers'. I do not think that Brown presents the tinkers as representative of poets. Rather, the poet and tinker are at opposite ends of the array of mankind that Brown decides to present to us, though both have certain elements in common and are brought together in the figure of the Blind Fiddler — a wandering outcast, an angel in disguise whose music is essential for the processes of nature to proceed. The tinker is a vagrant, a furtive beggar whose ceremonies are viewed as both magical and disgusting by Orcadians. He is representative of untramelled freedom, a natural vigour, and his the only road that knows no bounds. He sleeps and mates in ditches, is a victim of the sheriff and church elders and his movements are only dictated by the wind and rain. He dies as he has lived, untroubled by possessions, 'a length of bones in a ditch'. His clothes are threadbare but his pleasures simple: an egg, a scarecrow's jacket, and ale in front of a crofter's fire. He is linked with the oldest inhabitants of the islands, the builders of Maeshowe. In Brown's scheme of life he symbolizes a chaotic element, only mindful of his own needs, often violent, drunk and disdainful of authority. There are hints, however, that he is descended of a royal or supernatural lineage.

The poet in Brown's work is a craftsman like any other. His 'spell' is out to the service of the community. He is part of a hierarchy, honoured by kings and spared in battles and vengeful burnings, for his legends and art make life bearable. He does not, however, create an order that is parallel to worldly order. The sheriff in "The Ballad-Singer" suspects that the poet may lead the minds of the people into 'a labyrinth of happy images'. Clerics see the poet as a challenge to their authority, but all the officials rely on his skill. Poets in Brown generally use the elements of dissidence in their work to reinforce, not to undermine authority. They are the spokesmen for tribes, guardians of naming and interpreters of great events. Sometimes there is the example of a poet who is also of royal stock such as Rognvald Kolson; others are described as 'princes' who abandon their crowns for harps. They initiate the rhythms of seasonal events: honeymoons, summer fires, and they embellish the

the long winter nights with rich and re-lived histories. Poets, like tinkers, are wanderers, but their travels serve to bind lands together as Kolson's poets studied the love lyrics under masters at Narbonne, or as the narrator in the last story in *The Sun's Net* shares ideas with foreign poets. They are servants both of their Muse and, often, of a patron. Brown uses the poet, the patterner, on one hand, and the tinker, the impudent thief, on the other, to loan his vision of mankind a balance that extends outwards to the limits of his cosmology.

Within the great cosmic 'Dance' that matter performs, Brown envisages the forces of Chaos and Order forming one entity which is, paradoxically, both introspectively hostile and at rest. He purposely leaves contradictory elements in his work for he finds these contradictions manifest in the fibre of reality. The nature of man and of the human imagination are described as ultimately impenetrable. The 'bone' will only render a meaning after death. While a widow finds comfort in the medium of faith, the unheeding waves weave a formless pattern. This vast duality of meaning and meaninglessness is an equivalent of the other 'opposites' which Brown makes so much of: the constant overlapping of sea and land, the confrontation of North and South, Viking and monk, death and life, despair and hope. Within each of these opposed and complementary forces there is a small element of its 'opposite', recalling again the Chinese view of the universe. The darkest night is split by a ray of light, Christ appears in the world's most corrupt hour and, in *Fishermen with Ploughs*, Gudrun, like the grain in a jar, carries the hope of a whole community through storms and an alien environment. The principle of Order also holds a germ of chaos within it. Pilate finds a black heart to corn-ears in "Stations of the Cross"; there is chaos at the earth's core in "Peat-Cutting", and a worm gnaws at the heart of matter before Christ redeems the world.

The mysteries of Art, Religion and Love make this duality bearable. Even in these areas Brown has developed a fine sense of symmetry. A poem, instrument of the Word, and music is the medium of sound 'seeking silence'. This tendency of one extreme seeking to encapsulate another is constantly restated in his work. The sea, though warring with the land, is unable to alter the rhythm that cast it against the earth. The hawk and dove motif in *Fishermen with Ploughs* depicts how man craves the power of truth and beauty only to fall back into drudgery and violence. In "When You are Old" the hawk of time slays the 'dove' of an old love but, as Brown shows in a poem like "Carol" both hunter and hunted are necessary for the continuance of the 'Dance'. The hart which bends it head 'obedient to the arrow', associated with Christ's sacrifice, is another such emblem. The flesh and spirit constantly strain against each other, but they also seek a unity, a perfection resulting from their common origin. There will always be a schism in life and the real predator will never quite be the hawk on the shield. Poetry that is appreciated will never be silence. The final clause or 'side' to Brown's cosmology

182

is the reader and the reader's experimental world. In answer to questions concerning the effectiveness of the affirmative and redemptive elements in his work Brown says: 'It is left to the reader — as it always should be — to take out of it what he can'. It is because Brown places a primacy of interpretation upon his readers that his cosmology is difficult to view as a whole. However, hints of this larger and comprehensive scheme are found too clearly and too insistently in the writing to ignore them. Brown's poetic habits are too symmetrical, too concerned with patterning and too heraldic to leave so many loose strands. In this context I believe Robert Duncan to be right when he states:

> Back of each poet's concept of the poem is his concept
> of the meaning of form itself; and his concept of form,
> in turn, where it is serious at all, arises from his concept
> of the nature of the Universe, its lifetime or form, or even
> for some, its lifelessness or formlessness. A mystic cos-
> mogony gives rise to the little world the poet as creator
> makes.

Duncan's statement may be presumptuous in relation to the work of some poets, but this major correspondence is realised in Brown's writing. However, this relation between poetic world and perceived universe demands an act of translation from the reader. It is in confrontation with this difficulty and in the struggle to affirm the Word, that transcendent and unifying entity more splendid than simple language, that Brown becomes an important poet.

II

The recurrence of different Orcadian figures in Brown's verse is immediately evoked in *Fishermen with Ploughs*:

> ...the same people appear and reappear through many
> generations — laird, crofter-fisherman, shepherd, tinker,
> beachcomber, and the women who watch the sea with
> stony patience; all are caught up in 'the wheel of bread'
> that is both 'brutal and holy'.

The fortunes of the questing peoples seem to describe almost an exact circle. The book is 'A Poem Cycle' moving from the "Building of the Ship" to "The Return of the Women". Like Pound's *Cantos* it starts from a launching out upon the holy but unpredictable sea and ends in apparent failure and ruins with men delivered into the keeping of the 'Dragon'. The very act of stating these patterns is a crucial one for Brown. The two poems of drowning in the book make this obvious. Willag remarks to the open mouths on the shore:

> 'Drive old Bess, that fence-breaker, from the oats
> Back to her patch of clover.
> Yes, Breck can have my horse for his five goats.
> And Jeannie is wrong again.'

The small rounds of Willag's life become his overwhelming concerns.

Even in the face of death they inherit his language of affection, his simple but ceremonious rhythms of speech. "The Drowning Brothers" continually stresses the inter-relation of sea and land, fishing and crofting, and, finally, the burn becomes fervently praised in a psalm of drowning:

> The burn is our angel. He praises
> He fills our pails.
> He flames in the face of the drinking beasts.
> He carries the valley filth.
> Out to the seven brightnesses of the bay...

The poem ends:

> The tractor throbbed with one urgent image, bread.
> Heavy with images, the statues drowned.

The modern images pull against the psalm and serve to wrench the reader's attention between the idealised beauty of memories in personal death in an agrarian community and the paucity of the symbolic and looming machine. In both poems the rhythms of a community are affirmed even in the 'teeth' of death. These rhythms, the ceremonies of the poor and the great Dance of Life itself are derived from the central desire of human existence: 'What is the dance but a stylised masque of coupling?' What is coupling but a realisation of the unity to which all life aspires?

The 'shorthand of myth' is employed in "Dragon and Dove" and this literary and folk convention renders spectacular statements ('blacken the coast with yawls') in poetic terms. Thorkeld, lord of the tribe, 'lord of whales', is loaned the stature of a primeval figure (recalling the praise of Offa in the first Mercian Hymn):

> But Thorkeld appraised the hooves of oxen.
> Thorkeld handled the seed of the quartered sun.
> Thorkeld abode a Winter in Bergen
> With shipwrights, westerlings, weighers of bronze.

Gradually we see how the Blind Helmsman, almost a Homeric version of the skald, lessens Thorkeld's stature from the man who 'mingled his bronze with dragon flame' to 'What's Thorkeld? Torrents of silent fish'. Gudrun becomes the hope of the tribe and Njal, the new chief, is urged to 'Seek out Gudrun, the mountain bride./That small urn still has snow in it'. Gudrun's womb is the promise of generation and must come 'to a full fragrant barley girth'. The image of stalks and corn ends the section. The position of the skald is interesting. His first task is a statement of man's mortality, of the inevitability of decay, and yet he takes upon himself Thorkeld's role; just as Thorkeld supplied hope when his 'mouth of the poet guttered' so the poet stresses the need to turn from chaos and the 'black flame', 'to harness the passion of oxen'. Far from tribal fatalism, the poet praises man's assertiveness:

> Man goes, man voyages. His hand swings the star wheel
> This freedom is defeat for the Dragon.

But man does not long possess this vaunted free-will if he is totally at the mercy of the elements. A 'blind' rune starts the sequence. It is the skald who instructs Thorkeld, the tribe, Njal, and the shipwright; he defines their mental horizons and weaves a new myth for the fisher folk: 'Cornstalk unlocks the door of a great king..../....Lust, bread-kissed, becomes love.' But the community occupies the foreground. They are 'pilgrims with seed, vat bearers' and their different roles as sailman, skald and net-weavers are stressed. Their leaders, hymned by the skald till they occupy the full length and breadth of the tribal mind, become the seascape surrounding the ship. Thorkeld's wounds are 'a map of islands' and Gudrun's womb 'throbs from curve to curve' of the horizon.

In the 'Our Lady' section the verse opens with a chapel in the fields and already the jar — store of grain and malt — has become a holy vessel, a Lenten urn. The 'great king' of cornstalk is not only now a figure of sublimation replacing Thorkeld as a vision for the people but is also associated with Christ. Moreover, the very existence of the new generations of agriculturalists is a Crucifixion: 'To drudge in furrows till you drop/Is to be born' ("First Fall"). The land is the Holy Mother: 'Out of that mild mothering hill/And that chaste burn' ("Mother of God"). Rituals of bread-making and weaving are enacted around these centres of belief. The first three poems of the section are openly matriarchal. The Mother is invoked to 'fold' Christ and crofter from these furrows 'as a rapt bairn'. The twelve women (counterparts of the disciples) invoke 'Our Lady of the Atlantic' to save sailors and fishermen. Old earth and sea goddesses emerge, their outlines blending with that of the Christian Holy Virgin. Folk belief and superstition exist alongside the orthodox patterns: 'The knife is beside the stone jar'. One wonders if the 'three-masted' ship is not a symbol of a sailor's Calvary as we remember Stephen Dedalus in the "Proteus" section of *Ulysses* turning suddenly to see a similar vessel. The names of the ships "Trust" and "Bountiful" become attributes of the Mother. The women are shrouded in mystery; they stand 'in the darkening doors', like holy statues in niches, and are 'the makers of fire, preparers of smoke'. The Mother looks out from the appearances of everyday things: flails, candles, stones and kneeling oxen. The quality of incantation about the verses and the line-endings of "Stations of the Cross" — urn, turn, burn, thorn, morn, corn, etc. — are taken up in "Statue in the Hills" as fears of different groups of believers are expressed. Some charming and unusual images emerge: 'Fold of the Agnus Dei', '...Our Lady of Ditch Fires', '(...and you at the end Pieta, quiet chalice)'. Brown rarely closes a poem with Death, and these lines end with the Croft, where Mary and Joseph, angel, shepherd and king meet. There too the animal kingdom is reconciled and water and earth are joined in reverence:

> Our Lady of Dark Ploughs
> Our Lady of Furled Boats
> Our Lady of Kneeling Oxen.

"Helmsman" is a pivotal poem, taking us from a matriarchal setting to the 'Hall and Kirk' poems where the major foci are different external authorities. It is, on the surface, a poem about a shipload of pilgrims – a Bishop, an Earl, a poet, amongst others – sailing to Byzantium.

White domes, jade wine cups, the olive-skinned Greek girls, ikons, Arab mathematicians, Persian poets, ships from Ceylon and mosaics are the images Brown has used elsewhere in writing about this city. In *An Orkney Tapestry* he refers to one huge mosaic called "The Risen Christ", which covered a palace wall, where each tessera had been collected from scattered quarries of the east. This mosaic does not exist today, but if it ever did it could have been situated in the palace of Constantine Porphyrogenitus, which was originally an annex to the Blachernae palace. This extension, built by Manuel I.Comnenos, the emperor who entertained Earl Rognvald, is the only secular building of the ancient city that survives above ground-level in Istanbul today. This is not exclusively a city idealized by Brown then, but Yeats has linked Byzantium in our minds with ageless creativity, the profligate richness of the imagination and the splendour of artifice. The voyage of this poem is also that of life, the quest of state, religion, and art, towards their goal. But a common labourer, 'A sea troll' from Hoy, swings the rudder. Brown is fond of using the style and sentiment of the *Orkneyinga Saga* lyrics to give us this kind of medieval microcosm – the 'heads' of feudal life abstracted and juxtaposed to give the idea of a small kingdom. The labourer brings the isolated rulers together:

> And all this weighty pilgrimage,
> The harp, the sword, the psalter,
> I hurl at Cyprus.
> The sea tears like an acre of blue silk.

Cyprus was named after Cyprian Aphrodite, goddess of sensual love, and blue is of course the colour of the Great Mother's robe. The proto-myth of the Quest lies under this poem. Each figure strives for perfection, but the roses and seapink merely remind the helmsman of his woman. The common man, unpretentious and honest, still guides the great interpreters and mediators of life towards the holy city.

In *A Spell for Green Corn* Storm Kolson, a fiddler 'seen (and heard) in different parts of Europe', makes Sigrid Tomson pregnant. The fiddler's music is condemned by the kirk elders along with the pagan harvest fires. Sigrid is burnt as a witch due to the accusations of various church members. Storm is rumoured to be captured by trows. Sigrid, as she is led to the stake, says: 'I charge ye, O ye daughters of Jerusalem/that ye awake not my love till he please'. There are clear echoes of the "Song of Solomon", the Barleycorn myths, and the legend of the need for music in the earth here. Three horsemen ride between the hills in "Witch" – a staunchly masculine trinity. The mastery of the horse is popularly supposed to have spread from southern Asia into Greece with the Aryans, a racial grouping whose society was strongly patriarchal.

The horsemen that take Wilma are representatives of Protestantism, as
are the 'bible fishermen' who are cursed by their own suspicion, sexual
aggression ('launched their boat...with a wild shout'), and greed. Wilma's
laughter and her red shirt indicate that, like Hardy's Tess and Hester
Phrynne of *The Scarlet Letter*, she is linked with the old goddesses of
fertility and untramelled sexuality. Witch hunts took on a particular
severity in the first half of the 17th century in Orkney. Many were
accused by Scottish clerics and lawyers and later burnt on the Gallow
Hill of Kirkwall and Scalloway. Marwick writes of a Barbara Boundie
who, when questioned by the Orkney Presbytery in 1643, admitted
knowledge of 99 witches. A number of complete accounts of the witch
trials survive. In Norse tradition witches were supposed to gain their
knowledge from trows, but kirk and legal officials sought to link the
fertility rites with the Biblical Devil. The witches, obligingly enough,
began to acquiesce to these Protestant versions of their rites and pacts
and confess that they were allied with Satan. Brown is fully aware of
the grim ironies inherent in such falsifications.

In "Taxman" the horseman interrupts the reel, the girls dancing and
the ale-drinking to bring unwelcome news. The harvest is stored but
now the ruthless greed of a centralised authority is reaching further into
the islands. The Tinker Ikey, 'Egiptian', is castigated. He is a survivor
from an ancient culture and, like Christ and Wilma, he is at the mercy
of the executioner. The brief "Grave stone" reveals the gaunt but humourous epitaph of a fisherman. The humour might be darker than is at
first evident, though, if we see the 'hooves' as symbolic of the gentry,
the 'riding class'. "Buonaparte, the Laird and the Volunteers" reveals
the fate of seven Orcadian men enrolled against their will in His Majesty's
Service. Both the officers who ride into the valley and Buonaparte are
sternly masculine. Five men escape into 'troll-music' and whaling and
the women take up the essential tasks of ploughing and lobster-catching.

The section 'Foldings' shows Brown's impulse to insulate and preserve certain actions and events in Orcadian life and to 'fold' these into
the permanence of his art. 'Foldings' is a careful metaphor full of
maternal and tender associations:

> What they fold, what the shepherds fold,
> Is this, in March,
> A mothering huddle.

The ' Winter Bride ' finds a 'mother and a widow' co-existing within one
person balanced on a crag — this is both a statue and an ordinary woman.
Against the surge of time and 'progress' Brown saves these glimpses of
island life like the Laird desiring to '...from clutches of sea/Save a torn
net'. Poverty in these circumstances, the wearing down by hardship and
by the hunger of an agrarian existence, is a commonplace, even a virtue.
In "Then Four Great Angels, Air, Water, Fire, Earth, Being Summoned,
Fell From Their Eternal Circuits Unto Poverty At His Single Station,
To Be His Servitors", the elements are resolved in the desperate grinding

of food from a hard environment. As Poverty, the personification and capitalisation simultaneously reminding one of Traherne's meditations and Swift's savage satires on pompous governmental rhetoric, becomes, like Christ, a fixed point, aspects of the life of the poor gain the status of momentous, even transcendental, events. The 'meal' of the poem could refer to men and the first lines remind one of a Creation myth. "Black Furrow, Gray Furrow", a similarly dense poem, reveals the ploughing and meshing together of sexual, religious and folk motifs. It becomes a description of the Islander's coat-of-arms but the heraldic certainties are blurred by the synaesthetic effects of showing 'dust' as fecund and a coulter-blade emerging from the furrow. The inversion of ordinary associations emphasises the tenet of interpenetration.

In "A Winter Bride" we find that the different roles which a woman plays overlap in time of crisis: '(Girl and widow across a drowned wife/ Laid wondering neck on neck)'. The hard Orcadian namings and facts of Jock's death move through the soft and winding sounds of the twelfth and thirteenth lines to a sudden concentration of vulnerability and menace. 'She took the soundless choir of fish/And a sharp knife...' Her silence and awe throw the 'mouthing cuithes' and the blade into sharp relief. Nature seems an arbitrary flux here and the fine tension between uncomprehending shock, bitterness and reverence makes the ending admirable.

Brown splices what are ostensibly snippets of reportage into his poetry. (A recent collection, *Letters from Hamnavoe*, is made up of a selection of his newspaper articles). In Brown's hands the characters become 'lords of legend' beyond change or chance whereas the storytellers and their listeners are 'shadows'. The poet folds all into the permanence of art and, in this section, the actions and characters are dateless: a pre-Industrial aura of innocence, bravery and savagery surrounds them. In "A Jar of Honey", a prose-poem, the rhythms gradually co-ordinate the different characters, who, in their actions, both ordained and aimless, perform a magical and alchemical rite. The father has a 'holy' look and when he is eventually called in:

> He wouldn't move. He was afraid of the elemental women
> inside there, with their water and fire, the terrible priest-
> ess and her servers, swaddlers, shrouders, guardians of the
> gate of birth and the gate of death.

The chief midwife becomes a startling figure rather like a hieratic sculpture or a fertility fetish from the Cave Age: 'with huge hands and a face like stone'. The scene fills with lines of correspondence – some brief and others sustained. At times the allegory of birth is crude: the croft of Scar and the honey-leaking fissure are intrusive, demanding our attention for the sweetness, pain and danger of child delivery. The seven men, boy and old man are plainly embodiments of stages in human progress and the girls with circling arms and flame-red hair represent goddesses, or more specifically, vestals: attendants for the mystery. Brown folds and refolds images of life-in-death and death-in-life into one another. The boy has 'gray wax' at his mouth and the old man spits as he walks to the boats. The mother and child are offstage though they are plainly central presences in the poem and inhabit the thoughts of the watchers and the surrounding landscape. The scythe is the midwife's knife; the red stone, the mother's blood; and the jar of honey, the child and labour of all women, who, like worker bees, perpetuate life.

We have already acknowledged the unifying importance of the ceremonies of the people in Brown's work, but these rituals are also fundamental to this poet's vision of history:

> It is a ceremony that makes bearable for us the terrors and ecstasies that lie deep in the earth and in our earth-nourished human nature. Only the saints can encounter those 'realities'. What saves us is ceremony. By means of ceremony we keep our foothold in the estate of man, and remain good citizens of the kingdom of the ear of corn. Ceremony makes everything bearable and beautiful for us. Transfigured by ceremony, the truths we could not otherwise endure come to us. We invite them to enter. We set them down at our tables. These angels bring gifts for the house of the soul...

There is no need to indicate the suspect nature of the assumption: 'ceremony makes...everything beautiful for us' or the beguiling readiness with which the reader is drawn in to the 12th century collective pronoun. The words fold history together until 'we' all inhabit the allegorical 'estate of man'. Brown feels able to appreciate the

> terror and exaltation that came upon the first farmer who broke the earth. It was a terrible thing he had done to put wounds on the great dark mother.

He is conscious of the volition which drove the first tribal peoples to anthropomorphise the hills, deify men and fear the spirits they thought were latent in nature. This is a natural part of the planetary cycle for:

> The people themselves are moulded by the earth contours and the shifting waters they live among. They are made of the same dust as the hills they cultivate.

This abrupt assertion leads us to "Jock", a poem which marries the different traditions of seasonal rites, popular story and ancient myth. 'Winter' ends with a dazzling juxtaposition worthy of the Metaphysical poets' mordant wit: '...one ewe whose bones/Are lost again in a drift of daffodils'. In the 'Spring' section each rummaged article contributes to the reader's picture of Jock: 'Twelve lobster boxes, a fiddle bow,/A gun, and a coffin half-made'. In an ingenious twist, with a story of drunkenness, Brown aligns Jock with John Barleycorn, the legends surrounding Robert Burns and the members of the secret society, the Brotherhood of the Plough. Jock is a maker of ceremony; his perceptual frame of reference is shaped by that tendency which blurs and blends outlines till the Plough is creaturely, human, Jock's friend who has fathered the grain that nearly killed him. The 'plough-blade', 'that powerful curve' in its 'winter trance' seems an updated legendary and phallic sword stirring with spring warmth and the promise of new conquests. Burns' reputation as sexually voracious reinforces the impression of masculine strength and menace beneath the humourous voice of the poem.

With 'Summer' comes the recital of mock-heroic feats. It reminds us of Thorkeld, but there is a muffled laughter in the shift between: 'Who thronged the dinghy with bronze and silver/each sunset? Jock', and 'Who put Bella's Sunday hat on the scarecrow? Jock./Who got drunk at the seven agricultural shows? Jock.' Jock 'steals' fire from the winter and provides fertility for the cattle of twelve crofters, but the two final lines show how Bella shamed the so-called hero. Jock becomes Canute in the autumn seas of corn, but it is the women who salvage summer's 'cargo': 'Tall women stoop among sheaves/With bronze throats'. The 'bronze throats' are baling hoops, but it is a detail which adds a sense of wonder to the picture. The women's throats are 'bronze' with sunlight and the glow of wheat; the same throats might soon be sonorous with gossip or death keenings. It is an image repeated in the final section of the cycle calling to mind the association between 'bronze throats' and wombs, torcs and vaginas, especially those of Bronze age goddesses. These timeless Guardians are the conserving power in the community, storing seed and harvest in spite of and against the more prodigal strength of Jock, the Male Principle.

'Foldings', like 'Hall and Kirk', finishes on a note of renewal, but the penultimate poem in each section contains death. The black queen who enters "Funeral" seems the personification of Death who has dethroned her husband. Persephone appears in "Girl", a poem in the next section, but the widow of "Funeral" cannot be brought back from Hades with a 'dish of salt' or 'a jar of oil'. Each facet of life in the poem builds up to surprising juxtapositions. The cat's nose sniffing the dead man is 'Cold kissing cold', and this statement echoes backward and forward through the lines as the ritual action of neighbours (urged along by insistent 'Ands' and 'Cames') moves to the final stasis. Death sits, a still certainty in the middle of life's bustle and obsessional concerns.

Before we pass to the Age of the Machine, Brown gives us a powerful poem asserting the primacy of the plough and the furrow. In the final section whales are seen as 'tons of love', 'A winter of work for candle makers', 'thunderers' — they are a promise of plenitude, a bridge between two existences: 'Far back, those floating feast-halls belched./ Soon the stars flashed around like stalks of corn'. Tammag seems a reincarnation of Thorkeld, who was identified with oxen and the 'quartered sun'. The ploughman labours between the fire of the ox's mouth and a snow of gulls. The job is severe and intractable for the struggle with the ox is man's fight with the earth itself: 'a black block'. Between the elements Tammag is wrenched by the stony ground. The crowds run for the easy prizes of a vast promise and gulls like 'asylums' but Tammag remains. He and the ox '...tore from the black sun/Loaf, honey-comb, fleece, ale-jar, fiddle'. The 'black sun' is chaotic nature, a swift double-image of solar and telluric interchange that, like the block-like ox with a 'mouth like a furnace', also recalls the circle of peat. Is Tammag the potent counterpart of Jock, an actual hero revealing the waning but still active strength of the agrarian peasant? Such a relationship with the earth involves total commitment; Tammag is part of the plough and ox and when the blade strikes stone it tears at his shoulder. Bread, sweetness, clothing and life-enhancing ceremony are the gains of this exclusive relationship, but we cannot forget the dangers of male arrogance or the potential pride of Tammag once he feels he has laid the seventh furrow.

In "The Stone Hawk" the young have already been attracted by lipstick and gramophones: the meagreness of the haddock catch seems a vestige of a past life that machinery has superceded. In "The Laird's Falcon" the bird breaks from the stillness of heraldry hinting that the old rulers only emerge rarely from the paralysis that vitrifies them. Doves and the hopes of earlier peoples are killed, but their fate is a voluntary submission; they 'Took his bone circle in their throats'. The dove is a bird of love and spirituality in Brown. The hawk is linked with the onrush of time or predatory fate. The new boat in "Sea-Runes" is called 'Pigeon': 'Go gentle, dove/Among skuas, easterlies, reefs, whale-backs'. But even the falcon, 'lord of space', is lost now in 'a stone enchantment'. The heraldry is renewed but it is no longer linked with the fecund 'quarterings of the field', rather with loss, darkness, stone and enchantment. The motif of the bird of prey or dark angel and their victims runs through these poems, countering the small glimpses of promise linked with the children and old people. The beauty of the images: 'Rain. A sleeve dripping./Broken mirrors all about me' in "The Scarecrow in the Schoolmaster's Oats" elicits a tone of genuine wonder from the scholarly narrator and yet, by this stage of the book, the listing of different names – Canute, Midas, Ikey – has become tenuous and self-conscious. There is a distinct and self-depracating irony in the way the voice notes its desire to align Hogmany and the colour of whiskey with the old beliefs: 'I am – what you guess – King Barley-corn'. Elders still 'read' the sea and make 'orderly' furrows, but newer tensions are plainly realised in the recollections of "A Child's Calendar". At first we have the primeval and timeless impact of the land linked with the Feminine Principle:

> They stand about like ancient women,
> The February hills.
> They have seen many a coming and going, the hills.

Christianity is inculcated in the child's education:

> Daffodils at the door in April,
> Three shawled Marys.
> A lark splurges in galilees of sky.

In July the tourists arrive: '...cameras, binoculars, bird books'. Man's technology has not gained him the knowledge of plant and animal life which a child from the islands inherits. With December, the old connection between the families who have not traded poverty for material prosperity and Christ's story is renewed.

Fishmongers pay for fish with 'dull bits of silver', a beachcomber's idea of heaven is 'a seachest with a thousand gold coins', and the woman in "Butter" is left with only a 'scrape' of yellow to show for her churning. A note of desperation enters the poem: 'The old cow is giving me a mad/look'. In "Hill Runes" the natural thirsts of ploughman and horse, the ability of even well-lettered Orcadians to plough the soil, and the Smithy's 'flames of love' and, by implication, human sexuality, are threatened:

> The horsemen are red in the stable
> With whisky and wrath.
> The petrol-drinker is in the hills.
> ("Tractor")

The kenning-like construction for a machine, indicating a mind intrigued by runic connections, has no conception of how vast the upheavals of mechanisation will prove. Water and prices rise. Such innocents as the old couple in "Sabbath" endure the 'year of the submarine' and their story is a pastoral of hard labour and 'gaunt acre', but their generation is the last that will be able to lead such a life which has hardly changed since the rhythms of agrarian existence were established.

"The Drowning Brothers" is a crucial poem in this context; for the last time before the old crofts fall into disuse. the primeval Nature mysticism rears its head. Corn is personified. Christ and Barleycorn, Kings and Holy Fools, and angels in tinker's clothing, join together in the picture: '...a prodigal, stood in the door of the sun/Arrayed in harvest patches'. The brothers fear their sources: 'old sweat and dung', and the landscape broods as their attentions are focussed increasingly on water, denying the interpenetration of the elements. It is the tractor which finally drowns them. The very urgency of the machine ushers in another pace of life disturbing older work rhythms. The brothers become 'heavy' with lost images of their past lives and, cast out by the exclusive image of monetary gain, they drown. Statues can be symbols of art divorced from life in Brown's work, but here the idea of death-chilled limbs, a departing order closed into itself, and flesh vitrified by the approach of a foreign ethic merge in the sterile and cold stone.

In "Dead Fires" the first cold hearth is 'Burnmouth', a name encapsulating the ox's 'furnace', peat and the stream's strength ridding the villages of waste. 'Park', the croft where a community came to pay their respects in "Funeral", is now lost even to the healing touch of women. This was a human environment with a fire 'like a heart in each house' and the old names mix with and reinforce the impressions of the life going on around them even in their abandonment. They are names affirming the sacred bonding of human and animal life: Bunertoon

192

echoes the thrushes' song; Scar, once the croft of birth, is the rat's quick turn, and Reumin rolls off the tongue imaging the lonely, passing sheep. Each name is a cultural hieroglyphic. Bunertoon brings back the age of the 'toonships' — areas of good easily farmed land which has been in use for centuries. In many of these 'toonships' the Norse families had survived the encroachment of Scottish tyrants and this had continued up to the beginning of the eighteenth century. Scar and Park also sound as if they had their origins in the Norn language and do not simply hold the English meanings we associate with them. Brown finds the old farm names 'functional, powerful, beautiful'. But even a 'cold angel' is preferable to 'A Black Pentecost'.

The latter part of 'The Stone Hawk' section deals with a cultural conflict which Brown himself must have seen as a young child. Tractors were introduced to the islands during the 1930s. In 1939 there were still 6,250 horses in the islands, but by 1960 there were only 718, and half of these were ponies. The crofts of "Dead Fires" are a sight Brown must have seen, for the depopulation of Orkney has been at its worst over the last fifty years. However, in the first five sections of the book, Brown has produced a historical schema which is, at best, very uneven and shaped by his Catholic belief and, at worst, a one-sided and simplistic vision. In his introduction to the book he chooses to cite the Reformation, annexation to Scotland, foreign wars and compulsory education as those forces which altered the islanders' existence, mainly in a negative way. In fact, Adam Bothwell, Bishop of Orkney, made sure that 1560, the year of the Reformation, passed peacefully on the islands. The earls were often corrupt, and two Sheriffs, Robert and Patrick Stewart, had to be ousted with the help of central government and the British king. In 1651 Cromwell sent an occupying army to Orkney and these Protestants taught the inhabitants many useful crafts, such as improved methods of agriculture, weaving, and the use of the spinning wheel. It was the power of 'dull silver' and trading which finally put an end to the unproductive farms and crippling agrarian methods which had hardly changed since the Middle Ages. The 'Planking' system of the 1830s finally made large and prosperous farms possible by dividing more of the land up into fields. It was the timely response of government to local outcry which led to the 'Crofter's Magna Carta' of 1886, which must have been. as Shearer. Groundwater and Mackay have written, '...for the rank and file of Orkney people...probably the greatest event of the century...' This act made rents fairer, secured tenants from unjust eviction, and set up a commission to hear grievances.

Jock's 'golden spindrift' and the visionary harvests of 'Ploughman and Whales' must have been sometime during the period 1850-1910, but the idea of an Orkney where poverty and rich farms, tinkers and 'cargoes of summer', co-exist pervades the bulk of Brown's writings. *Fishermen with Ploughs* is supposed to show the 'slow evolution' of a people, but instead it shifts from poems about the 9th century through two 'bridging poems' concerning the pilgrimage of 1151 and the witch-burnings of the Reformation to Buonaparte and the beginning of the 19th century. If these dates were not noticed it might be easy for the reader to construct the picture of a late 19th century Orkney which stretches back to the Middle Ages with very little change; in fact, by grouping the poems as he has, Brown encourages us to do this. The 'Our Lady' poems deal with an unspecified period and, because of the historical 'blurring' due to the arrangement of the poems, these prayers seem to spread forward through the time-scale of the book. This myth of a continuum threatened only by the patristic cultures and the Machine Age is part of the method by which Brown creates the idea of the Catholic 'Dance of Life' and the desirability of the feudal and simple community in comparison with the gifts of progress. One only has to read the eye-witness accounts in Ronald Miller's *Orkney* to understand the painfully slow process by which the majority of Orcadians gradually worked towards some marginal comfort, security and health. Brown, it is true, has admitted the benefits of science, but he has, in these poems praising a hard but satisfying round of labour and rest, idealised the actual island into the kingdom of the Ear of Corn. What sets out to be a 'historical cycle' becomes a group of poems, some about a Norse tribe and the majority about a community of the last century, linked by devotional poems stressing a continuity and harmony which was only disrupted by the advent of machines. Mechanisation is the most concerted attack by the patristic, centralised and Male-dominted outsiders who take advantage of the islanders' greed and tip the scales towards ultimate Chaos and the need for another myth: that of the efficacious, primitive and terrible 'cleansing'.

III

"The Return of the Women" is a prose-poem narrated through the thoughts of seven women. Layers of attributes accumulate around the characters recalling the powers associated with gods, goddesses, heroes and heroines. For example, Jane is initially 'An ox-eyed Juno' in a classroom version of the Troy story, and she is shown directing the players' comings and goings. Siegfried, a bearded oarsman whose name reminds us of Germanic legend, enters into the Homeric or Dantesque landscape after the holocaust occurs and saves her. The nature of the disaster is not specified, but there are hints in the first passage (Helen looking from a tall turret, Ulysses breathing on a lens) that a bomb has been dropped. Jane is blinded but her man recognises the fact that: 'They can/generally see more than other folk, the blind'. Her baby dies when the survivors reach Hoy and she becomes convinced that only so much learning is good for men:

> ...but no history and no poetry, and only enough
> mathematics for them to count to a hundred. Beyond that,
> the black circle of Mephistopheles. We broke into it. We

were burned.

She is skilled in weaving and Brown gives her a great insight. She remains the teacher of the community but she is an instructor who determines the crafts which are essential and does not pursue knowledge for its own sake.

Natasha is a Latin name and originally meant 'Christmas-child'; she holds a grain of promise within her — the memory of old music which can ease the transition into the new existence. Her violin and statues are lost. These are significant items for Brown. His fiddler, stressing the primacy of utile art. asks '...What are all these statues and violins and calf-bound editions for?' Natasha loses her interest in artistic activity divorced from life, and finds herself listening for the natural sources of music: 'I love these birds, the lost cold drifting sea syllables'. The figure of Natasha enables Brown to renew the motif of Dove and Hawk in the narrative. The skipper eventually gives her a hawk and the pigeons move from her door. The hawk, symbol of lordship and physical mastery, asserts itself.

Bianca is an older woman, a vigilant and patient nurse. She is linked several times with the planet Venus. Because of her previous occupation she is intimately aware of man's animal nature: the 'narrow circle of the beasts'. She remains conscious of her vocation:

> I will have to be very patient, make myself a stone in the
> middle of these fires. Some day they may need me. I
> don't know. That's Venus, and I think up there, now,
> very faintly, the Plough.

Her fantasy of herself as a stone surrounded by fires reminds us of the Venuses of Asia Minor and the squat idols of the cave-dwellers. Eventually she lives alone, half way between the hills and the sea. The location of her home hints of her ultimate desire to unite the elements. She is a midwife, a cold sybil who gathers knowledge and delivers the children of the survivors.

Sophie is a Greek name meaning 'wisdom'. She is strongly connected with the land and inherits Brown's use of the Universal Dance motif. David, her husband, is a ploughman and his plough inspires a sense of wonder in Sophie (the sexual connections are obvious). David used to be a climber and Sophie is attracted by the names 'Jura with the three breasts' and 'Eriskay, island of music....Iona of the saints'. Her croft is called 'Greenhill' and is built under a hill between the horns of a bay. Her bodily curves are linked to 'the harder curve of the oar and plough'. She is soon pregnant; she was a singer and dancer before the Black Flame and now: 'Deep inside me a new heaviness stirs and sways, poised, the sea-begotten dancer'. The ambiguity of 'sea-begotten' (conceived at or by the sea?) supports Sophie's connections with an earth goddess. Her monologues are full of images of ripeness. The couple's 'green corn is tallest of all now' and David is naturally talented with animals. He and Sophie seem to recall the Lord of the Animals and his paramour who, in many cave paintings, bears a cornucopia. The skipper trying to steal their baby could be viewed as an allegory of the way tribal chieftains used to confiscate land and produce. The theft is thwarted and there is a tremendous primeval power in the picture of the father watching the attempt: 'David stood to his thighs in the/quaking earth'. Sophie also inherits Brown's idea of the 'Dance of Bread'. As harvesters once became dancers, Sophie now wonders when forced to reap: 'How can a dancer become a harvester in a day?' At sundown she can even hear the 'rapture of quick small hidden dancers' in the larksong, and this echoes the ancient superstition of trows, dancers under the hill.

Teresa is a Greek name meaning 'carrying ears of corn'. At the very moment that men are about to betray Christ in a play the Black Flame intrudes into her chapel and she is carried to sea. This woman, of a sensitive, religious temperament, searches for a resurrection: 'We never reached the empty tomb in the garden'. Already, in referring to Columba (whose name means 'Dove') and Magnus, she is beginning to endow the rituals of labour and sacrifice with a weight of localised reverence. Her muttering of the name Columbus perhaps refers to another voyage or enterprise which finally degenerated. Her prayer brings home with full force the import of what we are reading: '...have a care with the world's last few gutterings of breath'. She describes the arrival and the building of seven houses. She is convinced that 'we must live now as if we existed in some poor pagan ballad, unparadised'. The sacrifice of Good Friday is linked in her mind with the privations which the settlers endure. The analogy of music is used to convey the strength of her belief. The Mass has a 'transfiguring music' but in discarding her rosary Teresa turns to the oldest of songs in a childish rhyme: grave – wave – weave; thorn – mourn – corn. She soon learns that these two musics are inseperable. Primitive incantation turns into 'Gloria' as the now humbled community turns to consider the ancient joy of fertility. Teresa retrieves her rosary, newly aware of the pattern running through apparent chaos. The cries of happiness at childbirth are 'a Gloria of fisherman and shepherd and ploughman'. By the time of her last monologue Teresa has given voice to the full round of Brown's ideas about the Passion of all men, agricultural processes and new life. Her final worries about the 'unhallowed' status of her baby are assuaged by the God-bearer moving in a stone. She sees not only the divine presence in the rock but also the endless surge of grief and patience' that went into it from 'the girls, the young wives, the mothers, widows, the very old ones'. This could be the statue of Mary from Rackwick worn smooth by the sea. It mediates between earth and heaven and represents the sanctifying power of feminine care and love. Teresa's husband complains 'It is only a stone', but the woman wants her child to be born near it 'in the heart of Winter', recalling the solstice stone at Maeshowe and the 'seed of promise'.

Marilyn's name is a modern form of Mary which originally meant 'long-wished-for-child'. It is also, needless to say, the name of a screen idol admired predominantly for her sex appeal. Hollywood too has created its goddesses, its own particular brand of myth. She is a slant-eyed, voluptuous 15 year old, nicknamed 'Apple Blossom'; even her skin is pink and white. She seems the very embodiment of early and irresponsible sensuality. She also perhaps represents the oldest temptation — the apple that the skipper picks; the act that starts the downhill progress for the community as a whole.

Trudi's name is culled from Old German and means 'spear-strength'. She is literate and knows of Avalon, the Hesperides and Tir-Nan-Og, but possesses, as well as this mythic consciousness, an air of commonsense: 'We must study the life of otters'. Her second speech is a description of the skipper who quickly becomes the dominant figure in the story. Her intonation and recounting of feats of strength echo those of Thorkeld's admirers:

> He hewed querns from an immense boulder at the beach,
> stone circles out of a stone sphere. He has put new strakes
> in the Truelove....

Trudi's speech becomes a counterpoint to the skipper's actions. She is given the final monologue about Harvest. There is something of the Teutonic hero-worshipper in her — a grudging admiration of the super-man. The Harvest is blighted, and the skipper turns their attention to the sea. Just as the Blind Helmsman urged the Sea People to think of farming, so the skipper reminds these farmers of the whales, symbols of renewed wealth: 'Every whale is a storehouse of meat and oil'.

This group of people in the skipper's longhouse on Hoy are ostensibly at the closing-point of a great circle. The one jar of ale which has been saved is

> a lamp that lit the feet of men from Babylon to Hiroshima,
> a merry wayfaring, a sacred, storied centuries-long procession.

It is a strange language this, for the route from Babylon to Hiroshima — 'a merry wayfaring' — especially spoken in the desolate farmhouse on Hoy as the world's last corn is drunk away. Already the jar is 'ceremonial'. Saul, the lecherous, domineering tyrant, becomes 'patriarch, law-giver, priest, keeper of seed, measurer of the West, laird'. Old patterns begin to emerge and there is a touch of wonder in Trudi's voice as she sees Siegfried drink 'inclining his face towards Saul'. The skipper's speech, reminiscent of alliterative Anglo-Saxon or Norse, is scrupulously selective, mentioning only the bravery and hardships of the people. The skipper's dream has become the centre of the piece, but it is not the only dream of the people. David and Sophie are not present and must have defied him. His dreams of a stable society with himself as aristo-cratic head are smashed with the empty jar he dashes to the ground. Bianca, the childless midwife, wails: 'She alone, a cry like a woman in hard travail'. The birth of a new people is complete: 'The fish people sit round the table'. The lamp of fish-oil 'drips and glims and smokes'. It is a symbol of their existence, precarious, irregular and hemmed by

197

shadow. The 'enormous jerking masquerade' could refer to the immediate scene, but behind this whole section has lain the idea of history as a
masquerade: 'a merry wayfaring' from crisis to crisis. The 'Dragon' of
physical and psychic darkness and of primitive vulnerability to dark
impulses has mastered these people, yet to Brown this is not the end:

The great song must begin all over again, very far back,
beyond the oxen and millstones and bronze throats
of agriculture.

Darkness is seen as a nascent level of existence – a level at which the
oldest rhythms of life become meaningful again. In the short story "The
Seven Poets" the Siberian poet speaks of the need to return speech to
'elemental sound'. One of his listeners notes:

Always we feel that we are one with the earth. We understand the silence of stones. We re-affirm our kinship with
fish and stars.

There is no way in which the Hoy refugees can avoid their kinship
with the earth. Their collective recognition of this bond is part of the
darkness which they face. Later in "The Seven Poets" an Eskimo poet
recites the story of a hunt:

...They hunted down that whale
They filled a hundred lamps from his belly.
Just when the last lamp was empty
The sun peeped at us over a low rim of ice.
Dead whale, drowned hunters, devoured sun
Inside this circle all dances are made.

As a myth of seasonal change, of the discovery of artificial light and
of a kind of resurrection, the model of the whale is admirable. Just as,
in the story of Samson, honey comes from a dead lion, so here light
gleams out of death. Additionally, there are people moving like the post-
Apocalyptic fisherfolk among 'black times'. The circle of the final line
is that of lamplight, the sun, the all-encompassing bond of reliance between hunter, beasts and the elements. It is also the circle of primeval
life, where life is renewed. The Siberian must take the risk of bringing
the word back to the elements for purification. The fisherman must
face the darknesses, psychological and external, to renew the great
song with a fresh vigour. In such a setting word and ceremony must develop as proof against 'what seems to be the futility, pain and idiocy
of life'.

How successful is Brown's Apocalyptic vision? The final section and
Brown's introductory words about 'oxen, millstones and bronze
throats' remind of Muir's people who desert the tractors in favour of
oxen in "The Horses":

We make our oxen drag our rusty ploughs,
Long laid aside. We have gone back
Far past our father's lands.

Both Orcadians have idealised an island landscape of the late 19th century and both choose to show the destruction which ensues when machinery, science and centralised power interfere with that order. The names of the men and women gathered in Brown's story represent the major western civilisations: Greeks, Romans, Israelites, the Teutonic peoples, the Italy of the Renaissance and modern America. As in the picture of voyagers in the 'Dove' and 'Guthaland' we are presented with a microcosm of human existence. Additionally, each of the seven women seems to represent a particular human faculty. Natasha seems to parallel Euterpe, muse of lyric poetry, and each of the women can be associated with the daughters of Zeus. We are shown a scene of global disaster and the failures of the survivors emphasise the human need to return to the ancient sources for the Word and the ceremony. Brown offers us the circle as the basis for this 'history', but the story ends at one extreme of convexity. (Brown reveals his interest in this model for time in "When You are Old"). One feels at the end of "The Return of the Women" that the pendulum must, if painfully slowly, swing back to the hard Eden of "Foldings". There are many fine and moving poems in this volume, but there is a sense of strain in the schema as a whole which is emphasised, not vindicated, by the paradox of 'a merry wayfaring from Babylon to Hiroshima'. Brown's sacramental vision of history does not make these final scenes as convincing as those of the poems. The Orkney of his mind is so much more easily evoked in poetry than in this prose-poem with leanings towards realism. In "The Return of the Women" the allegories and analogues of the Trojan story, the voyage of the 'first people' and the Christian experience, rest uneasily around the actions of the characters. Brown's vision of a 20th century holocaust remains a sketch.

In the first stanza of "Bethlehem" we see a new stage in the development of a complex weave. Each statement is expressive not only of a person but of a whole mode of life. 'Gloria, Gloria, Gloria' is the angels' song, but it is significantly placed before the actual birth of the Christ-child. This is the 'Gloria' of Christians, but it is also the satisfaction of peasantry when all is 'folded' in for the Winter, the last of the ewes is safely gathered, the inn is 'full up' and the soldiers are mustering, but even in this atmosphere of safety and warmth there is the first sorrow: 'that the dove should vanish'. The inset list of names at the beginning gives clues to the identity of each speaker. The appearance of the star leads us to the next stanza and an explanation:

...the scrieving star
The star, alpha to omega, spells on
Gloria in excelsis Deo

The Magus seeks for the essential signs in all things: the Word, telling of the nature of God, written in the processes of the physical world. With the second sorrow a new desperation enters the work – the very tool with which man ekes his life out of the soil has been made crooked, perverted. The sky in its appearance reminds the watcher of 'psalms and angels'. This may suggest that the shepherds saw some imagined host or that the Gospel writers were merely using a metaphor for coldness in the word 'angel'. In fact, because Brown's writing depends so much on metaphor, the supernatural and natural become interchangeable, at points metaphors for each other. Christ Himself was a user of metaphors: Bread of Life, the Good Shepherd, the Rock and Living Waters. Brown is aware of the overlays which the story of the Nativity has collected in the form of analogues and devotional literature. The song of the angels in Latin breaks into the verse again and as the message grows in urgency we are told that the very 'seed', the hope of men, is black. However, as the soldier's mission becomes increasingly sinister, so the great cure for the world's sickness becomes more accessible and ordinary: 'A drop of mulled ale for winter bones'. 'Soldiers in a corn-field' presents an image of hostility at the very birthplace of life. The Holy Family arrives but the wise man is baffled at how a knowledge that transcends all his previously gained wisdom can be realised. The first two lines of the fifth verse show us the contending interests involved in the affair. There is both physical and spiritual hunger yet the State cannot allow reforms. The captain has his job to do just as urgently as those who suffer hunger-pangs. The Word is uttered but the child is a usurper to the Romans. The alliterative questions of the final two lines cast the issue forward into time: 'Whose bairn?' The interleaving of

different voices with no distinguishing pause between them reveals that
Brown is using character in the same way as he has used motif and symbol previously to stress unity. All these personae are implicated in
Christ's birth and death. Moreover, because of the lack of individuality,
the reader is encouraged to identify with both Magus and soldier, Shepherd and Angel. The gap between good and evil is not clearly defined:
the victim needs the executioner, the hart must turn obedient to the
arrow. The central 'personality' of the poem is both sinister and loving,
an amalgam of human traits, for Christ's compassion extends to all.
Brown, in folding voice into voice here, is attempting to convey new
subtleties by use of a form which is less static and more condensed than
those of his previous poems. The merging of personalities also makes us
aware of the artificiality of literature: how easy it is to manipulate details and persuade the reader to enter a tacit collusion with the fictive
poetic world.

There seem to be hints of at least three settings in "The Golden
Door": Heaven, the home of the Artistic Imagination, and the palace of
a Magus. Christ was exiled to a desert on a foreign planet. The mysterious black spiral could be the descent into a human birth. The ruler's
throne is withering because of man's sin, his determination to separate
himself from God. If, on the other hand, we take it to be an earthly
palace, all seems well in the king's rooms. The luxurious garments are
still being made but the scene within the golden door, within, perhaps,
the spiritual core of the kingdom, shows decay. The palace could also
symbolise the impotence stemming from artistic isolation, and the
stationary planet the need to be in contact with the natural world.

The shelterless 'boy' of the second section could be the Son of Man
who has no home, and the golden doors here symbolise the unrespons-
ive minds of men. The Christ who stands at the door and knocks is a
poignant image and one which Geoffrey Hill uses to fine effect in the
last poem of *Lachrimae*. The wise man waits with his charts but these
are part of the old knowledge which does not avail. The image requires
a different response.

The presence of the lawman in the Third section hints at the rule of
an old regime, governed by the legalistic demands of the Old Testament.
The names of the stars remind of the metaphysical sensibility of the
early tribes, of folklore, mysticism and ceremony. These stars are
'faithful' to the watcher; they obey his summons and are easily recognised, but the silent star like Christ, the thief or stranger in the night, is
an intruder. The wise man 'imagines' a title which could mirror the process of intuitive understanding or merely point out the possibility of
wishful thinking. The 'Door of Corn' is, to Brown, a redemption of the
oldest threshold of human settlement and a reminder of the sanctifying
power of the Bread of Life.

The third poem in this section, "Yule", seems at first to be a simple
overlapping between the Christian story and a cryptic parable involving

201

a detatchment of soldiers trying to cut down a tree. The hopes of the villagers: 'coloured tissue and paper lanterns', simple and non-aggressive pleasures, not only threaten hierarchic power by their communal appeal but also make irrelevant the old custom of the Yule log (which could be used as a feudal sop for the villagers). The soldiers represent the intrusion of external authority but, by a deft twist on Brown's part, they are also obedient servants of the old mythic legalism which demands a healing death. The reference to Blok reminds us of the stylised landscapes of the Russian symbolist poet, Aleksandr Aleksandrovich Blok, who also used folklore and peasant life to locate and invigorate his poetry. The 'New Covenant' of 'childishness' and 'crib' makes useless the strength of the executioner's arms, but the old demands for the death of a Lamb will assert themselves in time.

"The Keeper of the Midnight Gate" progresses through questions and analogies and, again, the different arrivals of the familiar personae are seen from a series of oblique angles. Translation is becoming the central poetic activity in these poems: the reader is invited to be a willing partner in the process. The Wise Men become: '...Daffodil-face, Ebony-face, Nut-face'. The speaker could be an ordinary gate-keeper, Death or one of the soldiers. The voices fluctuate between acceptance: 'Go in peace...', vicious temper: 'With your foreign stinks...', and the deliverance of sinister lists relating to childbirth. The names of the pregnant women are also those of great judges and heroines of the Jewish past. 'The Midnight Gate', Death, is shown to be at the very heart of life. The robin, arbiter of Spring, a speck of vivid colour recalling the flame of life in a bleak landscape, possibly Christ Himself, receives one crumb. The Biblical Christ only requires a grain of faith from a disciple.

"A Poem for Shelter" starts with subdued but passionate questioning, emphasising Christ's voluntary diminution. Here he is Father and Child of all. Childishness — Christ's assumption of the child's nature — is not enough and, suddenly, we are cast back to the Yule tree. He must become the 'rooftree', the 'axile-tree' of the Universe. Christ's splendour outshone the palaces of "The Golden Door"; now men, mindful of His sacrifice, should make Him their 'centre'.

In "Chinamen" the ceremonies of 'sweet sound' seem to be preferable to the formal gestures and discreet enjoyment of the human occasion, but there is also in Brown an admiration for precise arrangement of finger and bowl and lip and for the abstraction of elements. It is a very attractive vignette that the poet draws for us, but it is interesting that the scene is captured visually (much in the manner of a pattern on a Chinese bowl), and that no attempt is made to echo Chinese verse following such precedents as the work of Pound and Fenellosa. Water is the centre of our existence — milk for the young, mud for dwellings, and saliva, tears, blood, for the body. Here man has stylised his ancient and life-giving resource in a ceremony which is both formal and humourless. However, "Smugglers" and "Afternoon Tea" show Brown engaged

in humour and delighting in the sound and impetus of words:
> "You comm too litt," a Dutchman said,
> The words like a fankle of rusted wire.

and

> Drank Mrs.Spence, having poured in a tinkle, tinkle of
> whisky (I've such a bad cold!)

But the last line of the latter poem stalls the tone of gentle mockery, for the drinkers' mouths are also 'clay hollows' and the reader is invited to drift back over the images sensing the muted heartbreak and thwarted love in the scene.

"Fiddlers at the Harvest Home" reveals a poet who has become the master of the quick, well-observed flourish of description:
> A brightness across the jaw of the winter mouse...
> ...The ewe among red tatters of snow

and adept in his use of metaphor and formulae:
> And the midnight reel of seed and soul
> ...At last near the kirk
> The music is cut on stone ramshackle pages.

In the final stanza Brown extracts 'wheels' from each mode of life. Each section: 'Fish', 'Dance', 'Quarry' etc., seems to represent either the fiddlers' tunes or their styles of playing. Much of the repetition building up to the final stanza seems to echo the rhythms of fiddling culminating in the breathless: '...Stone to dust to corn to bread to breath', possibly the panting of dancers and lovers. These 'wheels' 'hallow ghost and bone'. No single circle of life is self-sufficient – the 'wheels' assume a primary importance in their inter-relation with and their sanctifying action upon men. As in the most 'primitive' beliefs the circles of ploughing, dancing and churning were connected with the sun's progress, so here the rounds and rhythms of life become intermingled.

The Earl Rognvald Kolson poems have their factual basis in the Medieval *Orkneyinga Saga*. Brown comments that these 'imitations' '...may disturb Norse purists. What I have tried to do is preserve some of the gaiety, savagery, piety of the originals'. He has made interesting amendments to two of the lyrics. In *An Orkney Tapestry* the hymn to Ermengarde is rendered:
> The small mouth of Ermengarde
> Commands two things –
> A sea strewn with wreckage
> As far as Jordan.
> And later, in autumn
> With other migrant wings
> A returned prow.

By 1976 the lyric has become:
> The summer mouth of Ermengarde
> Commands two things
> A sea of saga stuff, wreckage, gold,

As far as Jordan,
And later, at leaf-fall,
On patched homing wings
A sun-dark hero.

One must, of course, allow for the altered context; the former is within a narrative framework and the latter included in a series of lyrics. The lyric has become, on one hand more precise, and yet, on the other, more resonant, arousing fuller associations. 'Small mouth' is more personal but 'summer' subsumes personality in a splendour and sunny fertility associated with a pagan goddess. A 'sun-dark hero' is not only more human than the phallic 'a returned prow', but it conjures up the whole motif of the homing hero from Ulysses onward. The change can also be seen in "A Mass at Sea". Admittedly the lyric has added information to enchance the new setting but even so there has been a recconsideration of word and phrase. In the third line Brown has substituted 'green and blue tramplers' for sea horses, giving the image a new lucency and motion. Instead of:

May be worthy at last
for the glory of Christ the King
to break bread in the white churches.

we are given:

No end of sorrow, soultroth, seeking, still.
Kyrie Christe, kyrie eleison
The Golden Harvester
Comes out to grace, with robe and ring, the
swineherd.

The poet is using a specific language here: ecclesiastical Greek, but he is also stating less and allowing the images to urge the poem forward. The final four lines of "A Mass at Sea" capture the desperation and ecstasy of the ceremony whilst allowing none of the guilt to fade. Phrases in the later poem seem less mundane and surer: '....Into the lucencies of Christ. ....Sin darkens the grain-hold'.

The Norse lyrics, Viking harp songs and translation of "Deor" in this volume are Brown's finest attempts to render writings from ancient genres in a modern style which is just as terse and resonant as the originals. Kolson as Earl and Saint is an attractive figure to Brown. He brings together an eye informed by the feudal system: 'Brother wind, gentle sister raindrops'; a Northern wit: '...Here they come, in procession/ Demure and harmless as girls'; and an awe both spiritual and profane. Ermengarde seems to be the spirit of the South: the 'Domna' of the Troubadours whose ideal of courtly love makes it plain that this figure was a thinly disguised pagan goddess. She is 'rich and tall as starlight', and is characterised by images of summer and winter, kindness and chastity, peace and war. These paradoxes prove compulsive to the Northern invader. In *An Orkney Tapestry* Brown writes of the meeting:

...the mystery was suddenly sweet and fragrant, an opening

rose....

> Golden one
> Tall one
> Moving in perfume and onyx.....

Earl Rognvald and the Countess Ermengarde celebrated the Romance of the Rose all that Summer in Narbonne. The slow escalation of images: opening rose, tall one, perfume and onyx, and the reference to the great work by Guillaume de Lorris convince the reader that this is no Holy Virgin but the goddess of Love invoked in the figure of the mistress in Ovid's *Ars Amatoria*.

In "Vikings" the recording of life is shown as, above all, a process of selection:

> The men came home in the ships for harvest
> With wounds on them and bits of silver.
> One year my father did not come home
> The sea has him off Lindisfarne.

A dated trip to Largs (1263) rounds off the poem with a powerful image: 'A thousand sea-borne swords, a golden mask'. In these poems Brown is using a named historical persona to reveal the strange mixture of similarities with and incongruities between modern and ancient patterns. He binds traditions of popularisation and genuine historical perspective together and in this is unlike Hill who is both opposed to linguistic popularisation and the kind of empathic narrative which Brown achieves here. The convention of Norse wit, sometimes quite horrid in its juxtapositions, and the hearsay of battle (a common kind of reportage in Heroic literature) are present in "A Battle in Ulster". "Deor (from the Old English)" is unlike Pound's or indeed Brown's own previous attempts to echo alliterative verse. Brown uses a sestet of alternately rhyming lines with the seventh line injunctions as the only real concessions to older verse. There are distinct echoes of the early Yeats here. The intertwined images of snow, harvest and land, a battle and an unwanted pregnancy are captured in the subtle 'muted' music of the poem:

> Beadohild wept when death
> Cold on her brothers was snowing.
> And sorrow grew. No gown
> Could hide from public showing
> The glebe of her body rich
> From Weland's reckless sowing.
> That sorrow withered, so may this.

'Beadohild' is echoed in 'cold' and the vowel is softened in 'brothers', 'snowing' and 'showing', finally passing on with the gentle sounds of 'grew', 'gown', 'hide', and 'glebe'. The refrain reinforces a mood of hushed thoughtfulness. The third stanza shows Brown reinstating an old image in a new context. The words imitate Earmonric licking 'long, lazy chops' and, in retrospect, one even hears the action in his name.

"The Escape of the Hart" is a re-working of a theme we have discussed already: Christ and Bonnie Prince Charlie leaping '...to pacify the arrow' in the form of a deer. The first part of this poem is, however, also a plea for the free passage of human love. We pass from the beauty of the long line evoking the picture of a graceful, loping animal: '...Let the white beast move in power this evening across the/hunter's hill...' to the gusty and obscured moorland '...through shrouds and prisms of fog, we saw/the hunters...' In this version of the tale the Prince is not unfaithful; the elements fold him from harm. This is not the 'frightened stag' of "Prince in the Heather" but a Christ-figure who transcends fear: 'He looked at them with a cold eye'. This figure, an amalgam of Prince and transfixed stag, brings to mind the 'Lord of the Animals' from the Trois Freres caves — a spirit from the cavemen's ceremonies of 'sympathetic' magic.

"Eynhallow:Crofter and Monastery" is Brown's best poem celebrating the ruminations of a poor crofter to date. The statements and images are bluff and immediate. This is Brown's Orkney of the mind genuinely aligned with the historical island with its small unproductive fields and drudgery: 'I rent and till a patch of dirt/Not much bigger than my coat'. The switch to bitter humour is unexpected: 'The name of my wife is Hild./Hild has a bitter tongue'. The perceptions of the persona are wondering and ambiguous. 'A thousand stars' in this context seem beautiful but also chaotic and unproductive, especially when linked to the empty pail. In the fourth stanza the man's unconsciously ironic and unreasoning faith blurs the barriers between creed and legend but with the arrival of the Columbans he sees a new kind of reverence. Their ceremonies and words help to give a shape to the day and to tame the environment by insisting on a common kinship with fish, stone and earth. 'Drudgings' have become 'Dancings'.

We now approach those poems I consider Brown's best work to date: "The Sea, Four Elegies", "Sea Widow, Four Songs", "Seven Translations of a Lost Poem" and "Stations of the Cross: Nine Variations". "The Sea" opens with linguistic attention: 'A vast ancient terror is locked in the name/Like energy in an atom'. The act of naming, of translation into kenning and image is laid bare in the listing of heraldic pictures. Brown's kennings for death are 'woven' beautifully into the 'Door of Water' passage. The idea of innocence is associated with the Dove Door and ripeness with the Door of the Sheaf. These lines are assured and humane; Brown's images not only make concrete the fluid and unfixed natures of sea, life, and death, but they provide comfort in their insistence on man's significance. Old people are: 'Harvesters under a load of tranquil sorrows' We are left wondering. Are the 'names' on the lintel those of the drowned or swirls of the tide becoming legible hieroglyphics in the fixity of art?

'The Lost', restating Brown's analogies of sea and land, operates firstly on a level of brief and splendid surprise, effecting a synaesthesia of eye and ear. The first line: 'One stumbled on a grey hill, very steep', makes the reader almost giddy with the deceptive twist of image and delayed adjective. The narrator veers from a humour which exudes warmth, a capacity to stress the proximity of life and death in the 'carousel of angels' to the hissing sibilants of 'secretest cell of salt' imaging the spray. The Barleycorn myth is transposed to the sea: 'The Atlantic was veined all summer with slow pure glitters'. Orkney is personified in 'A Drowning'. The use of the 'I am' construction reveals the continuous 'present moment of the past' and echoes the sayings of Christ. The cadences are strongly Eliotic. The spirit of the poem seems to be both an individual caught half wondering in the recurrent patterns of Orcadian existence and also a vast entity incarnated in all children, young men and fathers of the islands. Many of these images have been used previously but because all life contains correspondences, foldings and recurrences and, to Brown, all existence is anagogical and related, these repeated motifs touch off memories and echoes in the reader's mind, enhancing the unity of the book.

Brown has chosen to employ the dialogue of dead lovers in "Sea Widow"; this form already has its notable precedents in the poetry of Hardy and Rossetti. The determination in the lost fisherman's promise to his beloved is powerful:

> I will build you a house with my hands,
> A stored cupboard,
> Undying hearth-flames, a door open to friend and
> Stranger

It is a mixture of sexual tension and aggression which is to bring Brown's finest exposition on, and exploration of, the Word and the act of translation in "Seven Translations". There is a strange if subdued sexual layer to Brown's work. In "King of Kings" the reader is shown Eros, the Romans' catamite '...swaying aloft like a tulip'.There are repeated references to women who sell their bodies because of loneliness and boredom, and in the short story "Celia" the alcoholic and sexually available female is given the unifying vision which finishes the narrative. In "A Winter Tale" the Doctor, repository of hopes and fears for a community, is regarded as 'queer', preferring the company of husky men to women. These references are too disparate and slight to mention in any connection with any theoretical schema, but in "Sea Widow" and "Seven Translations" the tensions surface. Thankfulness and regret mingle as the wife tells of the suitors she turned away in 'Lost Lovers'. The Fisherman is Christ, but also the archetypal male as progenitor:

> Spin out of me
> Into yourself, the stuff of life, secretly.
> Weave it on a sweet loom.

Strange afterworlds and anteworlds mingle as tenses are shuffled and the dead man re-lives his education, love and regret: 'I wished once I had not met you'. The voice is God's, the Primogenitor of wombs and seed, but it is also that of a taunting male: 'There are women whose love at last is all for cats'. However, the poem veers away from a confrontation with these paradoxes and from an examination of the medium of reconciliation: its own words and, by implication, the Word. There is the startling image of contemporaneity which suddenly circles in front of the woman when she acknowledges her limitations, her inability to grasp the essence of sexuality, love and life itself:

> I know the man only
> In flecks of salt and grains of sand,
> And when through the drifting pools of a child's face
> Looks back the skull.

The most ambitious and successful of these poems is "Seven Translations of a Lost Poem". Ostensibly, each of the seven sections is a different translation of three simple stanzas. The first stanza is addressed to a whore who gave the writer a disease, the second to an apparently unco-operative but inspiring older poet, and the third to death. On one level it is amazing how well Brown manages to change the outlook of each translation so radically. The range and intensity of emotional impact is remarkable. The narrator's resentment breaks through:

> She was a very luxurious lady
> She rotted my leg....
> ....I still get angry at the loss of five gold pieces
> And my boyhood
> And my ability to dance, to that madam.

It is interesting to remember Mann's predilection for depicting artists as sick or dying, and the distinct idea of the tribal seer or prophet as maimed or crippled in some way. The sixth section dealing with the overwhelming desires of man shows that even pain is forgotten in a rush of new passion:

> If Sandra would open her blue robe
> Nothing more. There is nothing
> I would ask or desire from the gods.

Sex, poetry and death are seen as ciphers, as translations of one another. Both whore and poet charge for their wares. In fact the second verse of the fourth section could still refer to the Bordel with the quick, evocative flourish of '...among privy noises'. The finalities, the small climaxes of sex and art, anticipate death here as the three processes are joined in one verse:

> She showed the silk under the silk
> He uttered 'plough-to-oven', a spell.
> Why have I lived another half-century?

The best poet in 'all that long street' (hence the world) cannot explain anything or rather 'could explain nothing'. The Word exists outside time and translation alerts us to this fact. The beauty of youth is an illusion; it co-exists with age: 'In one room a silver mirror./Toothlessness, scant hairs, peered back at me'. It is through confrontation with failure

208

and paradox that the Word is effective. The 'golden key' of sexuality, youth and even covert knowledge opens the door on a beauty already dead. After all the seeking through words the silence remains: 'The harp is hidden'. Love, beauty and death evade human attempts to place them chronologically. These recognitions: that of the ultimately hidden yet adequate nature of the Word, of the correspondence between desire and disappointment and of the power of translation through images to alert one to the fundamental illusion of time, are basically those of the mystic. It is, however, the sexual pressure of the poem which has worked these themes to such a pitch and formal complexity. The contrast between 'She was a very luxurious lady' and 'She rotted my leg' constitutes a direct confrontation with the destructive nature of the Feminine Principle: the sexual act is omitted from the poem (it is merely expensive entertainment); the pain of the speaker seems inherent in the nature of love itself. The anger of section Three changes to the longing of section Six, with its 'sighing' stop-and-start rhythm: '...Nothing more. There is nothing'. Anger and hate towards the woman who is sexually free are concomitant with possessive desire and love. Brown has allowed his narrator to break from the usual devotion to and archetypal vision of women (the prostitute of the poem, though not clearly defined, does not reach the stature of the Great Whore). The ensuing drama involves a powerful examination of the natures of time, language and death.

The First section of "Stations of the Cross" remains much as it appeared in *Fishermen with Ploughs* except for minor changes. The Second section shows the scene of Christ's progress shifting between Pilate's garden and the outside world where images, especially of women, seem to merge with natural objects revealing the travail of Creation at the Saviour's torment. The figure of Christ fluctuates in dimension from being a pitiful, sparsely-fleshed skeleton such as Giacometti might have sculpted to '...Four holes in the dust'. Or, at another point, a gigantic figure expressive of man's universal suffering: 'He clung close to the curve of the world'. Pilate's asides, like those of Hill's Offa, seem arbitrary and mundane, but each holds an immediate visual impact and, then, a delayed sense of imminent disaster. 'Pass the seal' is a closing dismissal of the whole pre-Christian world and the empire that empowered Pilate; 'That business is over' is a casual but frightening echo of Christ's cry from the cross.

Brown shows the 'Lesser Mysteries of Art' as having their source 'in that first garden'. Art like man is riddled with temptations, 'apple-fraught' but redeemable 'with pure rinsings'. The strength of music is revealed in a stanza where an Orphic figure (mimicking the harp's appearance) tames the 'seven red beasts' or emblematic deadly sins of the Miracle Plays. Each stanza is an act of translation: Christ's sacrifice, sexuality and death, attend every event in the physical world and in the world of the artistic imagination. Many of the images are hard and prismatic: ice, mirrors, brideboard, mask, obliterator. In "Potter and Jar"

209

however, the artistic imagination is feminine: 'Those humps and hollows are jars too, stranger'. The entry of a 'questing ghost' into birth, causing the Potter's amazement, is unprecedented. The craftsman is used to 'hump and hollow', lingam and yoni in the Hindu sense, but that this creation could be 'fountain for the thirst of angels' is beyond him. The Potter with his wheel, perhaps the oldest profession, images God in the total domination of his materials. The jar, like Christ, is a symbol of deathlessness and endurance and in the New Testament man is called a 'vessel' for the Holy Spirit. Finally, the jar contains wine for the continuity of life.

"Sea Village" on an obvious level is a description of the inhabitants of a village and how a boy rebels against a fishing monopoly and the almost feudal rights of the Laird. The people are a passive, yielding force. The compassion of the Female Principle (Mrs.Manson) is linked to its sexuality (the Slut) and its endurance (The Five Widows). These qualities contrast sharply with but also complement those of the dominant and intractable male Laird. This is no simple confrontation of 'types' like the Vikings and monks of "The Stone Cross". Brown has written elsewhere of the unity of hunter and hunted, hart and arrow, dove and hawk, but nowhere has the pattern seemed as complex and as convincing as in "Sea Village". Ollie is an individualistic rebel and a Socialist, an insurgent challenging the old order, but also a Catholic. All doctrines can be a kind of Crucifixion, an exploitation of the adherent: 'Paine and Blatchford, they'll bring him down'. The Laird is the aggressive ruler, but is also half feminine: 'One hand on the rein long and white and scented'. The sea voices which end the poem echo the conflict of ideologies which are not so well defined or sexually discrete as those Brown has previously shown. The nails hammered out by the blacksmith are for Ollie Manson (a play on 'Son of Man'), but also 'for the Hall', for the destruction of the ruling class which will duly follow.

In "Creator" Brown shows how the first constituents of the natural order: dust, rain, earth and water, had to combine to make 'Leaf and Forest and Fall'. Each succeeding sentence builds up images of the interrelation of all matter and of the interpenetration of Creator and creation. Christ, both man and God, is 'undone' on the 'loom of time', but will be observed like a 'Black Diamond' at the centre of the Universe when time has burnt out. Again, one is reminded of Eastern religion, especially Buddhism. Brown's insistency is blunt and challenging: 'He is the Winter Tree dragged by a peasant./He is Flax and Wheel and Fold of linen.' The capitalisation of Flax and Fold stresses the numinous condition of these material objects: the Godhead is realised in all things. The seventh statement is reminiscent of the Chinese principle of Yin and Yang: the supposed dualities of the Cosmos such as Hot/Cold, Chaos/Order, Hate/Love. Christ, representative of creativity, 'lay upon' chaos and, like the raindrop upon dust, proved vastly fruitful: '...then galaxies/grew from my fingers'. To the Christian, Christ is a firm rock, but the line 'He is the Hollow in the Rock' emphasises that both vacuity and fullness are necessarily related. The last line brings us to a meditation on the eternal principle in matter. In "Art and Sacrament" David Jones wrote:

> As it was the whole world that [Christ] was redeeming
> he involved all mankind, from before Swanscombe Man
> to after Atomic Man, in that act. If the very mean or
> channel of redemption is intricated in Ars we conclude
> that Ars and man are inseperable.

The Cross is therefore the sign which both links man to Art and redeems Art so that this is possible. For Brown, the successive 'translations' of Christ's loving act mirror that act, just as the 'folding' ordinance of poetry reflects that preservative capacity of the Great Mother.

Pound remembered the Europe of the First World war in the words: '...an old bitch gone in the teeth...a botched civilisation'. It is a language akin to this of tragic condemnation that Brown brings to bear on the earth: 'This is the inheritance — slaves and exhausted earth,/A botched kingdom'. Christ is a sower who dared to take over the tilth of the world from the seven corrupt stewards and was 'given to the heaviest mill-stones'. The empathy between Christ and the earth has rarely been so well depicted: 'He put the red mud of his face in a crumpled mirror./ The turning earth scraped at his hands, knees, eyes'. The seemingly indifferent sun burns on. Below, Christ has reduced himself to a state lower than the order of atoms, '...Starker than seed or star'. The Word has become a whisper in nothingness. He is locked away from the universal rhythms which mean so much to Brown, but the cave in earth is not a place of death here. It is John Barleycorn's furrow, the hollow where the Potter redeems his clay and the site of Resurrection. The imagery of this poem is strikingly beautiful, stressing the paradoxes of the narrative much as Hill's rhythms lay bare the apparent contradictions in "Lachrimae".

In "Carpenter" premonitions of Christ's birth and death mingle as the centurion and Mary vie for the craftsman's attention. The tree is marked like the powerful trunk of "Yule"; its root 'groans' in the earth and we soon discover that it is a symbol of, amongst other things, the Fall, cause of men's pain and death. Like the initial bartering of the apple for knowledge it proves 'A bad bargain'. Like the evil that Eve's act supposedly engendered, it is devious, difficult to unravel, inextricably tangled in man's nature: 'A length of gnarls and knots'. The tree of death and guilt will, due to the earnest pleas of a woman, become a cradle for the Saviour. His birth meant the uprooting of the Old Law, but this symbol of man's fallen nature will still prove potent enough to crucify the Christ. The Carpenter himself is a redeemer — he muses:

> I could drag out of the darkness of it, I suppose
> A board
> Or wash tub or shelf or churn, for the village women

The connection of women and trees in the poem seems to evoke ideas of the pagan past: the goddesses and the memories of their sacred groves disturb Mary: 'One glance among trembling branches'. Brown makes conscious associations between the tree that cradled Christ, gave him apprenticeship, filtered his view of the world (both psychically and physically) and provided his gibbet, and women who are mothers, lovers and, traditionally, the mourners and disposers of the dead body.

One could also see the poem as a metaphor for the artistic process. The artist '...went into a multitude of green shadows, early/I came to the marked tree at last'. Unfortunately he 'lops' at the material and it becomes death-like, intractable. Mary, in this context, is the influence of true inspiration, a Muse about to give birth.

Winterfold starts and ends with 'Our Lady' as 'a loaded lass'. She is the winter fold of the title containing new life. The volume is the work of a sensibility instilled with a reverence for and wonder at these images. The cross is the 'axle-tree' of his vision, but in "Carpenter" it becomes transmuted into a growing tree and into Mary with hands like leaves. The book is pervaded by a sense of ripeness attendant upon, subsequent to, and negating, the sting of death. The actual Resurrection is rarely shown — we are left poised on the edge of life after death or before the birth which will make death powerless. The cradle, cave and House of Dust of the last three poems are the various 'folds' where winter will be translated. Christ the Word is the great translator: of death to life, dust to grain, water to wine. He alone can unlock the kingdom where all words, in realising their kinship to the Word, render up a meaning 'from the bone'. The latter poems in this book sound like catechetical responses or sacred songs. They instate Christ as Lord of Brown's chosen language and, when the images are at their most terrible or beautiful, seek to persuade us that Christ is Lord of all language, the words that are his hidden self.

AFTERWORD

I have shown how Hill has moved out of the strident and vacillating narrative voices of his first two books into a poetry saturated with the music and sentiment of mystical songs. It has been a progress away from what seems to be a poetic sensibility twisted against itself. The checked and re-summoned responses of the early narrators seemed to breed a strange and profligate imagery of demons and 'loathly neckings' and this was offset by the tendency towards 'sacramental' art, or rather, that art which aspires to the condition of the sacramental. This progress has been achieved not through the signa and juxtapositions of *Mercian Hymns* but through an engagement with devotional sources and a new clarity of imagery and diction. The voices of "Lachrimae" and "Three Mystical Songs" are centripetal in that they initiate a drama in an absence of an identifiable speaker or speakers. This is no longer the crabbed obtuseness and self-hecklings of the first two books or the centrifugal voices of the Hymns which centre on historical artifacts and the dark entity of a genius loci. Hill's progress is in some ways comparable to that of the Jesuit martyr, Robert Southwell, who moved from concettism to a direct and uncluttered profundity in his art. Hill has moved from poems portraying the gods as psychic mechanisms and the juxtapositions of "Doctor Faustus" and "Of Commerce and Society" to deceptively simple songs and 'Pavanes'. The later voices are no longer ones of scholarly prevarication but of resignation to those forces which make up the 'matter of Christ'; they are resigned both to belief and unbelief, sure of the paradoxes and contradictions:'...there is no end/to such pursuits', 'You are beyond me, innermost true light,/uttermost exile...' The refined and obsessive confrontation with the crucified Lord rivals that of Brown in *Winterfold*. The pagan statues of *For the Unfallen* and the earth cults and fire-dragon motifs of the Hymns are discarded for a more unified vision. The Mercian artifacts and historical events are, however, recalled in the 'small worlds' and sensuous, amoral dreams of "An Apology for the Revival of Christian Architecture in England". Hill has written that his sense of history is 'neither Whig nor Marxist'. This could mean that he does not believe man is determined by the class struggle or other material factors. It could also mean that he is equally sceptical of the ideas of total freedom or unfreedom. He could also be saying that he is not sympathetic either to the vision of liberal or moderate progress from within a state or to the theory of equal distribution of ownership and re-alignment of economic strategies. His sense of history from "Of Commerce and Society" to "A Short History of British India" has been involved in revealing the racial and cultural myths which sustain a particular view or views of history and the tre-

213

mendous impetus that these versions gather. If history is to possess a focus it is a moral and personal one for Hill and relates to the individual striving for wholeness and clarity of intellect in relation to the structures that have shaped his society rather than to movements and neat divisions of class.

Heaney has used the Smith figure of "Forge" to move from poems of initiation and respect for nature to poems which concentrate on the darker aspects of masculine and phallic power. Heaney's sense of myth has always been inextricably linked with fear and darkness and those gods and goddesses, spirits, legends and parts of the human psyche which as yet remain obscured by that fecund dark. He has continually sought after those emblems which are adequate to the terror and confusions of modern Irish life while also relying heavily upon a background of historical events and artifacts. He has developed a fine etymological sense, and this, allied with his vision of the Irish past, has produced some fine poems of recovery of mythological and folk motifs. The formal arrangement of his poems has been adapted to deal with each subject as it arose, stressing the link which he sees between literary creation and the chanelling of vital psychic energy. He has desired to construct the assuaging ceremony of words to bridge the schisms between North and South, Catholic and Protestant, and form the circle where opposites are reconciled. He has become keenly aware of the power of referentially related images and his poems have often acquired the texture of a mesh of symbols which recall and anticipate those used in his work as a whole. In *North* the poet has shown how a warlike and bloody tradition of Irish life may also be used as a faculty to alter our perceptions of the present situation. In the same book Heaney's search for a more conscientious style has meant the disruption of his previously sensuous diction and concern with the interaction of man with nature; in Part II there emerged a verse at once colloquial and Augustan, where the voice of the narrator commented wryly on the inability of a poet to deal with Ireland at all, though, '...I believe any of us/Could draw the line through bigotry and sham...' "Exposure" ends the book with an attempt to reconcile this new voice with Heaney's older and traditional motifs of nature imagery, legend and 'weighting' of responsibilities.

Brown has developed an integrated and balanced mythological and material schema. He has used a wide variety of legends and conventions: Marian devotion, John Barleycorn, masques and ballads, to restore the patterns which he regards as potent to offset the decay of common words and their ancient power. He has moved from an idealisation of a pre-Industrial Orkney into a more realistic assessment of history, though his final glance backward from the Apocalypse of "The Return of the Women" is over a sacramental view of events – 'a merry wayfaring'. In *Winterfold* we have seen his development of a fine Norse lyric form and the use of a fluid and changing narrative perspective reinforcing his portrayals of the unity of men. Christ is seen as the great connector of life, the metaphor-maker, the 'tie that binds'. His 'folding' spreads outwards through matter and language: 'He put the red mud of his face in a crumpled mirror'. Just as in Hopkins' work the ideas of 'inscape' and 'instress' influence each word so Brown's notion of 'folding' is manifested with an increasing emphasis in the shapes and sounds of his verse. Eckhart makes the 'word' issue (seed) of the 'Word' and Brown, unlike Hill, relies heavily upon a growing and ultimate trust in this organic relationship and the conception of Christ as the great translator. God, the great 'I am', is forever being born in the humble lives of men. He is, in the Augustinian formulation, the good Good and thus, 'accordingly signified the unmixed and highest good which is grounded in itself, rests on nothing and 'returns full circle upon itself' '. Brown's motifs of the Great Dance and the circles of earthly life mirror this process. Brown too, like Heaney and Hill, has looked for a way of reconciling the different poles of existence. In "Kingdom of Dust" the extremities of life become folded within the sacrificial usurper-Christ figure: all sharpness, starkness, and, at the other extreme, nothingness, are deposited in 'that purest of urns' — the earth and Great Mother. It is in a renewed examination of the nature of desire, sexuality and the art of translation that Brown has achieved a rare combination of power and humour and a balancing of passionate commitment and detached observation in "Seven Translations of a Lost Poem".

Each poet has worked out of different responses to the land, its history or histories and myths, but, in doing so, they have raised some similar issues. How does one record or use the motif of the past without falsifying the actual patterns and feelings of those individuals now dead? Which poetic stance is fitting to confront the pain, violence and contradictions which seem inherent to our own lives and histories? How do the Christian tradition and the pagan cults which sought and seek to translate the texture of life into some meaning in relation to the Universe, relate to each other? What are the linguistic implications of the ways in which we answer these questions? Two of the poets have ostensibly admitted failure in their attempts to answer these queries. On another level, their respective answers to these problems have, at times, sounded similar, but their literary methods and habits of mind are so different that one cannot draw any strict analogies between their work. Hill is both sceptical and admiring in attempting faith in a sanctity of the human intellect. Brown seeks to fold, to wrap the apparently meaningless elements of life into a unified whole. He sees his art as both literary and sacramental. Heaney ends *North* with the figure of Incertus — a wood kerne taking colour and succour from his environment. This figure is an amalgam of his previous poetic personae and provides a temporary respite for a sensibility overwhelmingly engaged with the sensuosity and music of words and the ambivalence of his social stance that this entails.

Fundamentally, regardless of the different ways in which they have pressurised language and image to meet each poetic occasion as it arose, the aspect of their work which has proved most challenging and exciting has been the placing of the narrative or narratives and personae of the verse in relation to each writer's developing sense of imagery, form and diction. This has meant that their poetry, engaged with myth and history, has been 'inhabited', continually compelling the reader to an awareness of the crucial nature of these themes and perspectives. The personal or impersonal voices of the narrators have been dramatic. They have also been concerned, energised by the historical and mythological issues at stake.

Whatever changes one might like to predict in their work in the future, these three poets have made 'a shape out of the very things of which' they are themselves made. Even Hill, who I take to be the most chary of them about including personal material in his work, has written '...a poet must out a great deal of himself into his work'. Accordingly, they have not closed their examinations of myth and history off from their own lives and the world around them. The result is that their dealing with these themes assumes not only a broad and literary shape but also becomes immediately related to their own localised perceptions and the responses of the reader. It is the tension between these areas which make, at the very least, a core of their individual writings great, and the whole span of their work notable. For each of them has found in his separate way that his work has drawn in both the actual world and the mythic. Like Hill's Christian Neo-Platonist, they are compelled by both:

> On those pristine fields I saw humankind
> As it was named by the Father; fabulous
> Beasts rearing in stillness to be blessed.
> The world's real cries reached there....

NOTES

INTRODUCTION

INFLUENCES

12   'Buddha', however see Hill's "A Short History of British India"
12   'their own tongue', Brown does display a knowledge of Anglo-Saxon and French in some of his translations.
12   'Heaney's use of place names':
     Anahorish, soft gradient
     of consonant, vowel, meadow...
          ("Anahorish")
     My mouth holds round
       the soft blastings
      Toome, Toome...
          ("Toome")
     ...Broagh
     its low tattoo...
          ("Broagh")
13   Kenner, p.146. This etymological approach to myth was probably passed to Pound, and in turn Heaney, by Emerson's writings on literature and belief.
13   "Funeral Music:an essay", *King Log*, p.67
13   'assumes full depth', De Rachewiltz, p.179
13   'Pound progressively', ibid, p.197
14   'the marvellous thing', ibid, p.182-3
14   'Pisan Cantos', ibid, p.184-5
15   'imagine hearing', Hughes, "Myth and Education", *TLS*, 2.9.77, p.12
15   'The Cantos', Unfortunately, Pound sometimes relies on dubious sources for his mythological material, such as the work of the erroneous Egyptologist, Lt.Col.L.A.Waddell.
15   'Mass and its artifacts', De Rachewiltz, p.194
15   'For the net', Kenner, p.342
16   *Magnus*, pp.164-8
16   'rouse great masses', Ellman, *Yeats: The Man and the Masks*, p.252. Heaney, too, is aware of the mythic patterns underlying political parties, especially the Republican Party in Ireland.
16   'the "Heroes" ', ibid, p.125
17   'rapport with', ibid, p.119
17   'all my art theories', ibid, p.271
18   'Yeats had perceived', Kathleen Raine, "Hades wrapped in Cloud" *Yeats and the Occult*, p.86
18   'another Leda', Ellman, p.122
18   'a revelation',Raine, p.83
20   'allegorical bric-a-brac', see also T.S.Eliot, "A Game of Chess"
20   'If I had not made', August 1892, Ellman,p.97
20   'For Yeats', Tuohy, *Yeats*, p.77
20   'I think the term', *Selected Letters of Ezra Pound*, p.141
20   'is the poet', Emerson writes: "It is a secret which every intellectual man quickly learns, that, beyond the energy of his possessed and conscious intellect, he is capable of a new energy (as of an intellect, doubled on itself,) by abandonment to the nature of things." *Essays*, pp325-6. He goes on to talk of "that dream-power....by virtue of which a man is the conductor of the whole river of electricity."
21   'all words act', Kenner, p.223-31
21   Ibid, p.225
21   'Heaney has spoken', Haffenden, p.11
22   'The poet is the sayer', Emerson, p.310
22   'Like Blake', Kathleen Raine writes of this tradition. See *Defending Ancient Springs*.

22 'the circle is thus', Olney, "The Esoteric Flower", Harper, p.49
22 'we encounter', Olney, p.33
23 'She traces the change', Ure, "W.B.Yeats and the Irish Theme", *Yeats and Anglo-Irish Literature*, p.74
23 Tuohy, p.44
24 'It is the moon', Eliade, pp.214-5
25 'Yeats resigned himself', Albright, *The Myth Against Myth*, p.180
26 'The art of translation', Though for a consideration of Hill as a translator see A.A.Cleary, *Thames Poetry*, Vol.1, No.7, pp65-7

FOR THE UNFALLEN AND *KING LOG*

27 "Now and in England", p.483
27 'The word Hitler',Hughes, *TES*, p.12
30 'Now I lack', "God's Little Mountain"
31 'Tombs still extrude', "The Bibliographers"
31 'An idea', Coleridge, *Biographia Literaria*, p.100
31 'By using an emotive', *Penguin Contemporary Verse*, p. 392
32 'The highest philosophy', D.R.Dudley, "Plato", *Penguin Companion to Literature* 4, p.136
32 'Christianity, history', Wallace Martin, *Contemporary Literature*, 12 No.4, p.431
32 'is the impulse that makes', *Penguin Contemporary Verse*, p. 392
33 'Progress of an artist', *Selected Prose of T.S.Eliot*, p.40
33 '...humility of men', Stead, *The New Poetic*, p.145
33 'saturation', *Selected Prose of T.S.Eliot*, p.91
33 'Dante', ibid, p.230
33 'Hill's poem', W.S.Milne, *Agenda*, 17 No.1, p.70
33 'to create the closest unity', Hill, *Poetry Nation* 4 (1975) p.137
33 'drama of reason', Hill, *Agenda* 17, No.1, p.95
33 Milne, p.66
34 'a religious man', Christopher Ricks, *TLS*, 30.6.78, p.747
34 'a paradigm', Hill, *Agenda*, 17, No.1, p.15 & 23
34 'This is achieved', ibid, p. 16 & 21, p.91
34 'Hill has written', ibid, p.99
34 'But if a poem', Hill, *Poetry and Audience*, IX No.12, p.7
34 'To flesh and blood', "Genesis". Mircea Eliade writes: "The violent death is creative — in this sense, that the life which is sacrificed manifests itself in a more brilliant form upon another plain of existence."
34 'the violence of nature', *Contemporary Literature*, 12, No.4, p.435
35 'The world is not', Jeffrey Wainwright, *Agenda* 13, No.3 p.33
35 'A myth based', Martin, p.431
37 'protean', ibid, p.432
37 'she (Venus)', ibid, p.432
37 'groomed optimi', Heaney, "Freedman"
38 'Hill confesses', *Penguin Contemporary Verse*, p.391
38 'The ambiguity of the last line', Inasmuch as the poem deals with the artists recalcitrant materials we might consider Rilke's *Sonnets for Orpheus*.
39 Coupe,*Penguin Guide to European Lit.* Vol.7, ed.Thorlby, p.272-3
41 'By all means', (In the "Martyrdom of St.Sebastian" we find that history, the pitiless recurrence of the cruel god's vengeance, can be 'scraped clean' by the influence of art. Sacrifice like art crystallises pain, but this cleansing is shallow, a limited formulation.)
42 'The Word', *Penguin Contemporary Verse*, p. 392
42 'The Word becomes fashionable', Wainwright, *Stand*, 10, No.1.

pp. 46-7

43 'a prayer for contact', *Penguin Contemporary Verse*, p.392
43 'men mocked', Wainwright, *Stand* 10, No.1. p.48
46 'ornate heartlessness', *King Log*, p.68
47 'Yet sleeping and killing', The use of shadow imagery generally and especially in connection with the dark side of the persona is remarkable in Hill's work. For a discussion of the emblematic colours and motifs of the Baroque poets see Odette de Mourges "The European Background to Baroque Sensibility", *Pelican Guide to English Literature, 3.*

MERCIAN HYMNS

49 Eagleton, *British Poetry Since 1960*, ed.Schmid & Lindop, p.239
49 'History offers', Wallace Martin, pp.429-434
50 'drenched in flesh', Bacon, *Advancement of Learning*, p.28
50 'As Silkin', Silkin, "Poetry of Geoffrey Hill", Schmid & Lindop, p.158
50 'It was natural', Brooke, *Saxon and Norman Kings*, p.43
51 Hodgkin, *A History of the Anglo-Saxons*, p.386
52 Dodsworth, *Stand*, 13 No.1, p.63
52 'The Offa who figures', *Hymns*, p.36
52 'Whether on his parents', Brooke. pp.110-12
52 *Widsid*, see Brooke, pp.111-2
53 Graves, *White Goddess*, pp. 30-205
53 'Graves links pagan', ibid, p.180. (The holly-king appears in an Old English Christmas play, a survival of the Saturnalia, as the fool who is beheaded but rises again unhurt.)
53 'Hill does not enlarge', I think it apt to add the reservation that Hill would probably find *The White Goddess* at least as 'fantastic' a treatment of mythological material as *Mercian Hymns* is of its sources.
54 'tongue of the land', Bailey, p.44
54 'speech of the landscape', "Redeeming the Time", *Agenda*,10 No.1, pp.87-111
54 'Bran's buried head', Graves, pp.51-3
54 'England's well', see Heaney's "Helicon"
54 'one would hazard', Hill, *Agenda*, 9, No.1. p.21
55 'Offa's charters', Brooke, p.216
55 'In return, we know', Hodgkin, pp.386-91
56 'urine and ashes', see "East Coker", ll 38-47
56 'writing in 747', Weighall, *Wanderings in Anglo-Saxon Britain*, p.153
56 "Now and in England", pp.479-81
58 'Behind these women', There is a spell against them in "Saxon Charm"
58 C.H.Sisson, "Geoffrey Hill", *Agenda* 13, No.3, p.27
59 'Sir Cyril Fox', Hodgkin, p.390
60 Eagleton, p.235
61 'Mercia is glimpsed', The Greek 'eklego' means to pick out — a selection of scenes. The Hymns give us quick, selective glimpses of a wild countryside.
61 'Ruskin', *Fors Clavigera*, pp.149-157
61 'Heaney comments', "Now and in England", pp.482-3
64 'David Jones writes', "Preface to the Anathemata", *Epoch and Artist*, p.106 & 112
65 'We cannot hope', Steiner, *In Bluebeard's Castle*, p.98
65 'no definitive view', Hill, "Redeeming the Time", p.90

65 'It could be said', "True Conduct of Human Judgement", p.21
66 'The poet is hearing', *Agenda* 9, No.1, p.21
66 'Language gravitates', "Redeeming the Time", p.90
66 'There is in Hill', "Now and in England", p.480
67 'Moreover, they are', Though Hill is still dubious about timeless moments
67 'Offa, a boy at odds', 'House' in its Coleridgean sense as 'head' too.
67 Alexander, "Mercian Hymns", *Agenda* 13, No.3, p.30
67 'extraordinary justice', Sisson, p.27
68 'the dream convention', *Dream of the Rood*, "The Dream of Rhonab" and "The Dream of Macsen Wledig" are three examples from different ages of poetic growth in England and Wales.
69 'You know how much', Hodgkin, p.393

LACHRIMAE AND THE LATER POEMS

70 'Lachrimae are based', Sisson sets it besides Hill's work on *Ad Incensum lucernae*, the text of a cantata by James Brown. *Agenda*, 13 No.3, pp.27-8
70 'In Lachrimae', Milne, *Agenda* 17, No.1, p.66 & 71
71 Wainwright, *Agenda* 12, No.3, p.33
72 Ibid.
72 'parody of the exaggerated deliberation', ibid, p.35
72 'Lachrimae Amantis', ibid, pp.37-8. See also Cathmel Kazin, *Agenda* 17, No.1, pp.43-56
73 'your passion's ancient wounds', see E.L.River's translation of de Vega's poem "Que tengo yo que mi amistad procuras', *Agenda* 17, No.1. p.60
73 'to seek indirect utterances', Sisson, p.27
73 'the bulk of the words', In "Redeeming the Time" Hill writes that short words are the most elemental material, and they are the abrupt selving of prayer. *Agenda* 10. No.1, p.109
75 'stripped of all the baroque', Milne, *Agenda* 17, No.1, p.63
75 "On the death of Mr.Shakespeare", *Agenda*, 15, nos.2-3, pp.3-10
76 'This heartfelt wellbeing', Wainwright, *Agenda* 17, No.1, p.11
77 'If there is, as Peck', Peck, *Agenda*, 17, No.1, p.22

SEAMUS HEANEY INTRODUCTION

78 'Poetry lessons', *Worlds*, p.94
78 Alwyn & Brinley Rees, *Celtic Tradition*, pp.17-18
78 'He has, he tells us', *Worlds*, p.94
78 'As for his art', ibid p.95
78 'The Hidden Ireland', Corkery, pp.126-145
79 'Its elements', Heaney, "The Poetry of Patrick Kavenagh", *Two Decades of Irish Writing*, p.111
79 'pagan ritual', Corkery, pp.65-70
79 'such priestly function', Rees, p.17
79 'Before verse can be human', Clarke, "Anglo-Irish Poetry", *Literature in Celtic Countries*, p.161
79 Dillon & Chadwick, *The Celtic Realms*, p.129
79 'The Druid', Heaney writes of the work of Ted Hughes: "His poetry is most original and inclusive when it involves this process of entry and possession of another form of life or landscape, when it is a trance-like experience, a truancy of the consciousness, a shaman-flight." "Deep as England", *Hibernia*, p.13
79 Piggott, *The Druids*, pp.2-19

79   'Their souls were often', Eliade pp. 59-61, 86-94
80   'He has said that fear', Haffenden, p.21 & p.13
80   'I presume Eliot', "Now and in England", p.471
81   'There was some kind', Brown, *The Sun's Net*, pp.262-3
82   'Gods and goddesses', He has remarked to Haffenden: "One of Pound's 'A Few Don'ts' is 'Go in fear of abstractions', and I think I took that too literally for a long time." p.22
82   'One remembers Lawrence's', D.H.Lawrence, *Fantasia...*, p.7
82   'Now it is time', *D.H.Lawrence:a Selection from Phoenix*, p.493
82   'Yet they were made', P.V.Glob, *The Bog People*, p.7 & p.23
83   'They were sacrificial', ibid, p.132
83   'However, Glob's admiring', Bailey. p.44
84   'Jung has written', Haffenden, p.13
84   'However, there is profit', 1970-71, Guest Lecturer at University of California, Berkeley.
84   'nature mysticism stuff', Haffenden, p.20
86   'nothing will suffice', "Kinship"
87   'a poem is alive', Bailey, p.92
87   'In an interview', Haffenden, p.24
87   'much that is valuable', Bailey, p.93

DEATH OF A NATURALIST/DOOR INTO THE DARK

88   'Aye, the pen's', Bailey, p.39
88   'His poems are raids', Haffenden, p.13
88   'Digging' in fact was', Heaney, *Here and Human*, ed.Finn, p.57
89   'In spite of this', "Viking Dublin"
89   'Yet it was at Uisnech', Rees, p.156
90   'The dam brings', Lakes and pools were often revered by the Celts. Some were locations for sacrifice, either of human life or animals.
91   'Additionally', The frog is the disguised prince of fairytale, the wise familiar of witches and the rain of Jehovah on sinning Egypt.
91   'The 'nimbling' 'sliming', For a discussion of this rat imagery in relation to an earlier version of the poem in *The Irish Times*, 9.3.63 p.8, and the Myth of the Fall see McGuiness, *Eire*, pp.74-5
92   'rhyme 'rats to death', Graves, p.445
92   'The title of Heaney's poem', G.D.Josipovici, "Francis Bacon", *The Penguin Companion to Literature*, vol 1, pp.30-31
92   'The dating 'Late August', (To be accurate it starts on September 2nd). The Danaans, an Irish tribe, carried the tree north with them but 'since it could not be established as a wild tree, they will have used the bramble as a substitute: the fruiting season, the colour of the berries and the shape of the leaf correspond and blackberry wine is a heady drink.' Graves, pp.182-3. He also supplies a reason for the 'blight' at the end of the poem: "In all Celtic countries there is a taboo against eating the blackberry....in Brittany the reason given is 'a cause des fees' (because of the fairies). In Majorca....the bramble was the bush chosen for the Crown of Thorns and the berries are Christ's blood....'
93   'Heaney has written already', In *Poetry in the Making* he writes of his poem "The Thought Fox": "If I had not caught the real fox there in the words I would never have saved the poem. I would have thrown it into the wastepaper basket as I have thrown so many other hunts that did not get what I was after." p.20 For Heaney's modification of this view see Haffenden, p.25
95   'The influence of the famine', Becket, *Short History of Ireland*, p.145

95 'In his essay on Kavenagh', *Two Decades*, ed.Dunn, pp.104-6 & 111
96 'Among the Romans', Bailey, p.92
97 'By the time of the 13th', Rees, PP.140-1
97 'The rod points downwards', "Antaeus"
97 'The poem is permeated', These might be similar to ley-lines or the 'grids' of power mentioned by Carlos Casteneda.
97 'Trout recalls', see Hughes' "Pike" and Lawrence's "Fish"
98 'In the second stage', It is this merging which makes Heaney's scenes as vital and mysterious as:

> Whatever is fickle, freckled (who knows how?)
> With Swift, slow; sweet, sour, adazzle, dim;
>   "Pied Beauty"

Both Heaney and Brown wrote poems imitating Hopkins early in their careers.
98 Henderson, *Man and His Symbols*, ed Jung, p.15
99 'Hill has used':

> The starched unbending candles stir...
> ...As though the surging of a host
> Had charged the air of Pentecost.
> And I believe in the spurred flame,
> Those racing tongues...
>   ("The Bidden Guest")

99 'My sensibility', Haffenden, p.12
100 'Finding a voice', F.E.S.Finn, p.57
100 'The hawk was usually', Graves, p.338
100 'The conflation of the hawk-swan', There are some strong correspondences between the structuring of images in Heaney's poetry and Graves' 'findings'. In the final stanza of the poem Heaney links a thrush and a hawk in the March twilight. Graves, in glossing an ancient calendar, writes:

> Apr.16—May 13 — seg, hawk; sodath, fine coloured.
> Why is the hawk in the next place?
> Not hard. Amergin said of this month: I am a Hawk on a cliff. And Fine-coloured are its meadows.
> The same — SS — stmolach, thrush, sorcha, bright-
>   coloured
> Why is the Thrush joined with the Hawk?
> Not hard. The Thrush sings his sweetest this month. And Bright-coloured are the new leaves. p.298

It could be coincidence that Heaney's poem is dated only half a month earlier, but there does seem to be a similarity in the way both writers have chosen birds to express their dominant themes.
101 'Oisin in search of water', Rees, p.160
101 Sharkey, *Celtic Mysteries*, p.82
101 'all year the flax-dam', "Death of a Naturalist"
101 'Io, Io', "Canto XLVII"
102 'It is not merely', For link between roots and masturbation, McGuiness, pp.73-4
102 'Seminal impulse', F.E.S.Finn, p.59
102 'backward abysm', "Now and in England", p.471
102 'When I called', F.E.S.Finn, pp.58-9
103 'In mythology', Rees, p.232
103 'Ross talks of the dependence', Ross, pp.320-33
104 Graves pp. 203, 281 & 330. In Wales the Penkerdd or Chief Bard sat on the left of the Heir Apparent, "being reckoned equal in

honour with the Chief Smith." p.23
104 'husband of his forge', Rees, p.257
104 'The mysterious persona', For Heaney's link between artistry and Smithcraft see "King of the Dark", *The Listener*, 5.2.70, p.181
105 'a distorted version', A similar imagistic distortion is found in "King of the Dark", p.182
105 'Like a diving bell', The idea of the Otherworld or Annwn is very strong in Celtic belief. It can be a fairy mound, a land over or under the sea, but is mainly referred to as the Celtic Hades, and as such is underground. In *The Mabinogion* Pwyll encounters Arawn, King of Annwn. Like many heroes and magicians, he descends and finds Annwn to be a beautiful realm. As the Rees write' "...we return to the fact that the excluded, the wild, the dead, the young, the female, the Otherworld, have their place in the total scheme of things. The significant visit can be the last as well as the first, and it can be both at once." pp.203-4
106 'In the delectable Otherworld', Rees, pp.40-1. Dillon and Chadwick concentrate upon earthly feminine power: "Cartimandua is one of the outstanding women rulers of Celtic antiquity, comparable with her contemporary Queen Boudicca of the Iceni, and with the Heroic Age queen of Ireland, Queen Medb of Connacht. It is indeed impossible to have any true understanding of either Celtic history or Celtic literature without realising the high status of Celtic women and something of the nature of their place in society...." p.43
106 'The Morrigan', Dillon and Chadwick, p.183
106 'The recognition of water', Sharkey, p.7
106 'Rite of Spring', There is a close connection between this poem and "Sinking the Shaft", *Stations*, p.8
106 'In talking of Undine', In his lecture at Aberystwyth, 1977
106 '(a child) is much closer', Muir, p.20
108 'The insistence on diamond absolutes' see also "Exposure"
108 'The poem ends', Jung and Hesse culled similar beliefs from Indian and Oriental thought; some American Indian communities held the idea of a circular cosmos and the centripetal progress of the human psyche.
109 'The best moments are those', F.E.S.Finn, p.59
109 'I only write', Haffenden, p.23
109 'befitting emblem', Bailey p.44
110 'The clean and finely-honed', This haiku-like quality of image is, however, glimpsed again in "Good Night"

WINTERING OUT

111 'Terror was present', *Poetry Wales*, Summer 1975, p.92
111 'Any amount of dread', Haffenden, p.21
111 'When asked if', Aberystwyth (conversation), 1977
112 'out of everie Corner', *Spender's Prose Works*, p.158
112 'The Gaelic way of life', Becket, pp.55-6
112 'In an article', "The Trade of an Irish Poet", *Guardian*, 25.5.72, p.17
112 'whose lifeline', ibid
113 'Grove is a word', ibid
113 'The Dirraghs', ibid
113 'Heaney is allying', "falce aurea demetit" in Piggott's translation of Pliny, p.99
113 'He has mentioned', Buttel, *Seamus Heaney*, p.74
113 'of course an ancient', Chambers, *English Folk Play*, pp.218 & 225

113 'A line has been suggested', Gascoigne, *World Theatre*, p.17
113 'The ash-plant and stone', Though for a more detailed analysis of the origins of the straw mask, plant of ash or spiral wand, see Graves pp.168-9
114 'the man-woman', Chambers, p.153
114 'Graves writes extensively', The holly was honoured above the oak by many early tribes.
114 'This 'woman' gazes out', Graves writes: "The Kerry peasants still abominate hare meat, they say that to eat it is to eat one's grand-mother. The hare was sacred, I suppose, because it is very swift, very prolific — even conceives, Herodotus notes, when already pregnant — and mates openly without embarrassment." p.293
115 'Lewis Spence', *Magic Arts in Celtic Britain*, p.15. See also Taliesin and shape-shifting.
115 'To possess this science', ibid
115 'There have been various', See Plato's debate in *Cratylus* on the inspirational principles of 'nomos' and 'physis'.
115 'Moy' means plain', Joyce, *Origin and History*, vol.III, p.514
115 Ross, p.21
116 'the pleasure of the poem', Haffenden, pp.16-17
116 'In 1951 Mitchell', Herity & Eogan, *Ireland in Prehistory*, p.23
116 O Suilleabhain, *Handbook of Irish Folklore*, p.298
116 'They seem to have inherited', There are many stories of water serpents in Irish Literature. This might suggest, as Ross writes, that "in these traditions we have remnants, reduced now to mere folk episodes, of an earlier mythological tradition of composite, water-frequenting serpents, comparable with the imagery suggest-ed by the ram-headed, fish-tailed serpent of Celtic iconographic tradition." p.348
117 'He finds himself in bogwater', Gorgon heads are well-known features of Celtic remains symbolizing 'evil averting power'. In the hands of Celtic artists the gorgon-head motif came to be connect-ed with healing waters. In the persona of the elver-haired explorer Heaney has married the image of local superstition with that of Celtic statues and pillars. Ross, pp.90-92
117 'These patterns which bewitch', In passing through a maze one is not going in any particular direction, and by so doing one reaches a destination which cannot be located by reference to the points of the compass. Rees, p.346
118 'The circle maybe', Bain, *Celtic Art*, p.59
118 'it is because the cuckoo', Graves p.251
118 'as Culpepper says', ibid, p.173
119 'In spite of these weaknesses', Becket, pp.123-4
119 'a tradition of', ibid, p.127
119 'In 1799', ibid, pp.126-7
120 'The human head', Ross, p.126
121 'I have always listened', "Trade of an Irish Poet", *Guardian*, p.17
121 'In a similar way', Haffenden, p.8
121 'Cernunnos was supposed', See the sexual member of the Sheela-na-gig gargoyle at Sr.David's, Kilpeck, in this capacity too. (There is a photograph of the torc of the Goddess in Glob.)
121 'Consecrate the cauldron bog', The cauldron of Cerridwn is prob-ably the most famous of these vessels. It contained a brew of in-spiration and knowledge and the Triple Muse supposedly rose from its depths. It has passed down to us in popular legend as the witch's cauldron or the Holy Graal. But one must not forget that

the Graubelle man was found in a 'cauldron-bog' and that the Gundestrup bowl with its silver motifs of gods, goddesses, sacrifices and contests was pulled from a similar bog. The cauldron is both centre of sustenace for the community and the artists' mixing pot.

122 'The brand itself', Glob, p.126
122 'this goddess was being worshipped', ibid, p.116
123 'A 'kesh' is a causeway', Buttel, p.78
123 'The Burren mentioned', Herity and Eogan, pp.119-20
124 'The wind off the dumps', O Suilleabhain, p.256
124 'Cherry was connected', Graves, p.39. See also "The Cherry-tree Carol"
124 'It was the dawn', ibid, pp.175-6
125 'To 'tent' means', A ritual combat was enacted to decide who should abduct a girl; this was part of the whole ethos of 'maying'.
125 'Mirecea Eliade writes of', Eliade, pp.170-2
126 'His parents assured', Spence pp.110-14
127 'Heaney is well aware', Chadwick and Dillon, p.357
127 'Brown has used the weaving', Eliade, p.215
127 'lies in the summoning', Buttel, p.34
129 'California is a centre', Capra, *Tao of Physics*
129 'But organic life', For a similar version of a 'floating Christ' see Dali's "Christ of St.John of the Cross".
130 'To the Greeks', Jacobsthal, "Imagery in early Celtic Art", Dillon and Chadwick, p.32
130 'his calligraphy', "Viking Dublin"

NORTH

131 'Hughes sensibility', "Now and in England", p.474
131 'Nicking and slicing', "Digging"
131 'I am...', "Exposure"
131 'Moyola/is its own', "Gifts of Rain"
131 'I think of the persona', "Trade of an Irish Poet", *Guardian*, p.17
132 'I have simply presumed', "Now and in England", p.488
132 Deane, "Irish Poetry and Irish Nationalism", Dunn, p.13
132 'Description is revelation', "Fosterage"
132 'Those hobnailed boots', "Ministry of Fear"
133 'But, with the Joycean', "John Bull's Other Island", *Listener*, 29.9.77, p.397
133 'In fact it has become', "The Interesting Case of John Alphonsus Mulrennan", *Planet* No.41, January 1978, p.40
133 'the liturgical and the latinate', "Now and in England", pp.481-2
135 'Part II consists', Hooker, *Poetry Wales*, 11 No.1, p.90
136 'According to Diodorus Siculus', Graves, *Greek Myths* 2, p.33. (There might be an overlapping, in Heaney's mind, with the skull-cult here, especially as his persona becomes a 'Skull-handler' in "Viking Dublin".)
136 'I rise flushed', The colour 'rose' and dowsing with sand recall Yeats and Australian aboriginal hymns to a red father who burrows through the sand like a dog.
136 'One might say that', Eliade, p.187
137 'Anteaus/high as', "Hercules and Antaeus"
137 'Balor, also a giant', Squire, *Celtic Myth and Legend*, p.112
137 'and it suddenly struck me', Haffenden, p.22
138 'With a butcher's aplomb', reference to Torf Einar in *Orkneyinga Saga*.

138 'forming one 'world-tree', The 'world-tree' itself is a rich mythological motif, connecting heaven and earth and men to their
origins and 'innocence'.

138 'The speaker cannot allow', For Heaney's first explication of his
home's name see the *Guardian*, 25.5.72, p.17

139 'The 'serpent' formed', One recalls the 'sun-serpent' theory concerning the Stone Age remains at Avebury.

139 'The fiercest impact', Dillon and Chadwick, pp.160-2

140 'The longship becomes', (Some historians say the boat-shaped
long barrows reveal memories that ships were considered as
'wombs' carrying people to be reborn on new soil.)

140 'Jimmy Farrell', Heaney capitalises Farrell's 'Flood' to add a
touch of antiquity to the scene.

140 'The ship in the grass', One again thinks of the *Anathemata*.

141 'The aggressive chalk giant', see Hooker, *Soliloquies of a Chalk
Giant*, pp.52-5 for connections between giant and Haracles.

141 'She is, at once', The story of the stolen plait allies her with the
'Drumkeragh woman' (Glob, pp. 77-8). However, she could also
be associated with the Morrigan, Badb or Macha, the triple
goddesses of evil and destruction.

141 'The 'queen' in', There is an old Irish folksong with the refrain:
"Will you come to the Bower"

142 'who will say corpse', "Grabaulle Man"

142 'I almost love you....connive', "Punishment"

143 'The phallic nature', this recalls the 'nest imagery' of "Bone Dreams"

144 'Though aware of the defects', Dudley, "Tacitus, Cornelius",
Penguin Guide to Literature 4, p.160

144 '...from the time of Vergil', Dillon and Chadwick, p.182

144 'One of the fundamental', ibid, p.176

145 'I have often heard', ibid, p.46

145 'A society where girl's heads', Bailey, p.42

146 'queen of England', Hughes, *Choice of Shakespeare's Verse*, p.186

147 'I'm cauterised', "A Northern Hoard"

147 'Ile thinks like', Bailey, p.44

147 'changes the structure', ibid, p.93

148 'Hooker adheres', Hooker, *Poetry Wales*, p.90

148 'Caste marked annually', *Wearing of the Black*, ed.Fiacc, p.44

148 'The 'original' obviously holds', Heaney's remarks with reference
to *Stations* support this observation.

148 'The English and Northern Irish', R.H.Barrow's quotation at the
beginning of the poem is a blatant example of presumptuous hindsight with its highly suspicious use of the words 'backward',
'civilisation' and 'useful'.

148 'I was under', "Romanist"

149 'moved from Mossbawn', Bailey, p.38

149 'I was so homesick', "Ministry of Fear"

150 'Saturn is the Latin', Heaney probably uses the Latin forms of
Greek myths to leave the impression of Roman imperialism
behind the words.

150 'Another sky-god', This brings the second part of *North* round in
a circle as Zeus's son was Hercules, who in turn defeats Antaeus.

150 'Breughel is the presiding', Hooker, p.39

151 'There seems little attention', An 'obol' would signify a genuine
wealth for Heaney as it is Greek silver - the currency of Horace
and Homer.

151 'The two berserks', as in "The Ministry of Fear"

151 'By way of Glob', Bailey, pp.42-4
151 'In so far', *White Goddess*, p.171
151 'Graves goes on', ibid, p.168
152 'It is no wonder', "Knowledge to the Norse" because of Ygdrassil, the sacred ash.
152 'Those million tons', see Section V of "Kinship"
152 'Philistinian sky-worshippers', They worshipped Dagon, a fiercely male god imaged in phallic statues.
152 'The following line', For example, it reminds of one of Bob Dylan's ingenuously aggressive lines:
      In a soldier's stance I aimed my hand
      At the mongrel dogs who teach.
                      ("My Back Pages")
152 'each bank', "Kinship"
153 'Coherent miseries', "Whatever You Say Say Nothing"
153 'At Glanmore', Bailey, p.44 & p.46
153 'Heaney's statement about Sweeney', see "King of the Dark" p.182 for the influence of St.Patrick.
154 'geniuses who creep', "Bog Oak"
154 'small mouth', "Oracle"
154 'Nestrobber's', "Somnambulist"
154 'doubtful of his responsibilites', A return to the 'Incertus' of Heaney's adolescence.
154 'a poem is alive', Bailey, pp.46 & 92
154 'lies in the summoning', *Guardian*, 25.5.72, p.17

LOAVES AND FISHES, YEAR OF THE WHALE, NEW POEMS

155 'It is more the look', *Orkney Tapestry*, p.19
155 'Labour in the fields', ibid, p.15
155 'It is a word', ibid, pp.21-2
155 'Art must be used', ibid, p.130
156 'Poetry, art, music', *Magnus*, p.140
157 Campbell, *Hero with a Thousand Faces*
157 'Port of Venus', This confrontation is to prove an important focus in Brown's work.
157 'Events are never the same', *Magnus*, pp.139-40
158 'the Reformation killed', *Orkney Tapestry*, p.183
158 'The Heavenly Stones', In the tradition of "The Holy Well" and "The Bitter Withy".
158 'The body-spirit', *Magnus*, p.140. This 'one substance' sounds like a combination of ideas of 'prima materia' and 'sub specie aeternis' a memory of a pre-Cartesian vision.
158 'For the Catholic', Corbishley, *Roman Catholicism*, p.41
159 'Spirit and flesh', see *Magnus* pp.164-170
159 'The Indian beggar', *Greenvoe*, p.103
159 'The Sikh boy', *A Calendar of Love*, p.75
159 'Both salesmen', see Section III of Eliot's "The Dry Salvages"
159 'Surely no house', "A Winter's Tale", *The Sun's Net*, p.43
160 'Progress is seen', *Orkney Tapestry*, p.21
160 'Brown protests', ibid, p.20
160 'The monks at Eynhallow', "Eyin-helga" meaning "holy island" in Norse. Linklater, *Orkney and Shetland*, pp.33-4
161 'Bill in a "Time to Keep"', Reade, *Martyrdom of Man*.
162 'Even Christ, Son', Jones, *Anathemata*, p.75
162 'These women had', *Orkney Tapestry*, p.106
162 'for Brown there is', Interview with Brown, July 1976.

163 'In his story "Hawkfall"', *Magnus*, pp.164-6
163 'His world was infested', Marwick, *Folklore*, p.81
163 'In Orkney the world-serpent', ibid, p.20
163 'Through the arrogance', "The Seven Houses"
163 'Each particle', This does not mean that Brown cannot be exhilerated by a sense of immanent chaos (as in "Peat-Cutting") but it is not a ruling consideration in his work.
164 'Nowadays there is', *Orkney Tapestry*, p.21. This distinct departure from tradition is a central concern of *Fishermen with Ploughs*
164 'God, am I not dead yet', "Farm Labourer"
165 'The dance is a rising', *Orkney Tapestry*, pp. 130-1
165 'This second tradition', *Spell for Green Corn*, p.61. For a full discussion of the links between the Ballad Tradition and Fertility Rite see A.L.Lloyd, *Folk Song in England*, p.80
166 'Now our good ship', *Orkneyinga Saga*, tr.Palsson & Edwards, pp.31-2
166 'We watch o'er', *Orkney Tapestry*, pp.2-3
166 'After Sigurd', *Orkneyinga Saga*, pp.154-5
167 'That quality', *Fishermen*, p.1
169 'It (heraldry)', *Orkney Tapestry*, p.19
170 'Bernard's submission', Topsfield, *Troubadours and Love*, p.113
170 'Bernard was of poor', Topsfield, "Bernart de Ventadorn", *Penguin Companion to Literature 2*, p.109
170 'Men handle the jewel', *Magnus*, p.140
170 'the rood becomes fragrant', Resembling the ancient "Brotherhood of the Plough" ceremony in *Greenvoe*.
170 'In the ballad', *Penguin Book of Ballads*, pp.83-4
171 'A woman is given', She reminds one very strongly of Blok's Venus of Russia in "The Intellect Cannot Measure the Divine".
172 'First, the coat of the Estates', *Orkney Tapestry*, p.76-7
172 'This echoes the story', It is an ancient belief that music is a receptacle of vitality and energy and is needed by the earth.
172 'The Fiddler's Song', *Spell*, p.58
173 'By leaving the actual birth', Eliot's "Journey of the Magi" is strongly echoed in places.
174 'Christ around me', *Magnus*, p.52
174 'He takes very seriously', Corbishley, p.103

FISHERMEN WITH PLOUGHS

176 'Philip Pacey has', Pacey 'The Fire of Images", *Akros 11*, No.32, p.61
176 'This would not pose', Pacey only confuses the argument by comparing Brown unfavourably to David Jones, saying that Brown would be more 'convincing' if he folded into his poetry 'the authentic voice' of 'found material'.
177 'Myth comes bringing', Duncan, *Truth of Life and Myth*, pp.36-7
177 'There are indeed', "The Starlight Night"
177 'Yet however cohesive', As when man is turned into 'immortal diamond' after death and saved from the world of Heraclitean flux in "That Nature is a Heraclitean fire and of the comfort of the Resurrection".
178 'Believe me', *Poems and Prose of Gerard Manley Hopkins*, p.203
178 'So that what was', Jones, *Epoch and Artist*, p.167. And of course Brown uses anaphora in poems like "Our Lady of the Wastes".
178 'Knox and Melville', "Scotland 1941"
178 'Like Brown he belongs', "The Castle"

229

179 'Earth and man and sun', *Magnus*, p.140
179 'Men must never despise', ibid, pp.140-1
180 'Events are never', ibid, pp.137-40
180 'All voyages past', ibid.
180 'It is a process', ibid, p.14
181 'He abhors the loss', Interviewed by David Jones, Summer 1976
181 'The old stories', Pacey, p.64
181 'His 'spell' is put', Recalling the Scots word "makar".
181 'He is part of a hierarchy', The poet Niall in the story "The Burning Harp" is saved this way.
182 'While a widow', "A Winter Bride"
183 'It is left to the reader', David Jones, "Swatches from the Weave of Time", *Planet* 40, p.43
183 'Back of each poet's', Duncan, p.25
183 'Duncan's statement', It is also interesting that two so different poets should share the idea of a poem as a spell.
183 'the same people', *Fishermen*, p.1
183 'The book is', The singular "Poem" instead of "A Cycle of Poems", stressing the impulse for unity.
184 'What is the dance', *Orkney Tapestry*, p.129
184 'Man goes, man voyages', The "Dragon" or "black flame" is by no means simply Pride, Sin or Satan here. However, this is an image which takes us back to Dunbar's "Surrexit Dominus de Sepulchro" and the lines
　　　　　Done is a battell on the dragon blak;
　　　　　Our campioun Chryst confundit hes his force:
Brown has also inherited Dunbar's use of the Targe or shield motif, a love of allegory and translation of the Christian story into localised terms.
187 'Buonaparte, the Laird', this poem recalls "A Reel of Seven Fishermen"
187 'Both the officers', Napoleon passed laws reinstating the man as head of each household.
189 'It is a ceremony', "The Tarn and the Rosary", *Hawkfall*, p.198
189 'terror and exultation', ibid, p.196. See also Eliade on this subject
189 'the people themselves', ibid.
189 '...the metaphysical poet's', See the famous image of bone and bright hair in Donne's "Relique".
193 'Bunertoon brings back', Shearer etc. *New Orkney Book*, pp.24-5 Much of the following historical information is drawn from this book.
193 'Brown finds the old', *Orkney Tapestry*, p.22
193 '...for the rank and file', Shearer, p.36
194 'One has only to read', Miller, *Orkney*.
195 'What are all these statues', *Orkney Tapestry*, p.130
198 'Always we feel', *The Sun's Net*, p.266
198 'They hunted down', ibid.
199 'Natasha seems to parallel', Trudi with Calliope (Epic poetry), Sophie with Terpsichore (Dancing), Teresa with Polyhymnia (Sacred Poetry), Marilyn with Erato (Erotic poetry and mime), Jane with Clio (History) and Bianca with Urania (Astronomy).

WINTERFOLD
201 'The shelterless boy', An image with deep traditional resonances for the Jews. See *The Song of Solomon* 5 v.3.
201 'The names of the stars', see also George Herbert's "Artillery"

202   'The reference to Blok', The "snow", "Flagons" and "red seep-
      ings of sunset" also remind of Blok. Is Brown here half-humour-
      ously referring to Blok's initial enthusiasm for the Revolution and
      his unorthodox linking of Christ with Red soldiers in "The
      Twelve"? See the Introduction to *The Twelve and other Poems*
      tr. Stallworthy and France. Also Wainwright's "Poetry and Revo-
      lution' Alexander Blok and Osip Mandelstam" *Agenda* 12, No 4,
      pp.53-64

202   'The robin', The song "Who Killed Cock Robin" has also been
      identified as a concealed account of the Crucifixion.

202   'and that no attempt', Bold, p.44. I disagree with this assessment.

203   '...may disturb Norse purists', *Winterfold*, p.6

203   'The small mouth', *Orkney Tapestry*, p.111

204   'The mystery was suddenly', ibid, p.106

207   'The use of the 'I am', Eliot, "Tradition and the Individual
      Talent", p.41

207   'These recognitions', There is a link between these considerations
      and Eliot in the fifth section of "East Coker":

              ....Because one has only learned to get the better of words
              For the thing one no longer has to say.

      See also Brown's fine story "The Eye of the Hurricane" where
      disappointed sexuality and the conflict between carnal and sub-
      lime love bring a new apprehension of the Incarnation.

210   'The potter with his wheel', Isaiah 45 v.9-13

210   'Brown has written', This poem might be set favourably against
      Heaney's poems about sexual and national schism.

210   'Christ, both man', This echoes Hopkins' 'immortal diamond' in
      "That Nature is a Heraclitean fire..."

211   'As it was the whole', Jones, *Epoch and Artist*, pp.168-9

211   'an old bitch', Pound, "Hugh Selwyn Mauberly".

211   'Christ is a sower', Luke 20 v.9-19

212   'Brown makes conscious associations, see "Pilate".

AFTERWORD

213   'Hill's progress', Janelle, *Robert Southwell*, pp. 142-171

213   '...there is no end', "Pavana Dolorosa"

213   'You are beyond me', "Lachrimae Coactae"

213   'Hill has written', *Poetry Book Society*, p.64

214   '...I believe any', "Whatever You Say Say Nothing"

215   'He put the red', "Kingdom of Dust"

215   'Eckhart makes', *Meister Eckhart*, p.224

215   'accordingly signifies', ibid, pp.217-8

216   'Whatever changes', Jones, *Epoch and Artist*, p.108

216   '...a poet must put', *Poetry Book Society*, p.65

216   'On those pristine fields', "Funeral Music".

GEORGE MACKAY BROWN

A Calendar of Love, London, 1974
"The Cures of Saint Magnus", *Planet*, 40, November 1977
Fishermen with Ploughs:A Poem Cycle, London 1974
Greenvoe, London 1972
Hawkfall, London 1974
Ian Crichton Smith, Norman McCaig, George Mackay Brown, Penguin Modern Poets
"Incident in a Glen", *Poetry Wales*, 13, No.3, Winter 1977,
Loaves and Fishes, London 1959
Magnus, London 1974
An Orkney Tapestry, London 1973
Poems: New and Selected, London 1971
A Spell for Green Corn, London 1970
The Storm and Other Poems, Orkney 1954
The Sun's Net, London 1976
A Time to Keep, London 1972
The Two Fiddlers: Tales from Orkney, London 1974
Winterfold, London 1976
The Year of the Whale, London 1965

SEAMUS HEANEY

"Canticles to the Earth: The Collected Poems of Theodore Roethke".
The Listener.
Death of a Naturalist, London 1966
"Deep as England: Selected Poems by Ted Hughes", *Hibernia*, 1.12.72.
Door into the Dark, London 1969
Eleven Poems, Belfast 1965
"The Fire I' The Flint: Reflections on the Poetry of Gerard Manley Hopkins", *Chatterton Lecture on an English Poet*, Oxford, 1975.
"The Interesting Case of John Alphonsus Mulrennan", *Planet* 41.
"John Bull's Other Island", *The Listener*, 29.12.77.
"King of the Dark", *The Listener*, 5.2.70.
North, London 1975
"Now and in England", *Critical Inquiry*, Chicago, 1977.
"Patrick Kavanagh", *The New Review*, 1 No.10, 1975.
Stations, Belfast 1975
"Three Sonnets", *Poetry Wales*, 11 No.1., Summer q975.
"The Trade of an Irish Poet", *Guardian*, 25.5.72.
"Watermarks", *Stand*, 13 No.3.
Wintering Out, London 1972.

GEOFFREY HILL

Brand, A Version for the English Stage, London 1978
"The Conscious Mind's Intelligible Structure: A Debate", *Agenda* 9 No.4/10.No.1, Autumn-Winter 1971-2.
"Eight Poems", *Agenda* 13 No.3, Autumn 1975.
The Fantasy Poets: Geoffrey Hill, 11, Oxford 1952
For the Unfallen: Poems 1952-1958, London 1959.
" 'I in Another Place.' Homage to Keith Douglas", *Stand* 6, No.1.

King Log, London 1968

"Lachrimae or Seven Tears figured in seven passionate Pavans" *Agenda* 13, No.1. Winter-Spring 1975.

Mercian Hymns, London 1971

"Jonathan Swift: The Poetry of Reaction", *The World of Jonathan Swift*, ed. Vickers, London 1968.

"Perplexed Persistence: The Exemplary Failure of T.H.Green" *Poetry Nation* 4, 1975.

"The Poetry of Jon Silkin", *Poetry and Audience* 9, No.12.

"Redeeming the Time", *Agenda* 10 No.4/11 No.1, Autumn-Winter 1972-3

"Seven Sonnets", *Agenda* 15 nos.2-3, Summer-Autumn 1977.

"Three Mystical Songs", *Agenda* 11, no.4/12 No.1, Autumn-Winter 1973-4

" 'The True Conduct of Human Judgement': Some Observations on Cymbeline". *The Morality of Art: Essays Presented to G.Wilson Knight by his colleagues and friends*, ed. D.W.Jefferson, London 1969.

"We Close our Eyes to Anselm and Lie Calm" and "Ecce Tempus", *Poetry Nation* 3, 1974.

" 'The World's Proportion': Jonson's dramatic poetry in Sejanus and Catiline", *Jacobean Theatre*, ed. John Russell Brown and Bernard Harris, London 1960.

GENERAL

A Choice of Sir Walter Ralegh's Verse. sel. Robert Nye, London 1972

Albright, Daniel. *The Myth Against Myth: A Study of Yeats' Imagination in Old Age*, Oxford 1972

Alexander, Michael. "Mercian Hymns", *Agenda*, 13, 3, Autumn 1975.

Alexander, Michael. *The Poetic Achievement of Ezra Pound*, London 1979

The Anglo-Saxon Chronicle, tr & ed. Garmondsway, London 1972.

Auden, W.H. *Selected Poems*, London 1968

Bacon, Francis. *The Advancement of Learning*, ed. W.A.Wright, Oxford, 1935.

Bacon, Francis. *Essays*. Intr. Hawkins, London 1972.

Bailey, Anthony. "A Gift for Being in Touch: Seamus Heaney builds houses of truth", *Quest/78*, 2,2, January-February 1978.

Bain, George. *Celtic Art: The Methods of Construction*, London 1951

Becket, J.C. *A Short History of Ireland*, London 1975.

Blok, Alexander. *The Twelve and Other Poems*, tr. Stallworthy and France, London 1970.

Bold, Alan. *George Mackay Brown*, Edinburgh 1978.

Brooke, Christopher. *The Saxon and Norman Kings*, London 1975.

Brooke-Rose, Christine. "Lay me by Aurelie: An Examination of Pound's use of Historical and Semi-historical Sources". *New Approaches to Ezra Pound*, ed. Eva Hesse, London 1969.

Brown, Terence. "The Poetry of W.R.Rodgers and John Hewitt", *Two Decades of Irish Writing*, ed. Dunn, Cheshire 1975.

Buttel, Robert. *Seamus Heaney*, New Jersey 1975.

Campbell, Joseph. *The Hero with a Thousand Faces*, London 1975.

Capra, Fritjov. *The Tao of Physics*, London 1975.

Chambers, E.K. *The English Folk Play*, New York 1964.

Chaytor, H.J. *The Troubadours of Dante*, Oxford 1942.

Clarke, Austin. "Anglo-Irish Poetry". *Literature in Celtic Countries*, Cardiff 1971.

Clarke, Austin. *The Celtic Twilight and the Nineties*, Dublin 1969
Cleary, A.A. "Tenebrae. Geoffrey Hill", *Thames Poetry*, 1,7, July 1979
The Cloud of Unknowing, tr. Clifton Waters, Middlesex 1961.
Cohn Norman. *The Pursuit of the Millenium*, London 1962
Coleridge, S.T. *Animae Poetae*, London 1895.
Coleridge, S.T. *Biographia Literaria:Biographical Sketches of my Literary Life*, Vol 2, London 1817.
Coleridge, S.T. *Collected Works*, ed.David E.Erdman. Vol 3, London 1957.
The Common Muse: An Anthology of Popular British and Ballad Poetry ed. V.de Sola Pinto and Stewart Conn. "The Scottish Literary Revival" *Stand*, 10,4, 1969.
Cookson, William. "A Few Notes on Geoffrey Hill", *Agenda*, 9,2/3.
Copleston, F.C. *Aquinas*, Middlesex 1955.
Corbishley, F.J. *Roman Catholicism*, London 1950.
Corkery, Daniel. *The Hidden Ireland*, Dublin 1925.
Curtis, Simon. "Seamus Heaney: *North*", *Critical Quarterly*, 18,1.
Davie, Donald. *Ezra Pound:Poet as Sculptor*, London 1965
Dekker, George. *Sailing After Knowledge*, London 1963.
Deane, Seamus. "Irish Poetry and Irish Nationalism", *Two Decades of Irish Writing*, ed.Dunn, Cheshire 1975.
Dent, Peter. "North", *Agenda*, 13,2. 1975
The Dialogues of Plato translated into English with Analyses and Introductions, Vol.1, B.Jowett, Oxford 1893.
Dillon, Miles & Chadwick, Nora. *The Celtic Realms*, London 1973.
Dodsworth, Martin. "Geoffrey Hill's New Poetry", *Stand*, 13,1.
Donne, John. *Selected Poems*, ed.John Hayward, Middlesex 1968.
Duncan, Robert. *The Truth and Life of Myth*, Michigan 1968.
Dunn, Douglas. " 'Finished Fragrance': The Poems of George Mackay Brown", *Poetry Nation* 2, 1974.
Dunn, Douglas. "Manana is Now — New Poetry", *Encounter* 45, 1975.
Eagleton, Terry. "Myth and History in Recent Poetry", *British Poetry Since 1960*, ed.Schmidt and Lindop, Oxford 1972.
Eagleton, Terry. "New Poetry", *Stand*, 17,1.
Eliade, Mircea. *Myths, Dreams and Mysteries*, London 1976.
Eliade, Mircea. *Shamanism, Archaic Techniques of Ecstasy*, tr.Trask, London 1964.
Eliot, T.S. *Four Quartets*, London 1972.
Eliot, T.S. *Selected Poems*, London 1961.
Eliot, T.S. *The Use of Poetry and the Use of Criticism*, London 1933.
Ellmann, Richard. "Ez and Old Billum", *New Approaches to Ezra Pound*, ed. Eva Hesse, London 1969.
Ellmann, Richard. *Yeats:The Man and the Masks*, London 1949.
Emerson, R.W. *Essays*, London 1897.
The English and Scottish Popular Ballads,5 vols.,ed. C.J.Child, NY 1957
The English Poems of George Herbert, ed.C.A.Patrides, London 1974.
The Faber Book of Ballads, ed. Matthew Hodgart, London 1955.
Faber Book of Irish Verse, ed.John Montague, London 1974.
Farnell,Ida. *Lives of the Troubadours*, London 1896.
Feder, *Ancient Myth in Modern Poetry*, Philadelphia 1971.
Flannery, M.C. *Yeats and Magic*, New York 1975.
Focillon, Henri. *Art of the West 1: Romanesque*, tr.King, London 1963
Frazer, J.G. *The Golden Bough*, 7 vols., London 1914.
Gascoigne, Bamber. *World Theatre:An Illustrated History*, London 1968.
Gibbs, Barbara. "Seamus Heaney: 'Eleven Poems' ", *Stand*, 8,3.
Glob, P.V. *The Bog People*, London 1969.

Goodwin, K.L. *The Influence of Ezra Pound*, London 1966.
Grant, Damian. "Body Poetic: The Function of the Metaphor in Three Irish Poets", *Poetry Nation* 1, 1973.
Graves, Robert. *The Greek Myths*, 2 vols., Middlesex 1957.
Graves, Robert. *The White Goddess*, London 1961.
Haffenden, John. "Meeting Seamus Heaney", *London Magazine*, June 1979.
Hand and Eye: an anthology for Sachaverall Sitwell, ed.Elborn, Oxford 1977.
Handford, S.A. *Langenscheidt's Latin Dictionary*, Berlin 1960.
Here and Human:An Anthology of Contemporary Verse, F.E.S.Finn, London 1976.
Herity & Eogan. *Ireland in Prehistory*, London 1977.
Hodgkin, R.H. *A History of the Anglo-Saxons*, 2 vols., Oxford 1952.
Hoffman, Daniel. *Barbarous Knowledge*, Oxford 1967.
Hooker, Jeremy. "Seamus Heaney's North", *Poetry Wales*, Summer 1975
Hooker, Jeremy. *Soliloquies of a Chalk Giant*, London 1977.
Huberman, Elizabeth. "George Mackay Brown's Greenvoe: Rediscovering a Novel of the Orkneys", *Critique* 19,2.
Hughes, Ted. *A Choice of Shakespeare's Verse*, London 1971.
Hughes, Ted. *Crow*, London 1970.
Hughes, Ted. "Myth and Education", *Times Educational Supplement*, 2.9.77.
Hughes, Ted. *Poetry in the Making*, London 1967.
Hughes, Ted. *Selected Poems*, London 1972.
Irish Poets 1924-74, ed. David Marcus, London 1975.
Jackson, Kenneth. *A Celtic Miscellany*, Middlesex 1971.
Janelle, Pierre. *Robert Southwell, The Writer*, London 1935.
Jones, David. *Epoch and Artist*, London 1959.
Jones, David. *The Anathemata*, London 1952.
Jones, David. *In Parenthesis*, London 1937.
Jones, D.J. "Swatches from the Weave of Time", *Planet* 40, 1977.
Jones, Gwyn. *A History of the Vikings*, Oxford 1968.
Jordan, Furneaux. *A Concise History of Western Architecture*, London 1969.
Joyce, James. *A Portrait of the Artist as a Young Man*, Middlesex 1924.
Joyce, P.W. *The Origin and History if Irish Names of Places*, vol.3, Yorkshire 1976.
Kavanagh, Patrick. *Collected Poems*, London 1973.
Kazin, Cathrael. "Across a Wilderness of Retrospection: A Reading of Geoffrey Hill's 'Lachrimae' ", *Agenda*, 17,1.
Kennelly, Brendan. "The Rebirth of Irish Poetry", *Hibernia*, 33.
Kenner, Hugh. *The Poetry of Ezra Pound*, London 1941.
Kenner, Hugh. *The Pound Era*, London 1972.
La Belle, Jenijoy. "Vernon Watkins:Some Observations on Poetry", *The Anglo-Welsh Review*, 65.
Lawrence, D.H. *Fantasia of the Unconscious and Psychoanalysis and the Unconscious*, London 1961.
Levi, Peter. "History and Reality in David Jones", *Agenda* 11,4/12,1.
Linklater, Eric. *Orkney and Shetland*, London 1965.
Longley, Edna. "Searching the Darkness", *Two Decades of Irish Writing*, ed.Dunn, Chshire 1975.
Lucie Smith, Edward. *British Poetry Since 1945*, Middlesex 1960.
The Mabinogion, tr. Gwyn Jones and Thomas Jones, London 1975.
Mac Curtain, Margaret. *Tudor and Stuart Ireland*, Dublin 1972.
Mac Niocaill, Gearold. *Ireland Before the Vikings*, Dublin 1972.

Mac Liammoir, Michael and Eavan Boland. *W.B. Yeats and His World*, London 1971.
Man and His Symbols, ed. C.G.Jung, London 1974.
Martin, Wallace D. "Beyond Modernism: Christopher Middelton and Geoffrey Hill", *Contemporary Literature* 12,4. 1971.
Marwick, Ernest W. *The Folklore of Orkney and Shetland*, London 1975.
McGuiness, Arthur E. "Hoarder of Common Ground: Tradition and Ritual in Seamus Heaney's Poetry", *Eire/Ireland*, Summer 1978.
Meister Eckhart, Selected Treatises and Sermons, tr.James M.Clark and John V.Skinner, London 1958.
The Metaphysical Poets, ed. Helen Gardner, Middlesex 1957.
Milne, W.S. "Decreation in Geoffrey Hill's Lachrimae", *Agenda*, 17,1.
Milne, W.S. "The Pitch of Attention", *Agenda*, 17,1.
Miller, Ronald. *Orkney*, London 1976.
Miscellaneous Prose of Sir Philip Sidney, ed. Duncan-Jones and Van Dorsten, Oxford 1973.
Morgan, Edwin. "Scottish Poetry in the 1960s", *British Poetry Since 1960*, ed. Schmidt and Lindop, Oxford 1972.
Morgan, Kathleen E. *Christian Themes in Contemporary Poets*, London 1965.
Mourges, Odette de. "The European Background to Baroque Sensibility" *The Pelican Guide to English Literature* 3, Middlesex 1976.
Muir, Edwin. *The Letters of Edwin Muir*, ed. P.A.Butter, London 1974.
Muir, Edwin. *Selected Poems*, ed. T.S.Eliot, London 1965.
Muir, Edwin. *The Story and the Fable:An Autobiography*, London 1940.
O'Corrain, Donncha. *Ireland Before the Normans*, Dublin 1972.
Olney, James. "The Esoteric Flower:Yeats and Jung", *Yeats and the Occult*, ed.G.M.Harper, London 1976.
Orkneyinga Saga, tr. Palsson and Edwards, London 1978.
Orkney Miscellany 5, Kirkwall 1973.
O Suilleabhain. *A Handbook of Irish Folklore*, Dublin 1942.
Pacey, Philip. "The Fire of Images:The Poetry of George Mackay Brown", *Akros* 11, 32. 1976.
Peck, John. "Tenebrae", *Agenda*, 17,1.
The Penguin Book of Ballads, ed. Geoffrey Grigson, Middlesex 1957.
The Penguin Book of Contemporary Verse, ed.Kenneth Allot, Mdx.1950.
The Penguin Book of Irish Verse, ed. Brendan Kennelly, Mdx. 1970.
The Penguin Book of Spanish Verse, ed. J.M.Cohen, Middlesex 1956.
The Penguin Companion to Literature, vols. 1-4, Middlesex 1969-71.
Piggott, Stuart. "David Jones and the Past of Man", *Agenda* 11,4/12,1.
Piggott, Stuart. *The Druids*, Middlesex 1977.
Plato. *The Laws*, tr.Trevor S.Saunders, Middlesex 1970.
Plato. *The Republic*, tr. Desmond Lee, Middlesex 1955.
Poems and Prose of Gerard Manley Hopkins, ed. W.H.Gardner, Middlesex 1963.
The Poems of William Dunbar, ed.James Kinsley, Oxford 1979.
Poetry Book Society:The First Twenty-Five Years, ed. Eric White, London 1979.
Pound, Ezra. *The Cantos*, rev.edn. London 1975.
Pound, Ezra. *The Critical Heritage*, ed.Eric Homberger, London 1972.
Pound, Ezra. *Literary Essays*, ed.T.S.Eliot, London 1954.
Pound, Ezra. "Psychology and the Troubadours", *The Quest*, 4,1.
Pound, Ezra. *Selected Poems*, London 1928.
Pound, Ezra. *Selected Prose 1909-1965*, ed. William Cookson, London 1973.
Powys, J.C. "My Philosophy up to date as influenced by living in Wales"

Obstinate Cymric, London 1973.

Raine, Kathleen. *Defending Ancient Springs*, London 1967.

Raine, Kathleen. "Hades Wrapped in Cloud", *Yeats and the Occult*, London 1976.

Rachewiltz, Boris de. "Pagan and Magic Elements in Ezra Pound's Works", *New Approaches to Ezra Pound*, ed.Hesse, London 1969.

Reade, Winwood. *The Martyrdom of Man*, London 1932.

Rees, Alwyn and Brinley. *Celtic Heritage*, London 1961.

Ricks, Christopher. "Cliche as Responsible Speech", *London Magazine*, November 1964.

Ricks, Christopher. "Geoffrey Hill and 'The Tongue's Atrocities'", TLS, 30.6.78.

Roethke, Theodore. *The Collected Poems*, New York, 1961.

Rolle, Richard. *English Writings*, ed.H.E.Allen, Oxford, 1931.

Ross, Anne. *Pagan Celtic Britain: Studies in Iconography and Tradition.* London 1967.

Rimbaud, Arthur. *Poesies*, ed. Ruff, Paris 1978.

Ruthven, K.K. *Myth*, The Critical Idiom 31, London 1976.

Ruskin, John. *Fors Clavigera*, Vol.4, Orpington, 1896.

Saint Augustine:Confessions, tr. R.S.Pine-Coffin, Middlesex 1961.

Selected Prose of T.S.Eliot, ed. Frank Kermode, London 1978.

Seligman, Kurt. *Magic, Supernaturalism and Religion*. Herts, 1975.

Sharkey, John. *Celtic Mysteries*, London 1975.

Shearer, Groundwater and Mackay. *The New Orkney Book*, London 1966.

Silkin, Jon. "Bedding the Locale", *New Blackfriars*, London 1973.

Silkin, Jon. "The Poetry of Geoffrey Hill", *British Poetry Since 1960*, ed. Schmidt and Lindop, Oxford 1972.

Sisson, C.H. "Geoffrey Hill", *Agenda*, 13,3.

Sisson, C.H. "Poetry and Myth", *Agenda*, 15, 1/2.

Sisson, C.H. *In the Trojan Ditch*, Cheshire 1975.

Speirs, John. *The Scots Literary Tradition*, London 1940.

Spence, Lewis. *The History and Origins of Druidism*, London 1949.

Spence, Lewis. *The Magic Arts in Celtic Britain*, London 1945.

Spenser's Prose Works, ed.Greenlaw, Osgood, Paddelford Heffner, Oxford 1949.

Stead, C.K. *The New Poetic*, London 1964.

Steiner, George. *After Babel:Aspects of Language and Translation*, Oxford 1975.

Steiner, George. *In Bluebeard's Castle*, London 1971.

Squire, Charles. *Celtic Myth and Legend, Poetry and Romance*, London 1912.

Stock, Noel. *The Life of Ezra Pound*, Middlesex 1974.

Tacitus. *The Agricola and the Germania*, tr.H.Mattingley, Mdx. 1948.

Thurley, Geoffrey. *The Ironic Harvest: English Poetry in the Twentieth Century*, London 1974.

Topsfield, L.T. *Troubadours and Love*, Cambridge 1975.

Tuohy, Frank. *Yeats*, London 1976.

Ure, Peter. *Yeats and Anglo Irish Literature*, ed.C.J.Rawson, Liverpool 1974.

Vendler, Helen Hennessy. *Yeats' Vision and the Later Plays*, Harvard 1963.

Vickery, John B. "Myth and Methodology in Modern Literature", *Contemporary Literature*, 14, 3.

Wainwright, Jeffrey. "An Essay on Geoffrey Hill's Tenebrae", *Agenda*, 17.1.

237

Wainwright, Jeffrey. "The Speechless Dead:Geoffrey Hill's King Log", *Stand*, 10,1.

Wainwright, Jeffrey. "Poetry and Revolution: Alexander Blok and Osip Mandelstam", *Agenda*, 12,4/13,1.

Walton, James. "Megalithic Building Survivals", *Studies in Folk Life: Essays in Honour of Iowerth C.Peate*, ed.G.Jenkins, London 1969.

The Wearing of the Black, ed. Fiace, Belfast 1974.

Weighall, Arthur. *Wanderings in Anglo-Saxon Britain*, London.

Whitaker, Thomas. *Swan and Shadow: Yeats' Dialogue with History*, Chapel Hill, 1964.

Wood, Eric. *Collins Field Guide to the Archaeology of Britain*, London 1963.

Worlds:Seven Modern Poets, ed. Geoffrey Summerfield, Middlesex 1974

Yeats, W.B. "A Packet for Ezra Pound", *A Vision*, London 1938.

Yeats, W.B. *Autobiographies:Reveries over Childhood and Youth and the Trembling of the Veil*, London 1926.

Yeats, W.B. *Collected Poems*, London 1933.

Yeats, W.B. *Explorations*, London 1962.

Yeats, W.B., Penguin Critical Anthology, ed. William H.Pritchard, Middlesex 1972.

242

243